# Paul, Scripture,
## and Ethics

Biblical Studies Library

*The Descent of Christ: Ephesians 4:7–11 and Traditional Hebrew Imagery,* W. Hall Harris III

*Marriage as a Covenant: Biblical Law and Ethics as Developed from Malachi,* Gordon P. Hugenberger

*Paul, Scripture, and Ethics: A Study of 1 Corinthians 5–7,* by Brian S. Rosner

*The Structure of Hebrews: A Text-Linguistic Analysis,* George H. Guthrie

# Paul, Scripture, and Ethics

## A Study of 1 Corinthians 5–7

### Brian S. Rosner

 Baker Books

A Division of Baker Book House Co
Grand Rapids, Michigan 49516

© 1994 by E. J. Brill, Leiden, The Netherlands

Published by Baker Books
a division of Baker Book House Company
P.O. Box 6287, Grand Rapids, MI 49516-6287

First cloth edition published 1994 by E. J. Brill as volume 22 in Arbeiten zur Geschichte des antiken Judentums und des Urchristentums.

First paperback edition published 1999 by Baker Books.

Printed in the United States of America

Library of Congress Cataloging-in-Publication Data is on file at the Library of Congress, Washington, D.C.

For information about academic books, resources for Christian leaders, and all new releases available from Baker Book House, visit our web site:
http://www.bakerbooks.com

*To Leanne*

# CONTENTS

PART TWO

PAUL'S DEPENDENCE UPON THE SCRIPTURES FOR ETHICS
IN 1 CORINTHIANS 5-7

# PREFACE

This book is a revision of a doctoral dissertation submitted to the University of Cambridge in 1991. The dissertation was awarded the 1991 Kaye Prize. I am deeply grateful to my Cambridge *Doktorvater*, Dr. William Horbury, a model supervisor and scholar, for his kindness and friendship throughout and beyond the period of my research. Thanks are also due to Dr. Nicholas de Lange and Professor Morna Hooker, who each supervised the project for one term, for their searching questions and incisive critique and to Professor C.K. Barrett, one of my examiners, for the helpful and detailed comments he made on the Thesis.

I would also like to thank the members of the Cambridge New Testament Seminar, the Cambridge Early Christian and Jewish Studies Seminar, the Annual Seminar on the Use of the Old Testament in the New Testament, the Tyndale Fellowship New Testament Study Group, the British New Testament Conference Intertestamental Literature Seminar, the Aberdeen New Testament Seminar and the Edinburgh New Testament Seminar for their comments and criticisms of papers presented at different stages of the work. The provision of study leave by the Department of Divinity with Religious Studies, the University of Aberdeen, allowed me to complete the revisions. Many other friends have helped at various points. Mr. Gareth Davies, who lent me a new word processor for two years, deserves special mention. The editors of *NTS*, *JTS*, *ZNW* and *Tyn Bull* kindly gave permission to re-publish my short studies (listed in Bibliography) in revised form.

Without the financial assistance of the Overseas Research Scheme, Tyndale House Council, Cambridge University Board of Graduate Studies, the Bethune-Baker Fund, Clare College, friends from Blakehurst Baptist Church (Sydney, Australia), East Hills Baptist Church (Sydney, Australia) and Trinity Fellowship (Dallas, U.S.A.), Maurie and Josephine Kellahan, relatives, and especially my parents and parents-in-law, this project could not have been completed.

Finally, I wish to thank my wife Leanne, who is my partner in all things, and to whom this book is dedicated.

King's College
University of Aberdeen

## NOTES TO THE READER

The system of abbreviations of Biblical books as well as periodicals, reference works, serial publications and primary sources follows that of the *Journal of Biblical Literature* (95 [1976]: 335-38). Other abbreviations follow established usage.

Secondary sources are cited by the author's name and full title on first occurrence in the book, and by name and a short title thereafter. Commentaries on 1 Corinthians are cited by author only throughout (e.g., Barrett, 237).

# PART ONE

# PAUL'S DEPENDENCE UPON THE SCRIPTURES FOR ETHICS

CHAPTER ONE

# INTRODUCTION

## I. Paul's Ethics and Scripture
*"These things were written for our instruction"*

As a Jew who became the apostle to the Gentiles, Paul stood between the Jewish and pagan worlds. Consequently New Testament scholars have long debated the question of the sources of Paul's thought.[1] To which sphere was he more indebted? Once committed to the Gentile mission, did Paul jettison his Jewish heritage? In particular there is perennial interest in the extent to which Paul uses the Jewish Scriptures (the books comprising the Christian Old Testament) when he regulates conduct in his churches.

How important was Paul's Scriptural inheritance for his moral teaching? The view that Scripture did not play an important role in the formation of Paul's ethics is widely held. In 1928 Adolf von Harnack wrote:

> Paulus [hat] das Alte Testament nicht als das christliche Quellen- und Erbauungsbuch den jungen Gemeinden gegeben.[2]

Similar opinions continue to be expressed up to the present day. John Barton (1986):

> Paul . . . does not take much trouble to derive his ethical teaching from scripture.[3]

Andreas Lindemann (1986):

> [Paulus] versteht aber das Alte Testament, seine Bibel, gerade nicht mehr als Tora in eigentlichen Sinne; sie ist ihm nicht mehr die Quelle der Weisungen Gottes für das Verhalten der Menschen, soweit sie Christen sind.[4]

---

[1] E. Earle Ellis, 'Paul', 950, has observed that twentieth century studies of Pauline thought have devoted themselves primarily to three questions: "What is the relation between Paul and Jesus? *What are the sources of Pauline thought?* What is the role of eschatology in the mind of Paul?" (emphasis mine).

[2] Harnack, 'Das Alte Testament in den paulinischen Briefen und in den paulinischen Gemeinden', 137.

[3] Barton, *The Oracles of God*, 190.

[4] Lindemann, 'Die biblischen Toragebote und die paulinische Ethik', 263-64.

R. G. Hamerton-Kelly (1990):

> The Mosaic Law played no constructive role in his [i.e., Paul's] ethics.[5]

We could go on to cite a host of not only Protestant but also Roman Catholic and even Jewish students of Paul's letters who by and large concur with these sentiments, including J. Ph. Gloch (1885), E. Grafe (1893), E. Kühl (1894), M. Löwy (1903/1904), P. Wernle (1904), Rudolph Bultmann (1933), F. Prat (1945), L. H. Marshall (1946), B.S. Easton (1948), M. Buber (1950), S. Sandmel (1958), H.J. Schoeps (1959), J. Knox (1961), H. Ulonska (1964), P. Vielhauer (1969), E. Käsemann (1973), J.B. Hurley (1973), A. Strobel (1974), A. T. Hanson (1974), David R. Catchpole (1977), F.F. Bruce (1977), J. Murphy O'Connor (1978), John Boswell (1980), K. Schubert (1980), J.A. Fitzmyer (1981), Wolfgang Schrage (1982), Bruce Malina (1983), Peter Zaas (1984), F. Watson (1986), John Rogerson (1988) and Stephen Westerholm (1988).[6] This list is far from exhaustive, but it does demonstrate the range and strength of adherence to the position in question. Though differing in many details, and sometimes identifying Jewish traditions in Paul's letters, each of these authors share the conviction that the Jewish Scriptures and/or the Law of Moses no longer have fundamental practical significance for Paul, the Christian. Though no single figure or movement represents the root of this broad tradition of Pauline interpretation, Adolf von Harnack, the great student of Marcion,[7] probably exercised the greatest single influence on it, especially through his forcibly written essay, 'Das Alte Testament in den paulinischen Briefen und in den paulinischen Gemeinden' (1928).

Such scholars marshal evidence from many quarters. Indeed, there are at least eight reasons advanced for the conclusion that the Scriptures were *not* important for Pauline ethics (for an evaluation of these arguments see Chapter Seven, section III). First, Paul makes some very negative statements about the heart and foundation of the Scriptures' ethical teaching, the Law of Moses. These imply that the Law is not of value for Christians. According to Paul the Law "works wrath" (Rom 4:15), "increases sin" (Rom 5:20; 7:5,8-11,13) and even "kills" (Rom 7:5,8-11,13; 2 Cor 3:6). Christians are no longer "under the law" (Gal 3:23-25; 4:4-5,21; 1 Cor 9:20; Rom 6:14-15), having

---

[5] Hamerton-Kelly, 'Sacred Violence and "Works of the Law." Is Christ Then an Agent of Sin?', 74.
[6] See Bibliography under name and date.
[7] See Harnack, *Marcion*.

through Christ's death been released from it (Rom 7:1-6). The Mosaic Law has in fact come to an end (2 Cor 3:7ff; Rom 10:4). David R. Catchpole argues that, in Paul's mind, the Mosaic Law is irrelevant for Christian conduct:

> For him, Christ had in a real sense jeopardized Moses. One need only recall his adamant insistence on a salvation-historical continuity from Abraham to Christ, with the Mosaic law a marginal, inferior and temporary incursion due to be wound up when the first era of human existence ended with the arrival or revelation of Christ and faith (Gal. iii. 6-29).[8]

Concerning Paul and the Law Barnabas Lindars has observed that this conclusion is virtually a settled finding of Pauline studies:

> Modern critical scholarship, especially in Germany, has tended to work with a stereotype in which . . . Paul has been regarded as opposed to the law as fundamentally incompatible with authentic religion."[9]

Secondly, Paul openly abrogates many parts of the Scriptures, such as circumcision (1 Cor 7:19), food laws (Rom 14:14,20),[10] and festival days and the Sabbath (Rom 14:5; Gal 4:9-10). His practice seems to match his precept; not only does Paul at times appear to disparage the Old Testament, but, as James Dunn writes, Paul has "abandoned much of the Old Testament."[11]

Thirdly, when Paul does adduce Scripture to express or support a moral admonition, his use is commonly seen as haphazard and atomistic suggesting that the Scriptures are a minor rather than fundamental and formative source for his ethics. Such indiscriminate exegesis corresponds to a widespread characterisation of much early Jewish exegesis. In 1927 G.F. Moore characterised Jewish exegesis as "atomistic exegesis which interprets sentences, clauses, phrases and even single words independently of the context or the historical occasion, . . . combines them with other similarly detached utterances and makes use of analogy of expressions, often by purely verbal association."[12]

---

[8] Catchpole, 'Paul, James and the Apostolic Decree', 430. Galatians 4:1-10 is also cited. Catchpole considers that Paul could not have had anything to do with the Acts 15 decree because of its positive relation to the Torah and Noachian code.

[9] Lindars (ed), *Law and Religion*, xii.

[10] Cf. Leviticus 11; Deuteronomy 14:3-21.

[11] Dunn, *The Living Word*, 45; cf. E.P. Sanders, *Paul, the Law, and the Jewish People*, 162: "Paul had found a canon within the canon". Dunn himself does not deduce from this that the Scriptures are no longer a valuable moral guide for Paul.

[12] Moore, *Judaism in the First Centuries of the Christian Era: The Age of the Tannaim*, I:249-50.

Moore stated that: "the interpretation of the Scriptures in the New Testament is of precisely the same kind." Perhaps the most commonly cited example of such non-contextual exegesis in Paul's letters, 1 Corinthians 9:9, which quotes Deuteronomy 25:4 ("you shall not muzzle the ox") to support a case for financial support, falls into the category of Paul's use of Scripture for ethics.

Fourthly, Paul's churches are predominently Gentile. According to some scholars Paul was not concerned to correct the Scriptural ignorance of his Gentile converts. John Rogerson writes:

> In seeking to evaluate the significance of the comparative lack of reference to the Old Testament in the matter of providing guidance for Christian behaviour, we must bear in mind that most of the New Testament letters were written to Gentile Christian churches.[13]

Fifthly, 2 Timothy 3:16-17, the clearest affirmation of the centrality of the Scriptures for ethics in the traditional Pauline corpus is in the Pastoral Epistles, the theology of which is considered by many scholars to be post- if not un-Pauline. B. S. Easton, commenting on this passage, states:

> While Paul is adept at discovering 'spiritual' meanings in unlikely texts (1 Cor 9:9; 10:11; etc), he emphatically did not regard the Old Testament as the Christian's moral guide.[14]

Sixthly, other sources such as the words of Jesus and the non-Jewish ethics of Paul's day (even pagan law[15]) seem to exert a greater influence than Scripture on Paul's ethics. W.D. Davies argues that "it was the words of Jesus himself that formed Paul's primary source as ethical διδάσκαλος."[16] C.H. Dodd believed that:

> the ethical teaching given by the early church (especially Paul) was pretty closely related to the general movement in Graeco-Roman society towards the improvement of public morals as it was undertaken in the first century by various agencies.[17]

---

[13] Rogerson, 'The Interpretation of the Old Testament in the New', 10; cf. J. Barton, *People of the Book*, 6: "In commending the faith to Gentile Christians, Paul felt no need to begin with Jewish Scripture, or even to bring Scripture in at a later stage".

[14] Easton, *The Pastoral Epistles*, 68; cf. A.T. Hanson, *Studies in the Pastoral Epistles*, 46.

[15] Duncan Derrett, David Daube and Andreas Lindemann, for example, highlight Roman law as the key factor in Paul's decision to expel the sinner in 1 Corinthians 5 (see Chapter Three).

[16] Davies, *Paul and Rabbinic Judaism: Some Rabbinic Elements in Pauline Theology*, 136.

[17] Dodd, *Gospel and Law*, 23.

Seventhly, factors other than Scripture, including eschatology,[18] the Spirit,[19] love,[20] and social conditions,[21] appear to mould Paul's advice concerning conduct. The traditional and well entrenched Lutheran distinction between Law and Gospel, *Gesetz und Evangelium*, has exerted perhaps the strongest influence on the question of the relation, or rather non-relation, of Paul's ethics and the Torah in German scholarship throughout the twentieth century. Von Harnack argued that rather than giving the Old Testament as the Christian book of edification to the young churches Paul based his teaching and mission wholly and completely on the gospel: "er (hat) Mission und Lehre zunächst ganz und gar auf das Evangelium selbst gegründet und die Erbauung ausschließlich von ihm und das Evangelium begleitenden Geiste erwartet."[22] Lindemann likewise stresses that Paul derived his ethics not from the Old Testament but as "Konsequenz des Evangeliums."[23]

Finally, the most compelling reason given by those who doubt the importance of Scripture for Paul's ethics is the relative paucity of Scriptural quotations in Paul's ethics; Scripture is seldom quoted in Paul's paraenesis. The observation is sometimes made that in the sections of Paul's letters that concern doctrine and Christian belief Scripture

---

[18] Brevard S. Childs, *The New Testament as Canon: An Introduction*, 277 notes that "It is the relationship between the old and the new age in Paul's eschatology which has a consistent effect on his ethical instructions to the Corinthian church." Another way of explaining the apparent invalidity of the Mosaic Law for Paul which is related to his eschatology is his adherence to the apocalyptic and rabbinic idea that the Law would cease to operate in the messianic age—see Albert Schweitzer (*The Mysticism of the Apostle Paul*), Hans Joachim Schoeps (*Aus Frühchristlicher Zeit: Religionsgeschichtliche Untersuchungen*), L. Baeck ('The Faith of Paul') and W. D. Davies (*Paul and Rabbinic Judaism* and esp. *Torah in the Messianic Age and/or the Age to Come*).

[19] In answering the question of "the source of Paul's morality" John Ziesler, *Pauline Christianity*, 117, 124 stresses the guidance of the Spirit: "Paul is guided not by a rule but by the Spirit in the light of the concrete situation." Cf. Stephen Westerholm, *Israel's Law and the Church's Faith*, 209: "whereas the will of God for Jews was found in the statutes of Torah, Christians must discover it for themselves as their mind is 'renewed' and they grow in insight." In 'Letter and Spirit; The Foundation of Pauline Ethics' Westerholm argues that the role of the Spirit implies freedom from external law and in 'The Law and the "just Man" (1 Tim. 1:3-11)' he finds in 1 Timothy 1:8-9 a prohibition on the use of the Mosaic law in Christian ethics.

[20] According to many scholars "the law of love" or "the law of Christ" has taken the place of the law of Moses in Pauline ethics. Eg. P. Ramsey, *Basic Christian Ethics*, 77, argues that Paul's position in 1 Corinthians can be summarised as "Love and do as you then please."

[21] See Gerd Theissen, *The Social Setting of Pauline Christianity: Essays on Corinth*, and Wayne A. Meeks, *The First Urban Christians: The Social World of the Apostle Paul.*

[22] Von Harnack, 'Das Alte Testament', 137.

[23] Lindemann, 'Die biblischen Toragebote', 264.

is cited far more often than in the portions relating to conduct and Christian practice. A.T. Hanson is typical: "On the whole it is remarkable how little Paul uses Scripture for anything but proof," that is, to establish doctrine.[24] Andreas Lindemann makes the related point that where Paul could have cited relevant Scripture, he does not: in 1 Corinthians Paul "beruft sich . . . auf sie (die Tora) als verbindliche Autorität auch dort nicht, wo er inhaltlich mit ihrer Weisung übereinstimmt."[25]

It is true that there are relatively few quotations of Scripture in Paul's ethics. Of the approximately one hundred instances of Scriptural citation in the traditional Pauline corpus,[26] less than 20% occur in the ethical sections of the epistles.[27] Since Paul's ethics comprise, by any standard, significantly more than one fifth of his letters then one is justified in speaking about the relative paucity of Scriptural citation. If Scripture is a crucial and formative source for Paul's ethics, why then does he not quote it more often?

It is of course true that there have been scholars who have doubted many of the grounds just adduced for denying the importance of the Scriptures for Paul's ethics. Particularly important are those who investigated Jewish and early Christian catechetical teaching, A. Seeberg, G. Klein, P. Carrington and others, whose work we shall review in "The Influence of Jewish Moral Teaching on Paul's Ethics," Chapter Two, section II. Scholars who have argued directly that Paul characteristically turns to the Scriptures for moral judgements include C.K. Barrett, Otto Michel, Traugott Holtz, D. Moody Smith, E. Earle Ellis and Peter J. Tomson.[28] However, no-one to my knowledge has offered a sustained and convincing reply to those who deny a formative role for the Scriptures. Peter Tomson concurs with this judgment:

> Although today the axiomatically un-Jewish and thus anti-Jewish character of the Church is increasingly being questioned, the assumption

---

[24] Hanson, *Studies in Paul's Technique and Theology*, 174.
[25] Lindemann, 'Die biblischen Toragebote', 264.
[26] See D. Moody Smith, 'The Pauline Literature', 267-72. Cf. J.W. Aageson, 'Paul's Use of Scripture: A Comparative Study of Biblical Interpretation in Early Palestinian Judaism and the New Testament with Special Reference to Romans 9-11', 64-65; R. Longenecker, *Biblical Exegesis in the Apostolic Period*, 108-111; and E.E. Ellis, *Paul's Use of the Old Testament*, 150-152, who each define a quotation differently and detect up to six less instances.
[27] See Chapter Seven, section III for a list.
[28] Barrett, 'The Interpretation of the Old Testament in the New'; Michel, *Paulus und seine Bibel*; Smith, 'The Use of the Old Testament in the New' and 'The Pauline Literature'; Ellis, *Paul's Use*.

that the Jewish Law for Paul had lost its practical meaning has remained practically unchallenged in New Testament scholarship.[29]

Does paucity of Scriptural citation in Paul's ethics, coupled with these other reasons, necessarily betray a lack of dependence on Scripture? Were the Scriptures as Paul says in 1 Corinthians 10:11, "written for our ethical instruction," or is this statement, as von Harnack insists, only incidental ("nur beiläufig"),[30] and not indicative of Paul's practice? The present study is an attempt to answer these questions.

## II. The Need for the Present Study

Though there is no shortage of opinion on the question of the status of the Scriptures as a source for Paul's ethics, there is by comparison a dearth of substantive work on the subject. One might expect to find research into Paul's dependence upon the Scriptures for ethics in three types of studies: in investigations of the use of the Old Testament in the New Testament; in studies of Paul's ethics; and in the literature on Paul and the Law. However, in all three cases this subject does not form a primary focus of interest. Other concerns dominate the discussion.

Studies of Paul's use of the Old Testament almost invariably concentrate on Paul's use of the Scriptures to explain and defend his doctrine. This emphasis grows out of a preoccupation with the Old Testament quotations in Paul's letters,[31] which most often address matters of belief rather than conduct. The goal of C.H. Dodd's seminal work, *According to the Scriptures: The Sub-structure of New Testament Theology* (1952), was, for instance, "to discover just how the Old Testament was employed to elucidate the *kerygma*" (27). The relation of the Old Testament to the early Christian *didache*, to use Dodd's terminology,

---

[29] Tomson, *Paul and the Jewish Law*, 3.
[30] Harnack, 'Das Alte Testament', 138.
[31] Two previous studies of Paul's use of the Old Testament in 1 Corinthians, F.S. Malan, 'The Use of the Old Testament in 1 Corinthians' and H. Ulonska, 'Die Function der alttestamentlichen Zitate und Anspielungen in den paulinischen Briefen' only look at quotations and allusions. Gerhard Sellin's history of research on the problems of 1 Corinthians ('Hauptprobleme des Ersten Korintherbriefes') covers the origin and character of Corinthian problems (3001-15), and the originality (*Die Eigenart*) and structure of Paul's responses (apostle as model, Christ as model, love, corporeality and the new creation). The origin and sources of Paul's responses, it seems, has not attracted much scholarly attention.

was not on his agenda.[32] The title of Barnabas Lindars' book speaks for itself: *New Testament Apologetic: The Doctrinal Significance of the Old Testament Quotations* (1961). Likewise, F.F. Bruce's *This is That: The New Testament Development of Some Old Testament Themes* (1968), covers the rule, salvation, victory and people of God, and various Messianic themes, but ignores the subject of ethics.

Related to this concentration is the commonly voiced opinion that Paul read the Scriptures with Christ in mind (not unlike Jesus and the disciples on the road to Emmaus).[33] According to A.T. Hanson, *The Living Utterances of God: the New Testament Exegesis of the Old* (1983), whereas the Pharisees searched the Scriptures to help discover the right *halakha*, New Testament authors such as Paul did so in order to discover what light they shed on Jesus Christ (42).[34] What the Scriptures taught concerning conduct apparently did not arrest Paul's attention. That the study of Paul's use of the Old Testament has been dominated by this perspective is evident from the title of Dietrich-Alex Koch's recent and impressive work, *Die Schrift als Zeuge des Evangeliums: Untersuchungen zur Verwendung und zum Verständnis der Schrift bei Paulus* (1986), which he believes captures Paul's hermeneutical stance; Scripture is for Paul "witness to the gospel" (Rom 3:21). Only three pages of the book (296-98) are devoted to "die paränetische Verwendung der Schrift."

Studies of Paul's ethics by and large do not devote much energy to the question of sources and antecedents in general and to Scripture as a source in particular. The following studies, for example, do little with Biblical/Jewish background: A. Verhey, *The Great Reversal: Ethics and the New Testament*; J. L. Houlden, *Ethics and the New Testament*; W. Schrage, *The Ethics of the New Testament*; Ceslaus Spicq, *Théologie Morale du NT*; Heinz-Dieter Wendland, *Ethik des NT*; Siegfried Schulz, *Neutestamentliche Ethik*. In Schrage's twelve page introduction to New Testament ethics, which covers the subject of background, the Old Testament is not even mentioned! Hans Hübner's review of Pauline research ('Paulusforschung seit 1945: Ein kritischer Literaturbericht') *zur Ethik* (2802-8) touches upon its relation to the Old Testament only

---

[32] The same concentration is evident in James Barr's *Old and New in Interpretation: A Study of the Two Testaments* (1966).

[33] Luke 24:27, "Beginning with Moses and all the Prophets, he explained to them what was said in all the Scriptures concerning himself."

[34] Cf. Hans von Campenhausen, *The Formation of the Christian Bible*, 27: "Paul reads the Scriptures from the standpoint of Christ"; and Richard Longenecker, *Biblical Exegesis*, 206-9 on the "Christocentric Interpretation" of the New Testament authors.

once (2806), where the point is made (with reference to Schrage's work) that the Old Testament Law is not binding for Christians.[35] On the subject of New Testament ethics James I.H. McDonald offers a helpful distinction between three different types of parænesis: (1) traditional parænesis, which involves general moral themes (eg. Rom 12:1-13:14); (2) situational parænesis, which consists of *ad hoc* exhortations to specific situations (e.g., 1 Cor 5:1-11:1) and (3) ecclesiastical parænesis, which is related directly to the institutional needs of the church and the ministry (e.g., 1 Cor 11:2-14:40).[36] The Biblical/Jewish basis of Pauline traditional parænesis has received the serious attention of a number of scholars (see Chapter Two, section II). However, by comparison, the same roots of Pauline ecclesiastical and especially situational paraenesis, the present study's interest, have been neglected.

The enormous literature on the vexed question of Paul's attitude to the Law of Moses focusses almost exclusively on Paul's statements about the Law rather than the use he may have made of the Law; Paul's precept rather than his practice takes centre stage. In these studies, not surprisingly, Romans and Galatians figure most prominently, and the predominantly practical and ethical Corinthian epistles are neglected by comparison. Theories of development in Paul's view of the law are most often between Galatians and Romans, and the major interpretive cruxes, upon which entire monographs are devoted, are also confined to them.[37] In F.F. Bruce's, 'Paul and the Law in Recent Research', which covers the work of W.D. Davies, C.E.B. Cranfield, C.F.D. Moule, E.P. Sanders, H. Hübner, C.T. Rhyne, H. Räisänen and J.D.G. Dunn, Galatians and Romans not only dominate discussion, they are the discussion; there is not a single reference to 1 Corinthians.[38] Hans Hübner's review of Pauline research ('Paulusforschung seit 1945') on the question of the Law (2668-91), which

---

[35] A few partial exceptions are Victor Paul Furnish, *Theology and Ethics in Paul*, which devotes sixteen pages to 'The Old Testament and Judaism' as a source of Paul's ethical teaching (28-44), W. Meeks, *The Moral World of the New Testament*, which includes a chapter on "The Great Traditions: Israel" (65-96) concentrating on post-biblical Jewish moral teaching, and Eduard Lohse, *Theologische Ethik des Neuen Testaments*, which acknowledges *Altes Testament und Judentum* as part of the *Umwelt* of NT Ethics (13-17).

[36] McDonald, *Kerygma and Didache*, 89.

[37] For instance, on Romans 3:31, see C.T. Rhyne, *Faith Establishes the Law*; Romans 8:2, P. von der Osten-Sacken, *Evangelium und Tora: Aufsätze zu Paulus*; Romans 10:4, Badenas, *Christ the End of the Law: Romans 10.4 in Pauline Perspective*.

[38] The same is true of Douglas Moo, 'Paul and the Law in the Last Ten Years'.

covers the work of more than thirty scholars, mentions 1 Corinthians only with reference to J.W. Dranes's development hypothesis (2,687). Hans Hübner, *Das Gesetz bei Paulus*, is typical; the book has three chapters entitled, *Nomos im Galaterbriet, Nomos im Römerbrief* and *Verdichtung*.

Only three studies, to my knowledge, place first on their agenda an investigation of the status of Scripture as a source for Paul's ethics; Adolf von Harnack, Andreas Lindemann and Traugott Holtz have written independently, it seems, on this subject.[39] However, the question is not resolved by their work since they offer only (albeit seminal) articles and not full scale studies, and arrive at different conclusions (whereas von Harnack and Lindemann think Paul did not depend upon the Scriptures, Holtz conceives of significant indebtedness).[40]

A fourth study, Peter J. Tomson, *Paul and the Jewish Law: Halakha in the Letters of the Apostle to the Gentiles* (1990), which underscores the Jewishness of Paul's moral teaching and appeared after most of the research for this book was completed, is worth comparing with the present study. Tomson's book claims to be a forthright critique of three traditional assumptions of scholarship on Paul: "(1) the centre of his thought is a polemic against the Law; (2) the Law for him no longer had a practical meaning; and (3) ancient Jewish literature is no source for explaining his letters."[41] The book expends most of its energy in refuting the third assumption, exploring the roots of Paul's moral teaching in 1 Corinthians (5-14), Romans (14:1-15:13) and Galatians (2:11-14) in halakha, the legal tradition of Judaism. Tomson's findings are that Paul has a fundamentally positive relation to the halakha. A great value of the book is thus in its impressive assembly of post-Biblical Jewish parallels to Paul's practical teaching.

Tomson's work overlaps with the present study with its interest in the second assumption. *Paul and the Jewish Law* is not, however, a study of Paul's indebtedness to the Scriptures in the same sense as the present study. There is no mention in Tomson of von Harnack, Lindemann, Holtz or Koch on the subject, and no comment on 1

---

[39] Von Harnack, 'Das Alte Testament'; Lindemann, 'Die biblischen Toragebote'; Holtz, 'Zur Frage der inhaltlichen Weisungen bei Paulus'.

[40] Other scholars to have written about the relevance of Scripture to one aspect of Paul's ethics include Bernadette J. Brooten, 'Paul and the Law: How complete was the departure?', who perceives with reference to gender roles and gender relations continuity with the law, and R.G. Hamerton-Kelly, 'Sacred violence', which includes a survey of the non-relation of Paul's ethics to the Mosaic Law along the lines of von Harnack and Lindemann (though without reference to either).

[41] Tomson, *Paul*, 1.

Corinthians 4:6; 10:11; 9:9,10 or Romans 15:4 (texts which address Paul's attitude to the practical value of the Scriptures; Tomson prefers to highlight 1 Cor 7:17-24 and 9:19-23). Tomson also concentrates on different passages in Paul's letters than the present study. Whereas *Paul and the Jewish Law* devotes only nine pages to 1 Corinthians 5-6 (75-76, 97-103), issues related to 1 Corinthians 8-10 cover almost 70 pages (151-220). Tomson's interest is in Paul's relation to Jewish halakha, and the implications this may have for Law polemic and the practical value of the Mosaic Law in Paul's thought. The present study focuses first on Scriptural dependence, then on the influence of related Jewish moral teaching (see Chapter Two for a rationale for this method).[42] The present study is thus not as comprehensive as Tomson's work, concentrating as it does on only three chapters (1 Cor 5-7), but it is more radical, taking the Scriptures rather than Jewish halakhah as its starting point. Much of what Tomson concludes about the Jewishness of Paul the apostle to the Gentiles rings true with our own findings.

### III. THE PRESENT STUDY

The present study is an investigation of the dependence of Paul's ethics upon the Scriptures. It is not a study of Pauline hermeneutics. We are not concerned to tackle the fascinating question of *how* Paul used Scripture for ethics.[43] It is also not primarily an investigation of *why* Paul turned to certain parts of the Scripture's teaching and not others for his moral teaching.[44] Rather this book concentrates on the prior and more fundamental question of *whether* Paul is indebted to the Scriptures for ethics. To answer this question we shall focus not primarily on what Paul says about the Scriptures but what he does with the

---

[42] This different tack leads the present study to discover a key role in the formation of 1 Corinthians 5-6 in passages like Deuteronomy 23, Exodus 18/Deuteronomy 1 and Genesis 39 (to pre-empt some of our major results), texts which are conspicuous by their absence from Tomson's work.

[43] See Richard B. Hays, *Echoes of Scripture in the Letters of Paul*, and R.B. Hughes, 'Textual and Hermeneutical Aspects of Paul's Use of the Old Testament in 1 and 2 Corinthians', for such studies.

[44] E.g., Perhaps Paul saw the moral as against the ritual requirements of the law as still binding or maybe he understood the Noachian commandments as his hermeneutical key to the Old Testament vis-à-vis the Church (see Thomas R. Schreiner, 'The Abolition and Fulfilment of the Law in Paul' and Tomson, *Paul and the Jewish Law*, respectively).

Scriptures. Our findings will, it is hoped, be of interest to those investigating the questions of *how* and *why*, if for nothing more than supplying further data (previously unrecognised traces of Scriptural indebtedness) with which to test their theories. The challenge of the task at hand, in view of the considerable forces arrayed against a dependency hypothesis (see page four), is sufficient to engage our full attention.

We are also not primarily concerned with how Paul developed his ethics, strictly speaking. Eckhardt Schnabel has recently considered this question.[45] In his study of Paul's exhortations to overcome conflict in the church and to strive for unity Schnabel distinguishes motivations, norms and criteria. According to Schnabel, motivations to obedience in Paul's ethics include christological, salvation-historical, pneumato-logical, ecclesiological and eschatological bases. Valid norms for behaviour, guides to being and doing, consist of Old Testament teaching, the words of Jesus and apostolic teaching. And the realisation of Christian living is governed and led by certain criteria: the Holy Spirit, the governing powers and authorities instituted by God, love, reason, conscience and missionary effectiveness. We do not deny a valid place for these in Paul's ethical reasoning.[46] As vital as such discussion is, we are not so much interested in the *foundations* of Paul's ethics in the present study, what he uses to build his moral exhortations; the focus here is the *origin* of Paul's ethics, the basic tradition in which he stands.

The debate over the relation of Paul's ethics to Scripture is comparable to the question of the origins of halakhah in the Mishnah, in which two rival views also compete. Are the laws in the Mishnah largely derived from Scripture by exegesis or are they just laws which occasionally look for biblical support?[47] Though the Mishnah is only infrequently explicit about its Scriptural base some argue that, none-

---

[45] Schnabel, 'Wie hat Paulus seine Ethik entwickelt? Motivationen, Normen und Kriterien paulinischer Ethik'.

[46] Many of these elements are in fact themselves derived from Scripture; see chapter seven, III.

[47] M. Hagigah 1:8 takes the view that laws should have some Scriptural basis: "The rules about release from vows hover in the air and have naught to support them; the rules about the Sabbath, Festival-offerings, and Sacrilege are as mountains hanging by a hair, for (teaching of) Scripture (thereon) is scanty and the rules are many; the (rules about) cases (concerning property) and the (Temple-) service, and the rules about what is clean and unclean and the forbidden degrees, they have that which supports them, and it is they that are the essentials of the Law."

theless, most of the laws represent implicit exegetical tradition.[48] Other scholars contend that the source of the Halakha is in pure oral tradition which derives primarily from religious thought and custom, rather than Scripture.

A specific and current sample of this debate focuses on the rite of "the red cow" (Num 19:1-10), which is elaborated in Mishnah Parah. Jacob Neusner believes that such Mishnaic details of ritual embody a philosophy of holiness that is significantly different from that of the Scriptures, being a response to Jewish political helplessness after the A.D. 70 destruction of the temple.[49] H. Maccoby, however, has accused Neusner of special pleading and inaccuracy in reaching this conclusion, insisting that "the rabbis' main concern was to implement the attitudes they found in the Bible."[50] What Maccoby attempts to do for Mishnah Parah (with special reference to "the red cow") in response to Neusner (ie, rediscover and assert its Biblical basis), the present study attempts to do (perhaps less polemically) for Paul's ethics (with special reference to 1 Cor 5-7) in response to von Harnack, Lindemann, *et al* (ie., rediscover and assert its Biblical basis).

Do the Scriptures have practical/pragmatic/halakhic authority for Paul? Our concern in this study is to discover to what extent one can trace the chief lines of Paul's ethics (in the representative sample of 1 Corinthians 5-7) back into the Scriptures in most cases by way of Jewish sources. Thus this book considers *Paul's dependence upon the Scriptures for ethics in 1 Corinthians 5-7*. To introduce the study six subjects require some explanation.

## A. *Paul's Jewishness*

What justification is there for expending energy on searching the Scriptures, as opposed to some other source or factor, as a possible background to Paul's ethics? The first reason for this heuristic concentration

---

[48] Eg. J. Lauterbach, 'Midrash and Mishnah', 163-256; cf. Eckhard J. Schnabel, 'Law and Wisdom: in the Mishnaic System', who believes that the laws in question are "at once scripture-based, traditional and yet geared to the needs of real life Jewish communities" (104). For an introduction to the debate and major issues see Shmuel Safrai, 'Halakha', 121-86, esp. 123-25, 133-55, and H.L. Strack/G. Stemberger, *Introduction to the Talmud and Midrash*, 142ff. On similar questions asked of literature from Qumran see Philip R. Davies, 'Halakhah at Qumran'.

[49] Neusner, *A Religion of Pots and Pans*.

[50] Maccoby, 'Neusner and the Red Cow', 73.

is an obvious one: Paul was a Jew (Gal 1:13f; Phil 3:4-6; 2 Cor 11:22). The normal first century Jewish experience included considerable instruction in the Scriptures in the context of both home and synagogue (cf. Josephus, Ag. Ap. 2:178,204). Philo wrote that the Jews "consider their laws to be divine revelation and are instructed in them from their youth" (Legatio 210; cf. 115). According to Aboth 5:24 "at five years old one is fit for the Scripture." In 4 Maccabees 18:10 there is intimation that the model Jewish father gave much instruction in the Scriptures to his sons. The educational character of the synagogue service is stressed by Josephus (Ag. Ap. 2:175): Jews "gather together to listen to the law and learn it accurately."[51] In this light the present study represents an attempt to sound the depths of the Jewishness of Paul the Christian ethical teacher.

What was Paul's place in Judaism? Rather than needing to limit Paul's background to one corner or another of first century Judaism,[52] there are good reasons to believe that his exposure was broad indeed. The information about his pre-Christian career in Acts connects him both with Jerusalem and the diaspora. According to the sole surviving witness to Paul's education, Acts 22:3, Paul was educated at the feet of the honoured rabbi Gamaliel (possibly the grandson of Hillel).[53] Though trained in Palestine he maintained a living connection with Tarsus, his hometown (see Acts 9:30; 11:25), wrote his letters in Greek and used the Greek Bible. Indeed, in Acts 21:37ff, Paul is depicted as able to speak both Greek and Aramaic.[54] These indications of both double linguistic and geographical spread are closely paralleled by what we know of Josephus, who although born in Jerusalem, later lived in the diaspora and composed his writings in both Greek and

---

[51] Cf. Paul Barnett, *Bethlehem to Patmos*, 34-35.

[52] One cannot, of course, draw hard and fast distinctions between Hellenistic and Palestinian Judaism; as Horbury notes, summarising Schürer, 'Herod's Temple and "Herod's Days"', 105 "'Palestinian' Judaism can be found outside as well as inside Palestine, and 'Hellenistic' Judaism inside as well as outside." Cf. E. Schürer, *Geschichte des jüdischen Volkes im Zeitalter Jesu Christi*, III: 188-89. On reciprocal interchange of thought between Palestine and the diaspora see Davies, *Paul*, 1-16, esp. 6-7; Hengel, *Judaism and Hellenism: Studies in their Encounter in Palestine during the Early Hellenistic Period*; and Martin Goodman on Jewish literature composed in Greek, revised Schürer IIIi: 470-704.

[53] On Paul's relation to Pharisaic-Rabbinic tradition see Davies, *Paul*, and Daube, *The New Testament and Rabbinic Judaism*; and Hengel, *The Pre-Christian Paul*, 46-48, 133, n. 232.

[54] According to Martin Hengel, 'Zwischen Jesus und Paulus', 169ff. Paul, the ἑβραῖος (Phil 3:5; 2 Cor 11:22), spoke Hebrew/Aramaic.

Aramiac (see the opening of *The Jewish War*).[55] Paul's standard greeting to the churches to which he writes, χάρις καὶ εἰρήνη,[56] illustrates this combination of Greek and Hebrew influences; the phrase, as Max Zerwick and Mary Grosvenor note, "combines and Christianizes Gk and Hebr. greetings, χαίρειν and shalôm."[57] Tomson's description of Paul as a "hellenistic Pharisee" is thus not far from the mark.[58]

A second reason for our concentration on the Scriptures in this study is also an obvious one: Paul occasionally cites Scriptural texts in practical contexts (see Chapter Seven, section III for a list) and also states that in formulating his moral teaching he found the Scriptures to be useful. We shall save a discussion of the interpretation and theological import of such passages in 1 Corinthians and Romans to Chapter Seven.

In the search for the sources of Paul's thought, Paul's Scriptural inheritance may thus be regarded as having the priority over other sources, such as pagan law, Stoicism, Iranian religion and Graeco-Roman mystery religions. The case for establishing implicit connections between Paul's writings and the Scriptures even has an advantage over that which seeks to find echoes from Jesus-tradition. In this regard Richard B. Hays points out that "the Gospels are written later than Paul's letters, and Paul shows relatively little direct evidence of having known the traditions that they contain."[59]

## B. *Method*

Most studies of the use of the Old Testament in the New Testament concentrate upon explicit usage, looking only at quotations of and perhaps allusions to Scripture. The present study's interests are broader, including evidence of more subtle and perhaps less deliberate employment of Scripture. The word "use" is thus used in this book in its wider sense to include not only explicit use of Scripture but also what might be called implicit and instinctive use of Scripture. Our

---

[55] Cf. the Bar Kochba letters of instruction which were written in Greek, Hebrew and Aramaic.

[56] Cf. Apoc. Baruch 78:2; 2 Maccabees 1:1.

[57] Zerwick and Grosvenor, *A Grammatical Analysis of the Greek New Testament*, 458.

[58] Tomson, *Jewish Law*, 48-53. For a full and fair discussion of the pre-Christian Paul including questions of origin, citizenship, education, schooling and Pharisaic study of the Law in Jerusalem see M. Hengel, *The Pre-Christian Paul*.

[59] Hayes, *Echoes of Scripture in the Letters of Paul*, 30. For a full and more positive evaluation of Jesus-tradition in Paul's letters, especially Romans 12:1-15:13, see Michael Thompson, *The Example and Teaching of Jesus in Romans 12.1-15.13.*

concern is not just to catalogue how often Paul cites Scripture for
ethics, but to ask to what extent Scripture is the basis of Paul's ethics,
regardless of whether this is given explicit indication.

The following comments concerning method for our study of 1
Corinthians 5-7 (Part Two) apply equally well to other New Testament
passages. The first step in evaluating the use of Scripture for ethics
in any New Testament passage is to study the subject of that passage
in the Scriptures and related early Jewish literature (see Chapter Two).
For example, to study Paul's dependence upon the Scriptures for ethics
in 1 Corinthians 5:1-13, one must first study the Scriptures' teaching
on incest and on community exclusion; in 1 Corinthians 6:1-11—
on judges and judging; in 1 Corinthians 6:12-20—on fornication and
prostitution; and in 1 Corinthians 7:1-40—on marriage, sex, singleness
and asceticism. Obviously if a Biblical quotation is present (cf. 5:13b;
6:16) it should be investigated as a possible doorway into a larger
room of Scriptural teaching. Once this background material has been
assembled it should be held up as a mirror against the relevant New
Testament passage to see to what extent the influence of Scripture
may be reflected. Having listened to the Bible's teaching on a subject
one is ready to hear echoes (albeit with variations) in the New Testament. In the investigation of the influence of Scripture we shall consider
both why Paul objects to certain behaviour and the lines of instruction
he formulates to correct it.

In practice this process will involve the identification of Old Testament quotations, allusions, motifs, ideas, vocabulary, and so on. While
it is true that such levels of usage may be distinguished,[60] the main
focus of this work is not what kind of use is evident but whether
substantial use of Scripture can be identified at whatever level.

Objective criteria for the identification and evaluation of evidence
for Paul's dependence upon the Scriptures are not difficult to list.[61]
However, some subjectivity always enters in at the stage of application;
exegesis is never an exact science. Individual cases of Scriptural
dependence in Paul's ethics may be assessed by asking questions
concerning:

---

[60] See eg. William M. Schutter, *Hermeneutic and Composition in 1 Peter*, 35-36;
Thompson, *Jesus in Romans*, 28-36.
[61] Three of the most helpful discussions upon which our own builds are Hays,
*Echoes of Scripture*, 29-33; Thompson, *Jesus in Romans*, 28-36, and Watts, 'The Isaianic
New Exodus in Mark', 142-43.

*1. Verbal agreement.* What evidence is there of shared vocabulary? How rare are these terms both in the Scriptures and in Paul's letters? Are there unique combinations of significant words?

*2. Recurrence.* Does Paul cite or allude to the same Biblical passage, character or book elsewhere? Is it likely Paul knew of and regarded this passage highly?

*3. Tradition Indicators.* Is there evidence of stylistic or syntactical changes which can be explained by the presence of a Scriptural echo? Is there an introductory formula, particle (e.g., γάρ, δέ) or even asyndeton present?

*4. Intermediary Stage/Channel of reception.* What effect may early Jewish moral teaching have had on Paul's perception of this Scriptural text? Due to the foundational nature of the notion of Jewish mediation of Scripture to Paul's ethics to both the method and results of this study we shall devote an entire chapter, Chapter Two, to its elucidation.

*5. Thematic coherence.* How well does this alleged echo fit with the rest of the argument Paul is developing? Do the images and ideas of the proposed precursor text illuminate Paul's argument? Is some exegetical light shed on the passage?[62]

*6. Alternative sources.* Could Paul just as easily have derived the instruction in question from Jesus-tradition, Graeco-Roman philosophy, etc? Is the evidence for Scriptural dependence distinctive? The limitations of a single volume necessitate the selective application of this measure.

To ignore such criteria is to fall prey to the charge of 'parallelomania',[63] of jumping naively from similarity of thought to dependence. Any study of the Old Testament in the New Testament must endeavour not only to be creative, but cautious and judicious in its judgements, if it expects to win a serious hearing. However, although the six criteria undergird our study throughout, to run through them in each isolated case would be wearisome and is unnecessary.

Some of the connections between Paul and Scripture we shall propose are less certain than others. The argument of the study, it must be stressed, rests not upon individual items, but upon the cumulative

---

[62] See esp. Hays, *Echoes of Scripture*, 30.
[63] See Samuel Sandmel, 'Parallelomania'.

weight of the evidence. Rather than 'one bad apple spoiling the whole
barrel', when it comes to establishing Paul's dependence upon the
Scriptures for ethics, 'the more (connections between Paul's parænesis
and his Scriptural inheritance) the merrier'. Given the *a priori* likelihood
that Paul used Scripture for ethics (he did so explicitly on occasion,
claimed to have found it instructive, and was a Jew; see section IIIA
above), if enough of Paul's moral teaching can be shown to be *plausibly*
related to Scripture, coupled with a stronger case for several key features
(which are virtually certain or at least highly probable), then the scales
will be tipped in favour of a general dependency hypothesis.

I have approached the task in such a manner that the argument
of the present study does not stand upon evidence from the disputed
Pauline epistles, convinced that a strong case can be made even within
such restrictions. Though evidence from Ephesians and the Pastorals
is occasionally mentioned, it is never vital to the point at hand. Richard
Longenecker has observed that:

> while a precise determination of the Pauline corpus is of great significance
> for many historical and theological issues related to the apostle Paul,
> it is of lesser significance for a study of the apostle's use of the Old
> Testament [the great bulk of quotations are found in the *Hauptbriefe*].[64]

## C. *Paul's Old Testament Canon*

What does Paul understand by the term "the Scriptures"? Does he
have in mind what is now commonly labelled "the Old Testament"?
Unfortunately scholars are divided on this question. Whereas some
argue for a three-stage canonization theory (the Law, c.400 B.C.; the
Prophets, c.200 B.C.; and the Hagiographa, c.90 A.D. at Jabneh
[Jamnia]),[65] which conceives of a rather looser canon in Paul's day
than in ours, there is good evidence that the Old Testament canon
was effectively closed before the New Testament was written. E. Earle
Ellis contends that: "in the first century (Philo, Josephus) and even
two centuries earlier (Ben Sira) Judaism possessed a defined and
identifiable canon."[66] The notion of a certain number of books forming a fixed collection at an early date is supported, in particular, by
Josephus' Against Apion 1:38-42 and 2 Esdras (= 4 Ezra) 14:44-46.

---

[64] Longenecker, *Biblical Exegesis*, 107.
[65] This theory was popularised by nineteenth-century scholars and has been
developed by, *inter alia*, A.C. Sundberg, *The Old Testament and the Early Church*, and
J. Barton, *Oracles of God*.
[66] Ellis, 'The Old Testament Canon in the Early Church', 679; see 655-79 for

While it is not within the scope of the present study to enter fully into this complicated debate, we shall procede, as is customary in studies of Paul's use of the Old Testament, with the working hypothesis that the Hebrew Scriptures used by Paul comprised those currently printed in the Hebrew Bible.[67]

## D. *Paul's moral teaching*

Some may object that the concentration of the present study upon Paul's ethics imposes an arbitrary and artificial distinction onto the material.[68] Indeed, the dogmatic distinction between "doctrine" and "ethics" has at best a slender linguistic base in New Testament Greek; no term consistently captures the sense of "moral teaching" parallel to the modern term "ethics": ἦθος means habit or custom, and παρά-δοσις, κατηχέω, and παράκλησις while denoting basic instruction, often include not only piety and practice but also the content of the faith. The term παραινέω (advise/recommend; cf. paraenesis), though typically associated with moral education and practical ethical instruction, is not adorned with this technical sense in its few New Testament occurrences (see Acts 27:9,22). Even C.H. Dodd's distinction between κήρυγμα, content-oriented proclamation to outsiders, and διδαχή, moral instruction to believers, though dominant in British New Testament scholarship for decades, is upon closer inspection an oversimplification.[69] A straightforward comparison of Mark 3:14-15 ("he sent them out to preach," κηρύσσειν) with 6:30 ("they reported to him all they had done and taught," ἐδίδαξαν) demonstrates the significant overlap between the two terms. The New Testament language of communication is fluid and complex, with no single term corresponding precisely with what we mean by "ethics."[70]

---

evidence. S.Z. Leiman, *The Canonization of Hebrew Scripture: The Talmudic and Midrashic Evidence*, and R.T. Beckwith, *The Old Testament Canon of the New Testament Church and its Background in Early Judaism* offer full and convincing treatments. Barton reviewed Beckwith and labelled it an "apologetic for fundamentalism." Beckwith's criticisms of Barton's work are more substantive concluding that Barton "misrepresents part of the evidence and fails to do justice to the rest of it" (p. 395).

[67] This position is supported by Koch's investigation of Paul's practice of Scriptural citation, *Die Schrift*, 32-48.

[68] On the unity of the indicative and imperative (doctrine and ethics) in Paul's letters see Furnish, *Theology and Ethics*, 137-38, 157, 207, 211, 225-26, and *The Love Command in the New Testament*, 215.

[69] Dodd, *Gospel and Law*. See Furnish, *Theology and Ethics*, 106-14 on the inadequacy of Dodd's distinction in Romans.

[70] See McDonald, *Kerygma and Didache*, for a helpful discussion of these terms.

While a sharp distinction between doctrine and ethics in Paul's writings cannot be based on lexical grounds, there are several factors which suggest that for heuristic purposes a concentration on Paul's moral teaching is not entirely anachronistic and illegitimate. The perspicacious twofold structure of Romans and Galatians, the first part pertaining primarily to matters of belief, the second to questions of conduct, indicates that in Paul's mind the two, though related, are not indistinguishable.[71] Furthermore, the widespread first century concern with the interpretation of the Pentateuch, including legal decisions on conduct according to the law, likewise points to an interest in the broad category of moral teaching in Paul's day.[72] When we speak of Paul's ethics in the present study we are in no way endorsing a deep cleavage from his doctrine, nor do we mean to imply philosophical analysis; we simply have in mind his "ways which are in Christ" (1 Cor 4:17), his "instruction as to how one ought to walk and please God" (1 Thess 4:1).

## E. A Test Case

The significance of the present study for understanding Paul's dependence upon the Scriptures for ethics largely depends upon whether one can generalise from the case study of 1 Corinthians 5-7. Is 1 Corinthians 5-7 a representative sample from the diverse materials which comprise Paul's ethics? Is it a reliable sounding? There are several features of this passage which commend its adoption as a test case.

1 Corinthians 5-7 appears in an epistle described by Wayne A. Meeks as "the richest example of Christian parenesis that survives from the first century."[73] If Romans is Paul's fullest and most systematic exposition of his gospel, then 1 Corinthians represents his most thorough and vigorous ethical teaching. Furthermore, in 1 Corinthians Paul asserts the universality of much of his teaching, claiming that it is applicable to "all the churches" (see 4:17; 7:17; 11:16 and 14:33). In their studies of Paul's use of Scripture for ethics von Harnack,

---

[71] See Chapter Three, section V and Excursus 1 on the interrelation of the indicative and imperative in Pauline and Biblical thought.

[72] See Chapter Two, section III.

[73] Meeks, *The Moral World*, 130. Cf. also Davies, 'Paul and the Law': Reflections on Pitfalls in Interpretation, 9; and Tomson, *Paul and the Jewish Law*, 68-73, esp. 73: 1 Corinthians is "a letter replete with practical instruction . . . eminently suitable for the study of Jewish tradition in Paul."

Lindemann and Holtz, despite other differences, are at one in their high estimation of the importance of 1 Corinthians. Von Harnack writes:

> In keinem anderen Brief hat Paulus seine ganze apostolische Weisheit in Bekehrung und Pädagogie so vielseitig aufbieten müssen wie in dem 1. Korintherbrief. In keinem anderen Brief hat er zugleich so umsichtig das, was er zu sagen hatte, ausführen und begründen müssen wie in diesem Schreiben ... aber kein Thema ist in diesem Schreiben nur gestreift, vielmehr bewundert man in allen Kapiteln, wie es dem Apostel gelungen ist, pädagogische Eindringlichkeit mit sachlicher Vollständigkeit und Präzision zu verbinden.[74]

Lindemann believes that when it comes to observing Paul engaged with actual ethical conflicts, "solche Konflikte werden am klarsten im Ersten Korintherbrief sichtbar."[75] All three articles devote much attention to this epistle.

1 Corinthians 5-7 is not a narrow and unrepresentative selection from Paul's ethics. Within a relatively short compass (73 verses) several major topics of Paul's ethics are touched upon, including incest, exclusion, greed, sexual immorality, the state, and marriage.[76] It contains response to both oral (chapters 5-6) and written (chapter 7) reports from Corinth, and various forms appear, ranging from classic parænesis to vice catalogues and even a proverb (5:7).

1 Corinthians 5-7 is also not a selection from Paul's ethics which at first sight appears to have substantial roots in the Scriptures; the present study cannot be accused of choosing a sample that readily supports a thesis of Scriptural dependence. Johann Perk's ambitious listing of over two thousand Old Testament parallels in the New Testament, *Handbuch zum Neuen Testament: Alttestamentliche Parellelen*, lists only a handful for 1 Corinthians 5-6 (Lev 18:7-8; 20:11 for 5:2; Exod 12:15; 13:7 for 5:7; Deut 13:6; 17:7; 21:21; 22:24 for 5:13; Dan 7:21-22 for 6:3; Gen 2:23-24 for 6:16) and none for 1 Corinthians 7. There is only one undisputed quote from Scripture in these chapters (6:16). Most commentators indicate by their silence that the Old Testament has little to do with Paul's instructions here, and for each of the four sections (5:1-13; 6:1-11; 6:12-20; 7:1-40) several scholars emphatically

---

[74] Harnack, 'Das Alte Testament', 13.
[75] Lindemann, 'Die biblischen Toragebote', 243.
[76] Major concrete ethical problems in Paul's ethics not touched upon in 1 Corinthians 5-7 include the collection and issues relating to idolatry (cf. 1 Cor 8-10).

deny that Scripture has played a formative role. Indeed, some might wonder whether there are sufficient data to write a book on the use of Scripture in these three chapters. Von Harnack insists that 1 Corinthians 5-7 "hat zum A.T. kaum Beziehungen."[77]

## F. *Thesis*

The thesis of the present study is that in spite of the relatively few quotations of Scripture in Paul's ethics and other indications to the contrary (see the seven reasons listed in section I), the Scriptures are nevertheless a crucial and formative source for Paul's ethics. To use Paul's own words, Scripture was "written for our ethical instruction" (1 Cor 10:11; Rom 15:4; RSV).[78] The results of our research indicate that in 1 Corinthians 5-7 at least the debt to Scripture is much greater than has often been supposed.

The study is divided into two parts. Part One (chapters one and two) presents general considerations concerning the relation of Paul's ethics to the Scriptures.

Part Two (chapters three to six) investigates in detail Paul's indebtedness to the Scriptures in 1 Corinthians 5-7. The general thrust of our findings in Part Two is represented by the chapter titles; in 1 Corinthians 5-7 we shall discover significant links between Ezra and Paul excluding sinners (5:1-13; Chapter Three), Moses and Paul appointing judges (6:1-11; Chapter Four), Joseph and Paul fleeing immorality (6:12-20; Chapter Five), and between the Torah and Paul on the subject of marriage (7:1-40; Chapter Six). The nature of these links varies from case to case. For example, whereas we shall argue that the connection between Paul and Joseph is a literary one (Paul had the story of Genesis 39 in mind), the similarities between Paul and Ezra are probably due to mutual dependence on the Pentateuchal laws of exclusion. In no case does the title subsume everything there is to be said in the chapter about the Scriptural background to the passage in question. The titles serve in part a rhetorical purpose, highlighting a measure of the present study's contribution (Ezra, Moses, Joseph and the Torah barely rate a mention in treatments of 1 Corinthians 5-7) and its overall intent (to rediscover links with the Scriptures).

---

[77] Harnack, 'Das Alte Testament', 132.
[78] For comment on these passages and others that relate to Paul's attitude to scriptural teaching in relation to his ethics see Chapter Seven, section IV.

Chapters three to five close with an interpretative paraphrase, following the example of some earlier commentators (such as J.B. Lightfoot), which attempts to reflect our exegesis and also notes significant cross references to Biblical and Jewish literature discussed in the chapter. An appendix adds a small piece of evidence to the case, by tracing the Biblical/Jewish origin of 1 Corinthians 10:22b.

A Conclusion (Chapter Seven) draws together the results and teases out the implications of the entire study. The discovery that the Scriptures were in Paul's mind "written for our instruction" has considerable implications for the study of Christian origins as well for the interpretation of the New Testament.

# CHAPTER TWO

# INDIRECT DEPENDENCE
# SCRIPTURAL INFLUENCE THROUGH
# JEWISH MORAL TEACHING

## I. INTRODUCTION

*"you became obedient . . . to that form of teaching to which you were committed"*

The task of this chapter is to consider the influence of early Jewish moral teaching on Paul's ethics. To suggest that Paul's ethics should be seen against a Jewish background would not be new. Various scholars have argued that extra-Biblical Jewish moral teaching exerted a profound influence on Paul when he regulated conduct in the early churches (see section II for a selective review of this study).[1] The "form of teaching" (Rom 6:17) to which Paul committed his churches had much in common with early Jewish catechesis. The main point we wish to make in this chapter is that this Jewish influence can only be fully appreciated when considered in conjunction with the influence of the Scriptures. *Early Jewish moral teaching represents an intermediary stage which stands between the Scriptures and Paul and mediates Scripture to Paul.* Scripture (A) influenced Jewish moral teaching (B), which in turn influenced Paul's ethics (C); $A{\rightarrow}B{\rightarrow}C.$[2]

To examine this rather sweeping proposal we shall attempt to answer four questions, which correspond to four constituent parts of the $A{\rightarrow}B{\rightarrow}C$ process: (1) In what ways do scholars consider that Jewish traditions influenced Paul's ethics? (the link $B{\rightarrow}C$); (2) Where should one look for this Jewish moral teaching? (the entity B); (3) To what extent did Scripture influence Jewish moral teaching? (the link $A{\rightarrow}B$); and (4) What evidence is there that Jewish moral teaching mediated

---

[1] In Galatians 1:14 Paul states that "extremely zealous was I for the traditions of my fathers," which Longenecker, *Galatians*, 30, uncontroversially describes as referring to "(1) the teachings and practices developed in the Pharisaic schools of Second Temple Judaism . . . and (2) the interpretations of a more popular nature that arose within the synagogues of Paul's day." Section III gives an outline of this material that is extant.

[2] This proposal received its initial impetus from an analogous treatment of the indirect influence of the Scriptures upon the catechesis of the Church Fathers by William Horbury, "Old Testament Interpretation in the Writings of the Church Fathers", 736-40.

Scripture to Paul's ethics? (the whole process A→B→C).[3] Sections II, III, IV and V contain our answers to these questions.

## II. The Influence of Jewish Moral Teaching on Paul's Ethics (B→C)

An attempt to account for Paul's thought historically has always been at the heart of historical-critical study of Pauline theology. For well over a hundred years scholars have attempted to 'explain' Paul's thought by appealing to the influence of Hellenism, emphasising the centrality of Paul's conversion and/or by stressing his Jewish heritage. This being the case it is surprising that historical-critical endeavour has not given more attention to the Jewish origins of Paul's ethics. The early studies of the Jewish origin of Paul's thought ignore Paul's ethics. For example, Henry St. John Thackeray's *The Relation of St. Paul to Contemporary Jewish Thought*, 1900 has chapters covering Adam, the Law, Justification, Eschatology and Spirits, but not ethics,[4] and many studies of Paul's ethics, even some recent ones, offer little by way of Jewish background.[5] This *Forschungsgeschichte* would certainly contain many more entries if the subject were the Jewish background of any one of a number of aspects of Paul's doctrine, such as Christology, Eschatology or Soteriology.

The study of the Jewish background to Paul's ethics turns up in four types of research. Apart from (1) a few studies which set out to investigate Paul's ethics in light of his Jewish heritage, relevant discussion appears in: (2) studies of Jewish moral teaching (which may in a suggestive and seminal way refer to the applicability of their results for studies of Christian origins);[6] (3) commentaries on the practical sections of Paul's letters and studies of New Testament ethics

---

[3] Ground is covered in this chapter relevant to the debate over which elements in Paul's letters derive from Judaism and which from Hellenism. It is not our purpose to adjudicate or even further this discussion. Rather, the point to be underscored is that those elements which show some derivation from the ethical tradition of Judaism are to a great extent mediating Scripture to Paul.

[4] H.-J. Schoeps, *Paulus—Die Theologie des Apostels im Lichte der jüdischen Religionsgeschichte*, 1959 also passes over ethics, dwelling instead upon eschatology, soteriology, law theology and salvation history.

[5] See Chapter One, section II, "The Need for the Present Study."

[6] E.g., Max Küchler, *Frühjüdische Weisheitstraditionen*; Christov Münchow, *Ethik und Eschatologie: Ein Beitrag zum Verständnis der frühjüdischen Apokalyptik mit einem Ausblick auf das Neue Testament*; and Maldwyn H. Hughes, *The Ethics of Jewish Apocryphal Literature*.

(which sometimes include a discussion of sources and presuppositions); and (4) studies of specific New Testament parænetic forms such as virtue and vice catalogues and household codes (which often address the question of antecedents). Much of this study has been neglected and has remained on the fringes of Pauline scholarship. For example, Seeberg's pioneering studies (see section IIA below) fail to receive a mention in Stephen Neill/Tom Wright, *The Interpretation of the New Testament: 1861-1986*, and are ignored by Werner Georg Kümmel, *Das Neue Testament: Geschichte der Erforschung seiner Probleme*.

In the following short review of study of the Jewish background to Paul's ethics we shall mention some of the main contributions and a few dissenting voices in order to answer two questions. First, what evidence is there that Paul's ethics was influenced by Jewish moral teaching? Secondly, which texts comprise this crucial deposit of instruction? Limitations of space dictate that these goals be achieved without mentioning every turn and player in the several debates.[7] We shall aim at covering representative work in each of the various attempts to relate aspects of Paul's ethics to their Jewish background.[8] In line with our interest in the Scriptural roots of Paul's ethics, mention will also be made of work which, in addition to a Jewish influence, mentions the impact of the Scriptures.

The study of the Jewish background to Paul's ethics can be divided into four sections covering: (1) the early period; (2) household codes; (3) ethical lists; and (4) Paul's ethics in general. We shall include evidence from studies of letters which many scholars do not consider to be written by Paul, such as Ephesians and Colossians, in order to learn as much as possible about Jewish background relevant to moral teaching.

A. *The Pioneering Studies—the Christian Catechism Hypothesis*

In 1903 Alfred Seeberg's *Der Katechismus der Urchristenheit* initiated the serious study of the Jewish background to Paul's ethics with a grand and sweeping theory. He argued that much of Paul's ethical material

---

[7] Crouch's history of research on the Colossian Haustafel alone, *The Origin and Intention of the Colossian Haustafel*, 9-31 for example, amounts to some 10,000 words.

[8] Much work is still to be done in this area. Cf. James H. Charlesworth, *The Old Testament Pseudepigrapha and the New Testament: Prolegomena for the Study of Christian Origins*, 91 who, when discussing the importance of the Pseudepigrapha for New Testament studies, includes among "significant explorations left for future work . . . the study of paraenesis and ethics."

consisted of the modification of a Jewish catechism. This source had been formulated for the instruction of proselytes and was known to John the Baptist and Jesus. In its modified form the Christian catechism consisted of *Glaubensformel* and *Sittenlehre*. The latter supposedly contained ethical instruction including catalogues of virtues and vices and a household code. Seeberg's work was later refined by G. Klein and P. Carrington.[9] The Christian catechism hypothesis posed the problems and asked the questions with which later studies of the Jewish background to Paul's ethics were to grapple,[10] even though most scholars were not persuaded by Seeberg's reconstruction. Scholars took the task of research in several different directions. Some recognized the limitations by concentrating on the larger shape of the ethical material[11] and instead focused upon individual units such as Pauline household codes and ethical lists. The discovery of the Dead Sea Scrolls and the revival of scholarly interest in the documents of the Old Testament Pseudepigrapha occasioned more specialised investigations in certain quarters of the Jewish background.[12]

## B. *Household Codes—Stoic, Christian or Jewish?*[13]

Household codes supply good evidence for a Jewish inspiration at the level of both form and content of one aspect of "Pauline" ethics, namely, traditional parænesis. Colossians 3:18-4:1 and Ephesians 5:22-6:9[14] are relatively independent, self-contained, parænetic units which

---

[9] Klein, *Der älteste Christliche Katechismus und die Jüdische Propaganda-Literatur*, 1909; P. Carrington, *The Primitive Christian Catechism: A Study in the Epistles*, 1940.

[10] For example, in their major studies of the Jewish background to Paul's ethics, K. Weidinger, 1928, 4ff.; A. Vögtle, 1936, 3ff.; S. Wibbing, 1959, 4ff; E. Kamlah, 1964, 7, n.4; J.E. Crouch, 1972, 13ff.; and K.-W. Niebuhr, 1987, 1ff. all feel the need to come to terms with Seeberg's ground-breaking work.

[11] F. Hahn's survey and evaluation of Seeberg's works in the introduction to the 1966 reprint of Seeberg's *Katechismus* also criticises Seeberg on this point; see xii.

[12] The Jewish systematic theologian, Kaufmann Kohler, who wrote about the same time as Seeberg, also deserves mention as a scholar who was interested in the influence of early Judaism upon Christianity, especially in the ethical writings; see e.g., "Didache, or The Teaching of the Twelve Apostles" (1903).

[13] James E. Crouch, *Haustafel*, 9-31 organises his review of research into the pattern of ethical teaching upon which the Colossian Haustafel was based according to three competing hypotheses; either the code is (essentially) Hellenistic, Christian or Jewish in origin. This three part division is also followed by other *Forschungsgeschichten* such as R.P. Martin, 'ἀρετή', 929-32 and Peter O'Brien, *Colossians, Philemon*, 215-18. For a recent survey of the primary sources and some of the debates in the secondary literature see David L. Balch, "Household Codes".

[14] 1 Timothy 2:8-15; 6:1-2; Titus 2:1-10; (cf. 1 Clem 21:6-9) though sometimes

contain admonitions addressed to Christians according to their station[15] in life: wives and husbands, children and fathers, and slaves and masters.[16]

Whereas M. Dibelius and his pupil K. Weidinger argued that the codes in question are lightly Christianized forms of earlier lists drawn from Stoic moral philosophers (such as Aristotle, Seneca, Plutarch and Epictetus),[17] K.H. Rengstorf claimed that the Haustafeln are uniquely Christian, inspired by the home-life of John and Jesus described in Luke 1-2.[18] James E. Crouch, on the other hand, found the best precedents for the household codes in the literature of Hellenistic Judaism.[19] E. Schweizer, W. Schrage, and W. Lillie to a large extent concur.[20] The main sources to which Crouch points are Philo (Hypo.

---

included in the study of New Testament Haustafeln are better regarded as *Gemeindetafeln*, church-order regulations. These passages lack the pattern of reciprocal obligation and the household situation of the Colossian and Ephesian codes.

[15] D. Schroeder, 'Lists-ethical', 546 (cf. his 'Die Haustafeln des NT: Ihre Herkunft und ihr theologischer Sinn') aptly designates them "station codes."

[16] The relevance of the Haustafeln for Paul's ethics, even if Colossians and Ephesians were not written by Paul, is spelt out by Crouch, *Haustafel*, 29: "the content (though not the form) of the exhortations to the subordinate members of the Haustafel, is found in 1 Cor. 7—especially in vss. 17ff."

[17] Dibelius (*An die Kolosser*, 1913; see especially after his comments on 4:1) and Weidinger (Die *Haustafeln: Ein Stück urchristlicher Paränese*, 1928) appeal to expressions such as ἀνῆκεν (Col 3:18) and εὐάρεστον (Col 3:20), which are common in the Stoic literature. The motivation ἐν κυρίῳ (Col 3:20, etc.) is in their opinion merely a cosmetic Christian pendant. In spite of the popularity of the theory, especially in German scholarship (Crouch, *Haustafel*, 21 lists many adherents including Bultmann, Thyen, Conzelmann, Lohse and Merk) several factors weigh against it. There are considerable differences between the content, motivations, and settings of the Christian and non-Christian material, and their form is markedly different (the Stoic lists use neither direct address nor the imperative mood). The most that can be said is that the Haustafeln share certain characteristics with some Hellenistic codes.

[18] Rengstorf, 'Die neutestamentliche Mahnungen an die Frau, sich dem Manne unterzuordnen', 1954. In these narratives Joseph and Zechariah are clearly the heads of their respective families (a concept shared with the Ephesian and Colossian codes) and in Luke 2:51 Jesus is submissive, ὑποτάσσω, to his parents (a key term in both codes). Furthermore, an important Haustafeln motif, that of ἀγάπη, surely derives, he argues, directly from the example of Jesus. The influence of such Christian factors is difficult to weigh (though one wonders in what sense the family lives of Jesus and John were distinctively 'Christian'?). However, as a comprehensive theory of the origin of the Haustafeln material this view would become unsatisfying if some ancient sources, with which Paul may have been familiar, could be shown to contain some quite similar elements to the Haustafeln, which brings us to the theory of Jewish origin.

[19] Crouch, *Haustafel*, 1972.

[20] Schweizer, 'Die Weltlichkeit des Neuen Testaments: die Haustafeln', 1977; Schrage, 'Zur Ethik der neutestamentlichen Haustafeln', 1975; Lillie, 'The Pauline House-tables', 1975.

7:1-9),[21] Josephus (Ag. Ap. 2:190-219) and Pseudo-Phocylides (175-227). His opinion is that "each [of these] drew from a store of ethical material which was in current use in Jewish missionary activity."[22] He argues persuasively that the Hellenistic Jewish codes are significantly more similar to the Pauline codes than are the Stoic lists.

The influence of the Scriptures on the Pauline Household codes has not escaped the notice of a few scholars. D. Schroeder (who takes an eclectic view of the background to the Haustafeln) considers that the content of the Pauline codes is basically Old Testament-Jewish and argues that their form reaches back to Old Testament apodictic law (cf. Deut 5:16), which also uses direct address in the imperative mood supported by statements designed to motivate obedience.[23] Lillie also emphasises Old Testament-Jewish influences, noting the fifth commandment quotation in Ephesians 6:2-3 (and the example of Sarah cited in the equivalent Petrine code, 1 Pet 3:6).[24] Finally, Lars Hartman has recently argued that the Decalogue was a major "point of departure" not only for the relevant texts from Philo, Josephus and Pseudo-Phocylides but also for the Colossian Haustafel.[25]

## C. *Ethical Lists—Stoic, Iranian or Jewish?*

The origin of another form of traditional parænesis in Paul's letters has engaged the interest of scholars, namely catalogues of virtues and vices. The main examples are found in 1 Corinthians (5:9-11; 6:9-10), Romans (1:29-31; 13:13), Galatians (5:19-23) and Philippians (4:8). Three chief theories of the 'pre-history' of these lists, which are in fact a less specific class of household code, deserve mention. Whereas Anton Vögtle emphasised the indebtedness of New Testament ethical lists to Stoicism,[26] and Siegfried Wibbing and Ehrhard Kamlah both

---

[21] Schweizer, 'Haustafeln', has noted not only the influence of Hellenisitic Jewish sources on the Haustafeln, but also the impact of the Old Testament on the Jewish sources themselves. For instance, he points out that in Philo's instruction, unlike the (non-Jewish) Hellenistic codes, there are echoes of the Biblical concern for the welfare of the weak and disadvantaged in society. Parental authority is limited by the first commandment, Israel is reminded of her slavery in Egypt, and the married life of the neighbour is protected.

[22] Texts from 4 Maccabees, Sirach, Tobit and Aristeas are also cited.

[23] Schroeder, 'Haustafeln'; 'Lists-Ethical'.

[24] Lillie, 'House-Tables'.

[25] Hartman, 'Code and Context: A Few Reflections on the Parenesis of Colossians 3:6-4:1', 1987, 243. P. Stuhlmacher, 'Christliche Verantwortung bei Paulus und seinen Schülern', 177-78 also draws the decalogue into the discussion of the household codes.

[26] Vögtle, *Die Tugend- und Lasterkataloge im Neuen Testament*, 1936. The catalogues

found the roots of New Testament catalogues in the dualistic cosmology of Iranian religion,[27] E. Schweizer and P. Borgen are examples of those whose stress on the Jewish background to the Pauline vice catalogues has proved to be more convincing.[28]

F.F. Bruce and D. Schroeder have independently, it seems, offered a critique of the Iranian provenance theory which underscores instead the impact of the Old Testament.[29] They rightly question whether dualistic expression in the New Testament (such as found in Eph 5:6ff.) can be taken to reveal dualistic anthropology. Few scholars doubt that the New Testament God is an unrivalled Sovereign. Both the Community Rule and Pauline catalogues manifest rather the ethical dualism of the Old Testament prophets' Day of the Lord which promised salvation and judgement for different groups (eg. Jer 21:8; Ezek 18:5-9,15-17), and the blessings and curses of Deuteronomy 27.[30]

---

of Philippians 4:8 and 2 Peter 1:5-7 have more affinities with Stoic parallels than the other New Testament lists. A significant Stoic influence upon the New Testament catalogues in general, especially those in Paul's letters, has, however, not been established to the satisfaction of many scholars. Schroeder's conclusion, 'Lists, Ethical', 547 that evidence of such borrowing is crucially absent, though sweeping, is close to the mark: "The Stoic ethic is informed by what is natural, the New Testament ethic by love (agape) and faith; there is no Stoic parallel to Paul's identification of virtues with "fruit of the Spirit;" the four cardinal virtues and corresponding vices of Stoicism are not present in New Testament catalogues; and many of the virtues in the New Testament lists were regarded as vices in Stoicism."

[27] Wibbing, *Die Tugend- und Lasterkatologe im Neuen Testament und ihre Traditionsgeschichte unter besonderer Berücksichtigung der Qumran- Texte*, 1959 (originally a Heidelberg dissertation); Kamlah, *Die Form der katalogischen Paränese im Neuen Testament*, 1964. Wibbing considered that IQS, which contains virtue and vice catalogues in its section dealing with the governance of mankind by two spirits, found its roots in Iranian religion, and that Paul's ethical lists, also set in a dualistic framework, belong to the same milieu. Kamlah refined Wibbing's theory by distinguishing between "parænetic" catalogues, which describe putting off vices and putting on virtues, and "descriptive" catalogues, which close with a promise of salvation and/or a threat of destruction. He limited the influence of the dualistic cosmology of Iranian religion to the descriptive catalogues (parænetic catalogues were put down largely to Hellenistic syncretism with its dichotomy between the body and the soul).

[28] Schweizer, 'Traditional ethical patterns in the Pauline and post-Pauline letters and their development (lists of vices and house tables)', 1979; Borgen, 'Catalogues of Vices, the Apostolic Decree and the Jerusalem Meeting'. Martin, 'Haustafeln', 929 has also discerned that the discussion has shifted in the search for the provenance of the Pauline catalogues from Hellenistic sources "to the Old Testament Jewish tradition."

[29] Bruce, 'Review of Wibbing's *Die Tugend- und Lasterkataloge im Neuen Testament*'; Schroeder, 'Lists-Ethical'.

[30] Niebuhr, *Gesetz*, 234 has noted the pervasive influence of Deuteronomy 27 in Hellenistic Jewish paranesis.

Concerning the latter text's potential for explaining the origin of the catalogues, F.F. Bruce explains:

> So far as the solid ethical content is concerned more attention should be paid to Deuteronomy, where the shechemite dodecalogue of curses (xxvii. 15-26), with its implied companion-catalogue of blessings, is incorporated into a hortatory context which concludes with the admonition: 'See, I have set before thee this day life and good, and death and evil, . . . the blessing and the curse: therefore choose life . . .' (xxx. 15ff).[31]

The combined influence of Biblical and Jewish sources accounts for much of the background to the Pauline ethical lists.

## D. *Paul's Ethics—from Different Vantage Points*

We now turn to the final class of studies of the Jewish background to Paul's ethics. This brings Paul's ethics as a whole into consideration instead of one aspect of it. These studies may be distinguished according to the parcel of Jewish texts they bring to the task of comparison. Scholars have held Paul's ethics up to the background of Rabbinic literature (Selwyn, Daube, Davies), Qumran documents (Stachowiak) and Hellenistic Jewish parænesis (Holtz, Reinmuth, Niebuhr).

## 1. Paul's Ethics and Rabbinic Literature

W.D. Davies believes: "We can be sure that Paul would be familiar with ethical maxims and social conventions which the Rabbis propagated and that he used in his training of Christians."[32] David Daube's work on a puzzling grammatical feature of many of the hortatory sections of Paul's epistles (and 1 Peter) forms the primary basis for this statement.[33] Frequently in Romans (12:9-19, seventeen times; 13:11) and occasionally in Ephesians (4:2-3) and Colossians (3:16) the participle is used with an imperatival force.[34] Daube suggested that the imperatival

---

[31] Bruce, 'Review', 390. Cf. also Sebastian Brock, 'The Two Ways and the Palestinian Targum', who traces the origin of the "two ways" theme (cf. Didache, 1:1; the Letter of Barnabas, 18) to the Palestinian Targum of Deuteronomy 30.

[32] Davies, *Paul and Rabbinic Judaism: Some Rabbinical Elements in Pauline Theology*, 135.

[33] Daube's work appears as an appendix in E.G. Selwyn, *The First Epistle of St. Peter*, 467-88.

[34] This strange use of the participle had been explained by W. Sanday and A. C. Headlam, *The Epistle to the Romans*, 360, in terms of an elided ἐστε. J.H. Moulton agreed with this assessment (*Grammar of New Testament Greek*, I:180-83) seeing the construction as "established beyond question in the papyri" (cf. also M. Zerwick,

participle construction was due to Hebrew or, less probably, Aramaic
influence. He noted that the New Testament usage occurs solely in
regulations covering social behaviour within community and family,
which is one way in which post-Biblical Hebrew also used the participle
in the laws of Mishnah and Tosefta, and in baraitot. Davies sums
up what he considers to be the significance of Daube's position for
the study of the Jewish background to Paul's ethics:

> wherever in the Epistles of Paul we find the participle used instead of
> the imperative there Paul is certainly using material derived from Jewish
> sources, probably from some kind of Jewish codes of rules that had
> established themselves within Judaism as useful for the purpose of moral
> education.[35]

Davies suggests three possible sources for "the kind of material upon
which Paul drew . . . in drawing up moral rules," (only some of which
include the imperatival participle).[36] First, he mentions the Mishnah's
most familiar ethical tractate Aboth, as paralleling the matter, if not
the form, of Pauline parænesis. Secondly, reference is made to the
Jewish practice of drawing up codes to regulate contact with outsiders,
exemplified in the Zadokite Fragment (see eg. 9(B) vss. 11-30) and
Mishnah Demai (the first half of which goes back to the second Temple
period).[37] Thirdly, he turns to the derek eretz literature, especially
Derek Eretz Rabba and Derek Eretz Zuta (chs 1-4). While acknowl-
edging the limitations of this evidence,[38] Davies (and Daube, both
following Klein) claims that, in all likelihood, "every Rabbi had a
collection of such material, ethical and social maxims, rules for
conduct."[39] These three pockets of surviving literature give us some
idea of the kind of Rabbinic material which may have influenced
the hortatory sections of Paul's epistles.

Some details of the evidence for the Daube-Selwyn-Davies position
are, however, open to question. Nigel Turner points out that C.L.

---

*Biblical Greek*, 129-30). Daube, however, has pointed out that six of the seven examples
given by Moulton from papyri can be explained as normal usage of the participle
where it depends on a prior finite verb.
[35] Davies, *Paul*, 131.
[36] Davies, *Paul*, 131.
[37] Concerning Demai Davies, *Paul*, 132 adds this qualification: "the codes used
by Paul would differ in matter from the technicalities of Mishnah Demai, but would
be similar in form."
[38] The evidence is rather sparse, forms at best a general parallel to Paul and is
difficult to date—it may be Tannaitic but is it preapostolic?
[39] Davies, *Paul*, 135.

Mitton (in his Ephesians commentary) has shown that one example of the imperatival participle, 1 Peter 2:18, is comparable with Ephesians 6:5, which has the same injunction, but uses a straightforward imperative.[40] We could add that in 1 Thessalonians 5 Paul delivered many of the same commands using an imperative which he employed in Romans 12 using the participle. Alternative explanations of the imperatival participle in Paul (and 1 Peter) are also possible. Turner suggests that the Semitic influence in question may have come from spoken Jewish Greek in the Diaspora rather than Tannaitic Hebrew since "many apparent Semitisms are found in the secular Common Greek of Egypt, where there was a large Jewish population."[41]

Daube et al. make both a general and a specific point about Paul's ethics. The specific point, that passages like Romans 12:9ff. arise from a translation of Tannaitic rabbinical codes of conduct, is difficult to affirm with confidence in light of the misgivings expressed above; this conclusion may overstep the evidence.[42] The general point, that such hortatory passages in Paul's ethics bear some similarity to extant Rabbinic literature, sharing in the same tradition of ethical instruction, is, however, a more assured result.[43]

## 2. Paul's Ethics and Qumran documents

An example of a scholar who looks at Paul's ethics from the perspective of Qumran in a substantive way is L.R. Stachowiak. In 'Paraenesis Paulina et Instructio de duobus spiritibus in "Regula" Qumranensi', a summary of his German doctoral dissertation, he compares Pauline parænesis with the Manual of Discipline and concludes that both depend on a common basic Semitic tradition.

## 3. Paul's Ethics and Hellenistic Jewish Parænesis

In recent years two highly significant contributions to the study of the Jewish background to Paul's ethics have appeared. Both originated as dissertations at the Martin-Luther-Universität, Halle-Wittenberg

---

[40] Turner, *Grammatical Insights into the New Testament*, 167-68.

[41] Turner, *Grammatical Insights*, 168.

[42] Cf. Turner, *Grammar of New Testament Greek: Style*, IV:89: "it (the phenomenon of participles as imperatives) is not sufficient evidence for a Hebrew *Vorlage* to Romans 12."

[43] Cf. C.F.D. Moule, *An Idiom Book of New Testament Greek*, 180: "a strong case can be made for tracing at least some of these participles to Semitic influence."

under the direction of Traugott Holtz: Eckart Reinmuth, *Geist und Gesetz—Studien zu Voraussetzungen und Inhalt der paulinischen Paränese*, 1985; and Karl-Wilhelm Niebuhr, *Gesetz und Paränese—Katechismusartige Weisungsreihen in der frühjüdischen Literatur*, 1987.

In 1981 Holtz published an article, 'Zur Frage der inhaltlichen Weisungen bei Paulus' (referred to in Chapter One, section I), which asserted that the main source of the content of many of the ethical directives in Paul's letters was hellenistic Judaism. Several comments in this article chart the course which the later work of Reinmuth and Niebuhr was to take. The thesis of Reinmuth's study is found in seed form in a discussion of 1 Thessalonians 4:1-8, where Holtz notes the precedent of Jewish paraenesis in also prohibiting the common Pauline vices of sexual immorality and greed. Holtz contends:

> Inthaltlich entspricht der 'Wille Gottes' (V. 3) den auch mit seinem doppelten Inthalt, nämlich Enthaltung von Unzucht und keine habgierige Übervorteilung des Bruders, genau einem jüdischen Grundkatechismus des Verhaltens, der sich übrigens an einer ganzen Reihe von Stellen im Corpus Paulinum als zugrundeliegend nachweisen lässt.[44]

Reinmuth's study of the Spirit and the Law in Paul's letters presents the bold thesis that Paul advocated Law observance. Two sound observations of Paul's ethics and early Jewish paraenesis form the basis for the argument. First, Reinmuth notes that unchastity and greed are prominent vices in both Paul (see Rom 1:29-31; 2:21-22; 1 Cor 5:9-11; 6:9-10; and especially 1 Thess 4:1-8) and early Jewish literature (texts taken from Ps-Phoc, T. 12 Patr., Sib. Or., Men-Phil, 1 Enoch, Syr-Men, Ps-Herac, CD,[45] and esp. T. Jud. 18:2-6). Secondly, he shows that both Paul (1 Cor 3:16-17; 6:12-20; 2 Cor 6:16; Gal 5:13-6:10; Rom 8:1-11) and various early Jewish texts (T. Sim. 4:4; T. Ben. 8:2; Sib. Or. 3:698-701; 1QS 3:6-8) link the coming of the Spirit with obedience to God. Reinmuth believes that unchastity and greed were "a collective code word"[46] for general non-observance of the

---

[44] Holtz, 'Frage', 392. Three earlier articles of Holtz, 'Zum Selbstverständnis des Apostels Paulus', 'Zur Interpretation des Alten Testaments im Neuen Testament' and 'Die Bedeutung des Apostelkonzils für Paulus' are also of interest in tracing the development of his thought which would eventually blossom in the work of his academic progeny. They appear respectively as chapters 10, 6 and 11 of a collection of his articles, *Geschichte und Theologie des Urchristentums*.
[45] CD and 1QS are the only documents cited by Reinmuth which do not fit the category of Hellenistic-Jewish paraenesis.
[46] Robert A. Wild, 'Review of *Geist und Gesetz* by Eckart Reinmuth', 679.

Law among Jews in Paul's day. Since in the latter Jewish texts obedience to God amounts to obedience to the Law, Reinmuᵗh concludes that Paul advocates law observance when he opposes unchastity and avarice (remembering the caveat that 'the ceremonial law' was abrogated by the Christ event).[47]

Unfortunately, the most crucial point in this argument, that by prohibiting the two vices in question one advocated Law observance, is the weakest in Reinmuth's scheme. Very few of the Jewish texts offer genuine support for this hypothesis. It does not follow that to cite key moral emphases from the Law necessarily means that one is urging wholesale adherence to that code. If this were so one would expect, at least in Paul's case, more explicit indication for the sake of Gentile readers.[48]

Leaving aside the relevance of Reinmuth's work for the question of Paul's attitude to the Law, his major achievement in relation to the present study is the carefully documented assertion that sexual immorality and greed are two key vices in the Scriptures (A), Jewish moral teaching (B), and Paul's ethics (C). Although not labelled as such by Reinmuth, these data constitute a fine example of the mediation of Scripture via Jewish moral teaching to Paul's ethics. That Paul's ethics are pervaded by an opposition to these two vices is thus explicable in terms of indirect dependence upon the Scriptures.

Later in the article Holtz sends out a plea for further research into the theology of the Law in early Judaism, which Niebuhr was later to heed:

> In der Tat stehen wir hier vor einem zentralen Problem der Gesetztheologie nicht nur des Paulus, sondern des Neuen Testaments überhaupt und darüber hinaus des Frühjudentums, das einmal der genaueren thematischin Durchdringung bedürfte.[49]

Niebuhr's work will be discussed in section IVA.

---

[47] Cf. Test. Judah 18:2,6: "Guard yourselves therefore, my children, against sexual immorality and love of money . . . for two passions contrary to God's commands enslave him."

[48] Other problems for the work, such as the fact that Ps-Herac is a dubious text and 1 Thessalonians 4:1-8 may not in fact censure sexual immorality and greed, but only the former sin (πλεονεκτεῖν ἐν τῷ πράγματι τὸν ἀδελφὸν αὐτοῦ in verse 6 is a euphemism for adultery; cf. RSV and I.H. Marshall, *1 and 2 Thessalonians*, 110-12), are less telling.

[49] Holtz, 'Frage', 393.

E. *Conclusion*

A variety of scholars are thus convinced for different reasons that much of Paul's ethics is to be understood against a Jewish background.[50] How are we to conceive of this influence on Paul's ethics? Does Paul depend on a specific collection of material? How did he become acquainted with such teaching? It is not wise to attempt to prove the literary dependence of the ethical sections of Paul's epistles upon *certain* Jewish texts.[51] It is better to take the Jewish texts not as what Paul had in mind when he instructed his churches concerning proper Christian conduct, but as a witness to the ocean of Biblical moral teaching in which Paul was immersed, especially since much is undoubtedly lost. The texts of Jewish moral teaching involve common moral emphases and share standard features of ethical instruction to such an extent that we may safely assume that they witness to a widespread tradition of ethical teaching.

This tradition was in all likelihood diffused among Jews such as Paul by the exposition of the Scriptures in the synagogues.[52] Through such activity standard interpretations became attached to Biblical texts, so that when Paul thought of key texts in the Pentateuch, for instance, it was an interpreted Bible that he was considering. An existing Jewish ethic for Gentiles was already in place.[53] Paul had no reason to reject

---

[50] Outside of work focused exclusively on Pauline ethics A.E. Harvey deserves mention. In various publications he argues that the study of Christian ethics of the New Testament period has suffered from being approached with presuppositions derived from the western tradition of moral philosophy instead of being set in the context of the project of moral persuasion which was undertaken by others in and around the first century, especially Jews. On the Jewish background to the Sermon on the Mount see *Strenuous Commands* (esp. 150-53; 194-97); on 2 Peter see 'The Testament of Simeon Peter' (esp. 340-41; 350-52), where he argues that a Christian author, late in the New Testament period, appropriated "the form, the style and even the phraseology of hellenistic Jewish literature, and needed to add only a few cosmetic touches to adapt it for use within the church" (352).

[51] Cf. Charlesworth, *New Testament*, 78: "the documents of the Pseudepigrapha are not primarily important because they are cited by the New Testament authors; they are significant because they reveal the *Zeitgeist* of early Judaism and the matrix of earliest Christianity."

[52] John J. Collins, *Between Athens and Jerusalem: Jewish Identity in the Hellenistic Diaspora*, 162-63 also stresses synagogue preaching as the transmitter of the "common ethic."

[53] Collins, *Between Athens and Jerusalem*, 142ff. argues that "the characteristic feature" of the numerous 'minor' Jewish authors of the Hellenistic Diaspora (the book does not cover Philo) was an emphasis on "those aspects of Jewish law which were likely to get a sympathetic hearing from enlightened Gentiles—chiefly monotheism and the prohibition of homosexuality. . . . Distinctive aspects of Judaism such as circumcision and dietary laws were played down."

this interpretative tradition, as he might have done when the texts concerned the Messiah or the Gentiles or salvation by faith. He perceived no essential discontinuity between the moral demands of the Old and New Covenants.[54] The remarkable concordance between several of the texts of early Jewish paraenesis[55] is best explained in terms of standard traditions of Biblical interpretation. The likely prose-lytising function of much of the literature of Jewish moral teaching also renders Paul's acquaintance with it and high regard for its tradition not unlikely.

It is often objected that the task of comparing any New Testament writing with a text or texts of early Judaism is fraught with danger. Detractors warn that many texts are later than the New Testament, others include Christian expansions and/or interpolations and most cannot be reliably dated. The present venture into this treacherous territory subscribes to the principle that there is "safety in numbers". Our net of Jewish moral teaching is cast widely to include texts of both Palestinian and Diaspora provenance, texts of a sectarian and an establishment ethos and texts representing various genres drawn from several collections. In conjunction with other texts some texts of dubious date or character may be cautiously but legitimately consulted. Our concern is to observe standard features of ethical instruction. A broad sample is intended to confirm the existence of this common knowledge.

Others might object to the investigation on the grounds that talk of the Jewish position on any subject ignores the variety of religious expression and belief evident in the first century.[56] In reply it should

---

[54] Cf. Conzelmann, 101: "The fact that Christianity takes over the Jewish ethic must be theologically understood. Christianity regards itself not as a new system of ethics, but as a practical exercise of the will of the long-known God."

[55] Collins, *Between Athens and Jerusalem*, entitles his chapter on moral teaching, "The Common Ethic;" see 137-74. Cf. 162: "The common ethic which we have seen in such diverse writings as Pseudo-Phocylides, the sibyllines, and the Testaments was pervasive in Hellenistic Judaism." Cf. also, e.g., John Lewis Eron's study of the Testaments of the Twelve Patriarchs' views on sexuality, 'Ancient Jewish Attitudes', which concludes, 24 that they are "consistent with those found in the Apocrypha, Pseudepigrapha, and rabbinic literature." Eduard Lohse, *The Formation of the New Testament*, 42 offers a rationale for uniformity in ethics: "Parenesis, i.e. exhortation to right living, is always and everywhere largely determined by tradition." The complementary explanation offered here is that the texts shared the same biblical foundation.

[56] Eg. Charlesworth, *The New Testament*, 58 writes concerning only one collection of documents that there are far too many theologies in the Pseudepigrapha to speak of *a* theology.

be noted that widespread agreement in matters of conduct is possible
among the texts despite theological differences. For example, the fact
that Jubilees and the Testaments of the Twelve Patriarchs disagree
concerning the future of the Gentiles in relation to the kingdom[57]
does not negate their shared opposition to sexual immorality and greed.
Conservative and liberal theologies may have remarkably similar
standards of conduct.

### III. JEWISH MORAL TEACHING

Jews in the ancient world had incorporated the main ethical teachings
of their Scriptures in writings which presented the Jewish inheritance
to the reader (Jew or non-Jew) familiar with Greek traditions and
customs, such as Paul. Where might one look to find this Jewish moral
teaching (B)? In seeking to answer the question, what are the specifics
of early Jewish moral teaching with which Paul may have been familiar,
scholars may look in eight different directions: the Apocrypha,[58] the
Old Testament Pseudepigrapha, the Dead Sea Scrolls, Philo, Josephus,
Rabbinic Literature, the Jewish Greek Scriptures and archaeological
sources.

As stated in section IIE, the inclusion of a text in this list does
not indicate that we believe Paul necessarily had first hand knowledge
of it, but simply that it is a potential witness to the Jewish tradition
of moral teaching with which he was familiar. The sources could be
grouped according to one of several criteria: genre (testaments,
apocalyptic writings, and so on), provenance (Palestine or locations
in the Diaspora), date of composition, or even the explicitness of their
relation to the Scriptures (from the most explicit, the LXX, to the
least explicit, archaeological sources). Our map of the vast terrain
of early Jewish literature is arranged according to the traditional
collections of documents, which has the advantage of facilitating easy
access to the texts. The following list includes the most obvious examples
and is by no means exhaustive. Prominent studies of the relation of

---

[57] Whereas Jubilees argues that no Gentile will enter the kingdom, the Testaments
suggest that some Gentiles will be saved.

[58] 'Apocrypha' is used here in its conventional sense (as defined in the 39 Articles,
for example) to label those books sometimes included in the Old Testament which
are not in the Hebrew Bible.

a Jewish text or collection of texts to the Scriptures (A→B) or to the New Testament (B→C) are sometimes noted.[59]

A. *Apocrypha*

Catechetical material appears in:
1. Tobit (e.g., 4:3-18);[60]
2. The Wisdom of Solomon (e.g., 4:24ff.);[61]
3. Ecclesiasticus.[62]

B. *The Old Testament Pseudepigrapha*[63]

Listed roughly according to genre:
Instructional material
1. Pseudo-Phocylides (esp. 3-8,9-41,177-94);[64]
2. 4 Maccabees (e.g., 2:4-16);
Apocalyptic Texts
3. The Sibylline Oracles (esp. 3:36-45,185-91, 235-45, 377-80; 594ff., 726-66; 4:31-34; 5:165ff, 386-93, 430ff.);

---

[59] It is surprising that the relevance of many of these sources as background to New Testament ethics is so seldom recognised. For example, in Per Bilde's *Flavius Josephus between Jerusalem and Rome: His Life, his Works and their Importance*, 1988, ethics does not appear in the section on the significance of Josephus for New Testament studies.

[60] On Tobit's extensive exploitation of the narrative elements of the book of Job see Devorah Dimant, 'Use and Interpretation of Mikra in the Apocrypha and Pseudepigrapha', 417-19.

[61] On Biblical allusion in the Wisdom of Solomon see Dimant, 'Interpretation of Mikra', 410-17, and Georg Zeiner, 'Die Verwendung der Schrift im Buch der Weisheit'.

[62] S. Schechter and C. Taylor list nearly 400 apparent Biblical allusions and phrases in their edition of some Ben Sira fragments, *The Wisdom of Ben Sira: Portions of the Book of Ecclesiasticus*, 13-25. On the additions of Codex 248, which offer a window into the moral scruples of a scribe (or scribes) of Ben Sira (in much the same way as the translator's additions in LXX Proverbs; see fn. 79) see J.H.A. Hart, *Ecclesiasticus: The Greek Text of Codex 248*, 274ff.

[63] James H. Charlesworth, 'The Pseudepigrapha as Biblical Exegesis'; cf. 152: "The Pseudepigrapha, like all early Jewish religious writings, generally tended to be in some way exegetical."

[64] What sort of author wrote Pseudo-Phocylides? What was his purpose? A.E. Harvey's suggestion, 'Review', 545-46 that Pseudo-Phocylides is a self-consciously learned piece by a Jew in the style of a classical author intended to show that Jewish wisdom had always been the inspiration of the great non-Jewish Greek authors makes sense of the data and finds ancient precedent in Josephus and the Letter of Aristeas. On 'Pseudo-Phocylides and the New Testament' see the article by P.W. van der Horst.

4. 1 Enoch;[65]
5. 2 Enoch (e.g., 10:4ff.; 42:6-14);
6. The Testament of Abraham (e.g., [a]/10; [b]/12);[66]
7. The Apocalypse of Abraham (e.g., 24:5-8);
Testaments
8. The Testaments of the Twelve Patriarchs (e.g., T. Reu. 3:3-
6; T. Gad. 3:1-3; T. Levi 14:5ff; T. Jud. 18:2-6; T.
Iss. 3:3-8; 4:2-5; 7:2-6; T. Dan. 5:5-7; T. Ben. 4:1-5;
6:2-5; 8:1ff; T. Ash. 2:1-10; 4:2-5);[67]
9. Jubilees (e.g., 7:20);[68]
Pseudepigraphic Poetry
10. The Psalms of Solomon (e.g., 8:9-13; 4:2-5; 12:1?);[69]
11. Pseudo-Menander (esp. 9-15).

C. *Dead Sea Scrolls*[70]

1. The Damascus Document;[71]
2. The Community Rule;
3. The Temple Scroll;
4. Wisdom texts in 4Q series[72] (such as 4Q370[73]).

---

[65] 1 and 2 Enoch are based on Genesis 5:23-24 (cf. Sir. 44:16); see M.E. Stone, 'Apocalyptic Literature', 395-408, and G.W.E. Nickelsburg, 'The Bible Rewritten and Expanded', 90-97.

[66] See C.W. Fishburne, '1 Corinthians III. 10-15 and the Testament of Abraham'.

[67] H.J. De Jonge, 'The Testaments of the Twelve Patriarchs and the New Testament'; H. Aschermann, 'Die paranetischen Formen der "Testamente des zwölf Patriarchen" und ihr Nachwirken in der frühchristlichen Mahnung'. The crucial question concerning the nature of the Testaments of the Twelve Patriarchs relevant to our interests is whether it is, as James H. Charlesworth, *New Testament*, 108 puts it: "a major witness . . . to Jewish paraenesis just prior to Christianity, or to the profoundly determinative impact of Jewish ethics upon Christian paraenesis in the second century C.E." For a good survey of the problem and a defence of the former position see Geza Vermes and Martin Goodman in the revised Schürer, III1: 767-80.

[68] See John C. Endres, *Biblical Interpretation in the Book of Jubilees*.

[69] See Dieter Luhrmann, 'Paul and the Pharisaic Tradition', which concentrates on evidence from the Psalms of Solomon.

[70] The literature on the interpretation of Scripture in the Dead Sea Scrolls is very large. For a recent treatment see Michael Fishbane, 'Use, Authority and Interpretation of Mikra at Qumran'.

[71] See Jonathan Campbell, 'The Use of Scripture in CD 1-8,19,20'.

[72] See John M. Allegro, *Discoveries in the Judaean Desert of Jordan. V: Qumran Cave 4—I (4Q158-4Q186)* which needs to be read with J. Strugnell's review, 'Notes En Marge Du Volume V des "Discoveries in the Judaean Desert of Jordan"'.

[73] On 4Q370 see Carol A. Newsome, '4Q370: An Admonition Based on the Flood'.

## D. *Philo*

Moral teaching is scattered throughout Philo's apologetic writings and commentaries. A concentration occurs in Hypothetica.[74]

## E. *Josephus*

See especially Against Apion.[75]

## F. *Rabbinic Literature*

### 1. Mishnah

The Mishnah, a codification of rules for conduct according to the Law, *halakhah*, is, by definition, of interest for our subject.[76] Aboth and Demai have been studied by Daube, Selwyn and Davies with reference to Paul's moral teaching (see section IID1).[77] However, other practical material on subjects like idolatry and sexual offences is also scattered throughout the laws of Mishnah, and Tosefta and in baraitot. Such material could be explored from this angle, perhaps via topical summaries of the Talmud such as, *The Sages: Their Concepts and Beliefs* by Ephraim E. Urbach. It was not until the Middle Ages that the ethical principles and concepts of rabbinic literature formed the basis of a specific ethical genre. Tannaitic Rabbinic moral teaching is scattered throughout the vast rabbinic corpus.

### 2. Midrashim

The extensive commentary literature of Mekilta (of Rabbi Ishmael on Exodus 12-23), Sifra (on Leviticus) and Sifre (on Numbers 5-35 and Deuteronomy) could be assessed, via specific Biblical passages, for its moral teaching. It should, however, be used with caution due to its lateness.

---

[74] On the much studied question of the 'Authority and Interpretation of Scripture in the Writings of Philo' see Yehoshua Amir.

[75] Cf. E. Kamlah, 'Frömmigkeit und Tugend: Die Gesetzestypologie des Josephus in C.Ap, 145-295'; G. Vermes, 'A Summary of the Law by Flavius Josephus'; Louis H. Feldman, 'Use, Authority and Exegesis of Mikra in the Writings of Josephus', esp. 507-18.

[76] Halak means "to walk." Note the common Pauline metaphor for conduct, walking, in Galatians 5:16; 1 Thessalonians 4:1; Ephesians 4:1,17; 5:2,8,15; Colossians 4:5; cf. Ferguson, *Backgrounds of Early Christianity*, 391.

[77] On Aboth cf. also B.T. Viviano, *Study as Worship: Aboth and New Testament*.

3. Targumim
The Targumim, though quite late, reliably preserve many ancient traditions of Scriptural interpretation. Since they were transmitted through the synagogues, which were not places of radical innovation but of consensus, these interpretations in all likelihood commanded the support of a wide group. As with midrashim, looking up specific Biblical passages is a way of tapping their interest for early Jewish moral teaching.[78]

4. Extracanonical Tractates
In IID1 ("Paul's Ethics and Rabbinic Literature") we referred to the use made of the derek eretz literature in determining early Jewish ethical teaching. Aboth de Rabbi Nathan, which contains some sayings of the rabbis of the Tannaitic period, and Gerim, which concerns proselytes, are also of interest.

G. *Jewish Greek Scriptures*

Apart from shedding light on the way a certain Biblical passage with moral import was understood by many Jews, the Septuagint is also of interest for understanding early Jewish ethics by way of its occasional pietistic and moralising additions. Such phenomena have been noted and studied in LXX Proverbs by Gillis Gerleman, J. Weingreen and William McKane.[79] The additions to Daniel and Esther, and the expanded ending to Job are likewise LXX witnesses to early Jewish moral sensitivities.

H. *Archaeological Sources*

It may be possible to supplement the witness of literary sources to early Jewish morality with archaeological sources.[80] Saul Lieberman, for example, in *Greek in Jewish Palestine: Studies in the Life and Manners of Jewish Palestine in the II-IV Centuries C.E.* (68ff.), has used tombstones as a source of the ideals of early Jewish piety. Another archaeological source of ethical language are the epitaphs from Tell el Yehoudieh (*CPJ* iii), some of which are quite long and most of which are dated

---

[78] On the ethical teaching and tendencies of the Targumim see Etan Levine, *The Aramaic Version of the Bible: Contents and Context*, especially the chapters on holiness, repentance, prayer and the Torah.
[79] Gerlemann, 'Studies in the Septuagint: III. Proverbs'; Weingreen, ' Rabbinic Type Commentary in the LXX Version of Proverbs'; McKane, *Proverbs*, 33-35.
[80] See Ferguson, *Backgrounds*, 398-403.

in the Ptolemaic or Augustan epochs, a good time to have relevance to Paul. Other Jewish inscriptions, papyri, symbols and art could conceivably be put to the same service.

## IV. The Influence of the Scriptures Upon Jewish Moral Teaching (A→B)

The link between the Jewish texts and Scripture (A→B) may be seen on two levels: firstly, there is the evidence that many of the texts' authors consciously and deliberately wrote with the Scriptures in mind; secondly, we may observe the pervasive influence of two key Pentateuchal complexes.

### A. *Written with the Scriptures in Mind*

In the prologue to Ecclesiasticus the ancient translator describes his grandfather, the author of the book, as a man steeped in the Scriptures and concerned to secure obedience to them:

> My grandfather Jesus, after devoting himself especially to the reading of the law and the prophets and the other books of our fathers, and after acquiring considerable proficiency in them, was himself also led to write something pertaining to instruction and wisdom, in order that, by becoming conversant with this also, those who love learning should make even greater progress in living according to the law.[81]

Many of the authors of early Jewish moral teaching shared Jesus the son of Sirach's perception that they also stood in a Biblical tradition. For some secondary literature on the intimate relation of many of these sources to the Scriptures see the footnotes in section III. In particular it is worth noting (and supplementing) Karl-Wilhelm Niebuhr's conclusion concerning the Biblical roots of hellenistic Jewish paraenesis.[82]

---

[81] The last sentence of the Prologue is also noteworthy: "live according to the law". Cf. Andrew Chester, 'Citing the Old Testament', 160: "It is worth noting the way in which Ben Sira himself speaks (especially at 38:24-39; cf. also 32:15-16; 33:3) of the scribe as occupied with the constant study and interpretation of Scripture."

[82] Despite the fact that Niebuhr's book does not extend its results into the arena of New Testament studies, several factors suggest its relevance to our study of Paul's ethics. First, the publisher of the book obviously recognized its value for New Testament studies, placing it in the *Wissenschaftliche Untersuchungen zum Neuen Testament* series (J.C.B.

The major note of Niebuhr's impressive study, *Gesetz und Paränese*,
is that the traditional stereotypical form of early hellenistic Jewish
parænesis was shaped largely by the Torah (A→B).[83] The book attempts
to establish this contention in three movements. First, the formative
influence of Exodus 20-23, Leviticus 18-20 and Deuteronomy 27 upon
Pseudo-Phocylides 2-41, 177-91, Josephus' Against Apion 2:190-219
and Philo's Hypothetica 7:1-9 is established (a subject we shall take
up in section IIIB, "Written with Certain Scripture in Mind"). In
part II Niebuhr infers a similar Biblical influence upon the parænesis
of the Testaments of the Twelve Patriarchs, which he regards as basically
Jewish, with a Christian overlay. He stresses the similarity of its moral
emphases with those of Pseudo-Phocylides, Philo and Josephus. Part
III surveys a further ten early Jewish texts (apocalyptic texts: Syb.
Or., 2 Enoch, T. Abr., Apoc. Abr.; testaments: Tob., Jub.; instructional
material: Wis., 4 Macc.; and pseudepigraphic poetry: Ps. Sol., Gnom.)
concluding that these show a similar parænetic intent and implicit
reference to the Torah. The Conclusion draws together the main themes
of the fourteen texts (see section VA2, "Standard Virtues and Vices,"
following). The author does not ignore the presence of material in
the texts which was most likely not derived from the Scriptures, but
he does not see it as of primary importance.[84] Niebuhr is convinced
that this Torah-dependent type of parænesis was widespread in early

Mohr could have included it in a non NT series, such as *Texte und Studien zum Antiken
Judentum*, which shares its editor, Martin Hengel, with the *WUNT* series). Secondly,
the author of the book opens his final paragraph by implicitly inviting the use of
his work for understanding the New Testament: "Die untersuchte katechismusartige
Gesetzesparänese des Frühjudentums gehört zu den Voraussetzungen des Neuen
Testament" (243; cf. p.242: "Neutestamentlicher Glaube und neutestamentliche
Frömmigkeit sind daher wesentlich bestimmt durch die religiöse Gedankenwelt und
die Lebensaüsserungen der Synagoge."). Finally, reviewers of the book have noted
its relevance to the New Testament. James C. Vanderkam, 'Review', 514 is exemplary:
"the results of his study are of importance not only for the history of Judaism but
also for the interpretation of the New Testament because, in order to understand
the debates in it about the validity and function of the law, it is important to discover
just what that law meant to Jewish people at that time" (cf. also Van der Woude,
'Review', 104). We would add that the book is also important for the study of Paul's
ethics and especially Paul's dependence upon the Law of Moses for ethics (the use
to which we put it in sections IV and V).
  [83] One of the chief contributions of Niebuhr's study is, according to Collins, 'Review',
753 "his increased emphasis on the material correspondence of Hellenistic Jewish
parenesis with pentateuchal law."
  [84] On non-biblical influences upon early Jewish moral teaching see for example
D. Daube, 'Rabbinic Methods of Interpretation and Hellenistic Rhetoric', and
'Alexandrian Methods of Interpretation and the Rabbis', who sees Alexandrian
rhetorical and legal traditions heavily impacting much Jewish oral tradition.

Judaism, being understood in synagogues in Greek-speaking communities as the application of God's will to the practical problems of everyday life ("die praktische Lebensführung"[85]).

Niebuhr conjectures that the source which underlies the many texts consisted of legal exhortations in sentence form and included related Jewish and non-Jewish material (235-36). However, rather than speculating about the form of some treasure of early Jewish ethical instruction, it is better, in the light of the considerable spread of the common material, to be satisfied with viewing it as the actualisation of the Mosaic Law and to see synagogue exposition as the primary transmitter (see IIE).[86] The numerous parallels between Pseudo-Phocylides and the Rabbinic derek eretz literature pointed out many years ago by G. Klein would reinforce the impression that the tradition of Biblical moral teaching which Niebuhr has studied was widespread in Jewish circles.[87]

There can be little doubt that: "In the main, the approaches to ethics found in the Law, the Prophets and the Writings are continued in the intertestamental period."[88]

## B. *Written with Certain Scripture in Mind*

That Jewish moral teaching was built upon the Scriptures requires further explanation. It was not the case that every book and section of the sacred writings exerted an equal influence. On the contrary, as Niebuhr's study has shown, there is evidence that to a large extent a few key passages from the Pentateuch were the fertile soil from which much of the instruction grew. The Decalogue and Leviticus 18-20 are two such text plots.[89]

The significance of the Decalogue (Exod 20:1-17; Deut 5:6-21) in Israel's tradition would be difficult to overstate. Other collections of law, such as Leviticus 19, Deuteronomy 27:15-26, and Ezekiel 18 and 22, have been compared with the Decalogue,[90] but none can

---

[85] Niebuhr, *Gesetz*, 241.

[86] Niebuhr himself notes the flexibility of "die gemeinsame traditionsgeschichtliche Vorstufe" (236) and resists the temptation to reconstruct an "Urtext."

[87] Klein, *Der älteste Christliche Katechismus*.

[88] D.A. Hubbard, 'Ethics: OT Ethics', 2:169; cf. the title (and substance) of the second chapter of R.T. Herford's *Talmud and Apocrypha: A Comparative Study of the Jewish Ethical Teaching in the Rabbinical and Non-Rabbinical Sources in the Early Centuries*, "The Old Testament as the Main Source of the Later Ethical Teaching."

[89] Deuteronomy 27 may be a third example.

[90] See J.J. Stamm and M.E. Andrew, *The Ten Commandments in Recent Research*, 22-75.

match the Decalogue's simplicity, comprehensiveness and totality in not only containing the epitome of Israelite morality, but in declaring the conditions for membership in the people of God.[91] The Ten Commandments were reputedly spoken by God directly to his people (Exod 20:1,18,19; Deut 4:12; 5:4,22), written by God's finger on tablets of stone (Exod 31:18; 32:16; 34:1,28; Deut 4:13; 5:22; 9:10), placed in the Ark of the Covenant (Deut 10:1-4), celebrated annually at the feasts, and, at least during the Second Temple period, read daily (together with the Shema) in the Temple (m. Tam. 5:1).[92] J.J. Stamm and M.E. Andrew believe that one of the most important results of recent research on the Decalogue is the finding that "the Decalogue early held a central position in Israelite life."[93]

To discover that the "ten words" frequently informed post-Biblical Jewish moral teaching would hardly be surprising in view of their pervasive influence on many parts of the Jewish Scriptures themselves. Moshe Weinfeld has demonstrated that the first nine of the ten commandments are spread all over the law codes of the Pentateuch.[94] Indeed, Jewish philosophers like Philo and Saadia Gaon have tried to base all the Pentateuch's commandments on the Decalogue. Stephen Kaufmann has argued that Deuteronomy 12-26 is "a highly structured composition where major topical units are arranged according to the order of the laws of the Decalogue ... as it appears in chapter 5 [of Deuteronomy]."[95] Even more daring is David Noel Freedman's suggestion that embedded in the sequence of books from Exodus through Kings is a sequence of violations of the first nine command-

---

[91] The narrative framework of Deuteronomy stresses the finality of the ten commandments: (Deut 5:22) "These words the Lord spoke . . . and added no more." Weinfeld, 'What Makes the Ten Commandments Different?', 38 describes the Decalogue as "a fundamental list of concrete commands applicable to every Israelite, comprising the essence of God's demands from his confederates."
[92] Cf. M. Weinfeld, 'The Decalogue: Its Significance, Uniqueness, and Place in Israel's Tradition', 9-10.
[93] Stamm and Andrew, *The Ten Commandments*, 39.
[94] Weinfeld, 'Decalogue', 4-9: The first and second commandments are echoed, with considerable terminological overlap, in Exodus 34:14; 20:20(23); 23:24; 34:17; Leviticus 19:14; 26:1 (Deut 4:16,23,25; Psalm 97:7; 2 Kings 17:41; 2 Chron 33:7); the third in Leviticus 19:12; the fourth in Exodus 23:12; 34:21; 31:12-17; 35:1-3; Leviticus 19:3; 23:3; 26:2; Numbers 15:32-36 (cf. Jer 17:21); the fifth in Exodus 21:15,17; Leviticus 20:9; Deuteronomy 27:16; 21:18-21; the sixth in Exodus 21:12; Leviticus 24:17; Numbers 35:30-34; Deuteronomy 19:11-13; the seventh in Leviticus 18:20; 20:10; Numbers 5:11-31; Deuteronomy 22:22; the eighth in Exodus 22:1-12; Leviticus 19:11; and the ninth in Exodus 23:1; Deuteronomy 19:16-19.
[95] Kaufmann, 'Structure', 108; cf. John H. Walton, 'Deuteronomy: An Exposition of the Spirit of the Law'.

ments of the Decalogue in order.[96] B.S. Childs rightly asserts concerning the Decalogue that:

> The evidence that it was assigned a unique place of importance by the Old Testament itself . . . is manifold . . . the reflection of the commandments in the prophets (Hos. 4:1ff., Jer. 7:9ff.), and in the Psalms (50 and 81) testify to this influence upon Israel's faith.[97]

Such observations concerning the profound influence of the Decalogue upon the Jewish Scriptures, some admittedly more assured than others, illustrate an important point about the mediation of Scripture. The Scriptures were not only a collection of documents *for* exegesis but *of* exegesis.[98] Later portions of Scripture, and not just post-Biblical Jewish writings, may have mediated earlier portions of Scripture to Paul. In practice, whether the critical influence came directly from the Pentateuch, or the Prophets and Writings, or Jewish moral teaching may be difficult to determine. The stream of a given moral tradition may have flowed a fair way within the Scriptures before passing through Jewish moral teaching on its way to Paul.

For the considerable influence of the Decalogue (and the different summaries of the Law) upon the literature of early Judaism attention may be directed not only to K.-W. Niebuhr's study but also to the work of Klaus Berger and F. Dexinger.[99]

The critical role played by Leviticus 18-20 in the formation of three

---

[96] Freedman, 'The Nine Commandments: The Secret Progress of Israel's Sins'. Freedman claims, with some ingenuity and a little adjustment, that one can correlate the Decalogue with Israel's primary history: Exodus deals with apostasy and idolatry, Leviticus with blasphemy, Numbers with Sabbath observance, Deuteronomy with parental respect, Joshua with stealing, Judges with murder, Samuel with adultery, and Kings with false testimony. He explains that the final editor's purpose in this incredible redaction was not merely academic but theological, 42: "Israel's history could be told on two levels—as the story of its people, but also in terms of its successive violations of the commandments: one by one, book by book, until it ran out of options and possibilities, and was finally destroyed as a nation and its people taken into captivity."

[97] Childs, *Exodus*, 397. On the crucial role played by the Law of Moses in general in Amos, Micah, Isaiah and Jeremiah see Richard Victor Bergren, *The Prophets and the Law*, who argues that especially in the judgement speeches the Law is fundamental and binding; to transgress the Law was to break the covenant agreement between the Lord (the suzerain) and the nation (the vassal). See especially the table of some 85 texts from the four prophets which decry sins prohibited in Pentateuchal legislation, 182-83.

[98] This is the main point of M. Fishbane's *Biblical Interpretation in Ancient Israel*.

[99] Berger, *Die Gesetzauslegung Jesu: Ihr historischer Hintergrund im Judentum und im alten Testament. Teil I: Markus und Parallelen*, 258-77; Dexinger, 'Der Dekalog im Judentum'.

examples of hellenistic Jewish Parænesis, Pseudo Phocylides, Philo and Josephus, has been demonstrated by Karl-Wilhelm Niebuhr (see section IVA). The obvious dependence of Columns VI and VII of the Damascus Document upon Leviticus 18-27 would suggest that the influence of these chapters on Jewish moral teaching was more far-reaching than its purely Hellenistic range.

### V. The Influence of the Scriptures Mediated via Jewish Moral Teaching upon Paul's Ethics (A→B→C)

Having observed that the Scriptures significantly influenced Jewish moral teaching, A→B (section IV), and having noted several strands of evidence for the point that Jewish moral teaching significantly influenced Paul's ethics, B→C (section II), we are now poised to suggest ways in which Scripture may have been mediated via Jewish moral teaching to Paul's ethics, A→B→C. Some general observations will be followed by a list of specific examples drawn from 1 Corinthians 5-7 which are discussed in Part Two (chapters three to six).

A. *Some General Observations*

To what extent are the standard features of Jewish moral teaching, discernible trends in its handling of Scripture, reflected in Paul's ethics? We may consider six such features. In listing these features we are not suggesting that there are no exceptions. Obviously there is diversity within any tradition. Of course we do not presuppose unbroken continuity along an exegetical 'one-way-street'. At every stage of appropriation of tradition there is interaction between the tradition and its new interpretation. Here we are consciously making generalisations in order to reveal the type of evidence that may be gathered in more specific studies, such as our own in Part Two.

1. Standard Biblical Texts
We have already asserted that early Jewish moral teachers found certain passages from the Pentateuch indispensable for their parænesis. Did Paul also find such passages pertinent and profitable? A consideration of one example, Leviticus 18-20, would suggest that he did.

The parallels between Leviticus 18-20 and 1 Corinthians 5:1-11:1 alone are worth noting. Both sections oppose incest (Lev 18:6-18; 20:11; 1 Cor 5:1-13), homosexuality (Lev 18:22; 20:13; 1 Cor 6:9) and idolatry

(Lev 18:21; 1 Cor 10:7ff.). Both include a call to imitate God (Lev 19:2; 1 Cor 11:1), a command not to cause someone to stumble (Lev 19:14; 1 Cor 8:9), and a warning against spiritual prostitution (Lev 20:5; 1 Cor 6:12-20). Whether these similarities of thought and/or vocabulary indicate direct literary dependence is difficult to judge. In either case, that Paul and Leviticus 18-20 share so many concerns is testimony to the apostle's high regard for the teaching, if not the text, of these chapters from the Torah.

The impression of indebtedness to Leviticus 18-20 received from 1 Corinthians is strengthened in Romans. In Romans 13:9 he claims that Leviticus 19:18, a text commonly cited in Jewish moral teaching ("you shall love your neighbour as yourself"),[100] sums up the commandments. And in Romans 1:18-32 Paul closes his list of grievous sins with the remark that "those who do such things deserve death," an opinion reminiscent of Leviticus 20.[101] Although this is not noted by major commentators on Romans, Paul's list of sins which deserve death in Romans 1:18-32 has considerable overlap with those in Leviticus 20.

## 2. Standard Virtues and Vices

What are the main ethical concerns of Jewish moral teaching? To what extent does Paul echo these concerns? A fully documented answer to these questions would constitute a challenging and major study in its own right and is thus beyond our reach at this point. The difficulty in any attempt to compare Paul's moral emphases with Biblical and Jewish sources resides in the potential problem of selecting the evidence with Paul's ethics in mind, consequently enhancing the case for similarity. The temptation for a student of Paul's ethics, whether conscious or not, is to read the Jewish texts in the light of Paul's ethics, instead of the reverse. Pauline ethical categories and emphases might be given too prominent a place in the analysis. Karl-Wilhelm Niebuhr's summary of the "materialen Gehalt der frühjüdischen Paränese" is significant in this regard in that his conclusions were formulated without an eye to Paul's ethics, B←C (and with an eye to the formative influence of Scripture, A→B), thus marginalising this methodological pitfall. The main points of early Jewish paraenesis, according to Niebuhr, are:

---

[100] In *Gesetzeauslegung*, 100-36, Klaus Berger has traced Jewish exposition of Leviticus 19:18b in many Jewish texts. Cf. A. Nissen, *Gott und der Nächste im Antiken Judentum*, 258-77.

1. Sexual Ethics ("an erste Stelle der konkreten Mahnungen"). Included here are warnings against fornication, adultery, homosexuality and sexual perversions (incest, bestiality);

2. Compassion/Greed. A second important warning is the positive demand of compassion towards the weak and disadvantaged within society, the counterweight to which is the warning against greed and riches gained unlawfully;

3. Truthfulness. This category includes the prohibition of lying, slander, swearing false oaths and slyness;

4. Social Ethics ("verschiedene Verhaltensweisen im Umgang mit dem Nächsten"). In dealing with one's neighbour anger, envy, hatred, pride and strife are excluded.

That this list could well serve as a summary of the main emphases of Paul's ethical teaching suggests that the virtues extolled and the vices excoriated in the Scriptures, Jewish moral teaching and Paul's ethics are remarkably concordant.

3. Standard Arrangements of Ethical Material
A good example of the same configuration of ethical concerns occuring in both Jewish literature and the New Testament is the so-called double love commandment. The Old Testament commandments to love God and one's neighbour, though never bound together in the Scriptures, appear in that fashion both in the Testaments of the Twelve Patriarchs (T. Dan. 5:3; T. Iss. 5:2; T. Zeb. 5:1)[102] and the New Testament (Matt 22:37-40; Mark 12:29-31). Two possible examples of this phenomenon from Paul's ethics are: 1. the habit of hellenistic Jewish paraenesis (reported by Niebuhr[103]) to deal with sexual deviations, such as incest and homosexuality, and sexual relations in marriage in close proximity, an arrangement evident in 1 Corinthians 5-7; and 2. the

---

[101] Cf. Gordon Wenham, *Leviticus*, 281. On Paul's sexual ethic in Romans 1:18-32 it is worth noting Kenneth Hugghin's conclusion in 'An Investigation of the Jewish Theology of Sexuality influencing the references to homosexuality in Romans 1:18-32' that it is broadly consistent with the sexual ethic of Judaism, as found in the Apocrypha, Pseudepigrapha, Philo, Josephus, Mishnah and Tosefta. Since he also places the root of this teaching in the Torah, though not labelled as such, Hugghin's unpublished work supplies a fine example of Paul's indirect dependence upon the Scriptures.
[102] Cf. Philo's *Special Laws*, 263 for a comparable duty to God and man saying.
[103] Niebuhr, *Paränese*, 232.

well known correlation of law and wisdom in Ben Sira and many other Jewish texts, studied at length by Eckhard J. Schnabel,[104] which appears in Romans 2:17-20.

## 4. Standard Forms of Paraenesis

Common forms of early Jewish paraenesis include the 'two ways' motif, the household code, catalogues of virtues and vices, the paraenetic topic, topical figures, and the farewell discourse.[105] Each of these forms ultimately finds its roots in the Scriptures. The "two ways" motif brings Deuteronomy 27 or 30 to mind (see IIC). The germ of "the household code" is apparent in the Torah (e.g., in the fifth commandment) and in the wisdom tradition's respect for family ties, hospitality and other social obligations. Long before hellenistic influence upon Judaism, cataloguing of moral qualities and faults was an accepted device in Israel, as in Jeremiah's temple sermon (Jer 7:9; cf. Hos 4:1b-2).[106] The "Proverbs of Solomon" (Prov 10:1-22:16; 25:1-29:27) provide an ample and early precedent for the use of paraenetic topics and topical figures. And in the Bible farewell discourses are found on the lips of Jacob (Gen 49:29-50:14), Joshua (Josh 23:1-24:28), Samuel (1 Sam 12) and David (1 Kings 2:1-9; 1 Chron 28:1-29:28). These same forms are to a greater or lesser extent evident in Pauline paraenesis.

## 5. Standard Developments of Biblical Themes

In Jewish moral teaching certain themes are picked up from the Scriptures and coloured in a distinctive way. Idolatry, for example, is described several times as the origin, expression and consequence of indecent conduct.[107] This description is reminiscent of Colossians 3:5, which announces that "greed amounts to idolatry."

## 6. Standard Exegesis/Exposition of Biblical Passages

A key premise of the present study is that standard ways of understanding the significance of many passages of Scripture for contemporary conduct circulated in, were popularised by and gave rise to Jewish moral teaching. Many of the examples from 1 Corinthians

---

[104] Schnabel, *Law and Wisdom from Ben Sira to Paul: A Tradition Historical Enquiry into the Relation of Law, Wisdom and Ethics.*

[105] See James I.H. McDonald, *Kerygma and Didache: The Articulation and Structure of the Earliest Christian Message*, 73ff.

[106] McDonald, *Didache*, 78.

[107] Cf. Niebuhr, *Paränese*, 233: "Allerdings wird der Götzendienst mehrfach als Ursache, zusammenfassender Ausdruck oder Folge unsittlichen Verhaltens bezeichnet."

5-7 which follow (see VB below) illustrate the phenomenon of standard
Biblical exposition.

As the lens through which Paul perceived the relevance of Scripture
for ethics, Jewish moral teaching refracted the dynamic Biblical witness
in at least six different ways. In Jewish moral teaching certain Biblical
passages become prominent, certain Biblical moral scruples are
emphasised, certain Biblical ethical concerns are connected, certain
Biblical forms of paraenesis are popularised, certain Biblical themes
undergo development, and certain Biblical exegeses and expositions
are promulgated.

### B. *A List of Some Specific Examples from 1 Corinthians 5-7*

Some prime examples of the Scripture-mediating influence of Jewish
moral teaching on Paul's ethics in 1 Corinthians 5-7, along with the
section references from Part Two in which they are discussed, are
listed below. In all these cases, to a greater or lesser extent, we may
observe our A→B→C development. In examples 1, 2, 3, 8, 10 and
12 the influence of Scripture, A, would be very difficult, if not impossible,
to detect without knowledge of the intermediary stage of Jewish moral
teaching, B. It is not that Paul has simply been influenced by the
LXX. Later Jewish elaboration of Scripture also has a part to play.[108]

### *1 Corinthians 5*

1. The use of the Deuteronomy 23:2-9 (1-8) laws of assembly
   admission—ch. 3, IIIC.
2. The modification of the Pentateuchal penalty of execution—ch.
   3, IV.
3. The positive purposes of excommunication in verse 5—ch. 3, VI.

### *1 Corinthians 6:1-11*

4. The concern to maintain a good reputation before outsiders in
   1 Cor 6:1-11—ch. 4, IID.
5. The notion that the saints will judge the world in verses 2-3—
   ch. 4, IIE.

---

[108] Two of the clearest examples are the The Testaments of the Twelve Patriarchs
in no. 8 and the Targums in no. 12.

*1 Corinthians 6:12-20*

6. The notion that the future resurrection carries present moral demands in verses 12-13—ch. 5, III.
7. The use of κολλάω in verses 16-17—ch. 5, IVA.
8. The influence of Genesis 39 in verses 18-20—ch. 5, V.

*1 Corinthians 7:1-40*

9. The conception of marriage in verses 1-7—ch. 6, IIC.
10. The ascetic tendencies throughout the chapter—ch. 6, IIB.
11. The advice to Christian widows in verse 39-40—ch. 6, IIIC.

*1 Corinthians 10:22b*

12. The linking of idolatry, the jealousy of God and strength—Appendix.


## VI. CONCLUSION

The credibility of the major proposal of this chapter, the Jewish mediation of Scripture to Paul's ethics, is enhanced by noting analogous phenomena in early Christian art, the Church Fathers, modern theories of hermeneutics, and in studies of Paul's use of the Old Testament in the exposition of his doctrine.

The concept of Jewish mediation of Scripture to Paul's ethics finds a parallel with the probable Jewish origins of Christian art of the pre-Constantinian period which strongly attests Old Testament scenes and figures. Old Testament scenes turn up in Christian art in ways which suggest an indebtedness to earlier Jewish artistic interpretations of the same scenes. Henry Chadwick supplies an intriguing example:

> Late in the second century and early in the third, the town mint of Apamea (in Phrygia) issued a series of coins portraying Noah and his ark. The type so very closely resembles the manner in which Noah is portrayed in Christian catacomb art that it is very difficult to deny a connection. Probably, therefore, other Old Testament scenes in early Christian art were taken from Jewish models.[109]

The Church Fathers, who follow Paul in many respects, supply an even closer parallel involving many of the same Jewish sources

---

[109] Chadwick, *The Early Church*, 280. For introduction to and literature on early Christian art see, Horbury, 'Old Testament Interpretation', 755 fn. 138.

we have noted in this chapter. Christian catechesis (post-New Testament), according to William Horbury, was influenced by Jewish texts which developed the moral teaching of Scripture. For example:

> Commandments, exhortations and maxims from the Pentateuch and the Wisdom literature appear in the second century in combinations sometimes inherited from Jewish moral teaching.[110]

Modern theories of hermeneutics often employ analogous notions of "mediation" to the one developed in this chapter, when they treat the subject of preunderstanding and the role of tradition.[111] Such theories emphasise that history and tradition shape and dispose us in ways much deeper than we often realise. In the words of Hans-Georg Gadamer, "History does not belong to us, but we belong to it."[112] In other words, there is never any understanding which is not in some way shaped by our preunderstandings. There is, in short, no unmediated understanding. We arrive at an understanding of ourselves and our world indirectly, through the mediation of cultural, linguistic and religious signs, symbols and forms that permeate our everyday lives and which provide the tacit background which both predisposes and orients our lives. As Paul Ricoeur puts it, "the self does not know itself immediately, but only indirectly, through the detour of cultural signs of all sorts, which articulate the self in symbolic mediations."[113] Hence this chapter's stress on a Jewish mediation for Paul's knowledge and understanding of the Scriptures is in line with what many philosophers speak of as integral to any knowing and understanding.

The notion of a mediated use of Scripture for Paul's ethics which we are proposing is not far afield from a common view of Paul's use of Scripture for doctrine. Rendel Harris's primitive Christian testimony book proposal (*Testimonies*) and C.H. Dodd's more modest notion of traditional text plots (*According to the Scriptures*) proposed that Paul's use of Scripture to explain and defend his doctrine was indebted to early Christian Old Testament interpretation. The present proposal of a Jewish mediation of Scripture for ethics is thus paralleled by

---

[110] Horbury, 'Old Testament Interpretation', 737; see also 736-40.
[111] Discussion with Dr. J. Fodor has helped me in the formation of this paragraph.
[112] Gadamer, *Truth and Method*, 245. Cf. Paul Ricoeur, *Hermeneutics and the Human Sciences*, 68: "History precedes me and my reflection: I belong to history before I belong to myself."
[113] Ricoeur, 'Narrative Identity', 80.

the notion of an early Christian mediation of Scripture for doctrine. Both for doctrine and ethics, in his 'κήρυγμα' and 'διδαχή', Paul relied in part on a prior traditional use of Scripture.

This raises an objection to the whole approach of the present study: why is this chapter not entitled "Mediation via Early *Christian* Moral Teaching"? Surely Paul the Christian apostle's understanding of the Scriptures owes more to his Christian connections than to his Jewish roots. A Christian mediation of Scripture for Paul's ethics is, or course, theoretically possible. Nonetheless, our investigations have uncovered evidence that favours an emphasis on Jewish sources when one traces the chain of connection between the Scriptures and an aspect of Paul's ethics. Jewish sources are far more numerous than Christian ones in the first century (especially prior to Paul). Furthermore, Paul had warrant to modify and follow early Christian modifications of Jewish interpretation of Biblical passages relating to Christology, for example, since Jews and Christians disputed the identity of the Christ. He had less reason to change long-established Jewish exegesis on questions of conduct. The enormous emphasis on moral teaching by Christians in the late first and second centuries is commonly recognised,[114] and there may well have been Christian moral teaching prior to Paul. However, if the later Christian instruction is anything to go by, pre-Pauline Christian moral interpretations would have been in large measure a particular manifestation of the Jewish moral teaching covered in this chapter.

This chapter contends that the Scriptures not only directly influenced Paul's ethics through his use of Scripture, but also indirectly through his familiarity with Jewish moral teaching, which itself distilled and developed Scripture. In part, Paul heard the moral demands of Scripture through this Jewish 'filter' when he formulated the ethical instruction recorded in his epistles.[115] He did not receive his Bible in a vacuum. When Paul regulated conduct in the churches he used a "diffused"

---

[114] Cf. H.J. Carpenter, 'Popular Christianity and the Theologians in the Early Centuries', 296: "When Hermas or Second Clement spend a free half-hour in a little theological excursion it is sure to end abruptly in an earnest moral precept."

[115] Several of the authors in the recently published symposium *Paul and the Scriptures of Israel* (eds. Craig A. Evans and James A. Sanders) concur with this general point. E.g., Evans, 48: "Paul has heard more than Scripture itself; he has heard Scripture as it has been interpreted in late antiquity"; Davies, 33: "between the Tanak and the New Testament lies a vast exegetical-interpretive activity within Judaism. . . . it was to these traditions of exegesis and interpretation rather than to the Tanak itself in its textual nudity that they [the early church] related."

Bible. Though as simple as 'a, b, c,' this point has considerable significance for three areas of New Testament study. By ignoring it, focussing exclusively on *either* the Scriptures *or* Jewish moral teaching, scholars fail to tell the whole story of the origin of Paul's ethics, impoverish their exegesis of Paul's parænesis, and most significantly for our present concern, they underestimate Paul's dependence upon the Scriptures. Some elements of Paul's ethics which do not at first sight appear to have been influenced by the Scriptures turn out to be related to them indirectly via the mediation of Jewish moral teaching.

PART TWO

# PAUL'S DEPENDENCE UPON THE SCRIPTURES
# FOR ETHICS IN 1 CORINTHIANS 5-7

CHAPTER THREE

# EZRA AND PAUL EXCLUDING SINNERS
## 1 CORINTHIANS 5:1-13

### I. Introduction
*"Drive out the wicked person from among you"*

These words dramatically summarise and conclude Paul's solution in 1 Corinthians 5:1-13 to a problem of gross immorality[1] in the Corinthian church which had come to his attention.[2] Paul was scandalised to learn that the Corinthians were condoning the ongoing sexual relationship[3] of a member of their congregation with his unbelieving stepmother.[4] The command to evict the sinner in 5:13b echoes an expulsion formula found in Deuteronomy and suggests Paul's dependence on Scripture in this chapter. How indebted to the Scriptures is Paul in the expression and support of his urgent insistence that the man be removed? To what extent may Paul's discipline in 1 Corinthians 5 be compared with community exclusion taught in Paul's Bible?[5]

Several scholars have minimized the significance of the use of the Deuteronomic formula in 1 Corinthians 5:13. Though it is italicised in NA[26], three students of Paul's use of Scripture, E. Earle Ellis,[6] Richard

---

[1] The reason Paul considered incest unacceptable is addressed in section IV.

[2] Paul had received a report perhaps from Chloe (1:11) or Stephanus (16:15).

[3] Present tense ἔχειν indicates an ongoing relationship. However, the word does not necessarily denote marriage as in 1 Corinthians 7:2,29 (*contra* Mare), since ἔχω can be used to refer to a nonmarital relationship (cf. John 4:18; Robertson and Plummer). Barrett and Conzelmann's conclusion is preferable: in 1 Corinthians 5:1 marriage and a concubinate are both possibilities.

[4] That the woman was an unbeliever is clear because she received no rebuke from Paul (cf. verse 12: "For what have I to do with judging outsiders"). Most commentators agree that she is the man's stepmother: there is no explicit mention of "incest" and marriage (if it is in view) was illegal between mother and son (cf. The Institutes of Gaius I.63; Héring, 34). Both the Old Testament (Lev 18:7-8) and Judaism (m. San. 7:4) appear to have acknowledged the distinction between a mother and a stepmother in the context of sexual relations.

[5] For a sociological analysis of 1 Corinthians 5 in terms of deviance, norms and sanctions see Gerald Harris, 'The Beginnings of Church Discipline: 1 Corinthians 5'.

[6] Ellis, *Paul's Use*, 153.

Longenecker[7] and Herbert Ulonska,[8] do not consider it a quotation but merely an allusion, or verbal parallel, perhaps due to the absence of an introductory formula. If Paul is not explicitly citing Deuteronomy then the link between Scripture and 1 Corinthians 5 may be superficial and even illusory. David Daube,[9] Duncan Derrett[10] and Andreas Lindemann[11] implicitly play down the importance of 5:13b with their contention that the real issue in the chapter was not Scripture but pagan law, as reflected in the rebuke of verse 1 that even pagans do not tolerate incest.

Peter Zaas discounts the connection between the testaments suggested by Paul's command in 5:13b on exegetical grounds.[12] Zaas contends that Paul uses the expression from Deuteronomy to invoke the kindred ethos of expulsion from a community and to exploit the play on words between πόρνος (5:9,10,11; cf. 5:1) and πονηρόν (5:13b). He insists that this rhetorical function exhausts the contribution of the formula in 1 Corinthians 5: 13b:

> This apparent invocation of biblical law as a buttress for apostolic authority seems at least misplaced, given Paul's attitude to the law and given the Gentile composition of his audience. We can make a strong case, however . . . that the apostle is not citing scriptural law for church law here.[13]

Most commentators on 1 Corinthians 5, while not explicitly endorsing discontinuity between the testaments, make little attempt to investigate the link between it and the teaching of Scripture on community

---

[7] Longenecker, *Biblical Exegesis*, 110.

[8] Ulonska, 'Die Funktion der alttestamentlichen Zitate und Anspielungen in den paulinischen Briefen'.

[9] Daube, 'Pauline Contributions to a Pluralistic Culture: Re-creation and Beyond', 223-27. It would appear that the rabbis believed that in conversion the former relationships of a proselyte were dissolved, since a proselyte is like a newborn child. Pagan law (including the prohibition of incest) was imposed on proselytes to modify this scheme in order to prevent promiscuity. Daube thinks Paul adopts this rabbinic teaching in 1 Corinthians 5.

[10] Derrett, '"Handing over to Satan": an Explanation of 1 Cor. 5:1-7', 175 contends that Paul's church was "a sect . . . guided by the spirit and power of Jesus and not by the written word of Torah or its rabbinical interpretation. . . . the fact that such incest was criminal amongst the pagans at Corinth was highly significant in his [Paul's] eyes." In developing this point Derrett, 179 identifies the σατανάς of 5:5 with the Corinthian proconsul ("Paul consigns the incestuous man to the mercies of the Roman judge").

[11] Lindemann, 'Die biblischen Toragebote', 247.

[12] Zaas, '"Cast Out the Evil Man From Your Midst"', 259.

[13] Zaas, 'Cast Out', 259.

exclusion. It is the contention of this chapter, however, that the investigation of this link not only unveils Paul's profound indebtedness to the Scriptures but also opens up a fuller understanding of the reasons for the expulsion in 1 Corinthians 5. Scripture in 1 Corinthians 5 is not peripheral, but integral and germane to the formation of Paul's ethics and ecclesiology. The very heart of Paul's instructions to remove the offender is best conceived in terms of Pentateuchal covenant and temple exclusion, and many of the details find their roots in Scripture.

There is good evidence for concluding that 1 Corinthians 5:13b is indeed a quotation of a favourite expression of the LXX of Deuteronomy, where it is used on six occasions to signal the execution of a variety of offenders (13:5; 17:7; 19:19; 21:21; 22:21; 24:7; cf. Judg 20:13). The texts are identical, apart from the verb, changing from a singular future indicative to a plural aorist imperative, presumably to suit the epistolary context. Furthermore, ἐξαίρω is a New Testament *hapax legomenon*, suggesting Paul's intentional and explicit use of the formula from Deuteronomy.

The absence of an introductory formula is not a compelling objection to the notion that 1 Corinthians 5:13b is a quotation. Perhaps due to the lack of an apologetic purpose in the predominently ethical Corinthian epistles, stereotypical introductory formulae (such as καθὼς γέγραπται and the verb λέγω with various subjects) are not as common in 1 and 2 Corinthians as in Romans and Galatians. As D. Moody Smith notes, "Paul seems a bit less careful in the Corinthian letters (than in Romans and Galatians) to always make it clear that he is citing Scripture."[14] Ellis, Longenecker and Ulonska, for instance, admit a citation of the Scriptures in 1 Corinthians 15:32, where no introductory formula is present, and in 2:16; 10:26 and 15:27 where the only introduction is the conjunction γάρ. Quotations without introductory formulae are also present, according to NA[26], in 14:25 and 15:25. Paul's failure to introduce a quotation in 5:13 may be explicable on rhetorical grounds; the asyndeton suits the chapter's emotionally charged atmosphere.

Two further possible links between 1 Corinthians 5 and the scriptural teaching on community exclusion may be noted. Both appear in verse 5. The injunction "you are to deliver this man to Satan for the destruction of the flesh" has been compared by Adolf Deissman, Hans

[14] Moody Smith, 'The Pauline Literature', 274.

Conzelmann and others to pagan curse formulae.[15] Göran Forkman, however, has suggested an alternative background for this verse.[16] He describes it as "a solemn dynamic surrender to the power of evil," a "devotion," comparable to various Old Testament curses including the חרם of Deuteronomy 7:26 and 13:14-18[17] and ארר of Deuteronomy 27 and 28.[18]

Secondly, the verbal form of ὄλεθρος (destruction) in 5:5 is used four times in the Septuagint to translate כרת,[19] a prominent term in the teaching of the Scriptures on community exclusion. Although these four texts do not address community exclusion, the related compound ἐξολεθρεύω (destroy completely), does translate the majority of occurrences of כרת in the Pentateuchal community-exclusion formulae.[20]

## II. Community Exclusion in the Jewish Scriptures

The quotation of Deuteronomy in 5:13b, the possible allusion to Old Testament curses in 5:5 and the terminological links of ὄλεθρος (and especially ἐξολεθρεύω) in the LXX, taken together, suggest a link between 1 Corinthians 5 and Pentateuchal teaching on community exclusion. Is the connection confined to a few terms which perhaps appear only coincidentally? Or is there some similarity between 1

---

[15] Deissman, *Light from the Ancient East*, 303; Conzelmann, 97.

[16] Forkman, *The Limits of the Religious Community*, 143. That 5:5 constitutes a powerful curse and is not just the consignment of the offender to Satan's realm (synonymous with exclusion from the community) is supported by similar curses in 1 Corinthians 16:22 (ἤτω ἀνάθεμα) and 1 Timothy 1:20. G.W.H. Lampe's judgement is sound, 'Church Discipline and the Interpretation of the Epistles to the Corinthians', 352: "It seems likely, then, that the consignment to Satan is not simply to be identified with excommunication itself but that some kind of solemn curse is indicated."

[17] Cf. Exodus 22:19; Joshua 6:18; 7:12; Isaiah 43:28; Jeremiah 25:9; Zechariah 14:11; Malachi 3:24 concerning the "devotion" of Israelites and Leviticus 27:21,28; Numbers 18:14; Ezra 10:8; Ezekiel 44:29 on the "devotion" of Israelite possessions.

[18] In these chapters the curse leads to expulsion from the land of Israel and, ultimately, death.

[19] Numbers 4:18; Judges 6:25,28,30.

[20] Cf. Genesis 17:14; Exodus 12:15,19; 30:33; 31:14; Leviticus 17:4,9,14; 18:29; 19:8; 20:17,18; 22:3; 23:29; Numbers 4:18; 9:13; 15:30; 19:20. The verb, ἐξολεθρεύω also appears in Joshua 7:25, the only time in the LXX it translates צבר, in the story of Achan's expulsion from the community. This observation is further validation for William Horbury's suggestion, 'Extirpation and Excommunication', 36 (noting the terminological links of LXX Josh 7:12; Deut 17:7, etc and 1 Cor 5:13b) that "the LXX translator viewed Achan's removal as the paradigm of the expulsion . . . commanded in Deut.."

Corinthians 5 and the Pentateuch at a more substantive level? In particular, to what extent are the theological motifs of exclusion in the Scriptures reflected in 1 Corinthians 5? By 'theological motif' we mean the motivation associated with expulsion. What reasons are given for the removal of offenders? Three such motifs may be distinguished, which we shall call the covenant motif, the corporate responsibility motif and the holiness motif.[21]

## A. *The Covenant Motif*

Deuteronomic expulsion formulae involving the verb בער (*BDB*, 129.3: "utterly remove") are consistently associated with the covenant motif.[22] The word בער is translated by ἐξαίρω in the LXX of Deuteronomy. It is one of these formulae that Paul quotes in 1 Corinthians 5:13b. People are expelled by the בער formulae in Deuteronomy because of a breach of the covenant. Deuteronomy 17:7 makes this clear. The expulsion takes place because a person has "violated the covenant" of Israel's God (17:2; בריתו לבער). Commenting on Achan's sin Joshua 7:15 states: "He who is caught with the devoted things shall be destroyed. . . . He has violated the covenant of the LORD" (cf. 23:16: "If you violate the covenant . . . you will quickly perish"). In the Damascus Document expulsion from the community for a variety of offences is also consistently associated with the covenant.[23]

Another reason for expulsion in this material is the deterrence of a further breach of the covenant in the community. For example, Deuteronomy 19:19b-20a states:

> You must purge the evil from among you. The rest of the people will hear of this and be afraid and never again will such an evil thing be done in Israel.[24]

The dissuasion to sin further is also a reason for expulsion in 13:12-18; 17:2-7,12-13; 21:18-21.[25] In the בער formulae, the offender is expelled to maintain Israel's obedience to the demands of the covenant.

---

[21] Göran Forkman's study of community exclusion in the Old Testament, *The Limits*, identifies the covenant motif and the holiness motif.

[22] See Deuteronomy 17:7,12; 19:13,19; 21:9,21; 22:22,24; 24:7.

[23] Davies, *Paul*, 131.

[24] These verses are loosely quoted in 11QT LVI.

[25] This concern is illustrated, in a different context, in Esther 1-2 where, after disobeying the King, Queen Vashti is deposed to stop her example of disrespect spreading (see esp. Esth 1:17-18).

Deuteronomy teaches that Israel has certain obligations because of her covenant with the Lord. Customarily in the ancient Near East such a covenant is endorsed with blessings and curses. In Deuteronomy the curses listed in chapters 27 and 28 (cf. Lev 26), using the term ארר, censure virtually the same offences as in the בער formulae.[26] Failure to keep the covenant obligations results in discipline, whether it be the execution of the בער formulae, or misfortune and ultimately death in the ארר curses. In both cases offenders must be removed because of covenant disloyalty.

## B. *The Corporate Responsibility Motif*[27]

A second motif is associated with בער formulae in Deuteronomy 19:13 and 21:9. In both cases, the expression, "you must rid Israel of the guilt of innocent blood," is the penalty for the crime of murder. That "blood guilt" touches the whole community is made clear in Deuteronomy 19:13 where the motivation for the expulsion is "so that it may go well with *you* [i.e., the nation]" (cf. Deut 21:8). The notion of "blood guilt" introduces the motif of corporate responsibility, in which the community is held responsible for the sin of an individual.

The Old Testament affords widespread evidence for a corporate responsibility motif in relation to community exclusion.[28] In the following prominent examples the entire nation suffers, or is threatened with, some degree of divine displeasure on account of the presence of a gravely sinning member: (1) In Exodus 16:27-28 after "*some people*" broke the Sabbath, the LORD said to Moses: "How long will *you* [i.e., the nation] refuse to keep my commands and my instructions?"; (2) In Numbers 16:24-27 the people are warned to distance themselves from the tents of Korah, Dathan and Abiram, lest they be "swept away because of all *their* sins";[29] (3) In Deuteronomy 23:14b the nation is warned: "Your camp must be holy, so that the LORD your God

---

[26] These include idol worship, contempt of Yahweh, sexual offences and social crimes (cf. Forkman, *Limits*, 27-28).

[27] A shorter version of this section and section IIIB appeared as "'οὐχὶ μᾶλλον ἐπενθήσατε'—Corporate Responsibility in 1 Corinthians 5".

[28] Cf. Calvin Roetzel, *Judgement in the Community: A Study in the Relationship Between Eschatology and Ecclesiology in Paul*, 116: "The Old Testament often speaks of the judgement of an individual offender for the purpose of purifying the community, and how the entire community can be implicated by the sin of one of its members." Only Deuteronomy 13:6 and 17:7 are supplied in support of this statement (see page 58).

[29] Moses' and Aaron's prayer is instructive (16:22): "O God . . . will you be angry with *the entire assembly* when only *one man* sins?"

will not see *among you* anything indecent and turn away from *you*."
(4) In Deuteronomy 29:19-21 (18-20) "*a* person" going "his own way . . .
brings disaster on *the watered land as well as the dry*"; (5) In Joshua 7:1
the report of Achan's sin is introduced with the words: "But *the Israelites*
acted unfaithfully in regard to the devoted things." The Lord accused
all Israel (7:1: "*Israel* have sinned, *they* have . . . "), yet his "fierce anger"
(7:26) was turned away after the removal of only one individual, Achan
(and his house); (6) When the eastern tribes built their own altar by
the Jordan in Joshua 22, a delegation from the Israelites told them
(22:16-18), "the whole assembly of the LORD says: 'How could you
break faith with the God of Israel like this . . . If *you* rebel against
the LORD today, tomorrow he will be angry with *the whole community
of Israel*";[30] (7) In 1 Samuel 14:37-38 Saul assumed that some sin had
been committed in his army because God did not answer his request
for guidance which would affect the course of the nation; (8) Association
with the guilt of others is a feature of the prayers of Ezra 9, Nehemiah
1, 9 and Daniel 9, texts to which we shall return later; (9) In Nehemiah
13:18 Nehemiah rebukes the sabbath breakers with the words: "Now
*you* are stirring up more wrath against *Israel* by desecrating the
Sabbath".[31]

At various points in her history, Israel, like the pagan sailors who
felt compelled to eject Jonah in order to restore a safe passage for
their ship, removed certain offenders as an exercise in corporate
responsibility. While such persons remained, the nation was implicated
in their sin and, it seems, impending punishment.

## C. *The Holiness Motif*[32]

The holiness motif is associated with the two terms, חרם and כרת,
which we previously argued have links with 1 Corinthians 5:5. In
the Scriptures חרם is associated with holy war and is a curse directed
against people and objects which must be excluded because of contact
with foreign gods. In Deuteronomy 7:26 and 13:14-18 the 'ban' is

---

[30] The delegation goes on to cite the example of Achan in 22:20: "When *Achan*
son of Zerah acted unfaithfully regarding the devoted things, did not wrath come
upon *the whole community of Israel?*"
[31] Passages such as 2 Chronicles 7:19-20; 12:12; 32:25 represent special cases of
corporate responsibility where a leader has sinned. For New Testament examples
of corporate responsibility, see Revelation 2:14; 2:20.
[32] A shorter version of this section and section IIIC was published as 'Temple
and Holiness in 1 Corinthians 5'.

imposed because of the illicit spoils of war and outright idolatry respectively (cf. בדל in Deut 29:20-21 [21-22]). Along with the common כרת formulae of the first four books of the Pentateuch,[33] this material emphasises the holiness of God and the need for Israel to be holy. Contamination is also a common theme. Whoever takes possession of a devoted thing must himself be devoted, along with his house and even his town. In the holiness motif, a person or thing must be removed because of the holiness of God who has sanctified the community.

## D. *Conclusion*

Breach of the covenant, guilt by association, and the maintenance of holiness are thus three major reasons for exclusion from the community taught in Scripture. Three corollaries of these motifs have also been noted: the dissuasion from further disobedience, the prospect of impending judgement and the reality of contamination. These three motives are not, of course, mutually exclusive. Rather, they form a package of three perspectives on the identity of Israel. People are excluded because Israel is the sanctified (holiness motif), covenant (covenant motif) community (corporate responsibility motif) of the Lord, the holy God.

## III. THE COMMUNITY EXCLUSION MOTIFS IN 1 CORINTHIANS 5

This section attempts to demonstrate that the three motifs associated with community exclusion in the Scriptures are reflected in Paul's instructions to expel the sinner in 1 Corinthians 5:1-13.

## A. *The Covenant Motif*

The vice catalogue of 5:11 represents an obvious point of contact with the covenant motif.[34] The representative list of sinners which the church is to judge (5:12b) is in one sense a list of covenantal

---

[33] Whereas social crimes are associated with the בער and ארר penalties, the כרת formulae are distinguished by ritual offences (Gen 17:14; Exod 12:15,19; 30:33,38; 31:14; Lev 7:20, 25,27; 17:4,9,14; 19:8; 22:3; 23:29; Num 4:18; 9:13; 19:13,20; 1 Sam 2:33) which have points of contact with the cult and holiness.

[34] Neither E. Gräßer, *Der Alte Bund im Neuen: Exegetische Studien zur Israelfrage im Neuen Testament*, nor C.H. Talbert, 'Paul on the Covenant' note the relevance of this verse to the covenant theme in Paul's thought.

norms which, when broken, automatically exclude the offender.[35]

Paul lists "immorality" first, since that is the issue at hand. However, what governs his choice of the next five vices in the catalogue? From what source did Paul derive his list? Despite the pessimism of most scholars about the search for such a source,[36] in the case of 1 Corinthians 5:11 David Prior and Paul Ellingworth and Howard Hatton make a passing and undeveloped suggestion which has considerable merit.[37] Prior mentions that the sins to which the formula "drive out the wicked person from among you" is connected in Deuteronomy form "a remarkable parallel to the particular sins mentioned in 1 Corinthians 5:11." The LXX of Deuteronomy lists five such offences which in each case may be roughly compared with five of the six items in Paul's list: sexual promiscuity in Deuteronomy 22:21 (ἐκπορνεύω, LXX) is equivalent to Paul's πόρνος (fornicator); idolatry in 17:3,7 lines up with εἰδωλολάτρης (idolater);[38] malicious false testimony (19:18-19) with λοίδορος (reviler); the rebellious son who is a profligate and a drunkard (21:20-21) with μέθυσος (drunkard); and theft (24:7) with ἅρπαξ (thief). The only item in Paul's list without such a conceptual precedent is πλεονέκτης, which, as Leon Morris observes, is linked with ἅρπαξιν as one class in 5:10.[39] The five correspondences are difficult to pass off as coincidental. As Peter Zaas[40] observes, there is a distinct lack of overlap between any two of Paul's vice lists. Nor is there overlap between any one of Paul's lists and any list extant in ancient literature.[41]

Another possibility for the origin of the 5:11 list, made to me by

---

[35] Cf. Titus 3:10-11, "Warn a divisive person once, and then warn him a second time. After that have nothing to do with him. You may be sure that such a man is warped and sinful; he is *self-condemned*," αὐτοκατάκριτος.

[36] For example, Gordon Fee, 225 laments: "The Pauline lists are so diverse as to defy explanation."

[37] Prior, 85; Ellingworth and Hatton, *A Translators Guide on Paul's First Letter to the Corinthians*, 105.

[38] Idolatry and sexual immorality occur frequently in Paul's vice lists (eg. Rom 1:19-27; 1 Cor 6:9-10; Gal 5:19-21; cf. Acts 15:20,29; Rev 2:14,20). They are also associated in Wisdom 13-14. Cf. Sanders, *Paul*, 105.

[39] Morris, 88. Morris notes that "there is but one article, they are joined by *kai, and,* and separated from the rest by *ē, or.*" Though not cited by Morris, Maximilian Zerwick (*Biblical Greek*, 59: "the use of but one article before a number of nouns indicates that they are conceived as forming a certain unity") and Nigel Turner (*A Grammar of New Testament Greek*, III:181: the phenomenon portrays "a unified whole") support his point. Jean Héring's definition of πλεονέκτης suggests how the two words might be related: "one who uses brute force to enrich himself at the expense of his neighbour" (Héring, 38).

[40] Zaas, 'Catalogues and Context: 1 Corinthians 5 and 6', 623.

[41] The five correspondences, though remarkable, do not fit perfectly: only in 22:20-21 is the same terminology used; the key issue in 21:21 is disobedience (drunkenness

M. Goulder, is that the sins pick up the main themes of 1 Corinthians.
Either Paul had material from Deuteronomy in mind and the overlap
with sins dealt with in 1 Corinthians is coincidental or vice versa.
Since the list does not cover every sin in the letter (e.g., terms for
discord and disunity, found in the Gal 5 list of vices, are absent) the
link with Deuteronomy is to be preferred.

It appears that the contents of this Pauline vice catalogue can thus
be explained in terms of the *prima facie* purpose of 5:11, namely, to
list those persons warranting exclusion from the Christian community
according to the legislation of Deuteronomy.[42] This also suggests that
5:13b is a deliberate Deuteronomic citation. Prebaptismal catechesis
is commonly presented as the likely *Sitz im Leben* of such catalogues
in Paul's letters. In the case of 1 Corinthians 5:11, the more likely
provenance is some now lost Jewish or Christian summary of rules
for community exclusion based on Pentateuchal legislation. However,
there is no reason why this catalogue is not original to Paul himself
and specific to these circumstances.

The corollary of the covenant motif (that sinners must be excluded
to stop disobedience spreading in the community) can be seen in the
proverb in 5:6, "a little leaven leavens the whole lump."[43] The force
of this saying in 1 Corinthians 5 (as also in Gal 5:9) is similar to
the modern proverb, "one bad apple spoils the whole barrel."

## B. *The Corporate Responsibility Motif*

A striking feature of the instructions of 1 Corinthians 5 is that they
are not directed to the sinner himself but exclusively to the believers
in Corinth as a group.[44] Paul addresses the church as a body throughout
(the second person plural pronoun occurs nine times in thirteen verses).

---

is only a symptom); and 24:7 concerns theft of persons (though ἅρπαξ may denote
robbery of any description).

[42] Contrast Ziesler, *Pauline Christianity*, 121 who contends that Pauline vice and
virtue lists stand "for all bad things and all good things respectively."

[43] Cf. 1 Timothy 5:20, "Those who sin are to be rebuked publicly, so that the
others may take warning."

[44] Paul S. Minear, 'Christ and the Congregation: 1 Corinthians 5-6', 343, observes
that "in chapter 5, one verse deals with the incestuous person and twelve verses
deal with the culpability of the congregation." Weiss, 144-45 argues that in 5:13b
Paul substitutes plural ἐξάρετε for singular ἐξαρεῖς to make the Deuteronomic formula
address the whole community. The presupposition of corporate responsibility, Christian
solidarity, is introduced in 1 Corinthians in 3:23a, ὑμεῖς δὲ Χριστοῦ, developed by
3:16-17 and 10:17, and receives its classic statement in 12:12-31.

He wants the discipline to be carried out when they are assembled (συνάγω - literally "brought together"; 5:4)[45] and rebukes them in 5:2,6 as a group. The metaphor of cleansing by the removal of leaven is applied in a corporate fashion; the Corinthian Christians are to be "*a* new lump" (5:7), not new lump*s* of dough. Even the picture of the sacrifice of "Christ our passover", though possibly expanded in Romans 3:24-26 with individuals in mind, is in 1 Corinthians 5:7 applied, as Hans Conzelmann states, "to the collective body of the community."[46]

However, does this weight of corporate reference imply the notion of corporate responsibility? Are the Corinthians in some sense implicated in the offence of the sinner?[47] A possible intimation of collective responsibility is found in Paul's rebuke of Corinthian arrogance[48] and his call for the body to show passionate grief that will lead to action, ἐπενθήσατε, in 5:2. The word πενθέω is used in the New Testament of mourning over the death of a loved one (Matt 9:15; Mark 16:10; cf. Gen 50:10) and for grief over a great loss (Rev 18:11,15,19). Hence most commentators, including Robertson and Plummer, Lightfoot, Morris, Héring, and Pfitzner,[49] understand πενθέω in 5:2a as a mourning over the impending loss of the sinning brother, whose sin will lead to his destruction.[50] It could also be taken as grief at the shame brought on the church by the incest. However, these views seem out of keeping with the fact that πενθέω is only used elsewhere by Paul in 2 Corinthians 12:21[51] (cf. Jam 4:9; 1 Clem 2:6), where its sense closely parallels "the concept of godly sorrow or repentance."[52] If Paul did not have godly sorrow/repentance in mind in 5:2a, he could have used a word other than πενθέω, such as ταλαιπωρέω (Jam 4:9) which denotes sorrow

---

[45] E. Schweizer, *Church Order in the New Testament*, 192, notes that in verses 3-5 Paul is "obviously striving to establish the church as the real bearer of responsibility."

[46] Conzelmann, 99.

[47] No commentator, to my knowledge, has fully investigated this possibility.

[48] Whether their boasting was in spite of or because of the incestuous man is open to question. In either case, G.W.H. Lampe's description of their attitude, 'Church Discipline', 343 is close to the mark: "truly enlightened believers are beyond the reach of any defilement from sinners."

[49] Victor C. Pfitzer, 'Purified Community—Purified Sinner: Expulsion from the Community according to Matthew 18:15-18 and 1 Corinthians 5:1-5', 34-55.

[50] Cf. Moffat's translation: "you ought much rather to be mourning the loss of a member."

[51] The circumstances prompting the mourning in 2 Corinthians 12:21 also involve πορνεία.

[52] T. McComiskey, 'πενθέω', 2:422.

in wretched circumstances, δακρύω (John 11:35; cf. δάκρυον in 2 Cor 2:4) or κλαίω (1 Cor 7:30) which signify weeping and crying, or even λυπέω (1 Thess 4:13), ἀλαλάζω (Mark 5:38; cf. 1 Cor 13:1) or θρηνέω (John 16:20; Luke 23:27) which mean weep, especially in mourning for the dead.

The use of πενθέω in the LXX lends further support to the idea that in 5:2a Paul thought the Corinthians ought to "mourn" in the sense of confessing the sin of the erring brother as if it was their own.[53] The word only occurs six times in the LXX with reference to sin. In Ezra 10:6; Nehemiah 1:4; 1 Esdras 8:72; 9:2 and Daniel 10:2 it refers to sorrow over the sins of others and in Nehemiah 8:9 (cf. T. Reub. 1:10) it refers to sorrow over personal sin (but still in a corporate context). For example, in Ezra 10:6, Ezra "mourned over the unfaithfulness of the exiles." In the former references the grief is given expression in prayers by Ezra, Nehemiah and Daniel, in which the sins of others are confessed as if they are their own. Ezra 10, in particular, represents a distinct parallel to 1 Corinthians 5. It is an Ezra-like Paul who deals with the expulsion of the sinner. Just as Ezra mourned (πενθέω) over the sins of the community, so Paul enjoined the Corinthians to mourn (πενθέω) over the sin of the incestuous man. Just as Ezra demanded that the sinners separate from their foreign partners or else suffer expulsion themselves (10:8), so Paul demanded the expulsion of the sinner unless he separate from his illicit partner.[54]

The corollary of corporate responsibility, the fear of God's active displeasure over sin in the community, which we observed in Joshua 7 and other Old Testament texts, is also present in the incidents involving Ezra, Nehemiah and Daniel. All three assumed that the nation stood under the covenant and that breach of responsibility could jeopardize the whole group before God. A sense of urgency gripped these leaders' dealings with God and the nation. In each case

---

[53] If the offender in 2 Corinthians 2:5 and 7:12 can be identified with the incestuous person of 1 Corinthians 5 (see Colin G. Kruse, 'The Offender and the Offence in 2 Corinthians 2:5 and 7:12', for a summary of the evidence), then it is noteworthy in 2:5 that the sinner caused pain (λυπέω) to *all* the Corinthians (πάντας ὑμᾶς). The fact that in 2 Corinthians 7:9 λυπέω and μετάνοια are associated supports the supposition that the pain the sinner caused the Corinthians may have involved their identification with his sin and need for godly sorrow.

[54] Both the taking of wives from pagan peoples (Exod 34:16; Deut 7:1-3; cf. Josh 23:12-13), the sin with which Ezra dealt, and incest (Lev 18:8; Deut 22:30; 27:20), the problem in 1 Corinthians 5, are prohibited by the Torah. The critical sin in Nehemiah was likewise illicit marriage (10:30; 13:27).

πενθέω translates אבל, which in the Hebrew Bible often describes the reaction of those aware of the threat of deserved judgement (cf. Exod 33:4; Num 14:39). As Jean Héring states, "in the OT, belief in the efficacy of mourning and fasting for warding off public misfortune is well attested by 1 Kings 21.9; Amos 5.16; 8.10".[55]

Though not explicitly stated in 1 Corinthians 5, the same notion of the need to deal immediately with the sinner in order to safeguard the standing of the community before God may underlie the urgency with which Paul addresses the problem. Paul's incredulity and disquiet at the Corinthians' complacency is signalled by his rather abrupt beginning using the word ὅλως (denoting "actually", BAGD, 565 or "undoubtedly", Jerusalem Bible; cf. 1 Cor 6:7; 15:29; Matt 5:34), by the unusual placing of τινα between γυναῖκα and πατρὸς (isolating and making both words emphatic),[56] by the emphatic οὐχί (instead of οὐ) in 5:2, and by asyndeton at the beginning of verses 7,10 and in the middle of verse 13.[57] The string of verbs, ἐπενθήσατε (v2), ἀρθῇ (v2), παραδοῦναι (v5), ἐκκαθάρατε (v7), and ἐξάρατε (v13), unfold the urgency with which Paul wants the Corinthians to act. Apparently Paul considered the expulsion of the sinner imperative to protect the church's felicitous existence before God.

## C. *The Holiness Motif*

Thus far we have been concerned with the Pentateuchal laws of covenant and related excommunication regulations. William Horbury, in his study of the practice of excommunication in pre-rabbinic Judaism, argues that, throughout the post-exilic period, not only the laws of covenant but also the laws of temple admission legislated in Deuteronomy 23:2-9 (1-8) carried the implication of community exclusion.[58] For example, Deuteronomy 23:2-9 (1-8) was used by Ezra and Nehemiah for the exclusion of foreign wives from the community (Ezra 9:1-2 and Neh 13:1-3,23-27 allude to the passage)[59] and the lamentation over the destruction of Jerusalem in Lamentations 1:10 also recalls it.[60] A holiness motif is most clearly perceived in 1 Corinthians 5

---

[55] Héring, 35. Cf. also 2 Kings 22:11-20.
[56] F. Blass, A. Debrunner and Robert W. Funk, *Greek Grammar*, 473(1).
[57] In each case the Majority text (and a few early witnesses) alleviates the asyndeton by supplying οὖν, καὶ and καὶ respectively.
[58] Horbury, 'Extirpation and Excommunication', 25.
[59] Fishbane, *Biblical Interpretation*, 116-17, 125-26.
[60] Fishbane, *Biblical Interpretation*, 128.

in the light of this development in the use of Deuteronomy 23:2-9 (1-8).

Horbury demonstrates that during the Second Temple period the scope of the laws of admission to the assembly found in Deuteronomy 23:2-9 (1-8) were expanded beyond stipulations of physique and descent to include moral requirements.[61] Biblical evidence for this evolution includes the "entrance-*torot*" (Pss 15; 24:3-5; Isa 33:14-17[62]), the exclusion of "rebels" (הפושעים) in Ezekiel 20:38-40 from the future congregation, and the indictment of Israel for admitting into the sanctuary aliens who are "uncircumcised in heart" in Ezekiel 44:6-9. Josephus and Philo build upon this Biblical background and "take Deuteronomy 23 to exclude not only aliens and defective Jews, but also gravely-offending Jewish sinners."[63]

The likelihood that Deuteronomy 23:2-9 (1-8) played a role in the formation of Paul's thinking in 1 Corinthians 5 is increased by the fact that the previous verse in Deuteronomy addresses the very question with which Paul is engaged: "A man is not to marry his father's wife (τὴν γυναῖκα τοῦ πατρὸς αὐτοῦ); he must not dishonour his father's bed." That Paul linked the two passages has every possibility since, as Horbury observes: "The admission-regulations of Deut. 23:2-9 (1-8) were linked in rabbinic exegesis with 23:1 (22:30), and correspondingly understood, as by Targum Pseudo-Jonathan, as marriage laws."[64] This exegesis may even have a basis in Deuteronomy. Michael Fishbane has suggested that Deuteronomy 23:1 and 23:2-9 (1-8) are linked through the mention of the Ammonites and Moabites, who, according to Genesis 19:31-38, are the offspring of incest (Lot and his daughters).[65]

It would hardly be surprising, therefore, to find in 1 Corinthians 5 the expulsion of the sinner connected with the theme of temple and holiness.[66] Why must the offender be delivered to Satan for "destruction" (5:5)? Surely the best explanation is given only 23 verses

---

[61] Horbury, 'Extirpation', 26-27.

[62] Though applied in the LXX to the qualifications of a prophet, Targum Isaiah 33:14-17 maintains the original context of admission.

[63] Horbury, 'Extirpation', 26. For example, both apply 23:2(1) to the voluntary effeminate (not just to the born eunuch). See Philo, Spec 1:324-45 and Josephus, Ant. 4:290f.

[64] Horbury, 'Extirpation', 25.

[65] Fishbane, *Biblical Interpretation*, 120. C. Carmichael, *The Laws of Deuteronomy*, 174-76, also argues that Deuteronomy 23:1,3,4-6 should be seen in the light of Genesis 19.

[66] Temple imagery is prevalent in both Corinthian epistles. The church is identified

before chapter five in the solemn affirmation:

> Do you not know that you are God's temple . . . If anyone destroys
> God's temple, God will destroy him. For God's temple is holy, and
> that is what you are (3:16-17).[67]

There are good reasons for thinking that Paul's comments in 1
Corinthians 3:16-17 find their roots in the Old Testament and are
part of the same temple/holiness tradition mentioned above (which
largely grew out of Deuteronomy 23:2-9 [1-8]).[68] The very conception
of the community as a temple is a Scriptural theme, where the divine
indwelling is not just of a sanctuary but of a people.[69] The Peshitta
of Jeremiah 7:9 states the thought explicitly: "the temple of the Lord,
the temple of the Lord, you (plural) are the temple of the Lord."[70]
That this seed-thought of the community as a building or temple was
nourished in early Jewish teaching is clear from The Community Rule
8:4-7[71] and Philo's *On Sobriety* 66 and *On Abraham* 56.[72]

Even some of the details of 1 Corinthians 3:16-17 have Biblical/
Jewish precedents. Paul's notion of "the Spirit of God" rather than
simply "God" dwelling in the Temple is found in Josephus' account
of Solomon's temple (Ant. 8:114). The connection of temple with

---

as the ναὸς θεοῦ in 2 Corinthians 6:16. In 1 Corinthians 6:19 (significantly for 1
Cor 5) the need for sexual purity is linked to individual Christians being the temple
of the Holy Spirit. Furthermore, Paul associates sexual chastity with temple in 1
Corinthians 6:12-20 (cf. CD IV where the three nets of Satan are greed, fornication
and profanation of the temple).

[67] In a forthcoming Oxford D Phil thesis, 'Paul, Salvation and the Temple of
Jerusalem: A Study of the Socio-Political Dimension of Pauline Soteriology', Tony
Cummins argues that the temple motif is a factor in Paul's response to the Judaizers
in Galatians and informs his decision in Galatians 4 (cf. 4:31) to exclude them from
the community.

[68] *Contra* H. Wenschkewitz, 'Die Spiritualisierung der Kultusbegriffe Tempel, Priester
und Opfer im Neuen Testament', who stresses the formative role of Hellenistic thought
about the individual being divinely indwelt as the major background for Paul's use
of temple imagery.

[69] Exodus 25:8; 29:45; Leviticus 26:11f; Ezekiel 11:16; 37:26-28; Psalm 114:2; cf.
W. Horbury, 'New Wine in Old Wine Skins: IX. The Temple', 36-42.

[70] Cf. F.C. Burkitt, *Early Christianity Outside the Roman Empire*, 32; William L. Holladay,
*Jeremiah 1: A Commentary on the Book of the Prophet Jeremiah Chapters 1-25*, 242.

[71] Cf. 5:4-7; 8:8-10; 9:3-6. See G. Klinzing, *Die Umdeutung des Kultus in der
Qumrangemeinde und im Neuen Testament*, 70.

[72] Cf. V. Nikiprowetzky, 'Temple et communauté,' and 'Le Nouveau Temple'.
On the idea of a temple-like community in the pesher on 2 Samuel 7:10-14 in 4Q174
see Devorah Dimant, '4QFlorilegium and the idea of the Community as Temple'
and George J. Brooke, *Exegesis at Qumran: 4QFlorilegium in its Jewish Context*. L. Nieder,
*Die Motive der Religiös-sittlichen Paränese in der paulinischen Gemeinde-Briefen*, 49-50 suggests

judgement in 1 Corinthians 3:16-17 is reminiscent of Numbers 1:51; 3:10,38; 4:20; 19:20 and 2 Chronicles 26:16-21. Paul's concern for a purified temple also brings to mind Israel's sin offering, which was designed to cleanse the tabernacle from defilement.[73] The warning in 1 Corinthians 3:17, as stated in terms of talionic justice (φθείρει . . . φθερεῖ, is reminiscent of the LXX of Joshua 7:25 (a key excommunication text in the LXX): "And Joshua said to Achan, 'why have you *destroyed* us? The Lord will *destroy* you as at this day'."[74] Indeed, appropriate judgement is a feature of other Old Testament discipline texts (e.g., Lev 26:23-25; cf. 26:27-28,40-41). In context, 1 Corinthians 3:16-17 is introduced by 3:9-15, the building imagery of which also fits an Old Testament sanctuary background.[75] Paul makes the connection of his temple metaphor with the Scriptures explicit in 2 Corinthians 6:16ff., where Leviticus 26:12 and Ezekiel 37:27 are quoted.

Two groups of observations support the case for reading 1 Corinthians 5 (especially 5:5) with 1 Corinthians 3:16-17 and an Old Testament temple/holiness motif in mind.[76] First, certain features of 3:16-17 suggest its affinity with chapter five. 1 Corinthians 3:16-17, in contrast to 6:19, describes the body corporate as God's temple ("you [plural]

---

that the image of the congregation as the temple of God originated in Jewish eschatological thought:—God will erect a perfect temple in the eschaton (Isa 28:16; 1 En 91:13; Jub 1:17; cf. J. Baumgarten, *Paulus und die Apokalyptik*, 45-49 and Christian D. von Dehson, 'Sexual Relationships and the Church: An Exegetical Study of 1 Corinthians 5-7', 157).

[73] See Leviticus 4:1-5:13; 15:31; 16:19; Cf. J. Milgrom, 'Two Kinds of Hatta't Sacrifice', and Gordon J. Wenham, *The Book of Leviticus*, 84-103, who translates חטאת as "purification offering." Cleansing the Temple from defilement is a common note in Biblical/Jewish tradition: Hezekiah cleanses the temple of the defilements of Ahaz (2 Chron 29:12ff.), Josiah of those of Manasseh (2 Chron 34:3ff.), Nehemiah of those of Tobiah (Neh 13:4-9), and Ezekiel's new temple must be cleansed before use (Ezek 45:18ff.). A most impressive cleansing is that of the Maccabees (1 Macc 4:36ff.; 2 Macc 10:1ff.). See Lloyd Gaston, *No Stone on Another: Studies in the Significance of the Fall of Jerusalem in the Synoptic Gospels*, 112-13.

[74] It is worth noting that a prominent word for "the apostates" in the twelfth benediction of the *Tefillah* (see Emil Schürer, *The History of the Jewish People*, 455-63), the Benediction of the *Minim*, is משומדים, "the destroyed ones." On the Biblical roots of this benediction see W. Horbury, 'The Benediction of the Minim and Early Jewish-Christian Controversy'.

[75] Cf. Archibald Robertson and Alfred Plummer, 60 who, commenting on ὡς σοφὸς ἀρχιτέκτων (3:10), observe that: "The same expression is found in LXX of Isa. iii. 3, and σοφὸς is frequent of the skilled workmen who erected and adorned the tabernacle (Exod. xxxv. 10,25, xxxvi. 1,4,8)."

[76] In their studies of the temple motif in Paul's thought, Raymond Corriveau (*The Liturgy of Life*, esp. 48-68,187-92), Ronald Y.K. Fung ('Some Pauline Pictures of the Church'), Ernest Best (*One Body in Christ*, 160-69), D.R. de Lacey ('οἵτινές ἐστε ὑμεῖς: The Function of a Metaphor in St. Paul') and I.H. Marshall ('Church and Temple

are God's temple [singular]"; cf. 3:9b: "you [plural] are . . . God's building"), which, we are claiming, is Paul's presupposition in 1 Corinthians 5. The characteristic of the temple to which Paul draws attention in 3:16-17 is its ἁγιασμός (holiness), which carries a demand for the maintenance of purity, a thought which Paul develops in 1 Corinthians 5:6-8. The punishment in 1 Corinthians 3:15 ("if any man's work is burned up, he will suffer loss, though he himself will be saved, but only as through fire") has been plausibly compared by C.K. Barrett to the "destruction" of 5:5: "the man's essential self will be saved with the loss not only of his work but of his flesh."[77] 1 Corinthians 3:17 and 5:5 are also linked in terms of genre/function: both texts are, as Robert M. Grant explains, holy law.[78]

Secondly, 1 Corinthians 3:16-17 may well anticipate 5:1-13 since it is not uncommon for Paul in 1 Corinthians and elsewhere to set up a later discussion in such a manner. That Paul is capable of anticipating later material in his epistles by way of terse, proleptic, summary remarks is clear from the intricately structured epistle to the Romans.[79] In spite of the conspicuously occasional nature of 1 Corinthians (Paul responds to verbal then written reports), the epistle evidences a greater degree of compositional coherence than is commonly recognized. Whereas most commentators admit development of thought within sections of 1 Corinthians,[80] links between sections may also be observed. The introductory thanksgiving in 1 Corinthians (1:4-9), as is customary in Paul's letters, presents the main themes of the entire epistle.[81] The theme of spiritual gifts (addressed in chs. 12-14) is introduced in 1:4 (χάριτι [cf. χαρίσματα, 1:7] refers here

---

in the New Testament') make no mention of 1 Corinthians 5. The only author to my knowledge who connects 1 Corinthians 5 with 3:16-17, Michael Newton, *The Concept of Purity at Qumran and in the Letters of Paul*, 89 does so in passing.

[77] Barrett, 127. Cf. The "destruction" in Joshua 7:12,15 which is also "by fire." See also testing by fire in Proverbs 17:3 and Wisdom 3:6.

[78] Grant, 'Holy Law in Paul and Ignatius'.

[79] On the structure of Romans Klyne Snodgrass, 'Spheres of Influence: A Possible Solution to the Problem of Paul and the Law', 104 comments: "Frequently he [i.e., Paul] introduces a point briefly only to return to it later for detailed treatment. In 3.1-4 he raises issues that are not dealt with in detail until chs. 9-11. In 3.8 he asks a question that is dealt with in 6.1f. In 3.31 he makes a statement that is explained in chs. 7-8. . . . in 5.20 Paul brings law into connection with sin, but what he means by that statement is not clear until 7.7-13."

[80] On the "A-B-A" form of argumentation in chs. 1-3, 7:25-40, 8-10, and 12-14, see J. Collins, 'Chiasmus, the "ABA" Pattern and the Text of Paul'. Cf. also Gordon Fee, 15-16.

[81] Peter O'Brien, *Introductory Thanksgiving in the Letters of Paul*, 261-63, has observed

specifically to spiritual gifts[82]), and 1:5 (cf. λόγος in 1:5; 12:8; 14:9,19,36; and γνῶσις in 1:5; 8:1,7,10,11; 12:8; 13:2,8; 14:6),[83] Paul's proclamation to the Corinthians in 1:6 (cf. μαρτύριον in 1:6; 2:1[84]), the return of Christ in 1:7 (cf. 11:26; 15:23,47,52; 16:22), and eschatological judgement (τῇ ἡμέρα τοῦ κυρίου) in 1:8 (cf. 3:13; 4:3; 5:5). The issue of unity (1:10-4:21; esp. 1:10-17) is anticipated in the address in 1:2: αὐτῶν καὶ ἡμῶν ("their Lord and ours";[85] cf. also ἡμῶν 'Ιησοῦ Χριστοῦ in 1:10).[86]

As Paul dictated the rest of the epistle, without detracting from the subject at hand, he occasionally made a point which would have secondary application to a subject to be dealt with later. In 2:7-8 the connection of believers' ultimate glorification to their union with Christ (note the repetition of δόξα) is a precursor of 1 Corinthians 15 where Paul's chief point is that Christ's resurrection guarantees the resurrection of believers.[87] Believers' possession of the Spirit, foundational to 3:16; 6:19; 12:13, is introduced emphatically in 2:12.[88] In 6:12-14 Paul makes some pregnant statements that are expounded

---

four functions of such sections in Paul's letters: they serve a pastoral (revealing concern), didactic, paraenetic, and epistolary function. Our concern here is only with the last purpose. K.E. Bailey, 'The Structure of 1 Corinthians and Paul's Theological Method', 157 believes that in 1 Corinthians 1:4-9 "Paul makes some mention of what is coming in each of the five essays to follow." (Bailey understands 1 Cor as comprising five essays, on the cross and wisdom, sex, idols, worship, and resurrection).

[82] See Gordon Fee, 37 for validation of this point.

[83] Michael Goulder in a forthcoming *NTS* article on 1 Corinthians observes that "the first two gifts of the spirit in 12:8 are λόγος σοφίας and λόγος γνώσεως; and these correspond with 1:5, 'you were enriched in everything, ἐν παντὶ λόγῳ καὶ πάσῃ γνώσει." Note also the repetition of Corinthian enrichment, πλουτίζω in 1:5 and 4:8.

[84] In 1 Corinthians 2:1 μαρτύριον is to be preferred over μυστήριον (contra Nestle-Aland[26]). Both external evidence (μαρτύριον has wider geographical distribution, with Alexandrian, Western and Byzantine attestation) and the context (1:17-31 concerns the message about Christ) favour the former reading. μυστήριον may have arisen due to the influence of the same word in 2:7.

[85] The phrase is better taken as a possessive genitive with κυρίου (most commentators) than with τόπῳ, "their place and ours" (cf. Ellicott and Conzelmann), an interpretation correctly labelled by C.K. Barrett, 34 as "trite." Ulrich Wickert, 'Einheit und Eintracht der Kirche im Präskript des ersten Korintherbriefes', contends that in using this phrase, Paul had in mind the exhortation to unity which follows.

[86] Other elements in the opening verses also alert the reader to the question of unity (cf. σύν in 1:2 and the repetition of ἡμῶν in 1:2,3,7,8,9).

[87] As C.K. Barrett, 78 explains: δόξα in 2:7 is that which "awaits men in the age to come (eg. xv. 43)."

[88] Cf. F.F. Bruce, 39.

later in the letter.[89] The question of unity addressed in chs. 1-4 resurfaces in 11:17-22.[90] In the course of reading the epistle, the reader is drawn back instructively to earlier passages. It is a connection of this sort which we are proposing between 3:16-17 and 5:1-13.[91] The fact that a letter like 1 Corinthians was probably read/listened to in its entirety lends further credibility to this proposal of a *cumulative reading* of 1 Corinthians. 1 Corinthians 3:16-17 would have been in the forefront of the minds of the letter's recipients when 1 Corinthians 5 was read.

If we are correct in assuming that 1 Corinthians 5 ought to be read with 3:16-17 in mind, then another element in the chapter, in addition to verse 5, should be mentioned as congruent with a temple theme, namely, verses 7 and 8. Having 'cleansed the temple', Paul calls upon the congregation to celebrate spiritually the festival of Passover/Unleavened Bread in 1 Corinthians 5:7-8. That this sequence of events occured to Paul's mind may itself testify to the influence of the Old Testament temple motif, since, in the Old Testament, there is an observable link between cleansing or restoring the temple and celebrating the Passover. Following the "removal of all defilement from the sanctuary" (2 Chron 29:5) in order to "reestablish the service of the temple of the LORD" (2 Chron 29:35), King Hezekiah in 2 Chronicles 30 calls upon the people to celebrate the Passover. Similarly, King Josiah, after removing the articles of idolatry from the temple and replacing the sacred ark in its rightful place, ordered the Israelites to celebrate the Passover and observe the Feast of Unleavened Bread (2 Chron 35:1-19; 2 Kings 23:1-23). Ezra followed the same pattern; Ezra 6 records first the completion and dedication of the temple (6:13-18) and then a joyous Passover and Feast of Unleavened Bread (6:19-22). It is intriguing that, even in the Gospels (Matt 21:12-13; Mark 11:15-18; Luke 19:45-47; John 2:13-22), as in

---

[89] J.B. Lightfoot, *Notes on Epistles of St. Paul*, 215: "It is noticeable that these three verses [12-14] contain the germ of very much which follows in the Epistle: (1) the great principle which is to guide the Christian's conduct, (2) the question of εἰδωλόθυτα involved in βρώματα, (3) the conflict with sensual indulgences, (4) the doctrine of the resurrection of the dead."

[90] Other less certain connections across the epistle could also be noted such as 3:10-15 in relation to the "disqualification" in 9:27, and the judgement in 11:29; cf. also 3:23a (ὑμεῖς δὲ Χριστοῦ) with 6:19b (οὐκ ἐστὲ ἑαυτῶν).

[91] That 1 Corinthians 3:16-17 serves more than just the paragraph in which it resides has been suggested, without specific reference to ch. 5, by Gordon Fee, 237 ("the church as God's temple dominates his [Paul's] perspective even when it is not expressed") and by Friedrich Lang, 69 who notes that 3:16-17 introduces the theme of the holiness of the church which, he insists, dominates chapters 5 and 6.

1 Corinthians 5, cleansing the temple and celebrating the Passover are connected.

There are good reasons, then, for thinking that 1 Corinthians 3:16-17 provides the theological framework for understanding perhaps the most fundamental reason for the expulsion of the sinner in 5:1-13:[92] the sinner must be "destroyed" because he has defiled the holiness of God's temple,[93] the church.[94] A corollary of this holiness motif, contamination, is also present in 1 Corinthians 5. The sinner must be removed because holiness and unholiness cannot co-exist, "a little leaven leavens the whole lump"(5:6).[95]

## D. *Conclusion*

At several points throughout our discussion of Paul's indebtedness to Pentateuchal teaching on exclusion we have noted the relevance of another Biblical leader who also felt compelled to call for discipline, namely Ezra. It is worth noting that not only 1 Corinthians 5 but also Ezra 7-10 bears the marks of the three motifs of Biblical exclusion; Paul and Ezra act in a comparable manner.

That Ezra, a man consciously seeking to obey the Law of God (see 7:6,10,11,12,21), conceived of the reform of the returned exiles in terms of a return to *covenant* obligations is made clear in Ezra 10:3 ("Now let us make a covenant before our God to send away all these

---

[92] The fact that ὄλεθρος is used in 5:5 and φθείρω in 3:17 does not undermine the connection between the two passages. Whereas the former word is better suited to a context of explicit excommunication because of its (previously noted) links with כרת, φθείρω usually translates שחת in the LXX, a word not commonly used for excommunication; the immediate context of 3:16-17 and its primary application concern the protection of the church from false teachers and division and not excommunication.

[93] It seems that Paul believed, along with Deuteronomy 22:21b, that πορνεία "defiles the house" (of one's father).

[94] Adela Y. Collins, 'The Function of "Excommunication" in Paul', 263 without drawing attention to temple imagery, comes to a similar conclusion: "the more or less explicit reason for expelling the incestuous man in 1 Corinthians 5 was to guard the holiness of the community and to avoid offense to the presence of the Holy Spirit." Hans Conzelmann, 96 recognizes the holiness motif in 1 Corinthians 5, but, in my view, mistakenly connects it with 6:19 rather than 3:16-17: "Paul does not explicitly state the ground of his judgement, because the ground is self evident: the community is the temple of God (6:19)." The findings of this study are in disagreement with Pfitzner, 'Purified Community', 48 who states that "Paul shows, perhaps surprisingly, little or no interest in preserving the holiness of the church on a neo-levitical foundation."

[95] G.W.H. Lampe, 'Church Discipline', 355 aptly explains the proverb as "moral contamination of the brotherhood."

women and their children. . . . Let it be done according to the Law;" cf. Neh 9:32). As mentioned above (IIIB), Ezra's prayer in chapter 9, which mourns the sins of the people, discloses the profound sense in which he subscribed to the *corporate* solidarity and *responsibility* of the newly formed community. Finally, a *temple and holiness* motif is also operative in the decision to exclude certain offenders; Ezra is concerned to maintain the holiness of the race and the temple (9:2,8-9), building (like Paul) upon the teaching of Deuteronomy 23 (see IIIC above). In Ezra, the temple, which the community returned to Jerusalem to re-establish, is never far from view (1:2,3,4,7; 2:42,43,58, 70; 3:6,10,12; 4:1,3; 5:3,8,9,11,12,14,15; 6:3,5,7,12,14,15; 7:7,16,17,19,20,23,24; 8:17,20).[96] Post-exilic Malachi 2:11 expresses well the attitude of Ezra to his situation: "Judah has desecrated the sanctuary the LORD loves, by marrying the daughter of a foreign god" (that is, a pagan woman).

Did Paul have Ezra's example in mind when he wrote 1 Corinthians 5? Whereas his use of πενθέω in 5:2a would suggest that he did to some extent, his quotation of the Deuteronomic expulsion formula in 5:13b cautions against underestimating the direct use of Pentateuchal legislation. Either way, that the two share the same rationale and motivations for excluding those members of the community involved in illicit sexual relationships urges the conclusion that they both stand in a discernible Biblical tradition.

## IV. The Influence of Jewish Exegesis on Paul's Use of Scripture in 1 Corinthians 5

Our examination of the holiness motif in 1 Corinthians 5 concluded that Paul's development of this theme was built upon the assembly admission regulations of Deuteronomy 23:2-9 (1-8) as interpreted by post-exilic Judaism. Thus Jewish exegesis and use of Deuteronomy 23:2-9 (1-8) mediated Scripture to Paul. Another feature of Paul's use of the Scriptures in 1 Corinthians 5 which betrays his Jewish heritage is the modification of the penalty of excommunication. In the Pentateuch, execution, whether by human or divine means, was the result of exclusion signalled by the בער or ארר formulae. In 1

---

[96] In the light of this data Gerald J. Blidstein's comment, 'A Greek Parallel to Ezra X 8', 357 that "punitive banishment from the community—first found in Ezra x 8 . . . has no substantial roots in Pentateuchal legislation" is puzzling.

Corinthians 5 it is debated whether expulsion was necessarily intended to lead to the death of the sinner.[97] If not, Paul's understanding of excommunication corresponds with the practice of second Temple Judaism which, as William Horbury demonstrates, regularly understood excommunication as a surrogate or preparation for execution.[98] Evidence for this substitution can be drawn from sources as diverse as Josephus, 3 Maccabees, the Damascus Document and Philo. A development in the translation of the Deuteronomic formula Paul quotes in 1 Corinthians 5:13 evidences this substitution of a curse of exclusion for the death penalty. Regularly in Targum Onkelos, Targum Pseudo-Jonathan and Sifre, and usually in LXX, we find written "the evil man" instead of "the evil"(הרע) "shall be put away." It is this interpretive translation of the LXX, constituting a curse of exclusion, that Paul quotes in 5:13. Paul does not quote the MT, which unambiguously signals execution. Paul's understanding of excommunication in terms of exclusion is thus traditional, reflecting "established rather than new procedure."[99]

The very fact that Paul thinks it imperative that the "man living with his father's wife" be disciplined is itself testimony to Paul's inherited knowledge of the Scriptures. Many commentators on 1 Corinthians 5 mention Leviticus 18:8 and 20:11 as the background of Paul's decision to expel the sinner, noting the shared terminology γυναικός and πατρός (1 Cor 5:2).[100] However, two verses in Deuteronomy are just as likely to have influenced Paul. First, Deuteronomy 27:20, "cursed is the man who sleeps with his father's wife," is perhaps the reason Paul "curses" the sinner in 1 Corinthians 5. Secondly, Deuteronomy 23:1 (22:30), "a man is not to marry his father's wife," may have been the impetus for Paul to quote the Deuteronomic expulsion formula in 1 Corinthians 5:13. A variation of that formula appears in

---

[97] 1 Corinthians 5:5 is a veritable exegetical labyrinth. Scholars who understand the discipline as not necessarily leading to death include Robertson and Plummer, Thiselton, 'The Meaning of ΣΑΡΞ in 1 Corinthians 5.5: A Fresh Approach in the Light of Logical and Semantic Factors', and Cambier, 'La Chair et l'Esprit en 1 Cor 5.5'. Hans Conzelmann and F.F. Bruce (cross referencing 11:30) equate the punishment of 5:5 with death. In the present work I understand 5:5 as an excommunication that does not disqualify the offender from final salvation, but includes physical affliction not necessarily culminating in death.

[98] Horbury, 'Extirpation', 27-30.

[99] Horbury, 'Extirpation', 28.

[100] Sexual intercourse with the 'wife' of one's father is also condemned in Genesis 49:4 (see 35:22) and Ezekiel 22:10-11.

Deuteronomy 22:22 ("If a man is found sleeping with another man's wife . . . you must purge the evil from Israel;" cf. 22:24) and is presumably the penalty for the incest prohibited in Deuteronomy 23:1 (22:30).[101] In quoting the Deuteronomic formula in 5:13, Paul, it appears, is simply following Torah. The cruciality of 23:1 (22:30) was previously noted with respect to its juxtaposition to the temple admission regulations of Deuteronomy 23:2-9 (1-8). Mishnah Sanhedrin 7:4 (incest is punishable by stoning); 9:1 and Kerithoth 1:1 (incest is one of the first offences listed for "cutting off"); Jubilees 33:10-13; Tosefta Sanhedrin 10:1; The Damascus Document 5; The Temple Scroll LXVI and Philo *Special Laws* 3:22-28 confirm that Judaism maintained this Deuteronomic resolve that incest be punished.[102]

## V. FURTHER TRACES OF BIBLICAL INFLUENCE ON 1 CORINTHIANS 5

Paul's indebtedness to Scripture in 1 Corinthians 5:1-13 is not exhausted by our identification of the three community exclusion motifs. Not only the major lines, but also many of the details of Paul's instructions bear the imprint of the Scriptures. Paul moves within the biblical world of thought, using its idiom and language. In line with the broader theme of Paul's indebtedness to Scripture for ethical teaching in 1 Corinthians 5 several of these allusions and ideas will be noted.

*Verse One.*
Paul's use of the term πορνεία in 5:1 (cf. 6:13,18; 7:2; πόρνη 6:15,16; πόρνος 5:9,10,11; 6:9; πορνεύω 6:18; 10:8), a flexible term meaning "prohibited sexual relations," is roughly equivalent to זנות ("unchastity/fornication"; cf. 1QS 4:10; CD 4:17,20) which πορνεία translates in Numbers 14:33; Jeremiah 3:2,9; 13:27; Ezekiel 23:27; 43:7,9.[103]

---

[101] On 'Quotation of Scripture as an Index of Wider Reference' see R. Rendall's article by that title.

[102] Tomson, *Paul*, 100-101 has shown that Strack-Billerbeck's *Kommentar* (3:358) is mistaken in its judgement that the majority of Jewish sages did not object to a gentile or proselyte marrying his stepmother. Strack-Billerbeck's conclusion on the matter is the opposite of the present study's findings: "Jedenfalls haben wir hier ein Beispiel, wie völlig bedeutungslos dem im Rabbinismus groß gewordenen Apostel Paulus die jüdische Halakha für die Entscheidung größer sittlicher Fragen geworden war."

[103] This connection was first proposed by Strack-Billerbeck, *Kommentar* 3:342; cf. also Tomson, *Paul*, 98.

*Verse One.*

The unfavourable comparison of the Corinthians to the Gentiles in verse 1, rather than determining Paul's opposition to incest, operates rhetorically to heighten Corinthian guilt. As John Calvin observes: "in making mention of the Gentiles . . . [Paul intends] to heighten the aggravation of the crime."[104] This rhetorical device is well attested in the Scriptures. For example, in Amos 1 and 2, the prophet heightens Israel's guilt by portraying her as worse than the surrounding nations.[105] Israel's indictment is the eighth and final, longest and most detailed judgement oracle.

*Verses Two and Six.*

In 5:2,6 Paul rebukes the Corinthians for arrogance and pride (cf. 1:29-31; 4;6,18,19; 8:1; 13:4), a chief sin in the Scriptures (eg. 2 Chron 26:16; 32:24-25; Job 40:11-12; 22:29; Prov 8:13; 11:2; 15:25; 16:19; 21:4; 29:23; Pss 10:4; 31:19 [18]; 40:5 [4]; 59:13 [12]; 73:3-9; 94:2-7; Isa 10:12-15; 23:8-9; 25:11; Ezek 28:2-10; Jer 48:29-30; 50:29; Zeph 2:10; Amos 6:8).

*Verse Four.*

The excommunication described in verse 4 is to take place when the Corinthians are *gathered together* in the name and power of the Lord Jesus. Whatever else this scene implies it is comparable to the judgement scene of Deuteronomy 19:16-20 which includes the command quoted in 1 Corinthians 5:13b. In Deuteronomy 19 the discipline also takes place in the presence of the congregation (19:20a) and the Lord (19:17: "in the presence of the LORD").[106] Numbers 15:35 ("the entire assembly must stone him," the sabbath-breaker), 35:24 ("the assembly must judge" a case of homicide) and Leviticus 24:14,16 ("the entire assembly is to stone him," a blasphemer) are comparable. The forum for the judgement of offenders is also the gathered community in The Rule of the Community 6-7. In Biblical criminal law the whole community is involved in judgement.

---

[104] Calvin, 180.
[105] Cf. 2 Kings 21:9,11. In Deuteronomy 12:29-31 and 1 Kings 14:24 the nations are used as a negative model for Israelite behaviour.
[106] Jean Héring, 35 notes that, in contrast to the corporate court scene in 1 Corinthians 5:3-5, in the excommunication "practised by the synagogue . . . the elders alone formed the tribunal."

*Verse Five.*
Satan is presented in 5:5 as God's agent for punishment (cf. 1 Tim
1:20; 2 Cor 12:7).[107] This contrasts with the usual portrayal of Satan
as God's supreme enemy in Romans 16:20; 2 Thessalonians 2:9, etc.
Timothy Thornton has traced the roots of this idea in Job and Exodus
(and in Jewish literature).[108] In particular the formulation "deliver to
Satan" recalls LXX Job 2:6 (both use παραδίδωμι): "The Lord said
to the devil, I deliver him to you."[109] Despite the obvious differences
(Job is a just man being tested, not an unjust man being chastised),
this background is a possible avenue for understanding 1 Corinthians
5:5. Göran Forkman has noted the similarity of the curses in Job
with the covenant curses of Deuteronomy 28 and suggests a possible
connection with the effects of the curse in 5:5—material loss, personal
tragedy, illness and possible death.[110] A.R. Millard makes a similar
point concerning this possible scriptural background of 1 Corinthians
5:5:

> Extruded from the Covenant's present benefits, the miscreant might
> be brought to realize his error, repent, and be received again. There
> is an obvious similarity with the machinery of the Old Testament covenant
> which delivered the disloyal nation to its enemies for a time, they acting
> as the unwitting agents of the Lord (so the Assyrians Is. 8:5f, etc.,
> Nebuchadnezzar Jeremiah 25:9 etc.).[111]

*Verses Six, Seven and Eight.*
The Exodus/Passover/Unleavened Bread allusions and imagery of
these verses are well known and have received considerable attention.[112]
It is enough to note for our present purposes that, when Paul wishes
in 5:6-8 to supply the theological basis for the expulsion of the sinner,
his raw materials, despite his predominantly Gentile audience, are
precisely drawn from the Jewish Scriptures. Gordon Fee's summary
of the argument of these verses is accurate:

---

[107] Cf. Barrett, 126: "Satan, in fact, was being used as a tool in the interests of
Christ and the church." Satan's implicit connection with sexual immorality in 1
Corinthians 5 is also evident in T. Reub. 4:7,11; 6:3; CD 4:15-17.
[108] Thornton, 'Satan: God's agent for punishing'.
[109] Cf. Lampe, 'Church Discipline', 353: "the work of Satan is evil, but it serves
God's ultimate object almost as in the book of Job."
[110] G. Forkman, *Limits*, 143-144.
[111] A.R. Millard, 'Covenant and Communion in First Corinthians'. Cf. 2 Kings
24:2-3,20.
[112] See for example J. K. Howard, 'Christ Our Passover: A Study of the Passover-
Exodus Theme in 1 Corinthians' and David Daube, *The Exodus Pattern in the Bible*.

Although the metaphors get slightly mixed (the church alternately is the purified house, the new batch of dough, and the celebrants of the Feast), Paul's point is clear. They must remove the man for their own sake, so that they may truly be the new people of God in Corinth.[113]

*Verse Seven.*
Paul customarily sets his imperatives in the context of God's prior action on behalf of believers in Christ. 1 Corinthians 5:7 is a case in point: "cleanse out the old leaven . . . as you really are unleavened" (καθώς ἐστε ἄζυμοι). In this verse, as C.K. Barrett observes, "the imperative rests upon an indicative."[114] Deuteronomy 4:20 is a specific parallel not only to the structure of 1 Corinthians 5:7 but also to its contents. In 5:7 Paul attaches two motivations to the exhortation to cleanse out the old leaven: first, because the church is now positionally clean (introduced by καθώς), and secondly, because Christ is our Passover (introduced by καὶ γάρ).[115] Deuteronomy 4:20, concluding an exhortation not to become corrupt (4:16) in idolatry, attaches two remarkably similar motivations in reverse order; first, because of the Passover, and secondly, because you [i.e., Israel] are now the LORD's inheritance (introduced in the LXX by ὡς).[116]

The identity of the Corinthians is to inform their behaviour.[117] In other words, "What they must become is what they already are by the grace of God."[118] This prominent notion in Pauline ethics, though central and much discussed,[119] is not normally linked to the Scriptures. Since we shall encounter it again in 1 Corinthians 6:9-11 and 6:12-20 a short excursus on its likely background at this point is expedient.

*Excursus 1:*
*The Interrelation of Indicative and Imperative in the Scriptures*
It is abundantly clear that Old Testament ethical injunctions and

---

[113] Fee, 215. On the leaven metaphor in the New Testament see C. Leslie Mitton, 'New Wine in Old Wine Skins: IV. Leaven'. Mitton, 340 correctly notes that the metaphorical use is absent from the Old Testament (חמץ in Psalm 71:4, a possible example of such a use, is a different root; see K. Kellermann, חמץ, 4:488).
[114] Barrett, 128. Or as Michael Parsons says in 'Being Precedes Act: Indicative and Imperative in Paul's Writing', "being precedes act."
[115] BDF, 452 (3) understands καί γάρ in 5:7c as "for also". In other words, it introduces a second reason for the explanation of 5:7a, "be cleansed".
[116] An emphasis on the present blessed status of God's people is also evident in Deuteronomy 10:22 (cf. 10:5,8).
[117] Note the emphasis on identity in 1 Corinthians 6:9-11 (καί ταῦτά τινες ἦτε).
[118] Fee, 217.
[119] See M. Parsons, 'Being Precedes Act', and P.J. Gräbe, 'Die verhouding tussen

prohibitions are, like those in the Pauline corpus, rooted in the redemptive acts of God. The preamble to the Ten Commandments indicates that the people to whom God gives the laws are those whom He has liberated from Egypt (Exod 20:2). Throughout the Pentateuch, a chief motivation to obedience is, as Numbers 15:41 puts it, "I am the Lord your God, who brought you out of Egypt to be your God." The book of Deuteronomy brings this out forcefully. Deuteronomy is basically a call to God's people to reflect upon their past history of salvation, while calling them to present obedience. Several texts state that God's people should obey Him because of who they have become:

Deuteronomy 7:5-6 (concerning Canaanite idolatry):

> Break down their altars, smash their sacred stones, cut down their Asherah poles and burn their idols in the fire. For you are a people holy to the LORD your God.

Deuteronomy 14:1-2:

> You are the children of the Lord your God. Do not cut yourselves or shave the front of your heads for the dead for you are a people holy to the LORD your God.

Deuteronomy 27:9-10:

> Then Moses and the priests, who are Levites said to all Israel, "Be silent, O Israel. and listen! You have now become the people of the LORD your God. Obey the LORD your God and follow his command that I give you today."[120]

An example from the historical books is Samuel's farewell speech to Israel (1 Sam 12:20-25). In these verses the command to serve the Lord wholeheartedly and not to turn away after idols (the imperative) is reinforced with the reminder that the Lord was pleased to make Israel his own and the encouragement to "consider what great things he has done for you" (the indicative).

Likewise in the Prophets, misconduct is not simply weakness or ignorance, but unfaithfulness to the God of the covenant. In Biblical thought human behaviour is always considered in the context of the underlying and overarching relationship with God.

---

indikatief en imperatief in die pauliniese etiek: enkele aksente uit diskussie sedert 1924', for recent surveys.

[120] See also Deuteronomy 10:15-16; 14:21; 15:15.

*Verses Two, Seven, Nine and Eleven.*
Four other terms in 1 Corinthians 5, apart from ἐξαίρω, πενθέω and ὄλεθρος, have a significant history of usage in LXX texts concerning community expulsion. Throughout the chapter Paul employs vocabulary that has associations with the teaching of the Scriptures on exclusion from the community. In connection with αἴρω in verse two, it is worth noting Leviticus 10:4-5, where the word is used to denote the carrying out of the dead bodies of the two laymen who had been destroyed for bringing impurity into the sanctuary by acting as priests.[121]

The sense of ἐκκαθαίρω in verse seven is paralleled by the use of the similar verb ἐκκαθαρίζω in Judges 20:13,[122] where the Benjamites are called upon by the other tribes of Israel to execute certain Gibeonite sexual offenders (see 19:22-26) and thereby to "put away (ἐκκαθαριοῦμεν) evil (πονηρίαν cf. 1 Cor 5:13) from Israel."[123]

In verses nine and eleven Paul prohibits mixing with serious transgressors using the term συναναμείγνυμι. The same term is used in two Biblical passages concerned with the purity of the people of Israel. Hosea 7:8 contains the warning: "Ephraim mixes (συνανεμείγνυτο) himself with the peoples;" and Ezekiel 20:18 (LXX) exhorts Israel: "Do not walk in the statutes of your fathers, nor observe their ordinances and in their ways do not mix (συναναμίσγεσθε) and defile yourselves."[124]

The verb συνεσθίω, which turns up in verse eleven, appears in Psalm 100 in a similar context. In Psalm 101:5 (LXX), as Michael Newton observes, "banishment is equivalent to [exclusion from] table fellowship"[125] in comparable fashion to 1 Corinthians 5:11:

> He who slanders his neighbours secretly, he is banished (ἐξεδίωκον)
> He who is of haughty looks and of a greedy heart,
>   with him food is not shared (συνήσθιον; MT אתו לא אוכל).

In both 1 Corinthians 5 and Psalm 101 the faithful are not to eat with those guilty of slander, arrogance and greed. In Psalm 101:7 the presence of God in the Temple and evil are said to be incompatible, supplying a further link with Paul's sentiments (see III C):

[121] Michael Newton, *The Concept of Purity*, 88; cf. Lev 11:25,28,40 and 15:10 where αἴρω refers to the carrying of unclean animal carcasses and objects affected by bodily discharge respectively.
[122] ἐκκαθαίρω is used in the LXX in Deuteronomy 26:13; Joshua 17:15, Judges 7:4, but in a different way from 1 Corinthians 5:7.
[123] Newton, *Purity*, 91.
[124] Newton, *Purity*, 94.
[125] Newton, *Purity*, 95.

He who practices deceit shall not dwell in my house;
He who speaks falsehood shall not maintain his position before me.

At several points in 1 Corinthians 5 Paul could literally have quoted Psalm 101 to bolster his case for exclusion.

## VI. MATTHEW 18:15-20 AND 1 CORINTHIANS 5

Since 1 Corinthians is an epistle in which scholars find several references to the words of Jesus, it is important to consider the relationship between 1 Corinthians 5 and Matthew 18:15-20. Matthew 18:15-20 is, of course, itself Pentateuchally based (cf. Lev 19:17; Deut 19:15-19). The three Pentateuchal community exclusion motifs, which we have argued are clearly reflected in 1 Corinthians 5, are conspicuous by their absence from Matthew 18:15-20. In Matthew the main concern is for the restitution of the sinner rather than the purity of the church. As Victor C. Pfitzner contends: "Matthew reflects a gospel concern rather than interest in preserving the church as a community of the pure in the cultic sense."[126] Nevertheless, a modest comparison of 1 Corinthians 5 and Matthew 18:15-20 reveals three marked similarities that are worth noting:

First, in both passages, the whole church is involved in the process of excommunication (1 Cor 5:4; Matt 18:17). Secondly, in both cases, the Lord Jesus is the real agent of the judgement. In the tribunal envisaged in 1 Corinthians 5:3-5, if Paul is a judge, then the Lord Jesus whose name appears three times, is the supreme court judge. As G.W.H. Lampe observes, this conviction concerning Christ

> is similar to the belief expressed in Matthew 18:18-20; the verdict of the church is ratified in heaven, . . . because, when the congregation is assembled in prayer with the intention of exercising discipline, Jesus is in their midst and God will act in response to their petitions.[127]

In the third place, both 1 Corinthians 5 and Matthew 18:15-20 share a concern for the welfare of the sinner. The stated purpose of the handing over of the offender for destruction in 1 Corinthians 5:5 is "in order that his spirit may be saved in the day of the Lord Jesus." In Matthew the point of the cautious steps leading up to

---

[126] Pfitzner, 'Purified Community', 40; cf. E. Schweizer, Matthew, 370: "what matters is the sinner, not a 'pure community'."
[127] Lampe, 'Church Discipline', 344.

excommunication (private, then semi-private, then open rebuke before the church) is obviously to "gain the brother" (18:15b). As Lampe notes, "we are introduced to the Corinthian story at a late stage," possibly after such "appeals for penitence had taken place."[128] There is an implicit condition in the expulsion of the sinner in 1 Corinthians 5; if he repents, restoration will occur. That this is the case is perhaps seen in the fact that, whereas in the Pentateuch single acts of transgression brought exclusion, in 1 Corinthians 5 the character of the sinner, not an isolated offence, is the focus (cf. 5:10-11). The open door of reinstatement in Paul's thinking is made explicit in 2 Corinthians 2:1-11, even if the offender there is not to be identified with the sinner of 1 Corinthians 5.[129] Elements of pastoral concern can be found in both passages. This aspect of community exclusion is without a clear antecedent in the Scriptures.

However, to return to our earlier theme of Paul's Jewish heritage in terms of his handling of the Scriptures, two items should be mentioned with reference to the notion of the positive purposes of excommunication evident in Jewish exegesis of Joshua 7 and Numbers 15:34ff. First, Paul's eschatological concern for the sinner in 1 Corinthians 5:5 may to some extent be compared to Sanhedrin 6:2, where Achan's confession (Josh 7:20) is understood as making atonement for his sin and winning him a portion in the world to come. Second, the notion that exclusion might have a reformative effect is seen in the Qumran modification of the death penalty for gathering sticks on the sabbath (Num 15:34f) into seven years in a sectarian guard room (CD 12:4-6).[130]

## VII. CONCLUSION

*The Church as a Sanctified Covenant Community*
We are now in a position to identify the theological presupposition which underlies and facilitates Paul's appropriation of Scriptural

---

[128] Lampe, 'Church Discipline', 346.
[129] For the view that the two passages refer to the same person see Colin G. Kruse, 'The Offender and the Offence in 2 Corinthians 2:5 and 7:12', and for the alternative position, V. Furnish, *II Corinthians*, 159-66
[130] Cf. W. Horbury, 'Extirpation', 28. Cf. 1QS VII where, for different offences, different periods of penance are to be enacted, ranging from thirty days to two years. Exclusion from "the pure meal of the congregation" is also a punishment (cf. 1 Cor 5:11b; Ps 101:5).

teaching in 1 Corinthians 5. Paul's use of the three motifs associated with excommunication in the Scriptures indicates that he understands the church to be a sanctified (holiness motif), covenant (covenant motif) community (corporate responsibility motif). This 1 Corinthians 5 description of the church uniquely combines the image of church as a temple found in 1 Corinthians 3:16-17 and as a body developed in 1 Corinthians 10:17; 11:29; 12:12-27.

*Scripture as the Rule for Exclusion*
Why must the sinner be expelled in 1 Corinthians 5? Paul Minear concedes that "it may be easy to grasp the commands Paul gave, but it is far from easy to grasp the reasoning that lay behind these commands."[131] This chapter held the mirror of the Jewish Scriptures up to this question and discovered three answers, each reflecting a motif of Pentateuchal community exclusion. First, the man must be removed because he is guilty of covenant disloyalty, secondly, because while he remains, the church is implicated in his sin, and thirdly, because the community is the temple of the Holy Spirit. In short, he must be driven out for the sake of the church. A fourth reason for his expulsion, he must be ejected for his own sake, is not, it seems, related directly to the Scriptures.[132]

1 Corinthians 5:1-13 is an instance where an interrelated complex of Scriptural ideas converge to profound effect. We can make a strong case that the Scriptures in general, and Deuteronomy in particular, are foundational to Paul's ethics in this chapter. Paul's instructions are firmly anchored in the covenant and temple regulations found in the fifth book of the Pentateuch. As we navigated our course through 1 Corinthians 5 we discovered that the Deuteronomic expression in 5:13b was not a mirage but the tip of a veritable iceberg of dependence upon the Jewish Scriptures.

---

[131] Paul S. Minear, 'Congregation', 341; cf. Collins, 'Excommunication', 263 who identifies the holiness of the community but adds, "there may well have been other, unspoken reasons."

[132] This may well be the distinctively Christian and 'new' element in Paul's understanding of exclusion. However, to state the purpose of church discipline only in terms of motivating the repentance and restoration of the sinner (eg. J. Carl Laney, 'The Biblical Practice of Church Discipline', 356-57) is to miss much of Paul's (and his Bible's) teaching and seriously to truncate his ecclesiology.

*Interpretative Paraphrase*
*with Significant Biblical/Jewish Cross References*

It is actually reported that there is immorality among you, and of such a kind that even pagans condemn,[1] for a man is living with his father's wife![2] And you are still proud of yourselves! Ought you not rather to mourn, collectively confessing the sin of the erring brother as if it were your own?[3] Remove[4] the one who has done this from among you (1-2).

[1]Deut 12:29-31; 1 Ki 14:24; 2 Ki 21:9,11; Amos 1,2

[2]Lev 18:8; 20:11; Deut 23:1; 27:20; mSan 7:4; 9:1; mKer 1:1; tSan 10:1; Jub 33:10-13, etc

[3]Ezra 10:6; Neh 1:4; 1 Esd 8:72; 9:2; Dan 10:2 [4]Lev 10:4-5

For though absent in body I am present in spirit, and as if present I have already pronounced judgement[5] in the name of the Lord Jesus on the man who has done such a thing. When you are assembled,[6] and my spirit is present, with the power of our Lord Jesus you must deliver this man to Satan[7] for the destruction of the flesh.[8] (Do not forget that you are God's temple and that God's Spirit dwells in you. If anyone destroys God's temple, God will destroy him. For God's temple is holy, and that is what you are.[9]) Do this so that his spirit may be saved[10] in the day of the Lord Jesus (3-5).

[5]2 Sam 12

[6]Deut 19:16-20; Num 15:35; 35:24; Lev 24:14,16; 1QS 6-7

[7]Job 2:1
[8]Deut 27:20

[9]1 Cor 3:16-17; Deut 23:1-8
[10]mSan 6:2; CD 12:4-6; 1QS 7

Your boasting is not good. Do you not know that a little leaven leavens the whole lump? Cleanse out[11] the old leaven[12] that you may be a new lump, as you really are unleavened. For Christ our paschal lamb has been sacrificed.[13] Let us, therefore, celebrate the festival,[14] not with the old leaven of malice and evil, but with the unleavened bread of sincerity and truth (6-8).

[11]Ju 20:13
[12]Ex 12:15; 13:7

[13]Deut 4:20
[14]2 Chron 29,30; 35:1-19; 2 Ki 23:1-23; Ezra 6:13-22

I wrote to you in my letter not to associate[15] with immoral men; not at all meaning the immoral of this world, or the greedy and robbers, or idolators, since then you would need to go out of the world.

But rather I wrote to you not to associate[15] with any so-called brother who breaks covenantal norms, by being immoral,[16] greedy,[17] idolatrous,[18] abusive,[19] a drunkard[20] or a robber[21]— not even to eat[22] with such a one. For what have I to do with judging outsiders? Is it not those inside whom you are to judge? God judges those outside. "Drive out the wicked person from among you!"[23] (9-11).

[15]Hos 7:8; Ezek 20:18

[16]Deut 22:21 [17]Deut 24:7 [18]Deut 13:5; 17:7 [19]Deut 19:19 [20]Deut 21:21 [21]Deut 24:7 [22]Ps 101:5

[23]Deut 13:5; 17:7; 19:19; 21:21; 22:21; 24:7

CHAPTER FOUR

# MOSES AND PAUL APPOINTING JUDGES
## 1 CORINTHIANS 6:1-11

### I. Introduction
*"Brother goes to law against brother, and that before unbelievers!"*

In 1 Corinthians 6:1-11 Paul deals with the report that some of the Corinthian Christians were engaging one another in civil litigation[1] in secular courts.[2] Paul vigorously opposes this behaviour, judging it sheer audacity. Numerous rhetorical questions (disguised rebukes) and the use of τολμάω (6:1; cf. Rom 5:7) betray Paul's disdain. As verse 5a indicates, Paul writes to shame the Corinthians over such behaviour. The apostle's case against these lawsuits comprises two points:[3] in 6:1-6 he insists that Christians ought to be able to settle their own disputes,[4] and in 6:7-11, going a step further, he contends that Christians ought not to have disputes at all.

What role does Scripture play in the formation of these instructions? Unlike 5:1-13 there is no Biblical quotation in 6:1-11 which we may use as a possible way into a wider field of Scriptural background. If silence is any indication, most commentators on 1 Corinthians 6:1-11 apparently believe Scripture to have played only a minor role; in many cases only Daniel 7:22 is brought into the discussion (with reference to 1 Cor 6:2). Lukas Vischer's history of research, *Die Auslegungsgeschichte von 1 Kor 6,1-11*, contains hardly any reference to the Old Testament. When possible sources for Paul's instructions are discussed, Scripture is not accorded much weight. Concerning Paul's first point in 6:1-6 about the appointment of Christian judges, several modern commentators follow Hans Conzelmann's assertion that "the contemporary presupposition of Paul's ordinance is the Jewish court

---

[1] βιωτικός (6:3) and ἀποστερέω (6:7-8) suggest that a civil case and not a criminal case is in view (cf. Reginald H. Fuller, '1 Cor, 6:1-11. An Exegetical Paper', 100), involving perhaps legal possession, breach of contract, damages, fraud or injury.

[2] *Contra* A. Stein, 'Wo trugen die korinthischen Christen ihre Rechtshändel aus?', who makes the improbable suggestion that the Corinthians were submitting their cases to Jewish judges.

[3] Cf. Barrett, 135; Talbert, 28.

[4] 6:1 and 6:6 are an inclusio (note repetition of κρίνω and ἐπί).

of arbitration,"[5] a view previously tabled by Hugo Grotius.[6] The example and teaching of Jesus in 'turning the other cheek' is commonly cited as giving rise to Paul's second point concerning suffering wrong in 6:7-11.[7]

Nevertheless, this chapter attempts to evaluate the status of the Scriptures as a source for Paul's ethics in 1 Corinthians 6:1-11, by seeing whether one can trace the fundamental aspects of Paul's ethics in the passage back into the Scriptures (in most cases) by way of Jewish sources.


## II. CHRISTIANS OUGHT TO SETTLE THEIR OWN DISPUTES (6:1-6)

Unlike the case of the incestuous man in 1 Corinthians 5, Paul in 1 Corinthians 6:1-6 does not himself pronounce judgement, but instructs the Christian community to supply its own judges to adjudicate the dispute (cf. 1 Cor 6:1b, 5b). In spite of the virtual silence of the commentators concerning Old Testament antecedents, several aspects of these instructions may be explored with respect to their relation to the Scriptures.


### A. *The Appointment of Judges*[8]

Various attempts have been made to compare Paul's Christian 'courts' in 1 Corinthians 6:1-6 with contemporary Jewish judicial practices.[9] The analogy is appealing, for as Gordon Fee notes, "by the time of Paul, the Romans had granted the Jews liberty of settling internal matters, at least in Jerusalem."[10] In the name of Rabbi Tarfon, who flourished at the beginning of the second century, the following saying

---

[5] Conzelmann, 104. Cf. Lindemann, 'Die biblischen Toragebote', 247.

[6] Grotius, *Annotationes in Novum Testamentum*, 395.

[7] Eg. Fuller, '1 Cor. 6:1-11', 101: "Paul clearly echoes the teaching of the Sermon on the Mount (Matt. 5:39-42)." Cf. J. Piper, *Love Your Enemies: Jesus' Love Command in the Synoptic Gospels and in the Early Christian Paraenesis. A history of the tradition and an interpretation of its uses*, 59; Bruce, Fee, Findlay, Godet, Lang, NA[26] margin.

[8] An abbreviated version of this section was published in *Zeitschrift für die Neutestamentliche Wissenschaft und die Kunde der Älteren Kirche* under the title 'Moses Appointing Judges: An Antecedent to 1 Cor 6.1-6?'.

[9] See esp. M. Delcor, 'The Courts of the Church of Corinth and the Courts of Qumran'; Vischer, *Die Auslegungsgeschichte;* and B. Viviano, *Study as Worship: Aboth and the New Testament*, 18.

[10] Fee, 231. Josephus, Antiquities 14.17.235 is evidence that Jewish courts were also established in the diaspora.

is handed down.[11] It may well express a prevalent thought among
Jews in Paul's day:

> In any place where you find heathen law courts, even though their
> law is the same as Israelite law, you must not resort to them since
> it says, 'these are the judgements which you shall bring before them,'
> that is to say, 'before them' and not before heathens."[12]

There can be little doubt that Paul's concern that judicial matters
be settled internally is the common Jewish attitude of his day, though
there is evidence of some Jewish exceptions.[13] However, as a first step
towards exploring Paul's dependence upon the Scriptures in 6:1-11
it is advisable to look not only at contemporary practice but also to
the teaching of the Scriptures themselves on judicial matters.[14] It is
possible that the administration of justice in ancient Israel as presented
in the Scriptures may have influenced Paul's thinking in the appointment of judges in 6:1-6. Roland de Vaux[15] explains that Israel had
three different jurisdictions involving priests,[16] elders, and professional
judges instituted by the authority of the king. All three groups are
mentioned in the Pentateuch and take part in judicial affairs in other
parts of the Scriptures.

The communal jurisdiction of the elders was the notional model
upon which the Jewish Courts of justice were based in Paul's day.[17]
According to Mishnah Sanhedrin 1:6, the Great Sanhedrin had its
origin in the council of the seventy elders constituted in the time of
Moses (Num 11:4-31).[18] The New Testament also seems to make the
link, replacing συνέδριον with πρεσβυτέριον in Luke 22:66 and Acts

---

[11] b. Gitt. 88b; on Rabbi Tarfon see J. Gereboff, *Rabbi Tarfon*. See m. Sanhedrin
for the regulations.

[12] Cf. Exodus 21:1: "These are the laws you are to set before them."

[13] Some time before Paul the Elephantine papyri record Jews in Southern Egypt
using secular courts. Documents of the Jewess Babatha daughter of Simeon (found
in the Bar Kokhba caves) record similar activity in the early second century (see
G.W. Bowersock, *Roman Arabia*, 76ff.).

[14] On the diversity of judicial events in the Scriptures see Rolf P. Knierim, 'Customs,
Judges, and Legislators in Ancient Israel'; H.J. Boecker, *Redeformen des Rechtslebens im
Alten Testament*; Roland de Vaux, *Ancient Israel*; and D.J. Wiseman, 'Law and Order
in Old Testament Times'.

[15] de Vaux, *Ancient Israel*, 1:152-55.

[16] Priests functioned as judges in cases concerning the cult or religious practice.

[17] On the complex question of Jewish law-courts and the law they administered
in Palestine in the time of Jesus see Philip S. Alexander, 'Jewish Law in the Time
of Jesus: Towards a clarification of the Problem', esp. 46-53.

[18] Cf. Schürer, *The History of the Jewish People*, II:200,210.

22:5.[19] The lesser Jewish courts, sitting under the umbrella of the Sanhedrin, presumably also derive from the model of the elders.

Nonetheless, it is the tradition of the regal appointment of judges which provides the best background for 1 Corinthians 6:1-6.[20] Such judges find their prototypes in the competent laymen appointed to dispense justice by Moses upon the advice of Jethro, his father-in-law, in Exodus 18:13-26 and Deuteronomy 1:9-17. Deuteronomy 16:18-20 and 17:8-13 give further directions for these judges.[21]

The influence of the appointment of judges by Moses in the subsequent history of Israel as presented in the Scriptures increases the likelihood that Paul was aware of and thought highly of this ancient tradition. In 2 Chronicles 17:7-9 Jehoshaphat is depicted as ordering the teaching of the Law of Moses throughout Israel. King Jehoshaphat appoints judges in 2 Chronicles 19:5-11. The close relation of this passage to the relevant passages in Exodus 18 and Deuteronomy 1,16,17 has often been observed. H.G.M. Williamson, for example, contends for 19:5-11 that "it is hard to escape the suspicion that this may be directly dependent on Deuteronomy."[22] Raymond B. Dillard correctly concludes that in the Jehoshaphat narrative in 2 Chronicles 19:5-11 the Chronicler "shows a historical realization of judicial practices enjoined in Deuteronomy."[23] Shorter notices concerning the appointment of judges by Samuel, David and Ezra also occur in 1 Samuel 8:1, 1 Chronicles 23:4 and Ezra 7:25; 10:14 respectively (though without

[19] Cf. m. Shebu. 2:2: "the Sanhedrin of Seventy-one" (an allusion to Num 11).

[20] No commentator on 1 Corinthians, to my knowledge, mentions Moses in connection with 6:1-6. Neither do David M. Hay, 'Moses through New Testament Spectacles'; Tadashi Saito, *Die Mosevorstellungen im Neuen Testament*; Ernst Bammel, 'Paulus, Der Moses des Neuen Bundes'; nor Peter R. Jones, 'The Apostle Paul: Second Moses to the New Covenant community.'

[21] On the prominence of Moses in the Pentateuch generally see Dean S. McBride, 'Transcendent Authority: The Role of Moses in Old Testament Traditions'.

[22] Williamson, *1 and 2 Chronicles*, 288. cf. on v.6, 289: ". . . the start of the first parenetic section. Its sentiments are based largely on Deut. 1:17".

[23] Dillard, *2 Chronicles*, 150; cf. "the right of appeal to a higher judicial authority is found in Israel's most ancient traditions; Moses himself would hear cases too hard for the appointed judges (Deut. 1:8-18; Ex.18:17-26)." De Vaux, *Ancient Israel*, 1:154 concurs: "the literary expression of this text (2 Chron. 19:4-11) may have been influenced by Deuteronomy." Cf. also M. Weinfeld, 'Judge and Officer in Ancient Israel and in the Ancient Near East', 65 who, after discussing Exodus 18 and Deuteronomy 1, states: "The Chronicler's account of Jehoshaphat's appointment of judges throughout the land (2 Chr. xix:5ff) bears a similar stamp." The influence of Deuteronomy 1/Exodus 18 is surprisingly overlooked by Judson R. Shaver, *Torah and the Chronicler's History Work; An Inquiry into the Chronicler's References to Laws, Festivals and Cultic Institutions in Relationship to Pentateuchal Legislation*.

evidence of literary dependence on Deut 1,16,17 or Exod 18). The
appointment of judges by prominent Israelite leaders is a well attested
practice in the Scriptures.[24]

Contemporary Jewish custom also bears the imprint of the Moses
material.[25] Though the communal jurisdiction of the elders was the
notional model upon which the Jewish Courts of justice were largely
based in Paul's day, Exodus 18/Deuteronomy 1 and related passages
also exerted considerable influence in early Judaism. In 1QpHab 8,
for example, the wicked priest is effectively characterised as the antihero
of Exodus 18. The language of Exodus 18 also pervades the description
of judges and officers in the Temple Scroll 51,57. Josephus' description
of civic bodies of seven magistrates in Antiquities 4:214-16 recalls
Deuteronomy 16:18-20. Likewise, when Philo details the responsibilities
of a judge in 'On The Special Laws' he expounds Deuteronomy 1:17;
16:19 (70-71) and 16:20 (65-67).[26] Evidence may even be gleaned from
the Mishnah, where the usual designation of the sages, "the wise,"
probably derives from and refers to Deuteronomy 1:13-15. In rabbinic
tradition two of the 613 biblical commandments derive from Deuteronomy 1:17.[27]

Neither did it escape the notice of the early church that Moses
appointed judges.[28] The influence of Exodus 18/Deuteronomy 1 (and
Num 11) on the appointment of seven faithful men in Acts 6 has
been investigated by David Daube. Concerning the composition of
Acts 6 Daube concludes: "We may infer that the author drew directly

---

[24] Weinfeld, 'Judge and Officer', has demonstrated that the delegation of judicial
powers by the king was a common phenomenon in the organisation of justice in
the ancient Near East.

[25] On the influence of passages such as Deuteronomy 16:18-20 on Jewish Law
throughout the ages, with special reference to bribery, see Jacob Bazak, 'Judicial
Ethics in Jewish Law.'

[26] Cf. E.R. Goodenough, The Jurisprudence of the Jewish Courts in Egypt. Legal
Administration by the Jews under the Early Roman Empire as Described by Philo Judaeus, 201:
the Deuteronomy 1:17; 16:19 notion that "the judge ought to disregard personal
predilections in giving judgment . . . (is) always prominent in Jewish discussions of
justice."

[27] Abraham Hirsch Rabinowitz, 'Commandments, The 613', 779. "Judges of the
king", royal commanders in charge of jurisdiction, are also found in the Jewish colony
of Elephantine (Weinfeld, 'Judge and Officer', 72); see also R. Yaron, Introduction
to the Law of the Aramaic Payri, 27ff.

[28] The New Testament contains more explicit references to Moses than to any
other Old Testament figure (c. 80); David M. Hay, 'Moses through New Testament
Spectacles', 240.

on the Old Testament or, conceivably, on a fund of exposition accumulated outside Rabbinism."[29]

The situations in which Moses in Exodus 18/Deuteronomy 1 and Paul in 1 Corinthians 6:1-6 find themselves are not without similarity. Both Moses and Paul are overwhelmed by the judicial problems of the people of God.[30] Both leaders decide to handle the more difficult cases themselves,[31] with the Lord's help[32] (Paul pronounces judgement on the incestuous man in 1 Cor 5), and appoint judges to adjudicate the lesser cases[33] by deciding between their brothers.

The situations of Moses and Paul are of course not alike in every respect. Moses was not rejecting unsuitable judges, but appointing suitable ones. Without doubt, Paul's main task was more the former. This difference, however, is not so great that Paul could not have seen any relevance in the Moses incident to his own situation. Verses 6:1b and 5b indicate that Paul recommended as one option that some people from within the community settle the dispute. Furthermore, Patristic interpretation of 1 Corinthians 6:1-11 certainly saw the passage as relevant to the issue of the appointment of judges.[34]

The terminological links between 1 Corinthians 6:1-11 and LXX Exodus 18/Deuteronomy 1 (and related passages) also bear consideration. Both passages concern the activity of judging, κρίνω and διακρίνω (1 Cor 6:2,5; Exod 18:13,16) and detail the appointment of people to sit in judgement, καθίζω (1 Cor 6:4; Exod 18:14). Both define the chief qualifications of a judge as wisdom, σοφία, and righteousness, δίκαιοσύνη.[35] Moses appoints judges to arbitrate lawsuits, κρίματα, which Paul thinks the Corinthians ought to settle internally

---

[29] Daube, 'A Reform in Acts and its Models', 159. Thanks are due to Mr. J.P.M. Sweet for calling my attention to this article. Paul may well have known that what he was saying with respect to 'Christian judges' was in accord with other early Christian tradition, such as Matthew 19:28 which sees the disciples as judges modelled on the Mosaic constitution (see Horbury, 'The Twelve and the Phylarchs', for a survey of the Biblical and Jewish background).

[30] See Deuteronomy 1:12; Exodus 18:13,14,18, and Paul's disquiet in 1 Corinthians 5:1; 6:1.

[31] Exodus 18:22,26; Deuteronomy 1:17; 1 Corinthians 5:3-5; cf. Delcor, 'The Courts', 76: "In the Epistle to the Corinthians the office of supreme judge has fallen on the Apostle himself."

[32] Cf. Exodus 18:19b and 1 Corinthians 5:3-5.

[33] See Exodus 18:21-22; Deuteronomy 1:15, and 1 Corinthians 6:1b,4,5b.

[34] Bib. Pat. 1.452 and 2.381 assemble over 50 patristic discussions of 1 Cor 1:1-11 (or parts thereof), about which G.H.R. Horsley, *New Documents Illustrating Early Christianity*, 3:152, concludes correctly that "this passage provided the basis for what became the institution of the episcopal court set up under Constantine."

[35] Cf. esp. Deuteronomy 16:18-20.

(Exod 18:22; 1 Cor 6:7). The first case brought before the Exodus 18 judges is called a κριτήριον (Exod 21:6), the same term employed in 1 Corinthians 6:2 and 6:4 to describe the cases Paul thought the saints ought to adjudicate. In Exodus 22:8-9 the jurisdiction of the judges covers cases similar to that envisaged by many commentators as giving rise to 1 Corinthians 6:1-6 (namely, a civil rather than a criminal case). The specific grievance which apparently drove some Corinthians to secular courts was the defrauding of another person, ἀποστερέω[36] (1 Cor 6:7-8). According to Deuteronomy 24:14 (LXX-A) and 25:1 such disputes were supposed to be settled by the community's judges. A total of eight terms, then, some of which occur rarely in both the LXX and Paul's letters, can be traced from 1 Corinthians 6:1-8 to the tradition of Moses appointing judges in the Greek Old Testament.

That these data represent more than merely the coincidence of terms one normally expects to find in any two discussions of judicial affairs is suggested by the comparison of 1 Corinthians 6:5 with LXX Deuteronomy 1:16. In these two texts Moses and Paul appoint wise judges (cf. LXX Deuteronomy 1:15) to judge between their brothers:

| 1 Corinthians 6:5b | LXX Deuteronomy 1:16 |
|---|---|
| διακρῖναι ἀνὰ μέσον | κρίνατε δικαίως ἀνὰ μέσον ἀνδρὸς |
| τοῦ ἀδελφοῦ αὐτοῦ | καὶ ἀνὰ μέσον ἀδελφοῦ |

LXX manuscripts A, F, and M attest a reading which is even closer to Paul's words: ἀνὰ μέσον τοῦ ἀδελφοῦ αὐτοῦ. Ellis points out that Paul's explicit quotations of Scripture do not consistently follow one particular LXX text form. With reference to the case at hand it is worth noting that Paul's citations are sometimes quite close to LXX-A and LXX-F (eg. Rom 10:5; 2 Cor 6:16; Gal 3:10-12).[37]

A computer search of *Thesaurus Linguae Graecae*[38] confirms the significance of LXX Deuteronomy 1:16 in relation to 1 Corinthians 6:5. There are only three places in both literary and non literary Greek where (a form of) κρίνω plus ἀνὰ μέσον plus (a form of) ἀδελφός occur in that order: LXX Deuteronomy 1:16, 1 Corinthians 6:5 and

---

[36] The term is only used in the New Testament outside of Paul's letters in Mark 10:19, where it also appears in connection with the Scriptures, in an expanded list of "the commandments."

[37] Ellis, *Paul's Use*, 13. It is, of course, possible that LXX-A has been harmonised to the New Testament.

[38] *Canon of Greek Authors and Works*, ed. Luci Berkowitz and Karl A. Squitier.

Basil the Great's Commentary on Isaiah (102:9),[39] where 1 Corinthians 6:5 is quoted.[40] The Semitic flavour of the compound preposition ἀνὰ μέσον,[41] a *hapax* in Paul's letters, reinforces the impression that 1 Corinthians 6:5b contains an echo of the LXX.

Taken together, the terminological links between Exodus 18/ Deuteronomy 1 and 1 Corinthians 6:1-6, the influence and prominence of the tradition in the Jewish Scriptures and early Judaism, the similar situations of Moses and Paul, and the possible allusion to Deuteronomy 1:16 in 1 Corinthians 6:5 argue that Exodus 18/Deuteronomy 1 should be placed alongside 1 Corinthians 6 and some kind of influence between the texts investigated.

How are we to evaluate the connection between LXX Exodus 18/ Deuteronomy 1 and 1 Corinthians 6:1-6? Three possibilities suggest themselves. At the least we can say that Biblical language can be detected here. Perhaps Paul knew so well the thoughts and words of his Bible that when he wrote about appointing judges he could not avoid sounding a little like Moses doing the same. In that case neither Paul when he wrote 1 Corinthians 6:1-6, nor the Corinthians, when they read his instructions, would have been aware of the Scriptural tradition of Moses appointing judges. This is to minimise the connection. To maximise it is to suggest that Paul deliberately patterned his instructions after the Moses narrative, an allusion the Corinthians were intended to discover. A third position, located somewhere between these two extremes will be considered later.

The possibility of deliberate patterning in 1 Corinthians 6:1-6 is not without merit. The notion of using a segment of Scripture as a literary prototype or model after which to pattern a composition would not be new with Paul.[42] James L. Kugel describes a literary phenomenon of late Biblical (Old Testament) historiography and many post-biblical writings whereby "the present is encouraged to become part of biblical history . . . by describing current events, from as it were, the Bible's perspective."[43] This extension of Biblical history to

---

[39] See *Enarratio in prophetam Isaiam*, ed. P. Trevison, San Basilio. Commento al profeta Isaia, Turin 1939, 1,3-397; 2,3-575.

[40] That Basil's citation of 1 Corinthians 6:5 uses κρίνω, found in Deuteronomy 1:16, instead of διακρίνω demonstrates the synonymity of the two terms.

[41] Cf. F. Blass, A. Debrunner and Robert W. Funk (translator), *A Greek Grammar of the New Testament*, section 139, and Moule, *An Idiom Book*, 188 who compares ἀνὰ μέσον with Hebrew בֵּין (which it translates in Deut 1:16).

[42] Cf. G. Beale, 'Revelation', 323-25 on the use of Scriptural prototypes in Revelation.

[43] Kugel, *Early Biblical Interpretation*, 47-48.

the present can be illustrated from the book of Esther. Kugel explains:

> It [Esther] recounts the entertaining tale of a wicked courtier's overthrow and the salvation of the Jews in such a way as to make it sound like the great events of the past—and particularly the story of Joseph in Pharaoh's court on which some of its language is modelled.[44]

Sandra Berg's study of the motifs, themes and structure of Esther concurs with Kugel's comments describing the Joseph story as constituting "Esther's literary model."[45]

Traditional Moses material was not uncommonly the pattern for portrayals of Israelite history. In 1 Kings 17-19 it is a Moses-like Elijah that we encounter when Elijah turns the sword on the apostates and experiences the theophany.[46] The author of the book of Chronicles seems to model the succession of David and Solomon on that of Moses and Joshua,[47] and the building of the temple on the Pentateuchal record of the building of the Tabernacle (Solomon is a new Bezalel and Huram-Abi a new Oholiab).

Perhaps Paul is attempting to strengthen his own dealings with the Corinthians in 1 Corinthians 6 by a subtle but deliberate patterning of his instructions after the relevant Moses tradition found in Exodus 18/Deuteronomy 1. To portray himself as a Moses figure might enhance Paul's standing before the Corinthians.[48] As George Lyons observes, it is not uncommon for Paul to compare himself with the great leaders of Israel:

> he places his experience alongside that of the leading figures of Old Testament history—Abraham (in addition to Galatians, cf. also Romans 4), Isaiah and Jeremiah (cf. Galatians 1:15 and Isaiah 49:1; Jeremiah 1:5), Elijah (cf. Romans 11:1-5 and 1 Kings 19:4-18), and Moses (cf. 2 Corinthians 3:4-18 and Exodus 34:29-35).[49]

[44] Kugel, *Interpretation*, 47.

[45] Berg, *The Book of Esther: Motifs, Themes and Structure*, 186. On the stories of Joseph, Daniel and Esther and the genre of the Jew in the court of the foreign king see Lawrence M. Wills, *The Jew in the Court of the Foreign King*.

[46] William J. Dumbrell, *The Faith of Israel: Its Expression in the Books of the Old Testament*, 88-89; cf. esp. 1 Kings 19:9 (Heb) with Exodus 33:22 and Jeroboam's idolatry in 1 Kings 12:28 with Exodus 32:4.

[47] Williamson, *1 and 2 Chronicles*, 187-88; eg. cf. 1 Chronicles 29:23 with Deuteronomy 34:9 and Joshua 1:16-20, and 1 Chronicles 29:5 with Joshua 3:7 and 4:14.

[48] The attractiveness of Moses in the ancient world extended even beyond Judaism and Christianity—see John G. Gager, *Moses in Greco-Roman Paganism*.

[49] Lyons, *Pauline Autobiography: Towards a New Understanding*, 226. On the thesis that Paul conceived his apostleship and commission to preach to the Gentiles in prophetic terms see Karl Olav Sandnes, *Paul—One of the Prophets?- A Contribution to the Apostle's*

2 Corinthians 10-13 demonstrates that Paul was concerned to defend the divine source and authentic nature of his apostleship to the Corinthians. Furthermore, Peter Jones and Ernst Bammel have argued that Paul sees himself as a second Moses to the new covenant community.[50] Their two main passages are 1 Corinthians 3 (Jones), where Paul describes himself as the foundation-layer, and 2 Corinthians 3 (Bammel), where Paul as minister of the New Covenant compares himself with Moses, minister of the Old Covenant.[51] Should 1 Corinthians 6 be added to their case?[52] Extensive use of Deuteronomic legislation in 1 Corinthians 5:1-13 (see Chapter Three), Exodus/ Passover imagery in 5:6-8 and Exodus motifs in 7:22-23 and 10:1-13 render an allusion to another Moses tradition in 6:1-6 not unlikely.

Is it possible that in 1 Corinthians 6:1-6, when Paul appoints judges, it is a second-Moses whom we encounter? A softer version, balking at the title 'second-Moses', might see Paul simply following the pattern of Moses, rather like the Pharisees sitting in Moses' seat in Matthew 23:2. Although attractive and not implausible, there are insufficient allusional pointers in 1 Corinthians 6:1-6 to compel the adoption of at least the second-Moses identification. The indications that readers are meant to make a connection to the Moses tradition are too thin to be reliably designated allusion. Other factors, such as eschatological concerns in 6:2-3, take the reader's mind away from the Moses tradition. However, the marks that the Moses tradition has left are too distinct to be dismissed as merely the unconscious employment of Scriptural language; concepts as well as terms link 1 Corinthians 6:1-6 with Exodus 18/Deuteronomy 1. Thus, a third option, which sits between the maximalist and minimalist positions must be considered.

It is this: in 1 Corinthians 6:1-6 it seems that Paul applies the lessons of Exodus 18/Deuteronomy 1 (and related passages) to the problem of lawsuits in Corinth. This position conceives of a Paul who follows the implications of the Moses material (because Moses was the most important Biblical precedent for what he was doing), but one who

---

*self-understanding* (note in connection therewith that Moses describes himself in Deut 18:15 as a prophet).

[50] Jones, 'Second Moses'; Bammel, 'Der Moses'.

[51] Carol K. Stockhausen, *Moses' Veil and the Glory of the New Covenant: The Exegetical Substructure of II Cor. 3,1-4,6*, 169-75 also argues for the new-Moses identification of Paul in 2 Corinthians 3.

[52] 2 Timothy 3:8 may be compared with 1 Corinthians 6:1-6; the author likens his present troubles (false teachers) with the problems Moses faced (in the form of Jannes and Jambres).

does not find it necessary to signal his use of Scripture to the Corinthians either by quotation or allusion. Just as Moses appointed wise and righteous laity to decide lesser civil cases (including fraud) between their brothers, so also Paul rejected unrighteous judges and told the Corinthians to appoint wise laity to decide such cases between their brothers. Paul is, despite the absence of explicit indication, in effect, depending upon and obeying Torah as he understands its application to his new situation. To make this explicit he could have quoted Deuteronomy 25:1, which declares, "If there should be a dispute between [LXX: ἀνὰ μέσον] men, they are to take it to the judges," but he does not. Nevertheless, the weight of the evidence reviewed bears the conclusion that Exodus 18/Deuteronomy 1 had some influence upon the conception and expression of Paul's instructions to the Corinthians in 1 Corinthians 6:1-6 that disputes between brothers should be handled internally.

Reading 1 Corinthians 6:1-6 with this background in view sheds a measure of light on a couple of exegetical problems in the passage, namely, (1) the grammatical solecism in 6:5b and (2) the designation of non-Christian judges as "unrighteous" in 6:1, to which we shall now turn.

(1) A Grammatical Solecism in 1 Corinthians 6:5b.

1 Corinthians 6:5b contains a grammatical irregularity—singular ἀδελφοῦ—for which no satisfactory explanation has been proposed.[53] The Greek text reads ἀνὰ μέσον τοῦ ἀδελφοῦ αὐτοῦ, literally, "between his brother." Five ways of resolving the problem have been considered by scholars. First, one could adopt the reading of (more than one manuscript of) the Vulgate, the Syriac Peshitta and (more than one manuscript of) the Bohairic versions, which add "and the brother", the Greek *Vorlage* supposedly representing a primitive corruption of ἀνὰ μέσον τοῦ ἀδελφοῦ καὶ τοῦ ἀδελφοῦ αὐτοῦ.[54] However, this option amounts to no more than an emendation, since as G. Zuntz admits, the translators are "unlikely to have had at their disposal some genuine tradition unaffected by this fault,"[55] and it creates an awkward

---

[53] Fuller, '1 Cor. 6:1-11', 97 considers the phrase "normal in Greek," but offers no further examples to validate this assertion. Many commentators acknowledge the problem.

[54] Eg. G. Zuntz, *The Text of the Epistles: A Disquisition upon the Corpus Paulinum*, 15.

[55] Zuntz, *The Text*, 11. Cf. almost all modern English, German and French versions, which smooth out the text without textual justification.

redundancy with verse 6a (four occurrences of ἀδελφός would be unprecedentedly stilted Pauline style). Secondly, one may emend the text to the plural ἀδελφῶν.[56] While this solution removes the grammatical difficulty it is entirely fortuitous, lacking the warrant of internal evidence (it does not explain the origin of the more difficult reading). Thirdly, we may along with G. Zuntz, suggest that this is one place where the critic should correct the author.[57] Perhaps Paul simply made a grammatical blunder. This solution lacks appeal since as James Hope Moulton declares, "it is hard to believe Paul would have been so slovenly in writing or even dictating."[58] Fourthly, the text may be left as it stands and considered rare evidence of Paul's linguistic freedom and individuality.[59] Fifthly, J. Duncan M. Derrett relates the phrase to Psalm 82:1b (LXX: ἐν μέσῳ δὲ θεοὺς διακρίνει), and takes it to mean "in the midst of his brother."[60] However, a direct borrowing from Psalm 82:1 is unlikely since, if any Old Testament inspiration is to be sought, 1 Corinthians 6:5 has more points of contact with Deuteronomy 1:16. None of these solutions is satisfying, especially if a better one can be found.

The present study's juxtaposition of 1 Corinthians 6:1-6 alongside LXX Exodus 18/Deuteronomy 1 suggests two further avenues for solving the problem. First, an emendation on the basis of a possible allusion to Deuteronomy 1:16 in 1 Corinthians 6:5, reading "*between a man* and (between) his brother", is not without merit. This solution accounts for the origin of the more difficult reading with a common scribal error,[61] a point of favour which could also be claimed by the first solution noted above, and it also avoids the redundancy with verse 6 created by the first solution above. Neverthelesss, such an emendation remains pure speculation and is ill-advised in a study looking for links with the Old Testament.

A second and more likely (if less precise) solution also takes its starting point from the Greek Bible milieu which we have been proposing

---

[56] Cf. A.T. Robertson, *A Grammar of the Greek New Testament in the Light of Historical Research*, 409 and Findlay.

[57] Zuntz, 'The Critic Correcting the Author'.

[58] Moulton, *Grammar of New Testament Greek: Prolegomena*, I:99.

[59] Cf. Fee who says it may be an ellipse and A.T. Robertson, *Grammar;*, 409.

[60] Derrett, 'Judgement and 1 Corinthians 6', 27,30-31.

[61] The scribe's eye could have easily skipped from AI (the end of διακρῖναι) to AI (καί), an example of homoioteleuton: ΔΙΑΚΡΙΝΑΙΑΝΑΜΕΣΟΝΑΝΔΡΟΣΚΑΙΑΝΑΜΕ-ΣΟΝΤΟΥΑΔΕΛΦΟΥΑΥΤΟΥ

for 1 Corinthians 6:1-6.[62] Perhaps we may regard 6:5b as a loose
reminiscence of the LXX of Deuteronomy 1:16 which has led to rather
abrupt, but nevertheless comprehensible, Greek. It was sufficiently clear
to be taken without comment by people whose mother tongue was
Greek. Two fourth century Greek-speaking exegetes, Chrysostom and
Theodoret do not baulk at the Greek of 6:5b, quoting it without drawing
attention to it, and the Vulgate translates it literally. J.B. Lightfoot
asserts that "the sentence is much abridged."[63] The contribution of
this little digression is to suggest what it was Paul may have been
abridging, namely, Deuteronomy 1:16.[64]

(2) Going to Law before the "unrighteous"
Several commentators understand the ἄδικοι, in 6:1 standing in contrast
to the ἅγιοι, and synonymous with the the ἄπιστοι in verse 6, as denoting
the "unrighteous" in a religious not a moral sense, despite its appearance in a moral sense in 6:9. Friedrich Lang writes, for example:
"Dabei macht er den Begriff 'ungerechte', der jetzt im Unterschied
von 6,1 stärker im ethischen Sinn verwendet wird."[65]

However, Bruce Winter argues that ἄδικοι of verse 1 does refer
to the character of the honorary magistrates who presided and the
juries who pronounced verdicts in civil cases in places like Roman
Corinth.[66] Winter marshals both literary and non-literary evidence
for the conclusion that such jury-court practice warranted this adverse
evaluation: they could not be relied upon to administer justice
impartially since they were open to bribes and were partial to the

---

[62] Biblical influence on the Greek of 1 Corinthians may be detected throughout.
Three examples from chapter one make the point: In 1:20 αἰών and κόσμος are
used synonymously in a manner reminiscent of the double meaning of עולם in late
Hebrew (Barrett, 53); 2. πᾶσα σάρξ in 1:29 is clearly an Old Testament expression
(Barrett, 59); and 3. In 1:31, the use of the conditional participle as subject, ὁ καυχώμενος,
is due to the LXX (K. Beyer, Semitische Syntax im Neuen Testament, I:211-14). Near
1 Corinthians 6:5b is 5:13b, where ἐξ ὑμῶν αὐτῶν, is from the LXX, the classical
form of the reflexive (Zerwick and Grosvenor, An Analysis of the Greek New Testament,
507). Conzelmann's judgment (page 5) on the Greek of 1 Corinthians, that it is
good Greek with some LXX influence, is sound.
[63] Lightfoot, 212. Cf. Ellingworth and Hatton, A Translators Guide, 111: "this clause
is almost certainly a condensation of an idiom."
[64] This solution recognizes the Greek Bible milieu of 1 Corinthians 6:1-6 in general,
and of the preposition ἀνὰ μέσον in particular, and it does not resort to speculative
emendation, but nonetheless acknowledges the awkwardness of the phrase in koine
Greek.
[65] Lang, 79.
[66] Winter, 'Civil Litigation in Secular Corinth and the Church: the Forensic
Background to 1 Corinthians 6.1-8'.

status and power of the prosecutor or defendant or both. That Paul considers such judges unsuitable is explicable in terms of the qualifications of judges taught throughout the Scriptures, especially in Exodus 18/Deuteronomy 1 and related passages. Deuteronomy 16:18-20a states, for example, that judges must be righteous:

> Appoint judges and officials for each of your tribes in every town the LORD your God is giving you, and they shall judge the people fairly (κρίσιν δικαίαν). Do not pervert justice or show partiality. Do not accept a bribe, for a bribe blinds the eyes of the wise (σοφῶν) and twists the words of the righteous (δικαίων). Follow justice (τὸ δίκαιον) justly (δικαίως).[67]

That Paul labels the unacceptable secular judges in 1 Corinthians 6 ἄδικοι, whether in a religious or a moral sense, is consistent with the Scriptures' insistence that judges be δίκαιος.

## B. *Civil and Criminal Law in Ancient Israel*

Martin J. Buss argues that there is clear evidence in the Hebrew Bible for a distinction between civil and criminal processes of law.[68] Paul's indebtedness to Scripture is further revealed when 1 Corinthians 5:1-13 and 6:1-11 are read in the light of this distinction. Incest, the problem in 5:1-13, falls in the category of criminal law, and the dispute in 6:1-11 is covered by civil law which deals with relations within a group. Buss explains that criminal cases "were decided by the head of a community on his own authority or by the people as a corporate whole,"[69] both of which occur in 5:3-5, where Paul pronounces judgement and calls for the consent of the body corporate. Criminal legislation in the Hebrew Bible "speaks of the offender in the third person and addresses the breaching community in the second" (Exod 21:14,23, etc; page 59; 'he who does x, must be expelled' or 'put to death'). This is precisely Paul's style in 5:1-13. Civil cases in the Old Testament, on the other hand, were to be presented to the judges described in Exodus 18/Deuteronomy 1 and related passages. We

---

[67] Cf. Exodus 23:6-8; Leviticus 19:15; 1 Samuel 8:3; Isaiah 5:23; 32:1; Micah 3:9.

[68] Buss, 'The Distinction between Civil and Criminal Law in Ancient Israel'. The distinction has been independently recognised by Anthony Phillips, *Ancient Israel's Criminal Law* (followed by Wright, *An Eye for an Eye*, 152). G. Wenham, *Leviticus*, 284 on the other hand, thinks it is "somewhat artificial," but seems unaware of the distinctions mentioned above.

[69] Buss, 'Civil and Criminal Law', 53.

have argued that it is the model of these judges which informs Paul's discussion in 6:1-11.

It appears that Paul understood the Scriptural distinctions between civil and criminal law and appropriated them in response to Corinthian problems in 1 Corinthians 5:1-6:11. Many commentators struggle to discover a contextual link between 5:1-13 and 6:1-11, often regarding 6:1-11 as an aside interrupting Paul's discussion of πορνεία in 5:1-13 and 6:12-20. 1 Corinthians 5:1-13 and 6:1-11 may well be related in that they both concern law: in one case criminal law; in the other, civil law.

## C. *Settling Strife Between Brothers*

Paul insists on the inappropriateness and regrettable nature of the Corinthians' behaviour in 6:1-6 by depicting the situation as a family altercation between brothers. The word ἀδελφός is used three times in verses 5 and 6 for this very purpose.[70] It also occurs in verse 8. Such usage is of course not limited to Paul. The term "brother" was in standard Jewish use (see e.g., 1 and 2 Macc and many Rabbinic texts) and may well have enjoyed a relatively technical sense in early Christian communication (cf. ἀδελφός in semi-legal contexts in Matt 18:15 and Gal 6:1). A Biblical background to Paul's use of "brother" is also worth considering.

Exodus 18 and Deuteronomy 1 are not the only places in the Scriptures which share Paul's concern that disputes between *brothers* be settled peacefully. Genesis 13:6-13 records the legal controversy (ריב; μάχη) between Abram and Lot over the Promised Land. It is difficult to substantiate a connection between Genesis 13 and 1 Corinthians 6. Yet it is interesting that in Genesis 13:8 Abram says that there should not be strife between (בין; ἀνὰ μέσον)[71] Lot and himself "because we are brothers", ἀδελφοί. Verse 11 records the resolution of the dispute where "each man separated from his brother." Paul's concern that *brothers* in the family of God not squabble may well have been learned from Scripture. Psalm 133:1 (132:1): "Behold, how good and how pleasant it is for brothers (ἀδελφούς) to dwell together in unity."

---

[70] *RSV*'s "brother" (replaced in *NRSV* by "another") in verse 1 is not in the Greek.
[71] The preposition ἀνὰ μέσον is used five times in Genesis 13:6-11.

## D. A Good Reputation Before Outsiders

Many commentators assume that behind Paul's insistence that Corinthian lawsuits be handled internally rather than externally stands his concern for the reputation of the church.[72] Though disputed by some,[73] this contention is supported by Paul's rebuke in 6:5a: πρὸς ἐντροπὴν ὑμῖν λέγω. The only other place in the New Testament where this expression is used is in 1 Corinthians 15:34, where the cause for shame is the unhappy relation of the Corinthians towards outsiders.[74] When Paul writes to shame the Corinthians it is often, it seems, because of their loss of reputation before outsiders. In 1 Corinthians 6:5a he writes to shame the Corinthians at least partly because of the disrepute they have brought upon themselves by airing their dissensions in public before "unbelievers" (6:6). That Paul is concerned about what outsiders think of the behaviour of the Corinthian church is clear from 1 Corinthians 14:23-25 (οὐκ ἐροῦσιν ὅτι μαίνεσθε;). That he inherited from the Scriptures this concern for the reputation of the community before outsiders is the contention of this section.

Willem Cornelis van Unnik has traced the desire to make a good impression on one's heathen neighbours as an ethical motive in 2 Clement, the New Testament and the intertestamental Jewish writings.[75] He contends that there is both a negative and a positive reason in this literature for the motive: to protect the honour of God's name ("die Gefahr der Gotteslästerung," 232) and to win the heathen ("die

---

[72] Delcor, 'The Courts', 69 for example writes: "everything suggests that the Apostle wishes especially to prevent the private scandals of the community from being known by judges who did not share their faith."

[73] E.g., Fee, 232 stresses instead Paul's point that the Corinthians are "eschatological people". The two themes, eschatology and a good reputation, may, however, both be operating in the passage. Elsewhere, 229 Fee appears to admit the good reputation theme (Paul is aggravated because the Corinthian action "totally destroys the community before the world [v. 6]"). Those who concur with Delcor (e.g., Barrett, Talbert) do not validate their position.

[74] Though this is also disputed; cf. Fee, 774. Margaret Y. McDonald, 'Women Holy in Body and Spirit: the Social Setting of 1 Corinthians 7', 163 finds the good reputation theme elsewhere in Paul's moral teaching: "That Paul's instructions on marriage and sexual immorality reveals an interest in the relationship between church communities and the outside world is suggested by 1 Thessalonians 4.3b-5". O.L. Yarbrough, Not Like the Gentiles: Marriage Rules in the Letters of Paul, 86-87 has rightly noted the similarity between Paul's language in 1 Thessalonians 4 with early Jewish paraenesis, which served to distinguish the community from the outside world.

[75] van Unnik, 'Die Rücksicht auf die Reaktion der Nicht-Christen als Motiv in der altchristlichen Paränese'.

Motivierung ist die Missionsmöglichkeit," 229). He also hints that
Scripture may be the foundation of the tradition.[76]

That the Scriptures contain both threads of the concern that God's
people maintain a good reputation before the heathen is not difficult
to establish. Evidence can be gathered from sources as diverse as the
intercession of Moses on behalf of God's people in Exodus 32 (see
32:12,25; cf. 1 Kings 20:28; 2 Kings 19:14ff), Numbers 14:13-19 (see
vss. 15-16) and Deuteronomy 9:25-29, the prophets (cf. Isaiah 52:5;
Ezek 36:20) and even Wisdom literature (Prov 3:4; 22:1; 25:10; Eccl
7:1a—where a good reputation is highly valued). It is clear from Romans
2:24 that Paul knew and valued this tradition. In a discussion of Jewish
shortcomings, he states that "the name of God is blasphemed among
the Gentiles because of you, καθὼς γέγραπται," quoting Isaiah 52:5
(cf. Ezek 36:20).

Paul, it appears, inherited from Scripture, perhaps via Judaism, this
desire that the community make a good impression on outsiders both
for the sake of evangelism and for the honour of God's name. Evidence
may be gathered from across the traditional Pauline corpus. Paul
instructs the Thessalonians not to be busybodies nor idle "so that
your daily life may win the respect of outsiders" (τοὺς ἔξω; 1 Thess
4:11-12). He told the Philippians not to complain or argue "so that
you may become blameless . . . in a crooked and depraved generation
in which you shine like stars" (Phil 2:14-15). The Colossians are warned:
"Be wise in the way you act toward outsiders; make the most of every
opportunity" (τοὺς ἔξω; Col 4:5). An elder in the Pastorals must have
"a good reputation with outsiders" (τῶν ἔξωθεν; 1 Tim 3:7).[77] The
negative motivation, not to harm God's reputation, is seen clearly
in 1 Timothy 6:1: "All who are under the yoke of slavery should
consider their masters worthy of full respect, so that God's name and
our teaching may not be slandered." The positive evangelistic motive
is apparent in Titus 2:10, where slaves are to show themselves
trustworthy "so that in every way they will make the teaching about
God our Saviour attractive" (cf. Titus 2:5,8).

More importantly for an interest in detecting this theme behind
1 Corinthians 6:1-6 are two texts in 1 Corinthians itself. In 9:19-23

---

[76] Eg. van Unnik, 'Die Rücksicht', 224 observes that the author of 2 Clement
could have quoted Paul to support his case but instead cites Scripture (Isa 52:5 and
Mal 1:6ff).
[77] Cf. 1 Corinthians 5:12, τοὺς ἔξω, for the label "outsiders."

Paul claims that he behaves circumspectly before all outsiders so that he might save some (cf. 9:12b). This stands in contrast to the Corinthians who air their 'dirty laundry' with its consequent harm to the cause of the gospel's progress. 1 Corinthians 10:31-32, the conclusion to Paul's discussion of whether or not to eat meat sacrificed to idols (8:1-11:1), ties together both the negative and positive motives of this good reputation theme: "So whether you eat or drink or whatever you do, do it all for the glory of God. Do not cause anyone to stumble, whether Jews, Greeks or the church of God."

Thus, implicitly in 1 Corinthians 6:1-6 and explicitly elsewhere in the Pauline corpus, we find Paul developing a Scriptural theme, the concern to maintain a good reputation before outsiders. Such thematic use of Scripture, though more difficult to detect reliably than citations of and allusions to specific passages, should not be ignored in the evaluation of the Scriptures as a source for Pauline ethics. At least part of Paul's opposition to the Corinthians taking their disputes before pagan judges was that such behaviour damaged the reputation of the church, of the gospel and of God himself, a concern which Paul, in all likelihood, received from the Scriptures.

## E. *The Competence of Christian Judges*

In verses 2 and 3 Paul argues against the practice of taking disputes before secular judges by insisting on the superior competence (cf. ἀνάξιοι; 6:2) of the saints to handle such cases. A reason why the Corinthians ought to settle their feuds internally is that believers will judge the world (6:2) and even angels (6:3), to say nothing of (μήτιγε) ordinary earthly matters (βιωτικά). Most commentators acknowledge Scripture as the major source of Paul's conviction that the saints will judge the world (6:2), contending that it derives from the Jewish hope that God's people will participate in the judgement of the last days expressed in Daniel 7:22,[78] developed by post-Biblical Jewish writings (e.g., Wis 3:7-8; Jub 24:29; Sir 4:11,15; 1 Enoch 1:9,38; 38:5; 95:3; 96:1; 98:12; 108:12; 1QpHab 5:4-5) and picked up in early Christian teaching (e.g., Matt 19:28; Luke 22:30; Jude 14-15; Rev 2:26-27;20:4).[79]

The question of a source for the notion of judging angels is less

---

[78] Eg. C.H. Dodd, *According to the Scriptures*, 68: Daniel 7:22 "supplies the implicit scriptural authority for Paul's doctrine that the saints shall judge the world (1 Cor. vi. 2)."

[79] Cf. esp. Lietzmann, 25.

clear, since no extant antecedent text contains this thought.[80] Several commentators suggest that it is simply an extension from verse 2, "the world" including not only mankind on earth but heavenly beings. Though the Scriptures do not specifically speak of men judging angels, Paul could have deduced the idea from Psalm 8:5[81] (a psalm he quotes in 1 Cor 15:27), where a person's ultimate destiny in Christ is to be above the angels,[82] or as Norman Hillyer suggests, from Daniel 7:18, "where sharing the Kingdom would involve sharing the king's authority."[83]

The way in which Paul applies Scripture in 6:2-3 is worthy of note. Obviously, neither Psalm 8 nor Daniel 7, nor even the traditions they have spawned, concern settling disputes within the community. Paul infers a new significance from the authority of believers in the end time which is taught in the Scriptures. He reasons that since the saints will judge the world and angels in the future then they should be able to resolve everyday disputes in the present.

*Excursus 2:*
*The Origin of Paul's Positive Attitude to Government in Romans 13:1-7*

Many scholars believe that Paul espoused contradictory views of the state in 1 Corinthians 6 and Romans 13. However, as Bruce Winter argues, the two passages do not present conflicting views, since they address different questions.[84] In Romans 13 Paul discusses the attitude of Christians to government officials in general and their administration of criminal law, whereas 1 Corinthians 6 concerns the specific issue of civil litigation between Christians in secular courts. The origin of Paul's positive attitude to government expressed in Romans 13 is an interesting digression close to 1 Corinthians 6. In Romans 13, once again, Paul's Bible proves to be a major source for Paul's ethics.

Stated simply, Paul could have embraced the view which was brewing among many Jews and which came to a head in 66AD, that the Roman government was God's enemy. Instead Paul endorses the view

---

[80] 1 Enoch 13:10 speaks of reprimanding "the watchers of heaven," but not in the judicial sense.

[81] Cf. Hebrews 2:5 ("It is not to angels that he has subjected the world to come") and the quotation from Psalm 8:4-6 in 2:6-8.

[82] Though the LXX has "a little lower than the angels," not "God;" cf. Hebrews 2:7.

[83] Hillyer, 1,058.

[84] Winter, 'Civil Litigation'.

that government is God's servant. C.E.B. Cranfield is not alone among commentators in his opinion that "it is difficult to understand why Paul could write *quite* so positively about the authorities" (italics his).[85] Several scholars go as far as to question the Pauline nature of these verses, judging them an interpolation.[86] Perhaps with a view of Paul as 'the Christian Jew with Bible in hand' the Pauline nature of Romans 13 would be questioned less often.

In Romans 13:1-7 Paul reflects the theology of Scripture, especially sapiential traditions.[87] By insisting that government gets its mandate to govern from God, Paul's thought is in line with that of Daniel (2:21,37-38; 4:17,34-35; cf. 2 Chron 20:6), who declares that "the Most High is sovereign over the kingdoms of men and gives them to anyone he wishes" (4:25).[88] That submission to the authority of the state is a reflection of submission to God's authority and that government is a divine institution Paul could easily have learned from the Biblical teaching about kingship, powerfully exemplified, for example, in David's attitude of submission to King Saul (1 Sam 24:6; 26:9-11,23; 2 Sam 1:14-16; 4:9ff; 6:21; 15:25-26; 16:10; 19:21).

Certain details of the text of Romans 13:1-7 merit close scrutiny. The opening words, Πᾶσα ψυχὴ (cf. 2:9), are Hebraic, equivalent to כל-נפש.[89] Paul states that the proper relation of Christians to earthly rulers is one of submission, employing ὑποτάσσω in verses 1 and 5, and διαταγή in verse 2. David Mark Tripp points out that similar vocabulary is employed in comparable contexts in Wisdom 11:20 and

---

[85] Cranfield, *Romans*, II:653.

[86] J. Kallas, 'Romans xiii 1-7: An Interpolation'; E. Barnikol, 'Römer 13: Der nicht paulinische Ursprung der absoluten Obrigkeitsbejahung von Römer 13:1-7'; E. Käsemann, *Romans* ("an alien body in Paul's exhortation"); J.C. O'Neill, *Paul's Letter to the Romans*. Ernst Bammel, 'Ein Beitrag zur paulinischen Staatsanschauung', takes Romans 13 to be by Paul, but regards it as an exception to the way he most naturally thinks. He considers the apocalyptic destruction of the state to be more truly Paul's view, as in 1 Thessalonians 5 and 2 Thessalonians 2.

[87] Christopher J.H. Wright, 'The People of God and the State in the Old Testament,' distinguishes five different phases of Israel as the people of God in Old Testament history which correspond to different views of the relationship between God's people and the state. A common thread throughout the diverse Old Testament material is how "all human political authority and military power [are put] under the sovereign will of Yahweh" (page 8).

[88] Cf. the raising up of kings in Daniel 11 and Cyrus in Isaiah 45.

[89] Sanday and Headlam, *Romans*, 366; Morris, *Romans*, 460. Tripp, 'An Interpretation of Romans 13:1-7 in light of sapiential and apocalyptic traditions', 66-67 notes Acts 3:23, where the phrase occurs in a composite quote of Deuteronomy 18:19 and Leviticus 23:29.

Ecclesiasticus 10:1.[90] Wisdom 6:1-4 is especially close.[91] The idea of
"doing good" which appears in Romans 13:3-4 is a recurring theme
in Old Testament wisdom literature. Romans 13:3b, and the positive
advice to do good, τὸ ἀγαθὸν ποίει, recalls Prov 31:12 Eccl 2:3, 3:12;
7:20; Ecclesiasticus 42:14. Romans 13:3c's promise of rewards to those
who practice good behaviour is reminiscent of Proverbs 11:27; 12:14;
13:2,15,21; 14:22; 16:20; 25:22; 28:10; Ecclesiastes 9:7; Ecclesiasticus
12:1-2; 41:43 (contrast Job 21:13; 30:26; Eccl 7:15).[92] Support for
government in Romans 13:7 reminds one of Jeremiah 29:7. In Romans
13 Paul does not ground his exhortation in Christology but in the
Biblical doctrine of divine creation. As Tripp notes, "the ideas of
authority, wisdom, and ethics appear to move in a circle, both in
Romans 13:1-7 and in the Hebrew wisdom tradition."[93]

Affinities between Ecclesiastes 8:2-5 and Romans 13:1-7 have been
noted by several Old Testament commentators (reading the Old
Testament with its partner Testament in mind), including George Aaron
Barton (on verse 5, p. 150; ICC), E.H. Plumptre (on verse 2, p. 175;
Cambridge Bible for Schools and Colleges) and Michael A. Eaton
(on verse 3, p. 119; Tyndale Commentaries). It is indeed surprising
that the commentaries on Romans in the same series as the above
commentaries on Ecclesiastes, C.E.B. Cranfield (ICC), H.C.G. Moule
(Cambridge) and F.F. Bruce (Tyndale), do not sufficiently read Paul's
ethics with the Old Testament in mind to mention the parallel. It
appears that the obligation to look *back* (to the Old Testament) as
well as *forward* (to the New Testament) needs to be impressed upon
Biblical commentators.

Despite the lack of Old Testament references in most commentaries
on Romans 13, we need look no further than the Scriptures for the
origin of Paul's view in Romans 13 that government is God's servant.
Far from standing out as an alien or unexpected passage in the Pauline
correspondence, Romans 13 is the straightforward articulation of a

---

[90] Tripp, 'Romans 13:1-7', 74-75. Cf. Ecclesiasticus 10:40: "the government of
the earth is in the hands of the Lord, and over it he will raise up the right man
for the time."
[91] Noted by N.T. Wright, 'The New Testament and the "state"', 14; cf. 1 Enoch
46:5; Josephus, Jewish War, 2:140, "No ruler attains his office save by the will of
God."
[92] Tripp, 'Romans 13:1-7', 82.
[93] Tripp, 'Romans 13:1-7', 79.

view of government which finds its roots firmly planted in the Jewish Scriptures.

### III. Christians Ought not to have Disputes (6:7-11)

In verses 7-11 Paul shows the Corinthians an even more excellent way than settling disputes internally, namely, the refusal to dispute altogether. In the light of 6:7-11, the advice of 6:1-6 turns out not to be Paul's true preference but only a concession to human sinfulness. Four aspects of these radical instructions (6:7-11) may be explored in relation to the Scriptures: the alternative of righteous suffering; the idea that identity is supposed to inform behaviour; the ploy of reminding the Corinthians of their shameful past; and the opposition to homosexuality.

#### A. *Concession to Human Sinfulness*

Paul's argument for the use of Christian arbiters (6:1-6) is exposed in verse 7a as a compromise of basic Christian principles: Ἤδη μὲν ὅλως ἥττημα ὑμῖν ἐστιν ὅτι κρίματα ἔχετε μεθ᾽ ἑαυτῶν. Just as Moses tolerated divorce because of the hardness of the human heart (according to Jesus in Matt 19:8/Mark 10:5), so Paul has permitted Corinthian arbitration (in 6:1-6) even though it conflicts with the ideal order. David Daube has pointed out that the notion of a concession to human sinfulness is well established in Biblical and early Jewish literature.[94] A few examples will suffice to make the point here: The monarchy is presented in the Scriptures as instituted only reluctantly by God (1 Sam 8:7,9). The sale of land in the theocracy was only valid for a time since it upset the ideal distribution (Lev 25:23-24).[95] Various rabbinic texts view marriage to a Gentile woman captured in war as a somewhat inferior state of affairs (Sifre on Deut 21:10f and b. Qidd. 21bf.). And marriage itself was viewed as second best by the Essenes, as a concession to the lower instincts (Josephus, Bell. II: 160ff; cf. 1 Cor 7:6).[96]

---

[94] Daube, 'Concessions to Human Sinfulness in Jewish Law'; cf. Talbert, 21. Daube does not refer to 1 Corinthians 6.

[95] Cf. the reluctance evident in those passages which discuss the enslavement of fellow-Israelites (Lev 25:42, 55; Deut 15:12-15). Jubilees 11:2 similarly regards slavery as a deviation from the natural order of the world in general.

[96] Other examples are listed by Daube.

B. *The Alternative of Righteous Suffering*

LXX Leviticus 19:13a states: "You shall not wrong (ἀδικήσεις) your neighbour." Paul is in agreement, contending that it would be better for the Corinthian Christians to suffer wrong (ἀδικεῖσθε; 6:7). Several commentators confidently ascribe the source of Paul's teaching in these verses to the words of Jesus in Matthew 5:39-42.[97] For example, Gordon Fee describes it as "a sure instance" of how the teaching of Jesus has influenced Paul."[98] However, though true that Jesus' teaching about non-retaliation is conceptually akin to 1 Corinthians 6:7-8, to jump from similarity of thought to the conclusion of dependence may not be wise, especially in view of the fact that there are no terminological links.[99] Furthermore, Gordon Zerbe, *Non-Retaliation in Early Jewish and New Testament Texts*, has demonstrated that the non-relatiatory ethic of Jesus stands solidly in a tradition of non-retaliatory ethics of early Judaism. Jesus' teaching is not unique at this point.

A more judicious approach to understanding the background to Paul's instructions in 6:7-8 begins with the data of 1 Corinthians itself. In asking the Corinthians to be wronged and defrauded rather than compromise Christian standards of love Paul is, in effect, urging them to imitate himself. In 4:16 the exhortation to follow his example involves in its immediate context suffering for the sake of Christ (see 4:11-13). In 1 Corinthians 9 Paul exemplifies the attitude of being willing to suffer loss which he expects of the Corinthians in 6:7-8;[100] though possessing "the right of support" Paul says: "We did not use this right. On the contrary, we put up with anything rather than hinder the gospel of Christ" (9:12b). Indeed, the theme of suffering righteously and related notions punctuate the Corinthian correspondence (1 Cor 4:8-13; 15:3-8; 2 Cor 1:3-8; 4:7-12,16-18; 6:3-10; 7:5-7; 11:23-30; 12:7-10; 13:4). It is within the province of this material that the provenance of the sentiments expressed in 6:7-8 must be sought.

Karl Theodor Kleinknecht in *Der leidende Gerechtfertigte: Die alttestamentlich-jüdische Tradition von 'leidenden Gerechten' und ihre Rezeption bei Paulus* defends the thesis that the Biblical theme of the suffering righteous, which

---

[97] See footnote 7.
[98] Fee, 241.
[99] Paul could have made it clear he was following Jesus' teaching, as in 1 Corinthians 7:10, though the absence of such a note is not conclusive.
[100] The lesson of self denial exemplified by Paul in 1 Corinthians 9 was to be applied by the Corinthians to the problem of meat sacrificed to idols, but it is also applicable here in a secondary way.

can be traced through the intertestamental Jewish literature, forms the dominant background ("dominierenden Hintergrund"[101]) for the various Pauline discussions of suffering, including those found in 1 Corinthians.[102] Kleinknecht's net of Biblical and post-Biblical Jewish texts which incorporate the notion of suffering while standing in a positive relation to God is cast widely, and includes Job, Psalms, Isaiah, Daniel, Zechariah, Sirach, Wisdom, 1 Enoch, 2 and 4 Maccabees, Odes of Solomon, Testaments of the Twelve Patriarchs, Testament of Job and various Qumran texts. He notes that Paul applies this theme as a help to understanding not only the sufferings of Jesus but also his own sufferings and, of interest for our purposes, the sufferings of his churches. Kleinknecht argues that the majority of passages dealing with suffering in Paul's letters evoke the Biblical motif of the suffering righteous, whether by direct citation of or allusion to relevant Biblical texts or by the use of basic concepts, structures of arguments or vocabulary shared generally within that whole stream of tradition.

The above considerations suggest that in the discussion of possible sources for Paul's teaching in 1 Corinthians 6:7-8 concerning the alternative of righteous suffering, the Biblical theme of the suffering righteous should not be ignored. Although 1 Corinthians 6:7-8 does not allude to a specific Scriptural text, Paul's instructions here are built upon Paul's example of suffering which he definitely links to Scripture. The fact that Paul valued and endorsed the state of righteous suffering in 6:7-8 can thus to some extent be explained in terms of a thematic use of Scripture. This is not to play down the importance for Paul of the exemplary sufferings of Jesus, but these too were interpreted by Paul within the theological grid of righteous suffering in Scripture.

Recognizing the appearance of the righteous suffering motif in 6:7-8 brings to our attention a neglected contextual link between these verses and 6:9-11. This link is missed when one focuses exclusively upon the motif of non-retaliation and Jesus' saying in the sermon on the Mount for the provenance of Paul's thought in 6:7-8.[103] It is not uncommon in Paul's letters for the apostle to follow up the

---

[101] Kleinknecht, *Der leidende Gerechtfertigte*, 36.

[102] Kleinknecht, unfortunately, overlooks 1 Corinthians 6:7-8 in his treatment of suffering in the epistle.

[103] Non-retaliation and righteous suffering are obviously not mutually exclusive categories. Nevertheless, it is the latter motif which is connected in Paul's letters with inheritance.

thought of present suffering with the encouragement of future glory. Romans 8:17 demonstrates that in Paul's mind suffering is linked with inheritance: "Now if we are children, then we are *heirs*—*heirs* of God and co-*heirs* with Christ, if indeed we share in his *sufferings*." In 2 Corinthians 4:17 suffering and glory are also connected: "Our light and momentary troubles are achieving for us an eternal glory that far outweighs them all."

It is this notion that provides a bridge between 1 Corinthians 6:7-8 and the following three verses. Paul states in 6:9 that "the unrighteous *will not* inherit the kingdom of God."[104] The natural question to ask is, who *will* inherit the kingdom? The answer is, those who suffer righteously, by refusing to fight disputes with their brothers (6:7-8). 1 Corinthians 6:9-11 provides encouragement to the Corinthians to follow Paul's difficult advice in 6:7-8; those who choose to suffer wrong are the kind of people who will inherit the kingdom, a curious paradox.

C. *Identity Informs Behaviour*

In 6:9-11 Paul exhorts the Corinthian believers not to behave as the unrighteous whom God will exclude from final blessing, but according to their true identity as the cleansed, sanctified and justified people of God.[105] The Corinthians are to live differently because of whom they have become. It is widely recognised that this notion stands at the very heart of Paul's ethics. It is the stress of those who think Scripture (which they caricature as law) is not important for Paul's ethics (which they present as the antithesis of law, gospel).[106] Excursus 1 (Chapter Three) attempted to show that at this crucial point Paul is again indebted to Scripture; the same structure of thought (identity informs behaviour) pervades the book of Deuteronomy and is scattered throughout the Hebrew prophets.

---

[104] The future judgement of the unrighteous (cf. 1 Cor 4:5; 5:13) is a Biblical theme (Dan 12:1-2; Eccl 12:14; Ps 96:10,13; 98:9; Amos 5:18-20; Isa 24:1-23) which is developed in early Jewish literature: 4 Ezra 7:45-61; 2 Apoc Bar 30:2-5; 51:1-6; 1 Enoch 10:1-6; 22:11; 54:6;55:3-56:4; 91:6-9,19; 94:9; Jub 15:34; TLevi 4:1-6; TBenj 10:8-10; in Rabbinic literature cf. the phrase, "such and such have no share in the world to come," e.g., in m. Sanhedrin 10:1-4; m. Aboth 3:16; cf. Christian D. von Dehson, 'Sexual Relationships and the Church: An Exegetical Study of 1 Corinthians 5-7', 104.

[105] The alternative interpretation that the passage threatens self-disqualification from salvation (cf. Fee, Robertson/Plummer) is unlikely because: (1) verse eleven insists that the Corinthians will not fail to inherit the kingdom (ἦτε; cf. the threefold use of ἀλλά) ; and (2) in Paul's letters all believers are heirs of the kingdom (Rom 4:13; 8:17; Gal 3:29; 4:4-7).

[106] See Chapter One, section I.

## D. *Reminder of a Shameful Past*

In 6:9-11 Paul reminds the Corinthians of their shameful past before their conversion, presumably to motivate obedience by enhancing their love for the God who transforms and forgives; 1 Corinthians 6:11: "such were some of you." It is a device not uncommonly employed by the apostle (e.g., Eph 2:1-7; 4:17-24). It is also a ploy for which Paul could find ample precedent in the Scriptures, especially in the preaching of Deuteronomy (cf. e.g., 9:6,24) and the rehearsals of Israel's tainted history in Deuteronomy 32:16ff. and Psalms 78 and 106.[107]

## E. *Opposition to Homosexuality*

The vice list in 6:9-10 contains ten items, six of which are repeated from 5:11 (on these see Chapter Three, IIIA). Whereas one new term, κλέπται, belongs especially to the concerns of 6:1-11, the other three deal with sexual sin, and are thus in line with the main subject matter of the rest of 1 Corinthians 5-7. The μοιχός refers to a married person having sexual relations outside marriage, adultery. The same term is employed in the Decalogue (LXX Exod 20:13; LXX Deut 5:18 [17]) and the Holiness code (LXX Lev 20:10).

The two terms, ἀρσενοκοίτης (cf. 1 Tim 1:10) and μαλακός, call for some extended comment. That Paul here refers to homosexual behaviour (of one form or another) is clear.[108] Within the scope of the present study it is worth investigating whether this opposition may have been derived from relevant Levitical legislation (18:22; 20:13). J. Boswell is adamant that it did not:

---

[107] On these Psalms which give an extensive record of Israel's history, 'warts and all', see A.A. Anderson 'Psalms', 59-62. Cf. 61: In these Psalms "The people have been continuously and destructively rebellious while Yahweh has been increasingly constructive and faithful."

[108] Cf. RSV, "homosexuals"; TEV, "homosexual perverts"; NEB, "homosexual perversion"; NIV, "male prostitutes nor homosexual offenders"; KJV "effeminate nor abusers of themselves with mankind." On the complicated question of translation see Robin Scroggs, *The New Testament and Homosexuality: Contextual Background for Contemporary Debate.* John Boswell's thesis in *Christianity, Social Tolerance and Homosexuality* that ἀρσενοκοίτης refers to active male prostitutes ("male" being the subject rather than the object of the compound word) has been soundly refuted by J. Robert Wright, 'Boswell on Homosexuality: A Case Undemonstrated', and David F. Wright, 'Homosexuals or Prostitutes? The Meaning of ἀρσενοκοίτης (1 Cor. 6:9; 1 Tim. 1:10)'.

It would simply not have occurred to most early Christians to invoke
the authority of the old law to justify the morality of the new: the Levitical
regulations had no hold on Christians and are manifestly irrelevant in
explaining Christian hostility to gay sexuality.[109]

David F. Wright, however, presents a strong case for concluding that
with ἀρσενοκοίτης Paul in fact employed a new term which was
fashioned on the very basis of the Levitical prohibitions.[110] That these
verses were probably the inspiration of the neologism is quite plausible:

Leviticus 18:22     μετὰ ἄρσενος οὐ κοιμηθήσῃ κοίτην γυναικός
Leviticus 20:13     ὃς ἂν κοιμηθῇ μετὰ ἄρσενος κοίτην γυναικός

The only other occurrence of ἀρσενοκοίτης which is possibly contemporary with Paul (it may be a Christian interpolation) is Sibylline
Oracles 2:73. The relevant section of the Sibyllines is closely related
to Pseudo-Phocylides (suggesting its Jewish origin), the indebtedness
of which to Leviticus we noted in connection with Niebuhr's work
in Chapter Two (see section IVA).[111]

Thus, as Wright concludes, it seems likely that "the ἀρσενοκοίτ-
group of words is a coinage of Hellenistic Judaism or Hellenistic Jewish
Christianity."[112] Paul's opposition to homosexuality was not because
he had not thought about the subject (*contra* E.P. Sanders[113]). Neither
is it the whole story to say that he had simply taken it over from
a conventional list of vices from Hellenistic authors, whether Jewish
or secular (the view of Scroggs). Paul opposed homosexuality because
it is marked as a vice in the Torah and was stressed as a vice by

---

[109] Boswell, *Homosexuality*, 105.
[110] Wright, 'Homosexuals or Prostitutes', 126ff. The connection of Paul's ἀρσενοκοίτης
with Leviticus 18:22; 20:13 lends support to taking "male" as the object in the compound
word ("intercourse with males," that is, male homosexual). William L. Petersen's critique
of Wright's article, 'Can ἀρσενοκοίτης be translated by "Homosexuals"? (1 Cor 6.9;
1 Tim 1:10)', complements it in this area (187, "Wright has performed a service
in calling attention . . . to the LXX echoes in the word"). For Wright's response
to Petersen's criticisms see Wright, 'Translating ἀρσενοκοίτης (1 Cor 6:9; 1 Tim 1:10)'.
For an able and up-to-date survey of the Biblical data on homosexuality see Wright,
'Homosexuality: The Relevance of the Bible'. Cf. also G.J. Wenham, 'The Old Testament Attitude to Homosexuality', who convincingly traces Old Testament opposition
to homosexuality to Israel's doctrine of creation in Genesis 1-3.
[111] For surveys of the evidence of Judaism's uniformly negative attitude to homosexuality, employing other terms, see Scroggs, *Homosexuality*, 66-98; L.M. Epstein,
*Sex Laws and Customs in Judaism*, 134-37; Furnish, *The Moral Teaching of Paul*, 64-67,
and James B. De Young, 'A Critique of Prohomosexual Interpretations of the Old
Testament Apocrypha and Pseudepigrapha.'
[112] Wright, 'Homosexuals or Prostitutes?', 129.
[113] Sanders, *Paul*, 116.

Jews. That Paul had in fact given some thought to the subject can be seen from Romans 1:26-27, where he condemns both male and female same-sex conduct, the condemnation of which prior to Paul can only be found in Plato and Pseudo-Phocylides (according to Scroggs[114]).

## IV. CONCLUSION

The task of this chapter has been to evaluate the role played by the Scriptures in the formation of Paul's instructions found in 1 Corinthians 6:1-11. How important a source are the Scriptures to Paul's ethics in this passage? Despite the absence of any explicit citations, the evidence we have rehearsed supports the conclusion that the Scriptures were an indispensable and formative source for 1 Corinthians 6:1-11. In order to settle strife between brothers Paul followed the tradition about Moses appointing judges. He used the Scriptural motifs of righteous suffering and a good reputation before outsiders. He held to the Scriptural belief of the judicial role of the saints in the *eschaton*. He showed himself to have Scriptural structures of thought, such as the notion that identity must inform behaviour. He employed the Scriptural hortatory device of reminding people of their shameful past. Along the way he denounced homosexuality as a vice, in accordance with Scriptural teaching.

---

[114] Scroggs, *Homosexuality*, 131,141.

*Interpretative Paraphrase*
*with Significant Biblical/Jewish Cross References*

When any one of you has a dispute with another, does he dare seek judgement before the unrighteous[1] instead of the saints? Do you not know that the saints will judge the world?[2] And if the world is to be judged by you, do you not consider yourselves competent to settle such trivial cases?[3] Since we are also to judge angels,[4] how much more mere matters of earthly business! If therefore you have such cases,[3] why do you entrust jurisdiction[5] to those who have no standing in the church? I say this to your shame.[6] Is it possible that there is nobody among you wise enough[7] to judge between (a man and) his brother?[8] But instead brother[9] disputes with brother, and that before unbelievers (1-6)!

[1]Deut 16:18-20; Exod 23:6-8; Lev 19:15, etc

[2]Dan 7:22; Ps 8:5

[3]Exod 21:6
[4]Dan 7:18, Ps 8:5

[5]Exod 18:14

[6]Exod 32:12,25; 1 Ki 20:28; Isa 52:5; Ezek 36:20; Eccl 7:1, etc [7]Exod 18:18:19; Deut 1:15
[8]Deut 1:16 [9]Gen 13:6-13; Ps 133:1

To have such lawsuits[10] at all is a real defeat for you. Why not rather be wronged?[11] Why not rather be defrauded?[12] But you yourselves wrong and defraud, and you do this to your brothers![9] Do you not know that the unrighteous will not inherit the kingdom of God? Do not be deceived, neither the immoral, nor idolators, nor adulterers,[13] nor homosexual perverts,[14] nor thieves, nor the greedy, nor drunkards, nor revilers, nor robbers will inherit the kingdom. These are the sort of people some of you once were.[15] But you were washed, you were sanctified, you were justified in the name of the Lord Jesus Christ and in the Spirit of our God (7-11).

[10]Exod 18:22

[11]Lev 19:13
[12]Deut 24:14, 25:1

[13]Exod 20:13; Deut 5:17; Lev 20:10
[14]Lev 18:22; 20:13

[15]Deut 9:6,24; 32:16ff; Pss 78;106, etc

CHAPTER FIVE

# JOSEPH AND PAUL FLEEING IMMORALITY
## 1 CORINTHIANS 6:12-20

## I. Introduction
*"Flee sexual immorality!"*

In 1 Corinthians 6:12-20 Paul insists that the Christians in Corinth must maintain sexual purity, responding to the report that some believers were having sexual relations with prostitutes. This response has received an uneven evaluation from commentators. Some regard it as "a masterly presentation of the beauty of sexual holiness."[1] The majority of commentators, however, take another opinion, describing the paragraph as "disjointed," "obscure," "unfinished,"[2] "imprecise," "extravagant," and even "incoherent."[3] Our concern in this chapter is not only to attempt to unravel Paul's thought in these verses but to discover what relation, if any, this thought has to the Scriptures.

On the one hand, 1 Corinthians 6:12-20 might easily be regarded as evidence of the Jewishness of Paul's ethics. Contrary to being influenced by the view widely favoured in Graeco-Roman philosophy, that prostitution was a kind of middle way between asceticism and adultery, Paul's ethical stance in the Christian context maintains the Jewish position. On the other hand, the passage presents a formidable challenge to the present study's thesis of critical Scriptural dependence in Paul's ethics: if the Jewish Scriptures are the reason Paul is against going to harlots, why then does he not quote one of the relevant commandments from the Torah or Proverbs?

Andreas Lindemann makes two points about 1 Corinthians 6:12-20 to argue that the Bible and Jewish teaching have little to do with Paul's instructions here.[4] First, he notes that though the Scriptures (Prov 5:3; 6:23-7:27) and related Jewish traditions (Sir 9:6; 19:2) warn against sexual relations with the πόρνη, 1 Corinthians 6:12-20 stirs

---

[1] Prior, 94.
[2] See Héring, 47.
[3] T.A. Burkill, 'Two into One: The Notion of Carnal Union in Mark 10:8; 1 Cor 6:16; Eph 5:31', 118,120.
[4] Lindemann, 'Toragebote', 247-48.

up no memories of such texts.[5] Secondly, he believes that the text
which Paul does cite (in 6:16), Genesis 2:24, is employed in an altogether
unusual and unconvincing manner; whereas originally it functioned
as a declaration of the sanctity and value of monogamous marriage
(according to Lindemann), Paul employs it ingeniously to underscore
the danger of being joined to a harlot. Lindemann concludes concerning
the use of Scripture in 1 Corinthians 6:12-20: "als Kriterium für seine
konkrete Entscheidung spielt weder dieser [Gen 2:24] noch ein anderer
biblischer Text eine Rolle."[6]

It is fallacious on Lindemann's part to reason that the most fundamental ground someone is opposed to something will necessarily
be prominent and made explicit in their arguments against it. Traugott
Holtz believes this point has relevance to 1 Corinthians 6:12-20.[7] He
contends that Paul's arguments against fornication in this passage in
effect *presuppose* that fornication is wrong. This point is born out by
the observation of several commentators that Paul's proofs are so
strong that they could be used against all sexual activity, even within
marriage ("If fleshly communion with a '*porne*'='harlot' breaks the union
with Christ, why is the same not true of the fleshly communion in
marriage?"[8]). Paul's instructions, it appears, are designed to underscore
the severity and weight of the sin of πορνεία, and not so much to
show that it is sin. So, for example, a passenger trying to convince
the driver of a car that travelling at 90 mph on the motorway were
ill-advised may summon various proofs to their cause: safety, road
conditions, expensive fines, no need to hurry, and so on. However,
the use of such proofs does not necessarily betray a lack of interest
in or allegiance to the law against speeding. Indeed, the relevant law
may well rest at the heart of their opposition, even if left unmentioned.
Likewise, Paul's failure to cite a Biblical command does not necessarily
reveal the irrelevance of the Bible to his opposition to πορνεία.

---

    [5] Lindemann, 'Toragebote', 248: "Doch keiner dieser Texte klingt in der paulinischen
Argumentation auch nur an." We could add to Lindemann's references Exodus 20:14;
Deuteronomy 5:18; 22:22 and Leviticus 18:20; 20:10 which forbid extramarital sex,
and Exodus 22:16 and Deuteronomy 22:13-29, which censure pre-marital sex as
candidates in this regard. See also Genesis 34:31; Leviticus 21:7,9; Deuteronomy
22:21; Amos 7:17 and Deuteronomy 23:17 (see esp. LXX); 2 Kings 23:7; Jeremiah
2:20; Ezekiel 23:37,40,41; Hosea 6:9-10; 7:4; 8:9-10 which condemn mercenary and
religious prostitution respectively.
    [6] Lindemann, 'Toragebote', 248.
    [7] Holtz, 'Zur Frage der inhaltlichen Weisungen bei Paulus', 387-88.
    [8] Héring, 45. Paul seems to have anticipated this potential misunderstanding,
addressing the question of licit sexual union in the next chapter, 1 Corinthians 7.

In the case of 1 Corinthians 6:12-20 one reason Paul did not simply quote a Biblical prohibition to the Corinthians could be because he was obliged to deal with the theological justifications they were advancing in favour of their behaviour. Paul had to defeat the Corinthian libertines on their 'own ground',[9] for it was a misunderstanding of his own teaching which had led to the fault.[10] Most scholars agree that in 6:12-20 Paul is answering the libertine claims of a group in the Corinthian church.[11] It seems that some believers had misapplied Paul's teaching on Christian freedom (see their slogan, πάντα μοι ἔξεστιν, and Paul's qualifications in 6:12), extending it from food laws to relations with a harlot. They were apparently justifying their behaviour by insisting that since (they believed) the σῶμα was destined for destruction, to satisfy its appetites now, whether cravings for food or sexual intercourse, had no spiritual consequences (see Paul's response in 6:13-14). They may have felt safe from any possible defilement because of their close relation to Christ and the Spirit (a point Paul turns on its head in 6:15-19).[12] The shape of Paul's instructions in 6:12-20 is thus largely determined by Corinthian circumstances.

The findings of this chapter are the reverse of Lindemann's opinion. We shall argue that memories of both Scripture and early Jewish parænesis are in fact stirred up by Paul's instructions, in particular, Genesis 39:7ff., Hosea 3:1-3, and passages from Ecclesiasticus and the Testaments of the Twelve Patriarchs. Further, the use of Genesis 2:24 in 6:16, though in some respects novel, is a key to unifying Paul's thought in the section.

To many, however, 1 Corinthians 6:12-20 challenges the view that Paul depends upon the Scriptures in his moral teaching not simply because of what he omits (explicit reference to relevant Scripture), but because of what he includes. The passage is for many students of Paul's ethics a prime example of his clear preference for specifically Christian, rather than Old Testament, motives ("das christliche Wissen"[13]).

---

[9] Cf. Prior, 95: "Paul was compelled to take them up on their own presuppositions."

[10] Cf. Lang, 81-82: "Die Korinther haben die von Paulus gepredigte Freiheit des Glaubens mißverstanden als individualistische Willkürfreiheit und als schrankenlose Verfügungsgewalt gegenüber den materiellen Dingen dieser Welt;" and Conzelmann, 112: "in Corinth impulses emanating from Paul himself are at work."

[11] Whether this group are the Christ party or an early gnostic group or whatever is not important to our discussion.

[12] Cf. Fee, 264 on 6:20: "They thought the presence of the Spirit meant a negation of the body; Paul argues the exact opposite; The presence of the Spirit in their present bodily existence is God's affirmation of the body."

[13] Harnack, 'Das Alte Testament', 132.

126 CHAPTER FIVE

Verses 13-15, they say, show Paul's priorities; to persuade the Corinthians Paul stresses the resurrection of Christ and union with him. What are we to make of the so-called Christian motives in 6:12-20? The point we shall make repeatedly in this chapter is that Paul's Christian motives are themselves inextricably bound up with interpretation of the Jewish Scriptures. For the main lines of Paul's instructions there are clear Biblical precedents.

## II. SEXUAL IMMORALITY AND UNFAITHFULNESS TO THE LORD

No matter how difficult the interpretation of some of the particulars of 1 Corinthians 6:12-20, the general thrust of Paul's response to the problem of harlotry is perfectly clear: he treats it as a sin against God.[14] Assuming that some of the men resorting to harlots were married it is remarkable that Paul does not speak in terms of a sin against the wife. He says nothing of defiling the marriage bed, breaking a covenant or remaining faithful. Rather he conceives of the sin as fundamentally one of religious allegiance. In nine verses θεός and κύριος each occur four times, Χριστός twice and ἅγιον πνεῦμα once. Paul's concern is that the Corinthian offenders are joining Christ to a harlot, insulting the Holy Spirit and dishonouring God. The contention of this section is that there is every likelihood that Paul learned this decidedly theocentric orientation to the problem of πορνεία from the Scriptures.

In the Scriptures adultery is defined not primarily as a private matter, a sin against the spouse, but was regarded as an absolute wrong, a sin against God.[15] Genesis 39:9, a passage to which we shall turn later, makes this point clear: Joseph fends off Potiphar's wife's advances with the question, "How could I do such a wicked thing and sin against God?" David's sin against Bathsheba (and her husband Uriah) is

---

[14] Cf. Lang, 85: "In dem Abschnitt 6,12-20 argumentiert der Apostel christologisch (der Leib gehört dem Herrn V.13 u. 15), ekklesiologisch (die Leiber sind Glieder Christi, die ihre Aufgabe in der Kirche als dem Leib Christi haben V. 15), pneumatologisch (der Leib ist ein Tempel des heiligen Geistes V. 19) und eschatologisch (Gott wird unsere Leiber auferwecken durch seine Macht V. 14)."

[15] In their studies of the laws of adultery in the Old Testament Arnold A. Anderson ('Law in Old Israel: Laws Concerning Adultery'), H. McKeating ('Sanctions Against Adultery in Ancient Israelite Society with some Reflections on Methodology in the Study of Old Testament Ethics') and A. Phillips ('Another Look at Adultery') though divided on various issues, are agreed on this point. Regarding adultery in this way was apparently a unique perspective among the law codes of the ancient Near East.

confessed in Psalm 51:3 in similar terms: "Against you, you only have I sinned and done what is evil in your sight." "I committed this evil deed in the sight of the Lord," is how Reuben in Test. Reuben 1:9 confesses his sin with Bilhah (Gen 35:22), which is a kindred thought.

What the Scriptures teach about prostitution is, however, of even greater interest than adultery for Paul's instructions. The Hebrew Bible distinguishes two kinds of prostitutes: the secular harlot, זונה, whose motives are purely mercenary, and the female, קדשה, or male, קדש, cult prostitute, whose religious motives forge a connection between prostitution and idolatry.[16] Both harlots and cult prostitutes are condemned in the Jewish Scriptures, but on different grounds.

Secular prostitution is commonly opposed in Scripture by underscoring the personal and social stigma it carries. Dinah's brothers attacked Schechem because he had used her like a prostitute (Gen 34:31). Jephthah's brothers drove him out because he was a prostitute's son (Judg 11:2). Part of Amaziah's punishment is that his wife was to become a prostitute (Amos 7:17). In Leviticus 19:29 harlotry is said to lead to all kinds of evil (cf. Prov 23:28). The warnings against harlotry in Proverbs picture the harlot in highly uncomplimentary terms, depicting relations with her as the height of folly.

On the other hand cult prostitution is condemned throughout the Scriptures as disloyalty to God, in a manner not unlike Paul's stance in 1 Corinthians 6:12-20. Religious prostitution was commonly practised by the cults of the ancient Near Eastern fertility religions. Israelite participation was thus condemned as tantamount to apostasy. It was a problem for Israel from the moment they entered the promised land (Num 25:1; cf. Judg 2:17), becoming especially prevalent in Judah and Israel during the divided monarchy (from Reheboam, 1 Kings 14:24, to Josiah, 2 Kings 23:7). According to Exodus 34:11-16 the extermination of the inhabitants of the land was commanded so that the Israelites would avoid the practice. Deuteronomy 23:17(18) forbids cult prostitution for Israel (cf. Amos 2:7).

Is it then temple prostitution that Paul is combating in 6:12-20?[17] The link between idolatry and sexual immorality in 10:7-8, the fact that 6:18 ("flee immorality") is similar to 10:14 ("flee idolatry") and the temple imagery in 6:19-20 would suggest that it is. However, since

---

[16] On this link cf. Ezekiel 23:37; Syb. Or. 5:386-433.
[17] Manuel Miguens, 'Christ's Members and Sex', 41 for example, thinks so.

there is no evidence that cult prostitution existed in new Corinth, the question must be left open.[18]

Nonetheless, that Paul learned to equate prostitution, even of a secular sort, with unfaithfulness to the Lord from the Scriptures is suggested by three observations. First, though cult prostitutes and harlots are distinguished in the Hebrew Scriptures, the Greek Bible generally uses the πορν- group of words (including ἐκπορνεύω) for both. Thus in the LXX, a version with which Paul was undoubtedly familiar,[19] prostitution in general is viewed as apostasy.

Secondly, most of the references to prostitution in the Old Testament, even those using the זנה word group, turn out to be figurative referring to Israel's faithlessness toward the Lord and worship of other gods. This presumably exploits the association of cult prostitution with pagan worship and therefore apostasy (Lev 17:7; 20:5f; Num 14:33; 15:39; 25:1; Deut 31:16; Judg 2:17; 8:27,33; 1 Chron 5:25; 2 Chron 21:11,13; Pss 73:27; 106:39; Ezek 16; 23; Hosea; Jer 3:1-5).

A third and related point is that the words Paul uses for prostitution, πορνεία, and for the prostitute, πόρνη, are employed in Jewish literature not only for literal prostitution (e.g., Gen 38:24; Hosea 4:11; Sir 41:17), but also as a metaphor for unfaithfulness to the Lord (e.g., Num 14:33; Deut 23:17; Isa 47:10; Hosea 4:12; 5:4; cf. Isa 57:9; T. Sim. 5:3; T. Reu. 4:6-11; 6:1-6). Paul had ample Biblical precedent for regarding any type of prostitution as unfaithfulness to the Lord.

### III. A SIN AGAINST JEWISH AND CHRISTIAN HOPE: "GOD WILL RAISE US BY HIS POWER"

Reading Paul's letters is sometimes like listening to a tape recording of the question-answer time after a lecture in which the microphone has only picked up the answers, leaving the listeners to conjecture not only the substance of the lecture but the clarification sought by the questioners. In 6:13-14 it seems, to apply the analogy, that Paul had delivered a lecture to the church in Corinth on the irrelevance of food laws. Like the disciples of Jesus Paul's pupils were prone to misunderstanding.[20] Some, it seems, jumped from the notion of

---

[18] Jerome Murphy-O' Connor, *St. Paul's Corinth: Texts and Archaeology*, 55-57.

[19] Moody Smith, 'Pauline Literature', 272: "In Paul's quotation of the OT there are remarkable affinities with the LXX."

[20] The author of Hebrews faced similar problems (Heb 5:11).

Christian freedom with respect to food to freedom with respect to sexual relations.[21] Perhaps one questioner put it this way:

> Just as food is meant for the stomach and the stomach for food, so also the body is meant for sexual activity and sexual activity for the body. Furthermore, since God will one day destroy both the stomach and the body, is not what we do with our bodies now of no moral consequence?[22]

Verses 13-14 make sense in the light of such a reconstruction. Paul agreed with the questioner's comments concerning the stomach and food. However, he takes issue with both points about the body. First, the purpose of the body, he explains in 6:13b, is not immorality, but service of and communion with the Lord.[23] And secondly, in 6:14, he insists that the body is not temporary, but will be included in the *eschaton*; believers, like Christ, are destined for bodily resurrection.[24] In Paul's response he quotes one Corinthian slogan (6:13a, "Food is meant for the stomach and the stomach for food") and reformulates another (6:13b, "the body is not meant for immorality but the Lord").[25] Thus verse 14 demolishes Corinthian notions about the transience and consequent insignificance of the body.[26]

Brendon Byrne is probably correct in asserting that in 6:12-20 "the nub of the dispute between Paul and the Corinthians concerns the value to be placed upon present bodily existence."[27] Certain Corinthian Christians had embraced a body/spirit dualism, involving a low view of the purpose and future of the body, which opened the door to sexual licence. In 6:13b-14 Paul defends an exceedingly high view of the body, totally rejecting this dualism. In rejecting such a dualism

---

[21] Cf. Lightfoot. Talbert, 29 suggests that the Corinthians were influenced by a Greek view: "sexual intercourse is as natural as eating and drinking (e.g., Plutarch, 'Life of Solon,' 31)."

[22] A straightforward 'mirror' reading of 1 Corinthians 15:12-19 confirms that some Corinthian believers saw no future for the σῶμα. See John M.G. Barclay, 'Mirror-Reading a Polemical Letter: Galatians as a Test Case', on the pitfalls, problems and method of mirror-reading.

[23] Cf. Romans 12:1-2: "present your bodies."

[24] ἐξεγερεῖ, future, is preferred to ἐξεγείρει, present, and ἐξήγειρεν, aorist, both on external and internal grounds: it enjoys an Alexandrian-Byzantine manuscript alliance and fits the argument better.

[25] See the Interpretative Paraphrase at the close of this chapter.

[26] *Contra* Udo Schnelle, '1 Kor 6:14—eine nachpaulinische Glosse', who failing to relate 6:14 to the rest of the paragraph argues that it is a scribal gloss.

[27] Byrne, 'Sinning against One's Own Body: Paul's Understanding of the Sexual Relationship in 1 Corinthians 6:18', 611. The word σῶμα occurs eight times in nine

Paul is simply subscribing to the anthropology of his Bible. Friedrich Lang explains, commenting on 6:13-14:

> Dahinter steht ein welt-anschaulicher Dualismus von Körper und Geist, wie er in der griechischen Philosophie seit Plato lebendig war, aber der alttestamentlichen Tradition vom Schöpfungsgedanken her fremd ist.[28]

Paul's statement of belief in the resurrection of believers in 6:14b is one that could have been written by the pre-Christian Paul, since the same belief was reflected in Pharisaic and wider Jewish teaching.

The notion in these verses that the prospect of the future resurrection carries a demand for moral behaviour in the present is also a Biblical idea with a history of development. The doctrine of the resurrection hinted at in Psalms 49 and 73 and briefly stated in Daniel 12:1-3, is developed with an eye to ethical demands in 2 Maccabees 7:9,14; 2 Baruch 50-51; 2 Esdras 7; Test. Judah 25:1-4; Test. Benjamin 10:6-9; Test. Zebulon 10:4; 1QHymns 6:29-34.[29]

## IV. HOSEA FORBIDDING HARLOTRY

Going to prostitutes is ruled out for Christians according to Paul because of the sanctified status of believers: they have cleaved to and been bought by the Lord; He is their husband (6:16-17; see section A below) and redeemer/master (6:20; see section B). Not only do the Scriptures attest these two descriptions of the divine-human relationship, they also contain an instance (in Hosea) where they are combined in a warning against harlotry.

### A. *A Sin Against Christ: "united to the Lord"*

In verses 16-17 Paul continues his attack on the notion that fornication does not represent a vital and significant union by quoting (part of) Genesis 2:24, οἱ δύο εἰς σάρκα μίαν. The verse is quoted to support (note explanatory γάρ) the idea that sexual intercourse, even with a prostitute, creates a permanent bond: "the one who cleaves (ὁ κολλώμενος) to a harlot becomes one body (with her)."[30] The part

---

verses and is implied at several other points (see our interpretative paraphrase).

[28] Lang, 81. Paul's use of σῶμα throughout the passage to refer to the entire self, seen through the medium of the physical, is in line with LXX practice; cf. J.A. Ziesler, 'Σῶμα in the Septuagint'; Talbert, 30.

[29] Cf. D.A. Hubbard, 'OT Ethics', 2:169 for a similar list.

[30] D.S. Bailey, *The Man-Woman Relation in Christian Thought*, 10 explains: "he [Paul]

of LXX Genesis 2:24 which is not quoted also uses (a compound of) the verb κολλάω: "For this reason a man shall leave his father and mother and cleave (προσκολληθήσεται[31]) to his wife." In 1 Corinthians 6:17 the same verb is used to describe a believer's relationship with the Lord. Paul's presentation of the mutually exclusive alternatives of cleaving (κολλάω) to the Lord or to a prostitute in 6:16-17 testifies to his indebtedness to Scripture and early Jewish paraenesis.[32] Both cleaving to God and to an evil thing or person have precedents in the Scriptures. Deuteronomy 10:20; 2 Kings 18:6 and Jeremiah 13:11 speak of cleaving to God using κολλάω,[33] and Psalm 72(73):27(28); Deuteronomy 11:22 using προσκολλάω (translating דבק in both cases). Cleaving (κολλάω) to idols appears in 1 Kings 11:2, cleaving (προσκολλάω) to an evil thing in Deuteronomy 13:17 and to enchanters in Leviticus 19:31. Ecclesiasticus 19:2 is especially significant: "the man who cleaves to a prostitute is reckless." Ecclesiasticus 2:3 supplies the other alternative: "Cleave to him" (that is, God).[34]

That Paul in 6:16-17 presents the two alternatives of cleaving to a prostitute or cleaving to the Lord, has led a handful of commentators to suggest a second purpose for Paul's use of Genesis 2:24 in 6:16. Though he does not adopt it, John Calvin is among the first to articulate this view: Genesis 2:24 is used to "magnify the efficacy and dignity of the spiritual marriage which subsists between us and Christ."[35] Few commentators hold to the view that Genesis 2:24 is used by Paul

---

insists that it is an act which, by reason of its very nature, engages and expresses the whole personality in such a way as to constitute an unique mode of self-disclosure and self-commitment."

[31] Some argue that Paul uses κολλάω instead of προσκολλάω to remove the directly sexual reference from 6:16-17 (eg. J.I. Miller, 'A Fresh Look at 1 Corinthians 6.16f.', 127). However, κολλάω is used for a similar relationship with a harlot in Ecclesiasticus 19:2. That the two words can be used interchangeably can be seen in Matthew 19:5 and Ephesians 5:31 which, when quoting Genesis 2:24, employ κολλάω and προσκολλάω respectively. 1 Esdras 4:20 and Tobit 6:17 show that κολλάω continued to be associated with literal marriage.

[32] Sampley, "And the Two Shall Become One Flesh": A Study of Traditions in Ephesians 5:21-31, 79, correctly calls it "conventional."

[33] Cf. Psalm 118(119): 31: "cleave to God's testimonies."

[34] Sampley, One Flesh, 79 suggests that Paul may be directly dependent on Ecclesiasticus 19:2 and 2:3. However, the eight references to cleaving to God or to evil noted above (only one is mentioned by Sampley) render such an hypothesis unnecessary. Probably both authors, Jesus ben Sirach and Paul, learned about 'cleaving' from the Scriptures.

[35] Calvin, 218. Cf. Prior on 6:15-17, 101: "Paul uses the vocabulary, explicitly in connection with marriage, to describe the relationship between Christ (the Bridegroom) and the church (his Bride)."

in 6:16 not only to prove the seriousness of sexual union with a harlot but to introduce the notion of the believer's nuptial union with Christ.[36] Though none offers a sustained defence, there is, in fact, good evidence to support this view.[37] Several points need to be noted.

Paul's choice of words is significant. The use of κύριος in 6:17, rather than θεός, is congruent with spiritual marriage imagery. The appearance of κύριος in 6:13-14 ("God raised the Lord") indicates that by κύριος in 6:17, Paul means Christ. The hypothesis that he has spiritual marriage to Christ in mind would be seriously weakened if he had said believers are united to θεός in 6:17. He could also have used a word other than κολλάω to express how believers are united with the Lord, which did not recall the Genesis marriage text, such as ἀντέχω (1 Thess 5:14; Titus 1:9; Matt 6:24), στρεφόμαι (Acts 13:46), προσκλίνω (Acts 5:36) or προσκληρόομαι (Acts 17:4). Language characteristic of a marriage union also appears in verse 13, where Paul says that the body is meant for the Lord and vice versa. Talbert notes that comparable "to be for" language appears with reference to marriage in the Song of Solomon 2:16 and Romans 7:2-3.[38]

It would not be surprising if the bride image were implicitly present in 6:12-20, for though vital in his thought, it is customarily kept in the background by Paul. Claude Chavasse explains:

> He never puts it in the middle of the stage, but uses it as an argument always for something else . . . against fornication (1 Corinthians vi:15-20), for love in family life (Ephesians v.22ff), for spiritual docility (2 Corinthians xi.2).[39]

Spiritual marriage imagery also lurks in the 'atmosphere' of 1 Corinthians 7:32-35, where pleasing the Lord and pleasing one's marriage partner are compared, and is made plain to the Corinthians in 2 Corinthians 11:2 ("I promised you to one husband, to Christ, so that I might present you as a pure virgin to him"). In both passages, as

---

[36] An early advocate of this view is Hermann Olshausen, 110. Meyer's objection to seeing spiritual nuptial imagery in 6:12-20, 184 is that since in the marriage of Christ and the Church Christ is the husband, the contrast with cleaving to a prostitute would be unsuitable. This unnecessarily restricts the metaphor's potential for diverse application.

[37] In the light of this evidence it is surprising that Richard A. Batey's, *New Testament Nuptial Imagery*, and 'Paul's Bride Image' make no mention of 1 Corinthians 6:12-20.

[38] Talbert, 30.

[39] Chavasse, *The Bride of Christ*, 66. His identification of the image in 1 Corinthians 12:27 is less convincing.

in 6:12-20, Paul is concerned to secure the Corinthian believers' exclusive devotion to their husband, Christ.

The image of the church as Christ's bride/wife is appropriate to the problem of going to harlots since it implicitly calls (throughout its New Testament usage) for subjection, purity and faithfulness. Paul tells the Corinthians that they have cleaved to the Lord, a relationship which involves Christ owning them and having rights over their bodies. Such a description, read in the light of 7:1-7, where similar things are said about literal marriage, surely points to a marriage relationship. Indeed, 1 Corinthians 7:4, a verse describing conjugal rights in marriage, reflects back marriage connotations into 1 Corinthians 6:12b.[40] In 7:4 Paul remarks: "For the wife does not rule over (οὐκ ἐξουσιάζει) her own body (τοῦ ἰδίου σώματος), but the husband does; likewise the husband does not rule over his own body, but the wife does." As Byrne comments, "the sexual relationship in marriage involves a real making over of one's body to be the possession of the partner."[41] 1 Corinthians 7:4 shares a certain phrase with 6:12b, οὐκ ἐγὼ ἐξουσιασθήσομαι[42] suggesting that one reason Paul refuses to let his body be ruled by anyone is that "the wife does not rule over her own body, but the husband", that is, Christ.

Finally, the use of Genesis 2:24 on another occasion, in Ephesians 5:31, indicates that Paul (or in the view of many scholars, a follower of Paul) was not averse to finding in it an application to the marriage of Christ and the church. Ephesians 5:32 comments on the relevant phrase from Genesis 2:24: "This mystery is a profound one, and I am saying that it refers to Christ and the church."[43]

With the spiritual marriage image in view, some of the disconnected elements of 6:12-20 harmoniously converge. 1 Corinthians 6:13b,19b envelop the passage, protesting the Lord's right over the believer's body, a right given additional credence in the light of their nuptial union. In the Scriptures both physical (man to woman)[44] and spiritual (God to Israel)[45] marriage carry this ownership implication.

---

[40] See Fee, 250, 253 and Byrne, 'Sinning', 614.

[41] Byrne, 'Sinning', 614.

[42] The verb only occurs in 6:12 and 7:4 in Paul's letters.

[43] Cf. Ephesians 5:30 and 1 Corinthians 6:15.

[44] See 1 Corinthians 7:4 and a discussion of the Biblical background in Chapter Six, section IIC.

[45] See Ezekiel 16:8b: "you became mine" (verse 8 refers to a marriage covenant since "spread the corner of my garment" is symbolic of such a relationship in Deut 22:30 and Ruth 3:9); cf. 23:4: "they were mine."

That Paul derived the image of the spiritual marriage of Christ and the Church from the marriage of God to Israel depicted in Paul's Bible is surely beyond dispute. The Hebrew prophets Isaiah,[46] Jeremiah (e.g., 2:2), and Ezekiel (e.g., ch. 16) employ this image in some of their most famous passages and the entire book of Hosea is built around it.[47] Central in tying these traditions together for Paul was the fact that the marriage of God to His people was promised as a feature of the new covenant (e.g., Isa 62:5).[48]

D.E. Aune plausibly suggests that the application of this imagery to the relationship between Christ and the church by New Testament authors such as Paul was facilitated by four factors:

> (1) the messianic interpretation of some features of Old Testament nuptial imagery in Judaism, (2) the tendency in Judaism to depict the messianic age as a wedding feast, (3) early Christianity's functional substitution of Jesus for Yahweh, and (4) the Greco-Roman penchant for personifying corporate bodies with feminine imagery.[49]

## B. *A Treacherous Sin: "you are not your own"*

"The decisive argument against unchastity" in 6:12-20 is, according to Wolfgang Schrage, the question, to whom does your body belong?[50] In 6:19b-20a Paul decides the issue: οὐκ ἐστὲ ἑαυτῶν, ἠγοράσθητε γὰρ τιμῆς. The Corinthian Christians were not to do as they please, going to harlots, because they had been bought with a price by God in the slavemarket and he had become their master ( cf. 7:22-23). Now their main concern must be to please the Lord (1 Cor 7:32; 2 Cor 5:9,15; Rom 14:7-9; Col 1:10). Since to commit πορνεία is tantamount to being mastered by someone else (cf. 6:12b; τινος could be translated "anyone"), such behaviour would be a perfidious act, for no man can serve two masters.

Most commentators recognise a metaphorical reference to the slave market in the words, "you are not your own, you were bought with a price" (see 7:22-23). C.K. Barrett's judgement concerning the probable origin of this imagery points in the right direction:

---

[46] See C. Stuhlmueller, *Creative Redemption*, 103f, 115f; K. Krupp, 'Das Verhältnis Jahwe-Israel im Sinne eines Ehebundes'.
[47] See also 2 Samuel 17:3 (variant adopted by *RSV, NEB, REB, NRSV*)
[48] Other New Covenant passages such as Jeremiah 31:3,31-34; Ezekiel 36:24-30 speak of intimacy with the Lord but do not describe the relationship in marriage terms.
[49] D.E. Aune, 'Bride of Christ', I:546.
[50] Schrage, *Ethics*, 219.

The process of sacral manumission, by which a slave was bought 'for freedom' (cf. Gal. v.1) in the name of a god may well have served as an analogy and have supplied him with useful terminology, but the fundamental idea of ransoming Paul derived from the Old Testament, where the words are used in a wide variety of senses (eg. Exod. vi.6; xiii,13; Ruth iv. 4ff.; Ps ciii.4; Isa xliii.1).[51]

Indeed, if taken in isolation, 6:19b-20a could just as well have been said to Israel as to the church.[52] The Scriptures picture the Lord emancipating Israel from slavery in Egypt, describing the results of this rescue in terms of acquisition. Through this purchase Israel became his exclusive possession. Commenting on the use of ἀγοράζω in 1 Corinthians 6:20 (and 7:23) Lyonnet/Sabourin state:

> The term is Greek but the notion draws so close to the idea of 'acquisition', as it is found in the Old Testament, that it cannot really be understood unless we have in mind also that 'purchase' by which Yahweh, by virtue of the Sinaitic covenant, has already acquired for himself his people and which he promised to acquire in Messianic times by virtue of the new covenant.[53]

In 1 Corinthians 6:19b-20a we discover what is in the eyes of many one of Paul's new, specifically Christian, ideas thoroughly integrated with Scriptural background. In these verses Paul strengthens his case against πορνεία by drawing out ethical implications from the Biblical theme of the Lord's ownership of his people.

## C. *Conclusion*

Those who doubt that Scripture was important for Paul's ethics often suggest that something else is far more critical for Paul, namely, to recall Andreas Lindemann's words, "Konsequenz des Evangeliums" (i.e., the new life in Christ worked out in Christian behaviour).[54] It

---

[51] Barrett, 151.

[52] Exodus 19:5; Deuteronomy 26:18; Isaiah 43:21; Malachi 3:17 may be added to Barrett's references.

[53] Lyonnet/Sabourin, *Sin, Redemption and Sacrifice: A Biblical and Patristic Study*, 115. Lyonnet/Sabourin, 110-12 supply a review of this notion of purchase in the Old Testament, which we shall not duplicate here. They conclude, 112: "It is quite clear that such a notion of purchase or acquisition comes very close to the context of the N.T., much more so, certainly than that notion of purchase regulated among the Greeks and Romans, the profane and also the sacred manumission of slaves."

[54] Lindemann, 'Toragebote', 264. Cf. Lenski, 266 on 1 Corinthians 6:18: "Here we have an instance where Paul uses the gospel and not the law for inculcating a moral requirement."

is certainly true that in 6:12-20 Paul exhorts the Corinthian believers to sexual holiness on the basis of the great facts of salvation. Indicatives form the basis on which the imperatives of 6:18 and 6:20 stand. Otto Merk explains:

> sie [i.e., the Corinthians] sind bar erkauft, sie haben den Geist empfangen (6,19; vgl. auch Rm 8,11), der Herr gehört ihnen (6,13), sie stehen in der Christusgemeinschaft (6,15.17), Christus ist auferweckt (6,14). All das kann man als Begründungen für den „Indikativ" des σῶμα bezeichnen, aus dem der dem σῶμα auferlegte „Imperativ" gezogen wird für die Gegenwart: Fliehet die Unzucht (6,18); verherrlicht Gott an eurem Leibe (6,20).[55]

Indeed, 1 Corinthians 6:12-20 is a choice example of the interrelatedness of indicative and imperative in Paul's ethics.

However, to claim that *either* the Scriptures *or* the 'consequences of the gospel' influenced Paul's ethics is a false bifurcation. In Excursus 1 (Chapter Three) we established that the Scriptures (especially Deuteronomy and the Prophets) share with Paul the conviction that the call to obedience is grounded in God's prior salvific action. Identity informs behaviour in *both* the Scriptures *and* Paul's letters.

At the heart of Paul's call to sexual purity in 6:12-20 is the idea that God is the believer's husband (6:16-17) and redeemer/master (6:20). That Paul had been influenced by Scripture in this choice of indicatives upon which to base his imperatives, at least in a general sense, can be seen in the same combination of ideas in Isaiah and Hosea. Isaiah 54:5 states: "your Maker is your *husband*—the Lord Almighty is his name—the Holy One of Israel is your *Redeemer*."

An even closer parallel may be drawn with Hosea 3:1-3. Just as Paul exhorted the Corinthians not to go to prostitutes, so in Hosea 3:3 Hosea commanded Gomer not to be a prostitute ("you must not be a prostitute"). Both admonitions to sexual fidelity are argued on similar grounds. Hosea's demand is based upon his special relationship with Gomer: he is her husband (3:1) and having redeemed her from the slave market ("I bought her;" 3:2), he is her master. George L. Klein spells out the comparison:

> In Hosea 3 the prophet redeemed his wife out of a degrading life to a life bound by sexual decorum. Similarly in 1 Corinthians 6 the audience had been redeemed out of bondage to sin (including licentiousness) to a life in which sexual sin was unconscionable.[56]

---

[55] Merk, *Handeln*, 98-00; cf. Michael Parsons, 'Being', 122-26.
[56] Klein, 'Hos 3:1-3—Background to 1 Cor 6:19b-20?', 374.

An analogy from Hosea-Gomer to God-His people is made plain in 3:1 ("Love her as the Lord loves the Israelites"). Klein argues that in 1 Corinthians 6:19b-20 there is an "allusion (understood in broad thematic terms)" to Hosea 3:1-3.[57] However, lack of terminological overlap warns against too confident an identification of such an allusion. Nevertheless, for our present purposes, it is enough to note that it is an Hosea-like Paul whom we encounter when Paul deals with prostitution in 1 Corinthians 6. It is not that Paul has Hosea in mind in 1 Corinthians 6:12-20. Rather, the points of contact with Isaiah and Hosea demostrate that Paul is here standing in a discernible Biblical tradition. Calling God's people to repentance on the basis that He is their husband and master, far from divorcing Paul from his Scriptural heritage, places him in line with the best of Israel's prophets.

## V. JOSEPH FLEEING POTIPHAR'S WIFE[58]

With "vehement abruptness"[59] Paul exhorts the Corinthians in 6:18 to flee[60] immorality, φεύγετε τὴν πορνείαν. This is the paragraph's central injunction (along with and balanced by the more positive "glorify God with your body" [6:20]).[61] What is the origin or inspiration of φεύγετε τὴν πορνείαν? Two answers to this question have been suggested. Whereas F. Godet[62] and F.F. Bruce[63] claim that the command may recall Joseph's literal fleeing from Potiphar's wife, the margin of Nestle-Aland[26] notes the parallel of Test. Reuben 5:5, φεύγετε οὖν τὴν πορνείαν. It is possible that these two proposals may in fact both be right.

---

[57] Klein, 'Hos 3:1-3', 374.
[58] An abbreviated version of V.A,B and C appeared as 'A Possible quotation of Test. Reuben 5:5 in 1 Corinthians 6:18a'.
[59] Findlay, 821; note asyndeton.
[60] φεύγετε is a present imperative suggesting continual vigilance. Paul's exhortation in 6:18a underscores the perilous and menacing nature of πορνεία, φεύγω being a particularly emotive word. In the LXX people "flee" from enemies, snakes, the kinsman avenger and other dangers.
[61] In the traditional Pauline corpus believers are told on only three other occasions to flee sin: in 1 Corinthians 10:14 they are exhorted to flee idolatry; in 1 Timothy 6:11 men of God are to flee the love of money; and in 2 Timothy 2:22 Timothy is told to flee youthful passions.
[62] Godet, 1:311.
[63] Bruce, 65.

## A. *A Dangerous Sin: "flee sexual immorality"*

The question of whether Paul quoted from non-canonical Jewish literature has long been debated.[64] R.H. Charles' *Apocrypha and Pseudepigrapha of the Old Testament* (Oxford, 1913) claims that Pauline parallels can be found in Tobit (1:199), Wisdom (1:526f), Enoch (2:163f), Letter of Aristeas (2:92), 4 Ezra (2:559) and especially the Testaments of the Twelve Patriarchs (2:292),[65] a document Charles claims was Paul's *vade mecum*. However, E.E. Ellis and others are sceptical of such parallels, and claim that only similar phraseology is represented ("Paul's use of non-canonical Jewish literature is very doubtful at best ... in no case has a direct use of writings of the diaspora been established"[66]). The relation of 1 Corinthians 6:18 to Test. Reuben 5:5 is largely ignored in this debate,[67] and by commentators on 1 Corinthians. Apparently the repetition of a mere three words has not impressed scholars, who, if aware of the parallel, usually put them down to coincidence. Hans Conzelmann rightly calls φεύγω "a characteristic catchword in paraenesis,"[68] and there is certainly nothing distinctive about the term for sexual immorality in question, πορνεία (cf. 1 Cor 5:1; 6:13; 7:2; 2 Cor 12:21; Gal 5:19; Eph 5:3; Col 3:5; 1 Thess 4:3).

Despite such misgivings there are reasons to think that Test. Reuben 5:5 and 1 Corinthians 6:18 are related. The injunction in question occurs only fourteen times in ancient Greek literature:[69] Test. Reuben 5:5, 1 Corinthians 6:18 and in quotations of 1 Corinthians 6:18 in Epiphanius (*Adversus haereses* 31.483),[70] Gregory of Nyssa (*Contra fornicarios oratio* 9.211 [twice], 212, 213, 214),[71] John Chrysostom (*Ad populum Antiochenum* [hom. 14] 49.149; *Expositiones in Psalmos* [Ps 43:9] 55.182;

---

[64] Similar questions are asked of the writings of Philo and Josephus, who seem to know a measure of Biblical elaboration but do not give it the dignity of a source.

[65] Cf. Charles, *The Testaments of the Twelve Patriarchs*, lxxxv-xc.

[66] Ellis, *Paul's Use*, 77, 83. Cf. H.C. Kee, 'The Testaments of the Twelve Patriarchs', Charlesworth, 1:780 who comments concerning the relation of the Testaments to New Testament documents: "It is only in the Christian interpolations that there are direct links."

[67] Eg. Albrecht Oepke, 'Apocryphal Quotations in the New Testament', *TDNT* 3:988-92 in 'κρύπτω' discusses Jude 14, Hebrews 11:37, 1 Corinthians 2:9, Galatians 6:15, Ephesians 5:14, 1 Timothy 3:16, 2 Timothy 3:8, James 4:5 and John 7:38. Perhaps the two most discussed examples are Wisdom 12-14 in Romans 1:18ff, and Apoc. Eliae in 1 Corinthians 2:9.

[68] Conzelmann, 112; cf. Ecclesiasticus 21:2; m. Aboth 4:2; 4 Maccabees 8:19.

[69] According to an Ibychus computer search of *Thesaurus Linguae Graecae: Canon of Greek Authors and Works* (Oxford, 1986), ed. Luci Berkowitz and Karl A. Squitier.

[70] *Die griechischen christlichen Schriftsteller* (Leipzig, 1922), ed. K. Holl.

[71] *Gregori Nysseni opera* (Leiden, 1967), ed. E. Gebhardt.

In epistulam ad Romanos [hom. 24] 60.626; *In epistulam i ad Corinthios* [argumentum et hom. 18] 61.146),[72] and Origen (*Fragmenta ex commentaris in epistulam i ad Corinthios* 31;[73] *Secta in Psalmos* [Ps 30:16] 12.1301[74]). There is no reason to suppose that Test. Reuben 5:5 is a later Christian interpolation (itself influenced by Paul's words).[75] Neither is it an isolated thought in the paraenesis.[76] In context the injunction in Test. Reuben 5:5 concerns the same issue with which Paul is engaged, avoiding women "with a harlot's manner" (5:4). That Paul knew Test. Reuben 5 (or at least some of its traditions) is also suggested by its presentation of women as seducers even of angels (Gen 6:1-4) and consequent prescription of modest dress and hair style (cf. T. Jud. 15:5f) which brings to mind 1 Corinthians 11:10.

On the other hand, the Godet/Bruce connection of Paul's advice to flee immorality and the example of Joseph in Genesis 39 is also not without warrant. In fact Gregory of Nyssa (*Contra fornicarios*) recognised the link in the fourth century. His homily on 1 Corinthians 6:18, which quotes (as already noted) φεύγετε τὴν πορνείαν four times, uses Genesis 39:11-14 as its major illustration of what it means to flee immorality. In LXX Genesis 39:12 φεύγω is used (translating נוס) in the description of Joseph's successful escape from the clutches of Potiphar's wife: "he fled out of the house." LXX Genesis 39:13,15,18 use φεύγω a further three times in the recollections of Joseph's flight. Indeed, Paul would not have been the first to denounce sexual immorality with Joseph's example in mind. In *On Joseph* 43, Philo pictures Joseph, speaking to Potiphar's wife, as condemning "harlots (πόρναις) and strumpets and all those who make a traffic of their bodies."[77]

That Genesis 39 might have occurred to Paul as being relevant

---

[72] *Patrologiae cursus completus—series Graeca* (Paris, 1857-66), ed. J.-P. Migne.

[73] 'Documents: Origen on 1 Corinthians', ed. C. Jenkins, *JTS* IX (1908) 371.

[74] *Patrologiae cursus completus—series Graeca* (Paris, 1857-66), ed. J.-P. Migne.

[75] The bulk of accepted Christian interpolations are christological and/or anti-Jewish.

[76] Cf. Test. Reuben 6:1; Test. Levi 9:9; Test. Judah 18:2; Test. Benjamin 7:1; also Ps-Phocylides 146; Tomson, *Paul*, 76. Howard Clark Kee, 'The Ethical Dimensions of the Testaments of the Twelve Patriarchs as a Clue to their Provenance', 260 has observed that "the author (of the Testaments of the Twelve Patriarchs) deplores above all sexual immorality... πορνεία appears at least 25 times."

[77] *On Joseph* 43 and 1 Corinthians 6:18b may also be compared; Paul's assertion that πορνεία is unique is conceptually equivalent to Philo's description of adultery as "the greatest of crimes", τοῦ μεγίστου τῶν ἀδικημάτων. Both Philo (*On Joseph* 49) and Josephus (Ant. II.54) in their retelling of the Genesis 39 story maintain the crucial note of Joseph's flight, but instead of φεύγω use ἐκφεύγω and ἀποδιδράσκω respectively.

to the problem of prostitution is suggested by its position next to Genesis 38, in which prostitution occurs in the form of Tamar and Judah (πόρνη occurs in LXX Genesis 38:15,21,22; πορνεία in 38:24). R. Alter suggests that Genesis 38 and 39 as they are presently placed present a deliberate contrast between Joseph, who flees sexual temptation, and Judah, who succumbs.[78] If Judah's behaviour (sexual immorality) is the problem, Joseph's (fleeing) is the solution.

It is clear that Genesis 39 exerted some influence upon both Biblical and post-Biblical conceptions of sexual immorality. Its influence may even extend to certain details, such as the immoral lifting up of Potiphar's wife's eyes in 39:7 which may be compared with Isaiah 3:16; Ecclesiasticus 26:9; Test. Issachar 7:2 (cf. Didache 3:3).[79] Proverbs 7:6-27, where the seductress who casts her eyes on the young man and invites him to take his fill of her love while her husband is away, may also be compared with Genesis 39:7-20.

The question arises, then, when Paul wrote 1 Corinthians 6:18a did he have Joseph's example in mind or was he quoting Test. Reuben 5:5 (not as solemn Scripture but as an appropriate ethical maxim)? A closer look at the Testaments of the Twelve Patriarchs suggests a third possibility: Paul wrote 1 Corinthians 6:18a with *both* Test. Reuben 5:5 *and* Joseph's example in mind. In formulating the exhortation in question the author of Test. Reuben was himself thinking of Genesis 39, since only eight verses previously (T. Reub. 4:8) the example of Joseph in "protecting himself from a woman" is in view. Furthermore, two additional pieces of parænetical reflection upon Joseph's example in the Testaments of the Twelve Patriarchs have affinities with 1 Corinthians 6:19-20, suggesting Paul's sympathetic acquaintance with the document's moral interpretation of the Joseph story (see sections B and C following).[80]

---

[78] Alter, 'A Literary Approach to the Bible' 70-77; cf. also Walter Brueggemann, *Genesis: A Bible Commentary for Teaching and Preaching*, 312.

[79] Adolph Büchler, *Types of Jewish-Palestinian Piety from 70 B.C.E. To 70 C.E.*, 53-54. Büchler, 53 also mentions that R. Jose the Galilean applies Proverbs 6:17 to the adulteress: "Seven things are stated about the adulteress: high looks, for the adulteress raises her eyes to another man. . . ." On the essentially didactic nature of the entire Joseph story see Gerhard von Rad, 'The Joseph Narrative and Ancient Wisdom'; *Genesis, a Commentary*, 428-34; and, with qualifications, G.W. Coats, 'The Joseph Story and Ancient Wisdom: A Reappraisal'. For the remarkably wide distribution of and interest in the Genesis 39 incident in Jewish and world literature see Louis Ginzberg, *The Legends of the Jews*, 2:39-58 and E.I. Lowenthal, *The Joseph Narrative in Genessis*, 32-40; and J.D. Yohannan, *Joseph and Potiphar's Wife in World Literature: An Anthology of the Story of the Chaste Youth and the Lustful Stepmother* respectively.

[80] In the parænesis of the Testaments of the Twelve Patriarchs Joseph stands as

B. *A Sin Against the Spirit: "your body is a temple"*

Paul's use of the image of God's indwelling in relation to the chastity of individual believers in 1 Corinthians 6:19[81] is reminiscent of Test. Joseph chapter 10, where Joseph exhorts his sons on the basis of his experiences in Egypt, especially his escape from Potiphar's wife recounted in the two preceding chapters (8:1-9:5).[82] He states in 10:1-3:

> So you see my children, how great are the things that patience and prayer with fasting accomplish. You also, if you pursue chastity (τὴν σωφροσύνην) and purity (τὴν ἀγνείαν) with perseverance (ἐν ὑπομονῇ) and prayer with fasting in humility of heart, *the Lord will dwell among you, (κατοικήσει ἐν ὑμῖν) because he loves chastity.* And where the Most High dwells, even if envy befall someone, or slavery or slander befall one, *the Lord who dwells in him (κύριος ὁ ἐν αὐτῷ κατοικῶν) because of his chastity,* not only delivers him from evil but also exalts (δοξάζει) him, as he has done to me" [italics mine].[83]

"Chastity" here (sometimes translated "self control") clearly refers back to Joseph's exemplary behaviour in the face of the shameless advances of Potiphar's wife (see 9:2-3). This notion that God was specially present with Joseph after his successful flight is not without a basis in the

---

the chief example of moral excellence, being the only patriach cited as a positive example in a testament other than his own (Issachar and Zebulon are models to be emulated, but only in their respective testaments). Cf. Harm Hollander, *Joseph as an Ethical Model in the Testaments of the Twelve Patriarchs,* esp. 62-63; A.W. Argyle 'The Influence of the Testaments of the Twelve Patriarchs upon the New Testament', 256; M. Philonenko, *Les interpolations chrétiennes des Testaments des Douze Patriarches et les manuscrits de Qoumrân,* 50; J. Becker, *Untersuchungen zur Entstehungsgeschichte der Testamente der Zwölf Patriarchen,* 386ff. None of theses authors, however, mention the possible link of 1 Corinthians 6:18-20 with the Testaments' reflections upon Genesis 39.

[81] It is interesting that the parable of the two adulterous sisters in Ezekiel 23 connects prostitution and God's in-dwelling. The younger sister's name is Oholibah, which means "my tent is in her", implying that God's sanctuary is in her midst, though "tent" could stand for Canaanite high places. The suggestion that the temple imagery in 6:19-20 is loosely linked to the story of Joseph in Genesis 39 removes the need to find an ironic reference to temple prostitution ("Don't go to the temple, you are the temple . . .") in these verses.

[82] In 6:19-20 Paul explains that the reason it is so important that one does not "sin against his own body" (6:18c) is that the body has been granted a special status by God: believers' bodies are the temple of the Holy Spirit (6:19a); their bodies belong to God (6:19b-20; see section IVB). In Chapter Three (1 Cor 5:1-13) the subject of the church as the temple of the Holy Spirit was discussed at some length in relation to 3:16-17 (see section IIIC).

[83] The critical phrases in the above translation for the notion of divine indwelling (see italics; cf. H.W. Hollander and M. De Jonge's translation in *The Testaments of the Twelve Patriarchs: A Commentary)* are obscured in H.C. Kee's translation (in *The Old Testament Pseudepigrapha,* ed. by James H. Charlesworth) which reads: "the Lord will dwell among you" (10:2) and "the Lord who dwells with him" (10:3). The Greek preposition ἐν of course permits both translations.

Genesis narrative. Genesis 39:2-3 and 39:21,23 frame the 39:7-20
narrative with the information that God was "with Joseph" and Pharaoh
describes Joseph in 41:38 as "one in whom is the spirit of God."[84]

## C. A Dishonouring Sin: "glorify God in your body"

It is also possible that Paul's thought that a believer "glorifies God"
in 1 Corinthians 6:20 when he refrains from πορνεία is reminiscent
of a comment made by Joseph in Test. Joseph 8:5. After recounting
his successful escape from Potiphar's wife (T. Jos. 8,9), Joseph reports
in 8:5: "She came and heard the report how I gave thanks to the
Lord and sang praise in the house of darkness and how I rejoiced
with cheerful voice, *glorifying* (ἐδόξαζον) *my God*" [italics mine].[85] The
Genesis Joseph narrative does not explicitly state that Joseph glorified
God by fleeing, but it does underscore that Joseph's chief motivation
in the action was not to sin against God (39:9).

## D. Conclusion

Thus with the Biblical story of Joseph in mind, the Testaments of
the Twelve Patriarchs not only warned its readers to "flee immorality"
(cf. 1 Cor 6:18a; see VA), but also noted the relevance of God's
indwelling to the state of chastity (cf. 1 Cor 6:19; see VB), and concluded
that Joseph had glorified God (cf. 1 Cor 6:20; see VC). Whereas Morna
D. Hooker has suggested that when Paul wrote Romans 1:18-32 he
had the figure of Adam in mind,[86] we are proposing that behind 1
Corinthians 6:18-20 lurks the figure of Joseph. The three parallels
(T. Reub. 5:5 / 1 Cor 6:18a; T. Jos. 10:1-3 / 1 Cor 6:19; and T.
Jos. 8:5 / 1 Cor 6:20) are surely too remarkable to be written off
as sheer coincidence. Perhaps it is best to explain them in terms of
shared traditions.[87] In other words the Testaments of the Twelve Patriarchs witnesses to a traditional interpretation of Genesis 39 which

---

[84] Cf. Acts 7:9, "And the patriarchs . . . sold Joseph into Egypt, yet God was with
him."

[85] Harm W. Hollander, *Joseph*, 37 explains that "Joseph's action here described
is the usual action of the oppressed man after his salvation: he praises and glorifies
God who has saved him from his distress." Glory is also associated with Joseph's
chastity in relation to Potiphar's wife in Test. Joseph 9:3; Test. Benjamin 4:1; Test.
Simeon 4:5 and Wisdom 10:13f which report that Joseph himself received glory (δόξα).
δοξάζω is used in Leviticus 10:3 and Psalm 49(50):23 in a manner similar to 1
Corinthians 6:20.

[86] Hooker, *From Adam to Christ*, 85.

[87] Cf. James H. Charlesworth, *The Old Testament Pseudepigrapha and the New Testament*,

also influenced Paul. However, a simpler explanation, and the one that should probably be preferred, is that Paul was directly dependent on Test. Reuben 5:5 for the ethical maxim in 1 Corinthians 6:18a, a text to which he was drawn because of the Testaments of the Twelve Patriarchs' effective use of Joseph, a stock Biblical character, in its warnings against πορνεία.

## VI. A Unique Sin: "he sins against his own body"

1 Corinthians 6:18b supplies a reason why the Corinthians ought to flee immorality; the sin of πορνεία is a unique sin in that when someone commits it, unlike other sins, εἰς τὸ ἴδιον σῶμα ἁμαρτάνει. Paul's consideration that πορνεία is in some sense an exceptional sin strikes a cord with both the teaching of the Scriptures and with Jewish moral teaching.[88] Conzelmann contends that Paul "is plainly taking his cue from a Jewish saying which describes fornication as the direst of sins (Prov 6:25ff)."[89] Whether this text from Proverbs (or another, perhaps 7:1-27) specifically influenced Paul or not, there is no doubt that Paul's attitude is consonant with the tenor of the Scriptures. The Scriptures are uniform in their condemnation of sexual immorality and replete with instruction on the subject. In Chapter Two we mentioned the widespread and explicit opposition of early Jewish paraenesis to πορνεία (see section IID3). Sexual immorality is one, if not the most, prominent sin in these texts. For example, in the Testament of the Twelve Patriarchs it is presented, according to H.C. Kee, as "the grossest sin" (cf. T. Reub. 1:6; 1:9; 3:10-4:2; 4:7,8; 5:3,4; 6:1; T. Levi 9:9; 14:6; 17:11; T. Sim 5:3; T. Iss. 4:4; 7:2; T. Jud. 11:1-5; 12:1-9; 13:5-8; 17:1-3; 18:2-6; T. Dan 5:6; cf. Sir 23:16).[90] Test. Reuben alone describes Reuben's sexual sin as an evil deed (1:8), a great lawless act (3:11), a revolting act (3:12), an impious deed (3:14) and as a disgraceful act (4:2). The tone of such appellations may have been picked up from Biblical texts such as Deuteronomy 22:21b (the

---

78: "the documents of the Pseudepigrapha are not primarily important because they are cited by the New Testament authors; they are significant because they reveal the *Zeitgeist* of early Judaism and the matrix of earliest Christianity."

[88] The Biblical/Jewish explanation for the origin of Paul's view in 6:18b renders unnecessary T.A. Burkill's unsupportable idea, 'Two into One', 117 that it arose "because of a deep seated phobia of women."

[89] Conzelmann, 112.

[90] Kee, 'The Testaments', Charlesworth I:779.

144          CHAPTER FIVE

promiscuous girl "has done a disgraceful thing;" cf. 22:14).

Whereas the opinion of Paul, the Bible and Jewish traditions concerning the gravity of the sin of πορνεία is clear, the reason Paul supplies for this opinion in 6:18 is anything but clear. Some commentators (notably Murphy-O'Connor and Moule[91]) discover another Corinthian slogan in the words "every sin a man commits is outside the body," understanding it to mean, "the body has nothing to do with sin."[92] Though not without some support,[93] finding a slogan in 6:18 is not necessary if δέ is taken as exceptive (rather than contrastive):[94] "Every sin a man commits is outside his body, (δὲ) with the exception of the immoral man who sins against his own body."

The qualification concerning sin against one's own body has been variously interpreted.[95] Is πορνεία unique for Paul here because it is an internal sin (Meyer), because it alienates one from Christ,[96] because it is a sin against the personality (Godet, Ellicott) or against the body as "for the Lord," (Fee) or is Paul simply exaggerating[97] (other sins such as drunkenness, gluttony and suicide are against the body)? One view which is suggested by the immediately preceding context (6:16-17) is that πορνεία is a unique sin in that its effects on the body are irreversible; "the relation once established by πορνεία cannot be undone."[98] It is thus a sin against the ongoing well being of the body. This position reads 6:18 in the light of 6:16a ("do you not know that he who joins himself to a harlot becomes one body [with her]"), and with Genesis 2:24 (6:16b; "the two shall become one flesh)," in mind. Sexual immorality is a sin against the body because its legacy is

---

[91] Murphy-O'Connor, 'Corinthian Slogans in 1 Corinthians 6:123-20'; Moule, *Idiom Book*, 196-97.
[92] Murphy-O'Connor, 'Corinthian Slogans', 393. Cf. *NRSV*: "Every sin that a person commits is outside the body; but the fornicator sins against the body itself."
[93] See Fee, 261-63 for a detailed evaluation of this slogan hypothesis.
[94] Cf. Fee, 262 who takes this view and translates the verse: "All other sins a man commits are outside his body, but he who sins sexually sins against his own body;" and *REB*: "Every other sin that one may commit is outside the body; but the fornicator sins against his own body." Exceptive δέ in these translations is rendered by an "other . . . but" construction.
[95] However 6:18 is to be understood, Ecclesiasticus 23:16-17 suggests that fornication was already emphatically connected with the body in Jewish teaching.
[96] Robertson/Plummer cite blasphemy against the Holy Spirit as a point of comparison.
[97] Conzelmann, 112 states: "Paul at the moment has only this one instance, fornication, in view. Whether there may also be other offences against the body is not here considered." Cf. Barrett, Calvin.
[98] Bruce, 65; cf. Lightfoot, Alford.

permanent. It is an unacceptable legacy because the believers' bodies are members of Christ (6:15), indwelt by the Spirit (6:19) and have been bought by God (6:20). This interpretation finds Paul boldly working out the implications of Genesis 2:24 as he sees them in relation to πορνεία.

## VII. CONCLUSION

The present study asserts that the Jewish Scriptures and related early Jewish moral traditions played an important role in the formation of Paul's paraenesis. In 1 Corinthians 6:12-20 this can be observed in the way Paul conceives of the sin of πορνεία as unfaithfulness to the Lord, a sin against Jewish and Christian hope, a sin against Christ, a treacherous sin, a dangerous sin, a sin against the Spirit, a dishonouring sin, and a unique sin. It can also be seen in relation to Paul's appropriation of moral interpretation of the Genesis 39 Joseph story, with respect to the indicative/imperative structure of thought which informs the entire paragraph and in the use of Genesis 2:24 (in 1 Cor 6:16). Our exegesis of the paragraph discovered a central role for the Genesis 2:24 citation. Not only does Paul use it to warn against πορνεία, by proving that sexual intercourse with a harlot is no casual affair, but with it he spotlights the spiritual marriage of the believer with Christ, a union that calls for faithfulness and purity (see section IV). And in 6:18a Paul develops the thought introduced by Genesis 2:24, that of the intended permanence of sexual relationships, to highlight the uniqueness of the sin of πορνεία (i.e., its irreversible nature; see section VI). A serious look at Genesis 2:24 in 1 Corinthians 6:16 goes a long way towards recognising the unity of thought in the surrounding verses. Paul cited the text because it was pivotal to much of his argument in the whole paragraph.

It is true that Paul gives priority to Christian motives in much of his moral teaching. However, in the light of a deeper investigation of 1 Corinthians 6:12-20 one can see that these ultimately arise out of a Scriptural background. It is an Hosea-like Paul who forbids harlotry by reminding the wayward Corinthians that the Lord is their husband and master, and a Joseph-like Paul who calls on them to flee sexual immorality.

*Interpretative  Paraphrase*
*with  Significant  Biblical/Jewish  Cross  References*

(You say) "Everything is permissible
for me"—but (I say) not everything
is profitable. "Everything is permissible for me"—but I will not be
mastered by anything (or anyone).
(You say) "Food is for the stomach
and the stomach is for food—and God
will destroy both." But the body is
not for sexual immorality[1] (as you      [1]Gen 38:24; Hos 4:11; Ecclus 41:17
surmise), but for (service of and com-
munion with) the Lord, and the Lord
is for (the sanctity and future of) the
body. After all, just as God raised the
Lord (bodily) from the dead, so he
will also raise us (in our bodies) by
his power[2] (12-14).                      [2]Dan 12:2-3; 2 Mac 7:9,14; 14:46; Bar
                                             50, 51; 2 Esd 7; T Jud 25:1-4, etc

Do I need to remind you that your
bodies are members (making up the
body) of Christ? Shall I therefore take
members away from Christ and make
them members of a prostitute? Never!
Have you not considered that the one
who cleaves[3] to a prostitute[4] is one    [3]Gen 2:24 [4]Gen 38:15,21,22; Sir 19:2; 1
body with her? For as it is written         Ki 11:2
(in the Scriptures): "The two shall
become one flesh."[3] But one who
cleaves[3] to the Lord[5] (as you have      [5]Deut 10:20; 2 Ki 18:6; Jer 13:11; Sir 2:3
done) is one spirit with him (and these
two unions are incompatible)[6] (15-17).     [6]Hos 3:1-3

"Flee sexual immorality (as Joseph
fled from Potiphar's wife)!"[7] Every sin    [7]T Reu 5:5; Gen 39:7f
a man commits is outside his own
body, with the exception of the immoral
man who sins against (the ongoing
spiritual well-being of) his own body.[3]
Do not forget that your body is the
temple of the Holy Spirit,[8] who is in      [8]T Jos 10:1-3; Gen 39:2-3, 21, 23; 41:38
you, whom you have from God, and
(do not forget) that you are not your
own.[9] For you were bought with a           [9]Ex 19:15; Deut 26:18; Is 43:21, etc
price.[9] Therefore glorify God[10] with     [10]T Jos 8:5; Gen 39:9
your body (18-20).

# CHAPTER SIX

# THE TORAH AND PAUL REGULATING MARRIAGE
# 1 CORINTHIANS 7:1-40

## I. INTRODUCTION
*"I say this . . . to secure your undivided devotion to the Lord"*

In I Corinthians 7 Paul turns from divisions (1:10-4:21) and disorder (incest, lawsuits and fornication; 5:1-6:20) in the church about which he had heard, to difficulties the Corinthians had themselves raised with him in their letter concerning marriage (cf. 7:1, Περὶ δὲ ὧν ἐγράψατε). The chapter considers a number of different groups and issues. The apostle addresses:

1. The married concerning conjugal rights (7:1-7);
2. The unmarried (τοῖς ἀγάμοις) concerning marriage (7:8-9);
3. Christian married couples (τοῖς γεγαμηκόσιν) concerning divorce (7:10-11);
4. Christians married to unbelievers (τοῖς λοιποῖς) concerning divorce (7:12-16);
5. Female virgins (τῶν παρθένων) concerning marriage (7:25-38); and
6. Widows concerning remarriage (7:39-40).

Paul's basic advice in every case is not to seek a change in status (7:2,8,10,11,12-16,26-27,37,40); the married ought not to seek divorce and the unmarried ought not to seek marriage. The guiding principle of contentment in one's life situation is taken up directly and reinforced in 7:17-24.

At first blush 1 Corinthians 7 presents a serious challenge to the thesis of the present study; perhaps more than any other section in Paul's parænesis, 1 Corinthians 7 seems to supply the clearest evidence that Paul does *not* depend upon the Scriptures when he regulates conduct in the churches. Not only does Paul fail to cite relevant Scripture in 1 Corinthians 7, he depends on an alternative source (the words of Jesus), exhibits affinity with Stoic attitudes (according to several scholars), and even departs from clear Scriptural teaching on several counts. Many who read 1 Corinthians 7 claim that unlike the Scriptures

Paul is against circumcision (7:19), forbids divorce (7:10-13) and favours singleness. Andreas Lindemann draws the obvious conclusion from such evidence: "1 Kor 7 zeigt, daß die die Ehe betreffenden Toraaussagen für Paulus faktisch bedeutungslos sind."[1] Bruce J. Malina, commenting on 1 Corinthians 7, sounds a similar note:

> Since in Paul's Jewish world, norms about sexual behaviour . . . derived from the Torah, the Old Testament, and since Paul rejects the Torah as normative for Christians, he thus rejects Torah laws about sexual behaviour.[2]

In the face of these doubts about the relevance of Scripture and Jewish tradition for Paul's instructions in 1 Corinthians 7, we shall in this chapter nevertheless attempt to rediscover Biblical/Jewish background for the main lines and details of Paul's thought. Understanding Paul aright, we shall see, will prove to be crucial in this task. The thrust of this chapter will not, however, be that Paul nowhere departs from (any text of) Scripture in 1 Corinthians 7. Rather, it will be argued that there are many points of positive contact with the Scriptures, especially the Torah, and that when Paul felt compelled to disregard certain Scripture there were specific, identifiable circumstances behind such decisions. Whereas in chapters 3-5 (on 1 Corinthians 5-6) we attempted to answer the question of Biblical/Jewish background, in this chapter a further question seeks our attention: to what extent and under what circumstances does Paul *fail to use* Scripture as his moral guide?

Rather than working through 1 Corinthians 7:1-40 verse by verse, we shall deal with the material topically, organising the investigation around the three supposed departures from Scripture already mentioned (marriage, divorce and circumcision). These three sections are headed with what many would consider to be some of the most un-Jewish and non-Biblical things that Paul ever wrote.

---

[1] Lindemann, 'Die biblischen Toragebote', 253. Cf. von Harnack, 'Das Alte Testament', 132: "Sonst werden die Ausführungen, auch die Ehefragen, ohne Hinblick aus das A.T. erörtet—ausschließlich auf die Autorität des Herrn und das erleuchtete Urteil des Apostels selbst hin."
[2] Malina, *The New Testament World: Insights From Cultural Anthropology*, 113-14.

## II. "It is a Good Thing to Remain Unmarried"
## Marriage, Singleness and Asceticism (7:1-7,8-9,25-38)

On the question of marriage and singleness Paul could not be further from the Biblical/Jewish position, according to many scholars' reading of 1 Corinthians 7. Though differing in various details, the following authors consider that Paul, contrary to the Scriptures, subscribes in 1 Corinthians 7 to a low view of marriage—Godet, Lightfoot, Findlay, Grosheide, Morris, Conzelmann, Mare, Moiser, and Phipps.[3] Such authors point out that whereas Genesis 2:18 states that "it is not good for a man to be alone", 1 Corinthians 7:1b indicates the opposite: "it is good for a man not to touch a woman."[4] Whereas in 7:6 Paul regards marriage as a concession (κατὰ συγγώμην) to the weakness of human nature (7:2), sex and marriage were seen in a consistently positive light by Judaism which developed the Biblical witness. M. Yebamoth 6:6 argues on the basis of Genesis 2:18: "No man may abstain from keeping the law 'Be fruitful and multiply,'. . . for it is written, male and female he created them'."[5]

Indeed, in the light of 7:1,6-7,9,26,32-35 and 40 Paul has even been labelled an ascetic. For example, Rudolf Bultmann judged the sentiments of 1 Corinthians 7:1-7 as in keeping with ascetic tendencies of dualism rather than the Old Testament:

> Denn hier beurteilt er die Ehe im Sinne asketischer Motive des Dualismus als etwas Minderwertiges gegenüber dem γυναικὸς μὴ ἅπτεσθαι (V.1), ja als ein unvermeidliches Übel (διὰ δὲ τὰς πορνείας V.2).[6]

Jerome concluded on the basis of 7:1b that Paul thought it *evil* to

---

[3] Moiser, 'A Reassessment of Paul's view of Marriage with Reference to 1 Cor. 7', 103-4; Phipps, '1 Cor. 7:1', 129-30.

[4] Cf. Erich Fascher on 1 Cor 7:1; "Die Verse 7,1-8; 33-35; 38-40, aber auch 29-31 zeigen, daß Paulus weder der Gesetzlichkeit des Alten Testaments noch den Sitten der Heiden, die Geschlechtslust für ganz "natürlich" halten und dafür eigene Gottheiten haben, folgen kann." Concerning 7:1 S-B iii. 367 comment: "This fundamental proposition did not correspond to the ideas of the ancient synagogue."

[5] Several of the commonly cited standard proof texts, however, are not so unqualified in their approbation of marriage as one might suppose. Tobit 8:6 should be read with 8:7, which expresses a certain reserve for marriage (marriage for sexual desire is less legitimate). B. Kiddushin 29b, "He who is twenty years old and not married spends all of his days in sin," presents marriage as a remedy for fornication. Some of the passages appealed to are actually consonant with a low view of marriage (see section C below).

[6] Bultmann, *Theologie des Neuen Testaments*, 199. See D.L. Dungan, *The Sayings of Jesus in the Churches of Paul*, 1971, who also stresses Paul's asceticism in 1 Corinthians 7.

touch a woman. Ascetic tendencies, many would say, are not only absent from the Scriptures, but also from first century mainstream Jewry, with the single exception of the Essene movement.[7] Paul's views, according to Yarborough and David L. Balch, are much akin to Stoicism, especially that exemplified by Musonius.[8] For reasons of personal preference (7:7,40), eschatological urgency (7:25-31), and pietistic devotion (7:32-38), Paul, it seems, favours singleness and not marriage in opposition to his Bible and his Jewish background.

In response to this position, which conceives of the apostle in 1 Corinthians 7 as standing starkly against his Scriptural inheritance on the questions of marriage, singleness and asceticism, we shall attempt to establish the following points, which correspond to the ensuing sections A-E:

A. Paul in 1 Corinthians 7 is not as strongly in favour of singleness as some would assume;
B. Ascetic tendencies, such as those which are present in 1 Corinthians 7, though best known and focused in the Essenes, were not restricted to that Jewish group but are also in evidence in the Scriptures and other Jewish teaching of Paul's day;
C. Though Paul does not adopt the Biblical/Jewish preference for marriage, the way he conceives of marriage in 7:1-7 is very Biblical/Jewish;
D. Paul recommends singleness partly because of extenuating circumstances in Corinth (7:25-31); and
E. His insistence on the priority of devotion to the Lord in 7:32-38 probably arises from Scripture.

## A. *Paul and Asceticism/Singleness*

That 'first impressions do not always last' proves to be the case in 1 Corinthians 7. Upon closer inspection Paul is not nearly as ascetic and disparaging of marriage as many scholars seem to think.

The statement in 7:1b, καλὸν ἀνθρώπῳ γυναικὸς μὴ ἅπτεσθαι, a starkly

---

[7] Eg. Tomson, *Paul*, 106.
[8] Yarborough, *Not Like the Gentiles*; Balch, '1 Cor 7:32-35 and Stoic Debates about Marriage'. It is not within the purview of the present study to evaluate such Stoic parallels. However, it is worth noting in passing that the Yarborough/Balch case has been seriously undermined in a recent article by Roy Bowen Ward, 'Musonius and Paul on Marriage', which takes them to task over their best piece of evidence, namely, Musonius.

ascetic maxim which prohibits all sexual intercourse,[9] is in all likelihood a quotation from the Corinthian letter to which he is responding. Since the maxim concerns sexual intercourse it would be odd for Paul to coin it himself to introduce his comments in the rest of the chapter, which largely focus on marriage.[10] The abruptness with which 7:1b appears following the mention of the Corinthian letter in 7:1a also suggests that 7:1b is a quotation.[11] New topics in the rest of the letter are introduced less abruptly, save in 6:12, which is also probably a Corinthian slogan. Paul responds to the other texts regarded by many scholars to be of Corinthian origin, 6:12-13; 8:1 and 8:4, with a qualifying statement introduced by an adversative conjunction, which is precisely what we find in 7:2.[12] Though Paul does not entirely disagree with the slogan in 7:1b (it is true for those gifted with celibacy and with respect to πορνεία), he does reject it as far as married partners are concerned in 7:2, defending a full conjugal life in 7:3-5.[13] Paul is also opposed to it as a justification for divorce or 'spiritual marriage'.

On the basis of 1 Corinthians 7:6 ("I say this as a concession, not as a command") Lindemann asserts that Paul understands sexual relations "entgegen der biblisch-jüdischen Tradition, auch nicht als ein Pflichtgebot."[14] However, the concession (κατὰ συγγνώμην) in 7:6 is not to marriage (contra Godet, Mare and Findlay who take τοῦτο in 7:6 as referring to 7:2) but to temporary sexual abstinence in marriage (τοῦτο refers to 7:2-5; see Barrett, Bruce and, most clearly, Fee). Paul permits, but does not command, the practice of refraining from intercourse for the purpose of prayer.

On this score, the textual variants γάρ and δέ in 7:7 are worth noting. The former reading ties 7:7 to 7:6, assuming that the concession there is to marriage. Though both variants have considerable manuscript support, δέ is probably original on internal grounds—δέ ("but") is more natural since it signals a change in topic from 7:2-6, where

---

[9] Fee points out that the idiom "to touch a woman" occurs nine times in Greek antiquity, ranging across six centuries and a variety of writers, and in every other instance, without ambiguity, it refers to having sexual intercourse." See Fee, '1 Corinthians 7:1 in the NIV' for details.

[10] Christian D. von Dehson, 'Sexual Relationships', 168.

[11] Fee, 276.

[12] von Dehson, 'Sexual Relationships', 168-69; J. Murphy—O'Connor, 'The Divorced Woman in 1 Cor 7:10-11', 603.

[13] J.C. Hurd, *The Origin of 1 Corinthians*, 163 claims that in the rest of 1 Corinthians 7 Paul opposes the general principle which opens the chapter.

[14] Lindemann, 'Toragebote', 249.

Paul allows abstention in marriage; in 7:7 Paul turns to the broader issue of his personal preference for celibacy.[15] It appears that the scribe in question was more ascetic than Paul at this point. Several other textual variants in 7:1-5 also appear to be attributable to ascetic elements in the early church:[16] (1) In 7:3 the Majority Text and the later Syriac versions have ὀφειλομένην εὔνοιαν ("the kindness that is her due") instead of ὀφειλήν ("duty"), removing the reference to obligation in marital sexual relations; (2) In 7:5 the same manuscripts add νηστεία καὶ τῇ ("fasting and") before προσευχῇ ("prayer"); (3) In 7:5 p⁴⁶, Ψ and the Majority Text have συνέρχησθε ("coming back together")[17] rather than ἦτε ("being together"), which carries a weaker sense.

Paul's stance was also presented as starkly ascetic in early Christian interpretation. In the Acts of Paul, for instance, sexual continence plays a dominant role in practically every episode and the injunction to sexual purity is a central focus of Paul's preaching. On the whole, unlike some of his scribes and early interpreters, in 1 Corinthians 7 Paul generally opposes the Corinthian ideal of thoroughgoing asceticism.

On the question of Paul's preference for singleness, introduced in 7:7a, it is remarkable that throughout the chapter Paul's advice is tempered and tentative. He does not give a universal command on the subject. On the contrary, Paul states from the outset that it is his personal preference and not obligatory for others. He leaves room for personal choice on the matter, qualifying his instructions with phrases such as "I am sparing you" (7:28), "I wish" (7:32), "I say this for your good" (7:35), "Let him do as he wishes" (7:36) and "he shall do well" (7:37). He clearly sanctions marriage (7:28,36), accepting it as a necessary and legitimate option for others, and refuses to call it sin: ἕκαστος ἴδιον ἔχει χάρισμα ἐκ θεοῦ (7:7b). His advice about the "virgins" (7:25-38), though not without its interpretative difficulties, may safely be summed up as: singleness is preferable but not required.[18] Paul distinguishes in 1 Corinthians 7 between "commands of the Lord," his own instructions, and his own opinion (γνώμη). His preference for singleness falls into the last category.

[15] Cf. Metzger, *Textual Commentary*, 554.

[16] Cf. Fee, 272 and Wolfgang Schrage, 'Ethische Tendenzen in der Textüberlieferung des Neuen Testaments', 384-86.

[17] Fee, 272 explains the variant as an assimilation to Paul's usage in 1 Corinthians 11:20 and 14:23.

[18] Cf. Fee, 324. Fee, 32ff., lays out clearly the many exegetical problems in this passage.

Thus in 1 Corinthians 7, alongside a presentation of straightforward teaching on marriage and divorce we find Paul stating that in his estimation the state of singleness is preferable. This judgement, rather than disclosing a wholesale rejection of the majority Jewish opinion on the advisability of marriage, may, as Tomson suggests, belong to a category of instruction understood in early Judaism as 'personal preference':

> A distinction between the halakha accepted by all and the specific behaviour of the pious was common in ancient Judaism. The Sages called such 'extra' pious deeds commandments 'beyond the strict line of the Law'. . . . Hence it appears not only that Paul shared a similar tradition in the form of his preference for celibacy but was conscious of its distinction from the accepted halakha as it applied to society at large.[19]

In Anglician Christian tradition "works of supererogation" (voluntary works over and above God's commandments), article 14 of the 39 Articles, continue this same Jewish idea.[20]

## B. *Asceticism and Paul's Scriptural Inheritance*

Is it proper then to speak of ascetic tendencies in 1 Corinthians 7? The answer is yes, as long as 'ascetic' is carefully defined to exclude dualistic connotations and is not taken to signify a coherent way of viewing the world and acting in it. There is nothing in the chapter to suggest that Paul harboured a hatred for the body, nor that he denied the goodness of creation.[21] In fact, in 1 Corinthians 10:26 Paul affirms the goodness of creation, quoting Psalm 24:1, "the earth is the Lord's and all its fulness." However, some of Paul's sentiments do fall into the category of "rigorous self discipline and austerity," which is one way the Oxford English Dictionary defines "ascetic." For example, Paul gives qualified support to the Corinthians opinion, "it is well for a man not to touch a woman" (7:1b), generally favours singleness, advocates sexual abstinence (7:5), albeit "for a season" (πρὸς καιρόν), and admires sexual self control (7:5). Even so defined, many

---

[19] Tomson, *Paul*, 124. See also Urbach, *Sages*, 330-33.

[20] E.J. Bicknell, *The Thirty-nine articles of the Church of England*, 216-17 highlights 1 Corinthians 7 in his discussion of the basis of "works of supererogation" in the New Testament.

[21] Celibacy among the Essenes was also not an evidence of a dualistic rejection of the body as evil, according to A. Steiner, 'Warum lebten die Essener asketisch'

scholars would contend that such asceticism is alien to the Jewish
Scriptures and to ancient Judaism, with the single exception of the
Essenes.

Steven K. Fraade summarises the sharply differing views of two
eminent Israeli scholars of classical Judaism, Yitzhak Fritz Baer (*Israel
among the Nations*) and Ephraim E. Urbach ('Ascesis and Suffering in
Talmudic and Midrashic Sources'; and *The Sages*, 443-48) on the
question of early Jewish asceticism.[22] Baer proposed that pre-rabbinic
Judaism was typified by an ascetic idealism that left its mark on rabbinic
law and belief. He believes that remnants of the original "ascetic Torah"
lie embedded in the Mishnah and in baraitot. Urbach, by contrast,
believes that those ascetic movements and practices which do appear
in ancient Judaism are narrow, shortlived, syncretistic and to be
understood merely as responses to specific historical events such as
the destruction of the Temple, the Hadrianic persecutions and the
failed Bar Kokhba revolt.

It is not uncommon to find treatments of Jewish asceticism in the
second Temple period which describe it as a strictly Hasidaean-Essene
phenomenon, in agreement with Urbach. Outside this pocket of
Judaism asceticism is, it is asserted, only to be found in "a few isolated
passages in pre-Talmudic writings."[23] Two early scholars who adopted
this line were K. Kohler (1903) and A.E. Suffrin (1909). "Asceticism
was not suited to the Jewish temper," sums up the opinion of these
scholars.[24] George Foot Moore wrote (1929):

> in the manifestations of Jewish piety there is no ascetic strain . . . the
> premises of an asceticism such as was in vogue in certain pagan circles
> and early took root in the Christian Church were altogether lacking.[25]

"The strangely un-Jewish character" of Essene asceticism has even
led some scholars, rather than looking to the Scriptures, to speculate
about "the influence of Pythagoreanism, where celibacy, if not required,
was at least highly esteemed."[26] The fact that E.P. Sanders' highly
influential account of Palestinian Judaism (Part I of *Paul and Palestinian*

---

and H. Hübner, 'Anthropologischer Dualismus in den Hodayoth?'.
[22] Fraade, 'Ascetical Aspects of Ancient Judaism', 258-59.
[23] A.E. Suffrin, 'Asceticism, Jewish', 98.
[24] Suffrin, 'Asceticism, Jewish', 98.
[25] Moore, *Judaism*, 2:263-66.
[26] M. Black, 'The Tradition of Hasideaen-Essene Asceticism: Its Origins and
Influence', 29. Cf. Tomson, *Paul*, 105.

*Judaism*) also subscribes to the view which marginalises Jewish asceticism suggests that it still has considerable currency.

According to Fraade, "the generally accepted and often repeated view [is] that Judaism in its early stages eschewed asceticism root and branch."[27] The view that ascetical elements in early Judaism are at best marginal, is understandable if one looks exclusively at one 'section' of Judaism, such as that represented by the Pseudepigrapha or the Rabbinic corpus. However, the widespread attestation of such teaching in almost every corner of Judaism undermines the tendency to label it exceptional. Furthermore, a number of recent scholarly advances have led a number of scholars, including Fraade, to question the standard opinion. These include the discovery of the Dead Sea Scrolls, growing interest in non-Rabbinic early Jewish literature (such as the Pseudepigrapha), and the greater willingness to view even rabbinic Judaism in its hellenistic environment.

Adolf Büchler was among the first to challenge the consensus viewpoint, responding especially to K. Kohler. He accuses Kohler of identifying "the chaste" with the Essenes "without a shadow of evidence."[28] Büchler disapproved of the application of several Jewish ascetic passages to the Essenes, thus enlarging the group of 'apparent exceptions' to the rule of the non-ascetic character of Judaism, and noted a cluster of interpretations of the Biblical characters, Noah and Moses, which endorsed ascetic practices (see below). The following catalogue of evidence for asceticism in ancient Judaism builds upon Büchler's early work.

Though best known and focused in the Essene movement, Jewish asceticism was not limited to that group. The Therapeutae of Alexandria, known from Philo's writings, ought not to be ignored. Passages in pre-Talmudic writings which attached greater sanctity to virginity and celibacy include 2 Esdras 16:44; Wisdom 3:13; Sibylline Oracles 2:48; Test. Issachar 2.[29] In spite of the strong rabbinic preference for early marriage (m. Aboth 5:21; b. Qidd. 29b-30a; b. Sanh. 76a-b; Mek. Nezikin 3:112-14; Der. Er. Rab. 2:16),[30] even within Pharisaism

---

[27] Fraade, 'Ascetical Aspects', 257.

[28] Büchler, *Types of Jewish-Palestinian Piety*, 58. William Horbury, 'Paul and Judaism', 117 recognises the significance of Büchler's work for a critique of E. P. Sanders' presentation of Judaism.

[29] Cf. Suffrin, 'Asceticism, Jewish', 98.

[30] Cf. H. McArthur, 'Celibacy in Judaism at the Time of Christian Beginnings', 166-67.

there were those who preferred the solitary life. In rabbinic literature
there are regulations for unmarried men in society (e.g., m. Qidd.
4:13-14; and Qidd. 5:10; b. Qidd. 82a) and there is evidence of some
men marrying much later than the recommended age of twenty-five
in New Testament times.[31] Of Simeon ben Azzai, the only Tannaitic
scholar mentioned as a permanent bachelor, McArthur asks plausibly:

> But is it not possible that Ben Azzai was mentioned, not as a solitary
> exception but rather as the outstanding representative of a small group
> who were to be exempted from the normal marriage obligation?[32]

McArthur also reasons that since the bulk of evidence for a stress
on marriage is rabbinic, codified in the third century at the earliest,
"the silence of Sirach and Jubilees [on the subject], as well as 2 Baruch
and the apocalypse of Ezra, at least raises the possibility that stress
on marriage was more prominent after 70 C.E. than before that time."[33]

The Biblical basis for 'a negative view' of sexual relations may be
found in moral interpretation of the characters Noah and Moses.
Büchler lists a number of rabbinic sources which depict Moses as
having given up sexual intercourse with his wife in order to maintain
sanctified readiness to receive God's revelation (cf. Exod 19:10,15):
b. Yoma 4b; Baraitha Shabbath 87a; Aboth de-Rabbi Nathan recension
I, i and ii and recension II, ii; Targum Pseudo-Jonathan on Numbers
12:8; Sifre Numbers 12:1 (99, 27a); Sifre zuta Numbers 12:1, 81ff.[34]
That Philo, *Life of Moses*, II, 68, has the same tradition suggests its
broad and early attestation.

Büchler also notes the tradition that Noah and his sons lived
separately from their wives in the ark, Noah continuing this observance
for the rest of his life.[35] On a similar line several of the patriarchs
are presented as ascetics in Philo. Suffrin summarizes the evidence:

> Enoch was removed from sinful surroundings (*de Abr*, iii, 352). Abraham's
> call was accompanied with the command to depart from temptations
> of the flesh (*de Mig. Abr* i. 437). Jacob was the true ascetic who wrestled
> until he obtained a vision of God (*de Som.* i. 643). But the greatest ascetic

---

[31] See McArthur, 'Celibacy', 177-80 and T.C.G. Thornton, 'Jewish Bachelors in
New Testament times'. Economic conditions may also have played a part.

[32] McArthur, 'Celibacy', 170.

[33] McArthur, 'Celibacy', 175.

[34] Büchler, *Types of Jewish-Palestinian Piety*, 51ff.; As McArthur, 'Celibacy', 171 states
Exodus 19 "became the basis for further elaboration of the abstinence-from-sex motif."

[35] Büchler, *Types of Jewish-Palestinian Piety*, 50-51. See also McArthur, 'Celibacy',
172.

was Moses, whom self-discipline and continence qualified for the gift of prophecy, and raised to the nearest approach to God (*Vita Mos.* ii. 145ff).

There appears to have been a section in early Judaism, broader than the Essenes, which associated ascetic practices with the idea of the spirit and holiness. In Sifre Numbers 11:26-30 when Eldad and Medad with the spirit upon them began to prophesy, Zipporah, Moses' wife, exclaimed, "woe to their wives" - presumably because she believed they would now have to go without marital relations. Likewise, in Sifre, the seventy elders in Numbers abstained from sexual intercourse for a time.[36] Other evidence of traces of sexual abstinence includes the Midrash on Psalm 146, paragraph 4, building on Exodus 19:15, which asserts that sexual intercourse will be forbidden in "the time to come," and Jubilees 50:8, which prohibits intercourse on the Sabbath. Other Talmudic restrictions on intercourse include: on the Day of Atonement, during famine and in a room containing Torah scrolls.[37]

Analogous to evidence of sexual abstinence is evidence of other kinds of austerity and self denial. In this regard the popularity of the Nazirite vow and its abstention from wine and sometimes meat may be mentioned. Fraade asserts that:

> There is ample evidence that the practice of Nazarite vows, biblically prescribed in Numbers 6, was widely undertaken in Second Temple times for various durations and for a variety of reasons: penitence, divine favor, self-discipline.[38]

The apostle himself is seen taking such a vow in Acts 18:18; 21:23-24. Likewise, fasting in the Scriptures (Lev 16:29; 23:27, etc) and Judaism was a prevalent ascetic practice.

In the Septuagint the language of the dietary laws had an inward purificatory reference somewhat akin to the idea of asceticism; נפש being translated by ψυχή. Reading such laws as Leviticus 11:43-44 in Greek one is apt to think of defiling one's own soul or psyche.[39] Test. Asher 2:7, where ethical misconduct "defiles the soul," is roughly

---

[36] See also the excursus on "prophetic celibacy" in G. Vermes, *Jesus the Jew*, 99-102.

[37] See McArther, 'Celibacy', 172-73.

[38] Fraade, 'Ascetical Aspects', 273. Cf. 1 Macc 3:47-51; Josephus Ant. 19.6.1/ 294; War 2.15.1/313; mNazir 3:6; yBer 7.2 (11b).

[39] Cf. 1 Thessalonians 4; 2 Corinthians 7:1; Horbury, '1 Thessalonians ii.3 as Rebutting the Charge of False Prophecy', 501-2.

parallel to this notion. The reference in the Damacus Document 5:11-
13 to the defilement of the human spirit demonstrates that this Jewish
tradition was not restricted to teaching in the Greek language.

O. Zöckler has observed converging ascetic interests in Stoicism,
Cynicism, and Biblical/Jewish traditions.[40] Due to the widespread
influence of the Greek schools during the Roman period "philosophy"
and "asceticism" (τὸ ἀσκητικόν, cf. Epictetus, Diss. II. xii. 6) became
virtual synonyms. Thus Philo thinks of the ascetic element when he
calls Judaism "the true philosophy." In the New Testament the Jewish
roots of Christian asceticism are especially clear at Revelation 14:4,
a text which has links with Deuteronomy 23:9-14 (cf. 1 Sam 21:5).[41]

It seems true to say that ancient Judaism had considerable ascetic
tendencies, countered by other elements in the Biblical tradition, but
able to appeal to Biblical laws and examples. These ascetic elements
were shared with the pagan world, especially Stoicism, and were
inherited by early Christians. Those who find the ascetic tendencies
in 1 Corinthians 7 wholly averse to Paul's Scriptural inheritance fail
to take into account the many Jewish sources which witness to varying
degrees of asceticism. In particular, they fail to appreciate the way
in which passages from Torah were understood by many Jews in Paul's
day.

C. *Sexual Relations in Marriage*

In 7:1-7 Paul makes several points regarding sexual relations and
marriage, almost all of which have plausible roots in his Scriptural
inheritance. Paul's notion that sexual relations within marriage[42] ought
to act as a check on immorality (τὰς πορνειας) in 7:2 is reflected in
Proverbs and in ancient Jewish literature.[43] Proverbs 5:15,18 exhorts
its male readers to find sexual fulfilment exclusively with their wives:

---

[40] Zöckler, 'Asceticism, Christian', 73-74.

[41] John Sweet, *Revelation*, 222.

[42] To "have", ἔχω, one's own wife or husband is an idiom apparently drawn from
the LXX (see Deut 28:30; 2 Chron 11:21; 1 Esd 9:12,18; Tobit 3:8 [BA]; Isa 13:16;
54:1; cf. 1 Cor 5:1; 7:2a). It does not mean "to take a wife" but to "have sexually";
Fee, 278.

[43] Cf. Holtz, 'Zur Frage', col. 390: "In der Zulassung bzw. Empfehlung der Ehe
der Unzucht wegen (7,2) ist Paulus warscheinlich vom Judentum abhängig, denn
auch dort begegnet die Anschauung, daß die Ehe vor der Unzucht schützen soll."
See also W. Schrage, 'Zur Frontstellung der paulinischen Ehebewertung in 1 Kor
7, 1-7', 228.

THE TORAH AND PAUL REGULATING MARRIAGE

Drink water from your own cistern, flowing water from your own well. . . .
Let your fountain be blessed, and rejoice in the wife of your youth,
a lovely hind, a graceful doe. Let her affection fill you at all times with
delight, be infatuated always with her love. Why should you be infatuated,
my son, with a loose woman and embrace the bosom of an adulteress?

Test. Levi 9:9,10:

Be on your guard against the spirit of promiscuity (τῆς πορνείας) . . .
therefore take for yourself a wife.

Tobit 4:12:

Beware, my son, of all immorality (πάσης πορνείας). First of all take
a wife from among the descendants of your father.

The idea that husbands and wives owe one another conjugal rights
in 7:3 can be traced to Exodus 21:10, where it is said of the husband,
"he shall not diminish her food, clothing, or her conjugal rights",
a text which Tomson demonstrates was commonly cited in early Jewish
teaching on the subject.[44] N.Herz has even suggested the direct influence
of Exodus 21:10 on 1 Corinthians 7:3.[45]

In 7:4 Paul offers a cogent explanation for his insistence in 7:3
that sexual relations are due within marriage: in marriage one's body
belongs to one's partner. The Jewish Scriptures, along with many
sources from the Graeco-Roman world,[46] advocated a property code
for sexuality that is in line with Paul's thinking here.[47] That a wife
became her husband's property in Scriptural teaching is clear from
Deuteronomy 20:5-7 and 28:30 where the acquisition of a house, a
vineyard, and a wife are routinely equated.[48] That adultery was
considered an offense against sexual property is clear from Job's
assertion that the appropriate punishment of an adulterer would be
for the offender's own wife to become the servant and sexual property

---

[44] Tomson, *Paul*, 107. To his list we may add m. Gittin 9:3, where the phrase,
"you belong to yourself," describes the status of a divorced woman and m. Kiddushin
1:1, "she acquires herself by a divorce bill or by the death of her husband."

[45] Herz, 'A Hebrew Word in Greek Disguise: 1 Cor vii.3.', takes ὀφειλομένην εὔνοιαν
to be original and suggests ingeniously that εὔνοια could even be a transliteration
of the Hebrew, עונה, found in Exodus 21:11a.

[46] See Yarborough, *Not Like the Gentiles*, 31-63 for a survey of this material.

[47] L. William Countryman, *Dirt, Greed and Sex: Sexual Ethics in the New Testament
and Their Implications for Today*, has convincingly traced the notion of sexual property
in both the Scriptures (147-67) and Paul's letters (190-220). It is odd that Countryman
fails to cite 1 Corinthians 7:4, perhaps the best evidence for his thesis in Paul's letters.

[48] Countryman, *Dirt*, 155; cf. the excuses in Luke 14:18-20.

of another (31:9-10): "If my heart has been enticed to a woman, and I have lain in wait at my neighbour's door; then let my wife grind for another and let others bow down upon her." In this light the close proximity of adultery and theft in the Decalogue makes good sense (Exod 20:14-15,17). Incest was not so much an offence against the woman as against her husband; in Leviticus 18:7-8 (cf. Deut 23:1 [22:30]; 27:20) to have intercourse with one's mother was to "uncover the father's nakedness."[49] The problem with secular prostitution in Leviticus 21:9 and Deuteronomy 22:13-21 is the wrong done to the father of the harlot's household, since being unmarried she is the property of her father.[50] Paul's description in Romans 7:2 of a married woman as ὕπανδρος, "under a man," implying the ownership of the husband, reflects the same teaching. A later rabbinic tradition which praises "him who loves his wife as his own body and honours her more than his own body" (b. Yeb. 62b) directly parallels Paul's thought in 1 Corinthians 7:4.[51] The reciprocity of Paul's statement in 7:4 is the only thing which marks it as distinctive, though even this recalls the notes of mutual ownership in the Song of Solomon (2:16a; 6:3; cf. 7:10).

An even more specific proposal for the origin of the 7:4 affirmation that the two belong to one another in total mutuality is that Paul derived it from Genesis 2:24, "the two shall become one flesh", a text he quoted in 1 Corinthians 6:16. A full quotation of Genesis 2:24 is the basis of the statement in Ephesians 5:28, "Even so men should love their wives as their own bodies; he who loves his wife loves himself," a thought quite close to 1 Corinthians 7:4. This suggests, irrespective of questions of authorship, that Genesis 2:24 may have been in Paul's mind.

Periodic abstinence from sexual intercourse for the purpose of prayer is acceded to in 7:5. Abstinence in preparation for cultic activities is attested in Exodus 19:15; Leviticus 15:18; 1 Samuel 21:4-6 (cf. 2 Sam 11:8-13; Eccl 3:5; Joel 2:16; Zech 12:12-14). In early Jewish moral teaching Test. Naphtali 8:8 is especially noteworthy: "there is a time for having intercourse with one's wife, and a time to abstain

---

[49] Countryman, *Dirt*, 160-161.
[50] Countryman, *Dirt*, 164. C.J.H. Wright, *God's people in God's Land: Family, Land and Property in Old Testament Law*, 191-221 supplies of a full and balanced discussion of the evidence for the wife's status in Old Testament law and concludes that she is regarded as "an extension of the husband himself" (221).
[51] Tomson, *Paul*, 107 also cites this parallel.

for the purpose of prayer." Tannaitic halakha also referred to such abstinence, debating the maximum period a married man may abstain for various reasons before his wife had the right to divorce.[52]

1 Enoch 69:4 and the Damascus Document IV supply precedent for the thought of 7:5b that Satan can tempt one to acts of fornication. In the Damascus Document VI:11 Belial has three nets with which to entangle and snare mankind: *fornication*, riches and pollution of the sanctuary.[53]

## D. *The Present Distress*

In 7:25-38 Paul supplies two of his main reasons for recommending singleness to the Corinthians: because of the present distress and because of the priority of devotion to the Lord (see section E below). Though he does not forbid marriage (7:28a), he favours singleness διὰ τὴν ἐνεστῶσαν ἀνάγκην (7:26); in such circumstances those who marry will have θλῖψιν δὲ τῇ σαρκι (7:28b). The critical question in the interpretation of these phrases for our purposes is, do they apply to all Christians or is "the present distress" something peculiar to Corinthian believers in the mid A.D. 50's? In other words, is Paul's bias towards singleness in 1 Corinthians 7 entirely due to theological convictions or are there extenuating circumstances in Corinth which occasioned it?

In either case, the troubles are such that Paul thinks it expedient not to get married; "when high seas are raging it is no time for changing ships."[54] Since in the absence of contraception marriage inevitably led to children, the added responsibilities of the married state would be felt more acutely in times of persecution and trouble. As Bacon observed (cited by Robertson/Plummer), "children sweeten labours, but they make misfortunes more bitter." It is this context that may well explain why Paul's discussion of marriage, unlike many contemporary Jewish ones, does not focus upon propagation.

The vast majority of commentators understand Paul to be referring in these verses to the tribulation or messianic woes which are the lot of all Christians and will herald the second advent. Many see Paul here exercising his conviction that the parousia was imminent. Indeed, ἀνάγκη is used in Luke 21:23 in such an eschatological context,

---

[52] See m. Nedarim 5:6; t. Nedarim 5:6; Tomson, *Paul*, 107; m. Kethuboth 5:6, Talbert, 39.
[53] Cf. Jubilees 7:20.
[54] Morris, 116.

Mark's eschatological discourse presents similar sentiments to 1 Corinthians 7:25ff. (esp. 13:17,20), and 1 Corinthians 7:29, with its notion of "a shortened time," suggests an End Time setting.

The view that the trouble to which Paul refers is a local Corinthian situation is, nevertheless, a not unlikely interpretation. A.L. Moore points out that the key word, ἀνάγκη, does not have an established usage in eschatological contexts.[55] While Luke 21:23 employs it, Matthew 24:21,29 and Mark 13:19 prefer θλῖψις, and Paul uses ἀνάγκη in Romans 13:5; 2 Corinthians 6:4; 9:7; 12:10; 1 Thessalonians 3:7 and 1 Corinthians 7:37 (cf. 3 Macc. 1:16) with no thought of the End Time. The relationship of 7:26 to 7:29-31, which definitely speaks of the End, is the main hurdle for this view. Moore's suggestion that τοῦτο δέ φημι in 7:29 marks a clear break[56] and supplies a new point is not entirely satisfactory since 7:26-28 and 29-31 are obviously related in some way. Paul's point is that the present distress in Corinth is *like* that of the End, which is approaching; the present woes are in some sense typical of the parousia woes.[57] In this reading the thrust of 7:26ff. is that the unusually difficult circumstances in Corinth mean that staying single is advisable.

Bruce Winter has suggested that the present ἀνάγκη being experienced in Corinth was "dislocation in the city's life caused through a series of acute grain shortages and the attendant social unrest."[58] Extant evidence for grain shortages in the East during the forties and fifties includes the testimony of Eusebius, Pliny, Suetonius and several strands of non-literary evidence.[59] Tiberius Claudius Dinippus was three times curator of the grain supply in Corinth, *curator annonae*, during this period, an office only filled in times of famine.[60] That such famine invariably caused serious social upheaval in places like Corinth is also clear from Graeco-Roman sources. Seneca, Tacitus, Apollonius of Tyana and Dio Chrysostom speak of disorder and even riots during times of chronic food shortages.[61] P. Garnsey claims that "the fear of famine rather than famine itself was enough to send people on

---

[55] Moore, *The Parousia in the New Testament*, 115-117.
[56] Cf. Héring, 57.
[57] In a comparable fashion books 3 and 4 of the Sybillines (commonly regarded as Jewish in origin) list woes and disturbances with a natural explanation and view them in a light that puts them together with the End Time (see esp. 3:175; 4:140ff).
[58] Winter, 'Secular and Christian Responses to Corinthian Famines', 93.
[59] Winter, 'Corinthian Famines', 88-91.
[60] Winter, 'Corinthian Famines', 86-87.
[61] Winter, 'Corinthian Famines', 91-94.

the rampage."[62] Paul would not have been the first to describe such a situation as an ἀνάγκη. Thucydides, III. 82:2, 85:2, uses the term to describe occasions where cities faced conditions of dire necessity, which included severe famine.

More positive comments about marriage elsewhere in Paul's letters bolster the view that 7:26ff. indicates that his views in 1 Corinthians 7 on marriage are to some extent a "refraction" of his ethics, to borrow Helmut Thielicke's term;[63] they assume "the character of a necessary emergency measure,"[64] rather than being his sober direction for all the churches. 1 Corinthians 11:11ff; 2 Corinthians 11:2; Ephesians 5; 1 Timothy 2; Titus 2 see a more positive significance to marriage.[65] Even if one regards the Pastorals and Ephesians as inauthentic, there is no reason to think that their teaching on marriage is un-Pauline. It is unlikely that later 'Paulinists' would correct their mentor on this subject since, as Fee observes, "the entire history of the early church moves in the other direction" (i.e., towards asceticism).[66]

Verses 29-31 inject another factor into the question whether to get married or not. Paul makes the point that since believers know where the world is headed, they are not to allow the world to dictate their existence. In 7:31 Paul calls into question "the outward customs and ordinances of human life," τὸ σχῆμα τοῦ κόσμου τούτου.[67] Since possessions and relationships are doomed to pass away, Christians are not to be overly absorbed in them. These verses speak not so much of eschatological urgency, as an eschatological perspective. Their primary purpose is not to supply a reason to refrain from marriage, but to put the whole question into proper proportion. The prospect of heavenly existence, takes the edge off prevailing troubles and may even enable a believer to bear the disappointment of not getting married.

The provenance of Paul's comments in 7:29-31 is a matter of some debate. Both Stoicism and Jewish apocalyptic evidence comparable

---

[62] Garnsey, *Famine and Food Supply in the Graeco-Roman World: Responses to Risk and Crisis*, 31.

[63] Thielicke, *Theological Ethics*, 380. Thielicke does not discuss this concept with reference to 1 Corinthians 7, but in connection with Martin Luther's doctrine of the two kingdoms.

[64] Thielicke, *Theological Ethics*, 380.

[65] Cf. F. Lang, 106: "Der Apostel gibt in 1 Kor 7 keine vollständige Abhandlung über die Ehe, sondern setzt sich mit schwärmerischen Asketen in Korinth auseinander, die von allen geschlechtliche Enthaltsamkeit forderten."

[66] Fee, 276.

[67] Moore, *Parousia*, 112.

degrees of aloofness seen in these verses.[68] The influence of Jeremiah
16:1-9, an isolated incidence of celibacy in the Scriptures, though
ignored by this discussion, also deserves consideration. Lucien Legrand's
study of Old Testament antecedents to New Testament teaching on
celibacy finds a link between Jeremiah 16 and 1 Corinthians 7.[69] The
following parallels may be noted:

| Jeremiah 16 | 1 Corinthians 7 |
|---|---|
| 16:2a no wife | 7:29b |
| 16:5 no mourning | 7:30a |
| 16:8 no feasting/rejoicing | 7:30b |

Differences between the two passages, however, dissuade us from
seeing too strong a connection. Whereas Paul stresses the need for
moderation and a restrained participation in the affairs of this life,
Jeremiah is totally deprived of these things.[70]

### E. *Undistracted Devotion to the Lord*

In 7:32-35 Paul explains that he prefers singleness because marriage
makes life more complex by increasing one's anxieties about the affairs
of the world, thereby distracting one's attention from devotion to Christ.
Whereas Findlay and Conzelmann (fn. 36) draw attention to parallel
sentiments in Hellenistic Philosophy (Epictetus Diss. 3.2.69), and Paul's
sentiments might also be compared those exemplified in the Mary
and Martha story in the Gospels, it is also possible to understand
7:32-35 against a Biblical and Jewish background.

The priority of pleasing God in these verses may well have been
derived from Deuteronomy 6, a prominent text in both the Scriptures
and early Jewish literature, and one which was on Paul's mind only
a few verses later in 1 Corinthians 8:6. Martin McNamara has noted
the Palestinian Targum to the Pentateuch's treatment of Deuteronomy
6 and its relevance to New Testament teaching on "the undivided
heart" (including 1 Cor 7:32-35).

> Israel was commanded to love God 'with *all her heart*' (Deut 6:5). In
> the targum full devotion to God is described as a 'perfect heart', i.e.

---

[68] See Fee and Balch, 'Stoic Debates', on Stoic parallels and Schrage, 'Die Stellung
zur Welt bei Paulus, Epiktet und in der Apokalyptik: 1 Kor 7.29-31', on Jewish
parallels.
[69] Legrand, *The Biblical Doctrine of Virginity*, 31ff.
[70] Cf. William Heth, 'Matthew's "Eunuch Saying" (19:12) and Its Relationship
to Paul's Teaching on Singleness in 1 Corinthians 7', 37.

one completely set on God, not divided between him and created things. . . . At Sinai all Israel '*answered with a perfect heart*' that they would obey God's words (Pal. Targ. Ex 19:8). Finally, in the verse preceding the command to love God with all one's heart, the twelve tribes of Jacob answered together 'with a perfect heart and said; Listen to us, Israel our father, the Lord our God is one' (Pal. Targ. Deut 6:4).[71]

Deuteronomy 6 may well have played a role in Paul's thinking as expressed in 7:32-35.

The fact that Paul derives from this priority a warning for the married and an encouragement for the unmarried is interesting in the light of Jewish acknowledgment of the tension between the ideals of the study of Torah without distraction and the fulfillment of one's duties as a husband. In several Rabbinic texts worldly preoccupations, such as a wife, are seen as a potential distraction from the central religious obligation of ancient Judaism; namely, the study of Torah. Ben Azzai's explanation as to why he interpreted Torah well, but did not perform well in obeying the command to "be fruitful and multiply" (he was celibate), was "My soul clings in love to the Torah; let the world be sustained by others."[72] As Fraade states: "the ideal of complete, ascetic, continent availability to Torah is articulated in the *aggadah*."[73] An early example is found in Aboth de-Rabbi Nathan a. 20 which includes in its warnings against distractions from the study of and devotion to Torah, אשת איש, "the wife of a man."[74] Such comments ought to be seen in the context of wisdom literature, including Proverbs and Ecclesiasticus, where following the commandments of God is like the commitment of marriage; one is encouraged to "marry" wisdom and the Law.

Paul, it seems, inherited this teaching and applies it in 7:32-35 to devotion to commandments in a Christian context, that is, devotion to Christ. It would certainly not be the first time that Christ replaces Torah in Paul's exegesis and appropriation of traditional teaching. In Romans 10:6-8 he transforms Deuteronomy 30:12-13, a text that refers to the Torah, making it instead speak of Christ. N.T. Wright

---

[71] McNamara, *Targum and Testament—Aramaic Paraphrases of the Hebrew Bible: A Light on the New Testament*, 122-23.

[72] b. Yebamoth 63b (cf. also t. Yebam. 8:7; Gen. Rab. 34:14).

[73] Fraade, 'Ascetical Aspects', 275. For the combination of abstinence and hardship with Torah study see b. 'Eruv. 54a; b. Sota 21b; Aboth de-Rabbi Nathan 11; m. Aboth 6:4; Sifre Deut. 306; Fraade, 'Ascetical Aspects', 286.

[74] This phrase could refer to either one's own wife or the wife of another, in which case the distraction would not be marriage but adultery.

finds the same substitution in operation in Colossians, arguing that the underlying view of Christ there (esp. 1:15-20) is that he has taken the position which Judaism assigned to the Jewish Law.[75]

### III. "THE WIFE SHOULD NOT SEPARATE FROM HER HUSBAND ... AND THE HUSBAND SHOULD NOT DIVORCE HIS WIFE" DIVORCE AND REMARRIAGE (7:10-11,12-16,39-40)

Paul addresses the subject of divorce three times in 1 Corinthians 7. He instructs Christian married couples (7:10-11) and Christians married to unbelievers (7:12-16) not to dissolve their marriages. Finally, in verses 39-40, the Apostle restates his position to widows: "A wife is bound to her husband as long as he lives."

#### A. *Christian Married Couples*

In 7:10-11 Paul gives an authoritative command (παραγγέλλω) to the married in the Corinthian church: "the wife should not separate (χωρίζω) from her husband ... and the husband should not divorce (ἀφίημι) his wife." That in both cases Paul is forbidding divorce is suggested by the fact that both terms were used this way in ancient legal documents[76] and confirmed by the intervening clause which indicates that "separation" here leads to being "unmarried" (ἄγαμος).[77] Though the right of divorce was restricted to men in Judaism, in Greek and Roman Law either party could divorce.[78]

In Scripture and ancient Judaism divorce was a fact of life. Though no text in the Torah institutes divorce, Deuteronomy 24:1-4, dealing with a special case, presupposes it. Charles H. Talbert lists circumstances under which divorce occurred in Paul's Bible:

> It might be caused by a second wife's pressure (Gen 21:8-14), by the wife's father (Judg 14:19-20; 15:2,6), by a wife's leaving on her own accord (Judg 19:1-3), by a man's putting his wife away (Mal 2:3-16), and by religious leaders forcing termination of marriages (Ezra 10:3,9,17,44).[79]

---

[75] Wright, *Colossians and Philemon*, 25.
[76] Cf. Liddell-Scott, *A Greek-English Lexicon*, 2016 (χωριζω), 290 (ἀφίημι).
[77] Erasmus and many Protestant commentators take χωριζω to denote merely separation.
[78] Conzelmann, ftns. 18-22; Talbert, 44-46.
[79] Talbert, 44.

In post Biblical Judaism, m. Kiddushin 1:1 explains that the legal termination of the marriage bond was effected either by a divorce bill or by the death of a spouse. Josephus (Ant. 15:259; Life 414, 416, 427) and Philo (Special Laws III, 30) likewise allowed divorce. The well-known debate over the meaning of ערות דבר in Deuteronomy 24:1 between Beit Shammai and Beit Hillel demonstrates that the majority of Jewish opinion took the existence of divorce for granted even if the grounds for divorce were debated.[80]

That Paul here prescribes Christian conduct against this tide of Scripture and early Jewish moral teaching cannot be denied. However, several points militate against concluding that Paul's decision to depart from Biblical teaching here was endemic and taken lightly. First, as Tomson puts it, "Paul cites Apostolic, Jewish-Christian tradition as his source of authority."[81] In 7:10 Paul confesses his dependence on the words of the Lord Jesus for the prohibition of divorce, alluding to the teaching that was later preserved in Mark 10:2-12/Luke 16:18.[82] This is one of the few occasions in Paul's letters that a specific reference to the teaching of Jesus is made. What prompted Paul to quote Jesus here? Presumably he knew more sayings of Jesus than he cites in his letters.[83] C.K. Barrett has offered a plausible explanation:

> If Paul knew more but selected only a few, it may be that he chose only those where the teaching of Jesus differed sharply from that prevailing in Judaism: on divorce, the school of Hillel differed from the school of Shammai, but neither agreed with Jesus, who in his absolute prohibition of divorce differed from the Old Testament (Deut. xxiv) itself. It may be that it was this disagreement with the Old Testament that led Paul to claim the Lord's authority here.[84]

That Paul cites Jesus in 7:10 perhaps betrays his reticence, rather than his willingness, to alter the clear teaching of Scripture on matters of conduct.

Secondly, even though Paul decides against *much* Scripture in prohibiting divorce his instructions nevertheless bear relation to *some* Scripture. The context of the divorce sayings of Jesus in the Gospels

---

[80] For a discussion of divorce in ancient Judaism see Tomson, *Paul*, 108-11.

[81] Tomson, *Paul*, 117.

[82] On divorce in the synoptic tradition see Tomson, *Paul*, 112-16.

[83] See M. Thompson, 'Jesus in Romans 12,1-15,13', which argues that a great many sayings of Jesus influenced Paul's ethics in Romans 12-15 though without explicit indication.

[84] Barrett, 162.

is the interpretation of the seventh commandment, which on the basis
of Genesis 2:24, a verse Paul quotes only thirteen verses previously
(1 Cor 6:16), Jesus interprets as forbidding divorce.[85] Paul may well
have thought of the words of Jesus to which he refers as having some
basis in Scripture. Furthermore, Tomson has observed that in 1
Corinthians 7:10-11, "the terminology corresponds to the distinct legal
position of man and woman in Jewish law."[86]

Thirdly, it is worth noting that the Biblical-Jewish tradition is not
completely united on permission to divorce. Jesus and Paul were not
the first to dissent on this matter. In the Torah divorce is forbidden
under certain circumstances (when a man has slandered his wife, Deut
22:19; and when a man has seduced a virgin and is forced to marry
her, Deut 22:28,29) and Malachi 2:15-16, alluding to Genesis 2:24
("Has not the Lord made them one?"), decries it ("I hate divorce,
says the Lord God of Israel"). Outright opposition to divorce can
be seen in the Qumran scrolls, and not without a (supposed) Scriptural
basis: the Damascus Document 4:19-5:5 (quoting Gen 1:27 and Deut
17:17); the Temple Scroll 57:17-19 (expounding Lev 18:18). Paul was
not alone among Jews in his day when he proscribed divorce.

B. *Mixed Marriages*

In 7:12-16 Paul deals with a problem caused by the intrusion of the
gospel (cf. Matt 10:34-36: "I did not come to bring peace but a
sword. . . . a man's enemies will be the members of his own household").
Certain marriages in Corinth had become mixed because of the
conversion of one of the partners. Perhaps the Corinthians had been
taught by Paul that to enter into such marriages is ill-advised.[87] Maybe
some Corinthians had concluded that such a marriage resulted in
unholy contamination, to hazard an obvious 'mirror reading' of 7:14.
Paul's response is to reiterate 7:10-11 concerning no divorce and to
maintain, as Fee states, "mixed marriages are essentially Christian
marriages."[88]

In verses 12 and 13 Paul instructs believers not to divorce their

---

[85] Cf. von Dehson, 'Sexual Relationships', 146: "Gen 2:24 probably stands behind
the word of the Lord in 7:10."

[86] Tomson, *Paul*, 117.

[87] Cf. the teaching of 2 Corinthians 6:14-7:1, which is perhaps based on the Biblical
prohibition of mixtures, as in Deuteronomy 22:10. Note also the Old Testament
quotations, especially Leviticus 19:19.

[88] Fee, 298.

unbelieving spouses. This advice (λέγω ἐγὼ οὐκ ὁ κύριος) is no less authoritative than that in the previous two verses where Paul's judgement rests on a word of the Lord Jesus.[89] Paul's apostolic judgements derive their ultimate authority from Jesus even when a logion is not directly involved (cf. 1 Cor 7:40; 14:37; and esp. 2 Cor 10:8; 13:10). 1 Corinthians 14:34; 15:51 show that λέγω, as in 7:12, may introduce an authoritative word.[90] Simply that one's husband or wife is an unbeliever is no grounds for a divorce in Paul's eyes.

1 Corinthians 7:14 supplies a reason (note explanatory γάρ) why partners in mixed marriages ought to stay together; the entire family is consecrated through the believing spouse. The unbelieving partner does not defile the believer but the reverse is true (contrast Hagg 2:11ff. which states that uncleanness and not holiness is transferable). It is not that the unbelieving spouse and children are made holy in the technical sense of being saved;[91] in 7:16 it is clear that the unbeliever is not saved. Rather, the presence of a believer in the family produces a 'sacred environment' in which unbelievers exist and in which there is the potential for their salvation (7:16). Gordon Fee cites Paul's analogy in Romans 11:16 as providing a precedent for such an understanding of 'holiness': "If the part of the dough offered as firstfruits is holy, then the whole batch is holy; if the root is holy, so are the branches."[92] The consecration of a part sanctifies the whole.

How Paul may have arrived at his understanding of the 'holy family' is our present concern. However, to expect a lucid explanation for what is not entirely lucid would be asking too much. Nevertheless, it is possible to tentatively suggest the tenets or presuppositions upon which Paul's view was conceivably based. In each case it is apparent that these have their basis in the Scriptures, which is hardly surprising since 7:14 revolves around Jewish ritual language. In 1 Corinthians 7:14 it is conceivable that Paul has been influenced by three Biblical currents of thought which he has channelled into his teaching; the holiness of people in God's temple; the transferability of such holiness; and the interrelatedness of families.

Both "holiness" and "uncleanness" are terms drawn from the Scriptures which were current in Second Temple Judaism with vital connections to the temple. The cultic-ritual texts claim the majority

[89] Cf. Conzelmann, ftn. 25.
[90] Findlay.
[91] See Bruce for a cogent refutation.
[92] Fee, 301.

of Old Testament references to holiness.[93] Everything which belongs
to the cult is holy. It is this priestly-cultic holiness, which was maintained
in Qumran documents, apocryphal writings and also Philo and
Josephus, rather than prophetic-ethical holiness (see Rom 6:19-22; 1
Thess 3:12; 5:23), which Paul has in mind in 1 Corinthians 7:14.[94]
That Paul maintained the association of holiness with the temple is
clear from 1 Corinthians 3:16-17 and 6:19. The 1 Corinthians 7:14
use of the concept of holiness with reference to people is quite plausibly
indebted to this tradition.

The 7:14 notion that such holiness could be transferred by contact
is also not absent from this Scriptural tradition. Exodus 29:37 and
30:29 (contrast Num 4:15,20), though admittedly not with reference
to people, witness to such a contamination.

A vital notion in any understanding of 1 Corinthians 7:14 is that
of family solidarity. The marriage, though mixed, stands together.
At this point Paul is assuredly indebted to the Scriptures which are
replete with the concept of the interrelatedness of families. A consistent
pattern in the Scriptures is that God's loving concern extends to the
whole family. See, for example, Genesis 6:18; 17:7-27; 18:19; Deuteronomy
30:19; Ps 78:1-7; 102:28; 103:17-18; 112:1-2 (cf. Acts 2:39; 16:31).[95]
Rabbinic Judaism's view of proselyte children as constituting full
members of Israel is roughly parallel (see m. Ketub. 4:3; m.Yeb. 11:2).[96]

In 7:12-14 Paul has dealt with the possibility of the believing partner
in a mixed marriage desiring separation. But what if the unbelieving
partner wishes to separate? Such a scenario is addressed in 7:15. Paul
says, if this unfortunate situation arises, let your partner leave (χωριζέσθω).
There are several ways in which the next phrase may operate in the
passage: "But God has called us in peace" (ἐν εἰρήνῃ is emphatic).
Either this calling to peace refers to staying in the marriage (in contrast
to separation in 7:15a [Lightfoot; Barrett] and/or with reference to
7:16 [Fee]) or it signifies not being overly distressed if a divorce occurs
(as in 7:15b; Robertson/Plummer, Ellicott, Godet). Or perhaps, since

---

[93] See D. Procksch, 'ἅγιος', I:89-97.

[94] See D. Procksch, 'ἅγιος', I:89-97 and H. Seebass, 'ἅγιος', II:227-28.

[95] Cf. E. Best, '1 Cor 7:14 and Cildren in the Church', 163 on family solidarity
in 1 Corinthians 7:14: "It is found in contemporary Judaism. The clearest easily
accessible example comes in Dan 6:24 where not only are Daniel's accusers thrown
into the lion's den but also their wives and children."

[96] Fee, 302. cf. Barrett, 165 on 7:14b: "He is probably dependent on Jewish usage
and conviction here. The children are within the covenant; this could not be so
if the marriage itself were unclean."

7:15c embodies a principle capable of varied application, it applies both to keeping the marriage bond in peace and allowing a determined unbelieving partner to depart in peace (see Bruce). After all, 1 Corinthians 7:15c is sandwiched between references to both separation (7:15b) and a continuing marriage (7:16). Whatever the case, Paul's statement, as Fee, Barrett and especially Daube[97] have pointed out, reflects his Jewish heritage, "which for the sake of peace did certain deeds toward the less favored, or even towards the Gentiles, with a view toward winning the favour of Judaism with them."[98]

In 7:16 Paul ends his instructions to Christians in mixed marriages on an optimistic note, with the thought that perhaps they will be the catalyst to the salvation of their unbelieving spouse (γάρ connects back to 7:12-14 [the majority of commentators] rather than 7:15 [Ellicott, Robertson/Plummer]).[99]

## C. Christian Widows

In verses 39-40 Paul makes three points on the subject of the termination of marriage and remarriage for the benefit of Christian widows in Corinth. Peter J. Tomson argues convincingly that these "three distinct halakhot" use "formulations directly related to Rabbinic halakha."[100] The weight of the evidence for this assertion is such that it would be hard to find a passage in Paul's moral teaching in which he stands closer to the Rabbis.[101] In the following discussion the three elements in question will be taken in order. As throughout the present study, we shall stress the Biblical roots of the Jewish moral traditions to which Paul's thought bears some resemblance.

In 7:39a Paul indicates that the death of a husband terminates the marriage bond, so that a widow has the right to remarry: Γυνὴ δέδεται ἐφ ὅσον χρόνον ζῇ ὁ ἀνὴρ αὐτῆς. The death of a spouse is one of the ways a woman is released from marriage in Deuteronomy 24:1-4 (the other being divorce); Deuteronomy 24:3 stipulates this provision: ". . . if the latter husband dies. . . ." The influence of this text on early

---

[97] Fee, 304-5; Barrett, 16; Daube, 'Pauline Contributions', 234-35.
[98] Fee, 305. See esp. m. Gittin 5:8-9.
[99] The phrase οἶδα plus εἰ in the LXX is most often positive in thrust, "perhaps;" Lightfoot; Barrett.
[100] Tomson, Paul, 120-22.
[101] Cf. Tomson, 120: "this rule [ie., 1 Cor 7:39] presents us with the purest formulation of halakha in First Corinthians and in the whole of Paul's writings." Cf. Strack-Billerbeck, Kommentar, 3:377.

172 CHAPTER SIX

Jewish thinking regarding marriage was considerable. M. Kiddushin 1:1d reads: "the woman acquires herself by . . . the death of her husband", the basis of which in Deuteronomy 24:3 is spelt out in y. Kiddushin 1,58d. Similarly, the Temple Scroll 57:18 states, from the husband's point of view, that "she alone shall be with him all the days of her life; but if she dies he may marry another."

In 7:39b Paul states that a widow may marry whomever she wishes: ἐὰν δὲ κοιμηθῇ ὁ ἀνήρ, ἐλευθέρα ἐστὶν ᾧ θέλει γαμηθῆναι. The literary similarities to m. Gittin 9:3, "the essential formula of a letter of divorce is, behold, you are permitted to any man; you may go and be married to any man you want," have led Tomson to suggest that Paul is using here a standard Jewish halakhic formula.[102] Whether the nature of the tradition shared by 1 Corinthians 7:39b and m. Gittin 9:3 extends to the very words or is merely conceptual, is a difficult judgment in view of the paucity of available evidence. Nevertheless, either way, it is worth recalling that though the words in question are not found in Scripture, m. Gittin is a tractate whose self-confessed task is to clarify the halakhic implications of Deuteronomy 24:1-4.

Finally, in 7:39c Paul adds a restriction to his ruling that a widow may marry whomever she wishes, μόνον ἐν κυρίῳ. Christian widows are free to marry anyone, except an unbeliever. That similar restrictive clauses were in Jewish circulation in Paul's day is suggested by two sources. First, a Bar Kokhba divorce deed (early second century A.D.) exhibits analogous specifications: ". . . you may go and be married to any Jewish man you want."[103] Secondly, around 100 A.D. the Sages discussed a halakha of Rabbi Eliezer which has at least formal similarity to 1 Corinthians 7:39a-b: "If a man divorced his wife and said: you are permitted to any man, except 'so and so'."[104] They concluded that such a clause of exclusion invalidates the divorce unless those intended are persons without legal title to marry her, such as close relatives, slaves or non-Jews; m. Gittin 9:2: "You are permitted to any man except to my father and to your father, and to my brother and to your brother, to a bondman or to *a non-Jew*, or to anyone with whom she must not contract betrothal." The exclusion of marriage to a non-Jew is, of course, analogous to Paul's exclusion of non-

---

[102] Tomson, *Paul*, 121.
[103] *Discoveries in the Judaean Desert*, 2, no. 19; see further Tomson, 'The Names Israel and Jew in Ancient Judaism and in the New Testament', 271ff.
[104] See m. Gittin 9:1; t. Gittin 7:1-5.

Christians, and has a basis in the Scriptures (Deut 7:3; Josh 23:12; Ezra 9:2ff; Neh 13:23ff; Tobit 4:12ff).

## IV. "CIRCUMCISION IS NOTHING"
### CIRCUMCISION, SLAVERY AND KEEPING THE COMMANDMENTS OF GOD (7:17-24)

In 7:17-24 Paul turns aside from his discussion of marriage to reinforce the basic principle which punctuates his advice throughout the chapter, that of contentment in one's life situation. Circumcision and slavery, two great social dividers touching the questions of race and social class, appear as examples of Paul's point. One should not be anxious to change one's situation of life when the call of God to salvation is received, no matter whether such external circumstance relate to circumcision, slavery or, by implication, marriage; "let each person remain in that condition in which he was called" (7:20; cf. 7:24).

Paul's assertion of the irrelevance of circumcision in verses 18-19 is commonly seen as alien to both the Jewish Scriptures and Judaism. That Paul no longer recognised a distinction between Jew and Gentiles (cf. Gal 3:28) is of course a major departure from Biblical and Jewish teaching. Paul's stance that "circumcision is nothing" may, as in the case of his forbidding divorce (see IIIA), be due to the overriding influence of Apostolic, Jewish-Christian tradition. In this case the Jerusalem Council (Acts 15), which decided on the question of circumcision to allow a difference in practice between Jewish and Gentile believers, may have been a factor. Unfortunately the relation of Paul to the Council and his attitude to its teaching is a subject with proportions and literature too vast for the present study. An ideal place to take up such questions would be in a study of the Biblical/ Jewish background to Paul's discussion of the problem of idol meat in 1 Corinthians 8-10.

In one sense Paul's sentiments in 7:18-19 are, despite the obvious contradiction with Genesis 17:10-14, et al, in tune with the tenor of much Biblical instruction. With the motto, ἡ περιτομὴ οὐδέν ἐστιν, which also appears in Galatians 6:16, he asserts that what pleases God is not the external sign but the internal response. Galatians 5:6 and 6:15 make this clear: what matters is not circumcision but "faith working through love" and "a new creation" (cf. Rom 2:25-29; 13:8-10; Gal 6:2; Phil 3:2; 1 Cor 9:20-23). These ideas are in effect an amplification of passages like Deuteronomy 10:16, where membership in the covenant community depends on a mark that is not outward but a matter of the heart, and Jeremiah 4:4, where the prophet calls for membership based on ethical commitment rather than physical mutilation. Other figurative uses of "circumcision" in Exodus 6:30 ("uncircumcised lips"), Jeremiah 6:10 ("uncircumcised ears"), 9:26 ("uncircumcised heart") and Leviticus 19:23 ("uncircumcised fruit of the land") also point in Paul's direction. Of course, none of these texts imply a rejection of the outward sign, which we find in Paul (for Gentile believers).

In 7:21-22 Paul takes up the issue of slavery as a second illustration of his principle of contentment. The choice of slavery as an aside in a discussion of marriage and divorce has Jewish precedent. In m. Gittin, a tractate based on Deuteronomy 24 concerning the annulment of marriages by divorce, there is also incidental reference to the manumission and emancipation of slaves (see 1:4-6; 4:4-6).

1 Corinthians 7:21 is an interpretative *crux*, because the object of the phrase μᾶλλον χρῆσαι in 7:21 is unstated. Does Paul advise slaves to make use of their freedom *by going free* or to make use of their slavery *by refusing freedom*? Those who think he meant the latter observe that the context speaks of staying in your place, not of liberation, and take μᾶλλον to mean "instead" (BAGD, 489.3). The arguments for the former interpretation are, however, more compelling. The nearest antecedent idea is freedom (ἀλλ εἰ καὶ δύνασσαι ἐλεύθερος γενέσθαι), χρῆσαι means "to take advantage of the opportunity" (1 Cor 9:12,15), suggesting a change of conditions, and μᾶλλον may denote "rather." Bartchy adds the historical argument that a manumitted slave could not in fact stay a slave in Roman culture.[105] Paul teaches that believers should be content in slavery, but if the chance to go free arises, he advises the slave to seize it.

This teaching has been compared by David Daube to a Jewish explanation of the ceremony of piercing the ear-lobe of a slave who, at the end of seven years service, instead of becoming free chooses to remain with his master, Exodus 21:5-6. He claims that the Mekilta on this passage is "strictly parallel" to 1 Corinthians 7:21-23 in that it not only recommends that slaves become free if the opportunity arises, but it cites the notion that God is the master of every Jew

---

[105] Bartchy, *First Century Slavery*, 62-120. Robertson/Plummer, Findlay, Lightfoot and Godet note that Philemon 21 shows Paul with a positive attitude to a slave gaining his freedom.

on account of the Exodus-event (the Jewish antecedent of Paul's reference to the Christ-event in 7:23a, "you were bought with a price"[106]). The Rabbis point out that the ear which is pierced in the rite is the same one with which the slave heard God proclaim: "For unto me the children of Israel are servants" (Lev 25:55).[107] Daube explains: "A Jew voluntarily continuing in slavery thereby repudiates God who, by redeeming the people from the hand of Pharaoh, became their master in a very special sense."[108] Since it is unlikely that the rabbinic tradition would be dependent on Paul here, and if the two sources are to be connected, we must suppose that both have been influenced by some early Jewish teaching on slavery.

## V. Conclusion

Andreas Lindemann regards 1 Corinthians 7 as weighty evidence that Paul's ethics bear no positive relation to the Torah:

> In kaum einem Abschnitt seiner Briefe geht der Apostel so detailliert und in geradezu kasuistischer Weise auf (individual-) ethische Probleme ein wie hier in 1 Kor 7; umso wichtiger ist die Beobachtung, daß er sich dabei an keiner Stelle auf irgendeine Aussage der Tora zu diesem Themenbereich bezieht.[109]

The results of the present investigation indicate that, though no explicit reference to the Torah occurs in the chapter, there is good reason to think that several key Torah texts were influencial either directly, or indirectly via Jewish mediation, in the formation of its teaching; namely, Genesis 2:24, Exodus 19:15; 21:10, and Deuteronomy 20:5-7 (cf. 24:5); 24:1-4. The reasons Paul may have chosen not to cite texts such as these in his paraenesis will be explored in the following chapter.

The impression that Paul's instructions in 1 Corinthians 7 largely stand within a Biblical-Jewish tradition is strengthened by noting resemblances with m. Gittin, the rabbinic tractate based upon Deuteronomy 24.

---

[106] On the relation of 1 Corinthians 7:22-23 to the Exodus see David Daube, *The Exodus Pattern in the Bible*, 46; and Howard, 'Christ our Passover: A Study of the Passover-Exodus theme in 1 Corinthians'.

[107] I could not find this explanation in Mekilta, but it is in b. Kiddushin 22b.

[108] Daube, 'Concessions', 4.

[109] Lindemann, 'Toragebote', 253.

| 1 Corinthians 7 | | m. Gittin |
|---|---|---|
| 1. 7:21-22 | - aside on slavery - | 1:4-6; 4:4-6 |
| 2. 7:12-15 | - the interests of peace - | 5:8-9 |
| 3. 7:39b | - permitted to any man - | 9:3 |
| 4. 7:39c | - any man except . . . - | 9:2 |

Such parallels urge the recognition of the Jewish milieu of Paul's instructions.

Far from disproving the thesis that Paul's ethics seldom depart from scriptural teaching, 1 Corinthians 7 turns out to be 'the exception which proves the rule'. Our study revealed that Paul's occasional failure to follow the Scriptures as his moral guide in 1 Corinthians 7 is to a large extent due to specific, identifiable circumstances. In the cases of divorce and circumcision Paul had apostolic tradition which dissented from the majority Biblical/Jewish position. As regards his advice to the Corinthians in favour of singleness, extenuating circumstances in Corinth, "the present distress," largely determined his instructions. Simply noting Biblical quotations leads one astray; the total Biblical and Jewish background must be brought into focus if one is to assess reliably Paul's indebtedness to the Scriptures. There are no quotations of Scripture in 1 Corinthians 7. Nonetheless, Paul's teaching throughout the chapter, including the 'ascetical' notes, is fully comprehensible in terms of contemporary Jewish interpretation of Torah.

# CHAPTER SEVEN

# CONCLUSION

## I. PAUL'S SCRIPTURE AND ETHICS
### *"These things were written for our instruction"*

The findings of the present study support the conclusion that the Jewish Scriptures are a crucial and formative source for Paul's ethics. The major lines of Paul's ethics in 1 Corinthians 5-7 have been reliably traced back into the Scriptures, in most cases by way of Jewish sources. In 1 Corinthians 5 a case of incest is condemned and discipline employed because of the teaching of Pentateuchal covenant and temple exclusion. In 6:1-11 going to court before unbelievers is prohibited with the Scriptures' teaching on judges in mind. In 6:12-20 going to prostitutes is opposed using the Scriptural doctrine of the Lord as the believer's husband and master, and with advice which recalls early Jewish interpretation of the Genesis 39 story of Joseph fleeing Potiphar's wife. And in 7:1-40 several key texts from the Torah (as understood by much early Jewish interpretation) inform what is said about marriage. Connections to Paul's Scriptural inheritance for most of the details of 1 Corinthians 5-7 have been suggested which corroborate an indebtedness to the Scriptures. Thus the widely held view that Paul's dependence upon the Scriptures for ethics is negligible and incidental is seriously challenged by the present study.

Three things have been achieved for each of the four soundings in Paul's ethics: (i) neglected Old Testament background has been brought to the fore; (ii) the mediation of early Jewish moral teaching has been suggested; and (iii) with these two in mind a measure of light has been shed on the exegesis of the Pauline passages in question.

This concluding chapter attempts to do four things: (i) to make some general observations which, rather than focusing on one Pauline passage, take the entire test case into view (section I); (ii) to indicate important implications the research has for the study of the New Testament (section II); (iii) to anticipate and face the major objections to our thesis of critical Scriptural dependence in Paul's ethics (section III); and (iv) to explore whether or not Paul's dependence upon the Scriptures for ethics was deliberate (section IV).

Some general observations concerning Paul's dependence upon the Scriptures for ethics in 1 Corinthians 5-7 may now be made. First, it must be said that though Paul's use of Scripture for ethics is both extensive and impressive, it is not slavish. To underscore the employment of traditional materials is not, of course, to play down the creative originality and intellectual power of the apostle Paul. We do not charge Paul with plagiarism by speaking of sources for his ethics. It is Paul's saturation with Scripture which guides him in the shape and content of his ethical instruction, but which also leaves him free to be genuinely creative. Every section of 1 Corinthians 5-7 is in large measure unique. The edifice of instructions that Paul builds to instruct the Corinthians is Paul's indeed, but, to a large extent, the building blocks which he employed are drawn from his Bible.

Secondly, Paul seems to share the general Jewish view of the time that the Pentateuch is the fundamental Biblical text.[1] Whereas in 1 Corinthians 5 he could have cited Ezra, he quotes Deuteronomy. 1 Corinthians 6:1-6 recalls Moses, rather than Jehoshaphat or David, appointing judges. In 6:12-20 he quotes Genesis and not Hosea. Likewise, in 7:1-40 several Torah texts play an important role in the formation of the instruction.

Thirdly, when Paul regulates conduct in the churches, he is dependent on the Scriptures in general and on Deuteronomy, it appears, in particular. We have already mentioned the indebtedness of Paul's ethics to Leviticus 18-20 (see Chapter Two, section IVB). In the specific case of 1 Corinthians 5-7 at a remarkable number of points there are evident links with Deuteronomy:

| 1 Corinthians | Deuteronomy |
|---|---|
| 5:1 | 22:30; 27:20 |
| 5:5 | 23:1-8 (2-9) |
| 5:6 | 16:4 |
| 5:7-8 | 4:20 |
| 5:13b | 17:7, etc |
| 6:1-6 | 1:9-18; 25:1 |
| 6:5b | 1:16 |
| 6:12-20 | 23:17-18 |
| 7:39-40 | 24:1-4 |

---

[1] This is seen especially vividly in Philo, who almost invariably quotes from the Pentateuch only. The prominence of the Pentateuch continues in the Church Fathers:— on the basis of citations and allusions to the Old Testament, E. Junod, 'La formation

Apparently, Paul dealt with Corinthian problems in the light of Deuteronomic legislation. The fact that he quotes Deuteronomy eleven times (in the four main epistles), including 25:4 in 1 Corinthians 9:9, supports this observation.[2]

Our second and third observations, which stress Paul's dependence upon the Torah, contrast with the impression one gets from simply noting Old Testament quotations in Paul's ethics. Allen Verhey, for example, concludes on the basis of explicit citations that "in contexts of moral exhortation . . . [Paul] cited the Prophets and Wisdom more often than the Torah, and when he did appeal to the Torah it was more often to narratives than to statutes."[3]

Fourthly, both Paul's view of Christ and his view of the church are fundamental to his appropriation of Scripture for ethics. It is often suggested that Paul's hermeneutic is christocentric.[4] 1 Corinthians 6:12-20 is rightly held up as a prime example. We need to note the presence of a stress on the identity of the church in Paul's use of Scripture as a basis for ethics, alongside the usual christological motif.[5] In 1 Corinthians it is Paul's understanding of the community of the church, as well as his doctrine of Christ, which informs his handling of Scripture. Three examples bear consideration. In 1 Corinthians 5, Paul's view of the church as a sanctified covenant community facilitates his reading of Deuteronomy. In chapter nine, Christians are the recipients of Torah (9:10), and in chapter ten they áre those who learn from Israel's mistakes (10:6,11; cf. 10:1, "*our* fathers"). Thus Paul's doctrines of the church and Scripture go hand in hand.

Finally, though our study focused on only three chapters in 1 Corinthians, there are indications that the results are indicative of Paul's ethics in general.[6] Subjects dealt with in the study which have relevance to other parts of Paul's ethics include the indicative/imperative structure of thought, the good reputation before outsiders theme, the motif of righteous suffering and the vice of sexual immorality.

---

et la composition de l'Ancien Testament dans l'Église grecque des quatres premiers siècles' 109 has observed that the Pentateuch, Prophets and Psalms constituted the books to which reference was most frequently made in second century Christian literature.

[2] According to Moody Smith's count, "Pauline Literature", 268-71.

[3] Verhey, 'Ethics: NT Ethics' 2:179.

[4] Eg. Longenecker, *Exegesis*, 104 argues that "Paul understood the Old Testament Christocentrically."

[5] Cf. Hayes, *Echoes*, 86, 123, 162, 168, 177, 184 on Pauline ecclesiocentric hermeneutics.

[6] In Chapter One, section IIIE, we argued that 1 Corinthians 5-7 is a representative sample from Paul's ethics.

Furthermore, we also found it expedient to affirm the Biblical/Jewish roots of Paul's teaching elsewhere, including Romans 13 (Excursus 2, Chapter Four), Romans 1 (Chapter Two, section IVB) and 1 Corinthians 10:22b (Appendix).

## II. IMPLICATIONS OF THE PRESENT STUDY

There are important implications for the study of Christian origins as well for the interpretation of the New Testament arising from the present study. We have shown that Paul the Christian owes much more to his Jewish environment than has often been supposed, and that Pauline churches, for all their distinctiveness, appear historically as part of the broad spectrum of movements in ancient Judaism. On the side of interpretation, the Pauline writings turn out to be integrally related to the Scriptures regarded by Jews as normative, and not simply as documents brought into an artificial relation with the Old Testament by the later Christian Church.

Our investigation bears on the task of understanding Paul as a thinker. Scholars attempting to 'explain' Paul's thought fall into two groups. One group emphasises Paul's *context*, often appealing to the influence of Hellenism, and other factors external to his letters. A second group stresses Paul's *personal experience and religious heritage*, especially his Jewish training and indebtedness to the Scriptures. The results of our investigation side with the second group, advocating a 'paradigm shift' for many students of Paul. In stressing the Jewishness of Paul our study strikes a chord with some recent substantial work on the apostle, his theology and his ethics, such as, P. Tomson, *Paul and the Jewish Law*; M. Hengel, *The Pre-Christian Paul*; K.-W. Niebuhr, *Heidenapostel aus Israel: Die jüdische Identität des Paulus nach ihrer Darstellung in seinen Briefen*; and F. Thielman, *From Plight to Solution*.

The present study could be classified as a study in Paul's ethics, as an investigation of the use of the Old Testament in the New Testament, or even as research on Paul and the Law. Viewed from these three angles it has something to say to many practitioners of New Testament studies.

To those who study the *ethical portions of Paul's letters* (and of any other New Testament author), the study urges that the possible influence of Scripture and early Jewish moral teaching ought not to be ignored. When studied against this background, several obscure features of 1

Corinthians 5-7 received fresh treatment, such as the motives for the expulsion in 5:1-13, a grammatical irregularity in 6:5b, and the origin of 6:18a. Our study delivers a warning to traditio-historical studies of New Testament ethics which trace the ideas only back as far as the literature of second Temple Judaism and not all the way to the Scriptures.[7] These may be missing the crucial stage. The significance of many portions of the Pauline parænesis can only be appreciated by taking full account of Old Testament background *as well as* the conceptual development of Old Testament ideas in early Jewish paræ-nesis (see Chapter Two). This commonly-held conviction for many areas of New Testament doctrine (such as christology) must now be extended to Pauline (and New Testament) ethics.

Future studies of *the use of the Old Testament in the New Testament* might consider the distinction adopted in this study between the use of Scripture for doctrine and for ethics. The use of Scripture for ethics may occasion a qualitatively different use of Scripture. The circumstances under which Paul does and does not quote Scripture calls for further investigation. Such studies would do well in future to include in their considerations not only quotations of Scripture but also less explicit levels of Scriptural usage. Furthermore, the mediating role of Jewish exegetical and interpretative traditions must not be ignored (see chapter two). The task is to listen for "echoes of interpreted Scripture."[8]

The present study redresses the tendency to over-emphasise the negative function of *the Law in Paul's thought* (see chapter one, section I). Many commonly-held and cherished views of Paul and the Law will have difficulty explaining the results of our research, especially the considerable evidence of Paul's indebtedness to the Torah for moral teaching.

## III. Eight Objections

In Chapter One we rehearsed eight arguments which purportedly cast doubt on the view that the Scriptures are an important source for Paul's ethics (section I). We must now re-examine these arguments in the light of the conclusions reached in the present study. None

---

[7] The Scriptures were in one sense also intertestamental literature—not written, but widely read in that period.

[8] Craig A. Evans, *Paul and the Scriptures of Israel*, 47.

of the eight reasons, upon closer investigation, is sufficiently compelling to undermine fundamentally our thesis of critical Scriptural dependence in Paul's ethics. Many scholars doubt the importance of the Scriptures for Paul's ethics because:

1. *Paul makes some very negative statements about the Law of Moses.* However, it does not necessarily follow from these statements that the Law is therefore irrelevant for determining Christian conduct. There are several ways of understanding Paul's 'negative' statements about the Law which do not rule out the Law's ongoing validity in large measure for believers in Christ. There is a sense in which the Law as Mosaic covenant is abolished, but the Law as revealing God's will, the Law as Scripture, has ongoing value for Christians. Alternatively, Paul is opposed to the Law when it is usurped into the sphere of sin, the flesh and death, and approves of it in its proper sphere—that of faith, the Spirit and Christ.[9] We could go on to mention other possible distinctions which allow *both* the 'negative' statements about the Law *and* a proper use of the Law by believers to stand in Paul's thought.[10] Although at points Paul may be seen as against the Law, this does not mean that he has no time for the ethics of the Law.

2. *Paul openly abrogates some parts of Scripture.* That Paul regarded some customs prescribed in the Law of Moses as not binding on Christians, such as the laws concerning circumcision, food, festival days and the Sabbath, cannot be denied. However, this opposition is readily explained in terms of Paul's mission. The laws which Paul does not follow are those which restrict the people of God to the Jews by signifying distinctions between Jews and Gentiles.[11] In Paul's mind, the Christ-

---

[9] See Snodgrass, 'Spheres of Influence'.

[10] Scholars who, from a variety of angles, believe that for Paul the Law is in large part valid for believers include C.E.B. Cranfield, *Romans*, esp. II:845-62; George E. Howard, 'Christ the End of the Law: The Meaning of Romans 10:4ff.', and *Paul: Crisis in Galatia*; C. Thomas Rhyne, *The Law*; Robert Badenas, *The Law*; Ragnar Bring, *Christus und das Gesetz: Die Bedeutung des Gesetzes des Alten Testaments nach Paulus und sein Glauben an Christus*; Hans Conzelmann, *An Outline of the Theology of the New Testament*; Richard Longenecker, *Paul: Apostle of Liberty*; George Eldon Ladd, 'Paul and the Law'; and Thomas R. Schreiner, 'The Abolition and Fulfillment of the Law in Paul'; Klyne Snodgrass, 'Spheres of Influence'.

[11] See J.D.G. Dunn, 'Works of the Law and the Curse of the Law (Galatians 4:10-14)', and *Romans* (2 vols); H. Räisänen, *Paul and the Law*, 162-77; E.P. Sanders, *Paul, the Law and the Jewish People*, 17-64, J.M.G. Barclay, *Obeying the Truth: A Study of Paul's Ethics in Galatians*, 82; F. Watson, *Paul, Judaism and the Gentiles: A Sociological Approach*, 63-72 and 132-42.

event, especially the cross, made salvation available to all people—Jews and Gentiles—by faith. Even when Paul emphasised this position in Romans and Galatians he was anxious to assert that the Law as a whole still played a role. The Law continues to matter for Paul and is respected by him. All that can be safely concluded from his 'opposition' to the identity markers of the Mosaic covenant is that the literal application of *certain* laws of Torah was not regarded by Paul as universally binding.

*3. Paul's use of Scripture in moral contexts is haphazard and his exegesis atomistic, corresponding to a widespread characterisation of early Jewish exegesis.* Whether or not Paul's exegesis of the Old Testament texts which he cites in his paraenesis is flippantly non-contextual, betraying less than a serious regard for the Old Testament as a moral guide, is open to question. An evaluation of all the Old Testament exegesis in Paul's paraenesis is beyond the scope of this concluding chapter. However, if Paul's use of the Deuteronomic expulsion formula in 1 Corinthians 5:13 and his use of Genesis 2:24 in 6:16 have relevance in this context, it would seem that he treated the Scriptures' direction on moral questions with the highest regard (see chapters three and five of the present study respectively).

The question of Jewish precedent for Paul's supposed indiscriminate exegesis is also a matter for debate. David Instone Brewer recently surveyed the exegeses preserved in rabbinic literature which are likely to have originated before A.D. 70, and analysed them with regard to their exegetical techniques and assumptions. The results of his study demonstrate that to portray the predecessors of the rabbis, Paul's contemporaries, as extravagant and ingenious in their handling of Scripture is simply inaccurate:

> [they] did not interpret Scripture out of context, did not look for any meaning in Scripture other than the plain sense, and did not change the text to fit their interpretation, though the later rabbis did all these things.[12]

*4. Paul's churches are predominantly Gentile.* In the case of the Corinthian church at least, there is evidence that the Scriptures formed a large part of Paul's face to face instruction. 1 Corinthians assumes a good deal of Old Testament knowledge which Paul presumably imparted to the Corinthian believers in person. Understanding 5:6-8 requires

---

[12] Instone Brewer, Techniques and Assumptions in Jewish Exegesis before 70 CE, 1.

some knowledge of Passover and Unleavened Bread, comprehending
15:20 requires a familiarity with the concept of "first fruits" (Exod
23:16,19a; Lev 23:10-14; Num 18:8-13; Deut 18:4; 26:2,10; 2 Chron
31:5; Neh 10:37), and to grasp properly some terms in 2:6-9 an
acquaintance with Jewish apocalyptic/wisdom traditions is necessary.[13]
Furthermore, 16:2 mentions the Sabbath and 16:8 Pentecost, both
without explanation. It appears that Paul assumed that his readers
shared his culture and so recognised something of the Jewish nature
of his teaching and its Biblical background.[14] It is worth remembering
that Gentile adherence to Judaism in the first century was reasonably
widespread, the "Godfearers" phenomenon probably being only the
tip of the iceberg.

Ten times Paul rebukes the Corinthians for their ignorance or, more
likely, forgetfulness: οὐκ οἴδατε. Several commentators believe that what
Paul wants the Corinthians to "know" probably formed part of his
original oral teaching to them.[15] It is significant that in nine of these
instances, it is knowledge that is either found in or derivable from
the Scriptures that Paul wants the Corinthians to recall. Far from
tolerating Gentile lack of Biblical knowledge, Paul puts part of the
blame for Corinthian misconduct on their ignorance of the Scriptures!

| οὐκ οἴδατε ὅτι . . . | *Scriptural Source* |
|---|---|
| (1) 3:16 - "you are God's temple and God's Spirit dwells in you" | Exod 25:8; Pesh Jer. 7:9; etc (see ch. 3, IIIC) |
| (2) 5:6 - "a little leaven leavens the whole lump" | 5:7-8 demonstrate that this thought is connected to Exod 12:14-20; Deut 16:4 |
| (3) 6:2 - "the saints will judge the world" | Dan 7:22 (see ch. 4, IIE) |
| (4) 6:3 - "we shall judge angels" | derivable from Dan 7:22 (see ch. 4, IIE) |
| (5) 6:9 - "the unrighteous will not inherit kingdom of God" | Dan 7:9-14, etc |

[13] See R. Scroggs, 'Paul: Σοφός and Πνευματικός'.
[14] If one takes Acts as a starting point, then it is very likely that the audience
of 1 Corinthians was familiar with the Synagogue culture.
[15] Eg. Barrett, 90 comments on the phrase: "it is implied that they ought to know,
perhaps Paul himself had told them"; I.H. Marshall, 'Church and Temple in the
New Testament', 213 on 6:19: "the way in which Paul says 'don't you know?' may
well imply that he thought he was reminding his readers of teaching with which
they were already familiar; it could have formed part of his earlier oral teaching
to them." Cf. Hodge, 94.

| | |
|---|---|
| *(6)* 6:15 - "your bodies are members of Christ" | cf. notion of corporate personality/solidarity (see ch. 3, IIB, IIIB)[16] |
| *(7)* 6:16a - "the one who cleaves to a prostitute is one body with her" | derived from Gen 2:24 (see ch. 5, VI) |
| *(8)* 6:19 - "your body is a temple of the Holy Spirit" | Gen 39:2-3,21,23; 41:38; T. Jos. 10:1-3 (see ch. 5, VB) |
| *(9)* 9:13 - "those who work in the temple get their food from the temple, and those who serve at the altar share in what is offered on the altar" | Lev 7:6,15; Deut 18:1-4, etc |
| *(10)* 9:24 - "in a race all the runners run, but only one gets the prize" | No Scriptural Source[17] |

*5. 2 Timothy 3:16-17, the clearest affirmation of the significance of Scripture for ethics in the traditional Pauline corpus, is in the Pastoral Epistles, the theology of which is considered by many scholars to be post- if not un-Pauline.* Whereas 2 Timothy 3:16-17 may be the fullest statement of a positive attitude to the relevance of the Scriptures to questions of conduct, it is certainly not the only indication in the Pauline corpus. Though not commonly brought to notice, Paul makes some very positive statements about the Law of Moses and the Jewish Scriptures in 1 Corinthians and Romans. We shall save a discussion of these texts until section IV. Read in this light we find that 2 Timothy 3:16-17 to be, in fact, a fair summary of Paul's attitude to the Scriptures.

*6. Sources other than Scripture seem to exert a greater influence on Paul's ethics.* Several considerations point towards regarding the Scriptures as *fundamental* for Paul's ethics. First, as we argued in Chapter One (IIIA), the Scriptures have theoretical priority as a source for Paul since he was a Jew, used Scripture for ethics explicitly on occasion, and claimed to have found it instructive. Secondly, with the Scriptures in view we have been able to account (with varying degrees of certainty) for the greater part of our representative sample of his ethics, 1 Corinthians 5-7. Thirdly, we have on occasion been able to show that the

[16] Cf. also J.W. Rogerson, 'The Hebrew Conception of Corporate Personality: A Re-examination'.
[17] The tenth occurrence of οὐκ οἴδατε is not only exceptional in that it possesses no Scriptural source—it is also not so much a rebuke, as in the other nine uses, as an attempt to make the Corinthians' recollection of common knowledge vivid.

evidence for Scriptural dependence is not only plentiful but distinctive. For example, phrases in 1 Corinthians 6:5 (see Chapter Four, IIA) and 6:18 (see Chapter Five, VA) only occur in Biblical/Jewish material prior to Paul, and reading Matthew 18 alongside 1 Corinthians 5 (see Chapter Three, VI) confirmed the significance of Pentateuchal teaching on exclusion with respect to Paul's instructions. Fourthly, we found evidence where Paul and Biblical/Jewish ethics stand against prevailing Græco-Roman attitudes, namely on the question of prostitution (see Chapter Five, I). Fifthly, the words of Jesus ought not to be taken too quickly to be a rival source to Scripture, since in some cases the Jesus-tradition may operate as an intermediary stage between Scripture and Paul. Much of Jesus' teaching is simply an elaboration of Scripture. Finally, many of the hellenistic elements in Paul's letters may have come to him through Jewish sources. The overlap between Pauline and Græco-Roman morality is undoubted. What we wish to stress is the somewhat neglected likelihood that Paul received Greek ethical teaching largely through the connection with the Scriptures that they had already been given in Jewish morality. When Paul appears to be hellenistic, he may in fact be 'Jewish-hellenistic'. Taken together, these considerations suggest that, when Paul came to regulate conduct in the early churches, his most frequent recourse was to his knowledge of the Jewish Scriptures rather than what he may have known of teaching like that of Musonius or Epictetus or even an (early version of) the gospels.

That Paul drew upon sources other than the Scriptures is undeniable.[18] We do not doubt that Paul made use of what he found to be true and profitable in paganism and philosophy, in the style of his Acts 17 portrayal (cf. Phil 4:8). Our point is that Paul's ethics are primarily a development of the religion of Israel, not pagan religion. Likewise, that Paul was familiar with some Jesus-tradition and esteemed it highly is a given. However, our findings suggest that, nonetheless, Paul's debt to the Scriptures as understood in his day for ethics is much greater than has often been supposed.

---

[18] On Jesus-tradition in 1 Corinthians see C.M. Tuckett, '1 Corinthians and Q'; and D.C. Allison, 'The Pauline Epistles and the Synoptic Gospels'. On cultures (other than Jewish) which may have influenced the New Testament authors and writings see Charlesworth, *The Old Testament Pseudepigrapha and the New Testament*, viii-ix. A. Malherbe, 'Paul: Hellenistic Philosopher or Christian Pastor?', contends that the influence of hellenistic philosophy on Paul is more in the manner of his ministry than in the central issues of his thinking.

Our major argument with scholars who judge Scripture to have played only a minor role in Paul's ethics primarily concerns method. Too many studies merely count Scriptural citations and ignore indirect dependence upon Scripture via Jewish mediation (see Chapter Two). This approach invariably underestimates Paul's dependence upon the Scriptures. It is not surprising that what we have seen (manifold links with Paul's Scriptural inheritance), others have missed; many studies have not looked hard enough (beyond Biblical quotations to Biblical allusions, motifs, ideas, etc.) and have not looked in the right places (at Jewish as well as Biblical sources).

7. *Factors other than Scripture appear to shape Paul's advice concerning conduct.* Five factors are commonly cited. As with the words of Jesus and the non-Jewish ethics of Paul's day, one cannot deny a place for these factors in the formation of Paul's ethics. However, their influence worked together with, not instead of, the Scriptures.

It is important not to ignore the prior influence of the Scriptures with regard to the role of *eschatology* and *love* in Paul's thought. Paul's perspective on the End Times undeniably works with Biblical ideas that have undergone a development in apocalyptic Judaism.[19] Furthermore, the apostle confesses the source of his love ethic in Romans 13:8-10, namely Leviticus 19:18, which was an acceptable Jewish summary of the Law.

The importance of *social conditions* is difficult to assess without further extensive research. However, this factor does not necessarily displace the Scriptures. A full account of the complex phenomena of Paul's ethics recognises the interplay between a variety of factors. Our perspective is that often Paul responded to concrete, social situations with relevant Scripture in mind.

The fourth and fifth factors are also not rivals to Scripture. To pit *the Spirit* against Scripture, as if Paul saw the two as mutually exclusive approaches to ethics, is highly questionable. Thomas R. Schreiner contends:

> There is no evidence in Paul that the Spirit apart from the external word provides the norm from within the Christian. Rather, there is

---

[19] See Ellis, 'Biblical Interpretation', 710-13 on the similarities and differences between New Testament and Biblical/Jewish eschatology.

no necessary polarity between life in the Spirit and external demands. The Spirit and the Word work in harmony for Paul (Gal. 3,2; Rom. 10.16-17).[20]

It is a gross over-simplification to observe the many 'Christian' motives in Paul's parænesis and conclude that he based his ethics on *the gospel* as opposed to Scripture. Our research has shown that both generally (see Excursus 1, Chapter Three) and in specific cases Paul and the Scriptures reflect the same indicative-imperative structure of thought. For the main examples in 1 Corinthians 5-7 we advanced specific Biblical/Jewish parallels. Pauline law/gospel conflict is not in fact about ethics, but about salvation; when Paul says hard things about the Law (see III.1), therefore, he does not mean that its ethical precepts are of no value. There may be some validity to the Lutheran law/gospel distinction,[21] but it has become the proverbial procrustean bed when used to rule out Paul's dependence upon the Scriptures in his ethical teaching.

*8. There are relatively few Scriptural quotations in Paul's ethics.* Even though, as we pointed out in Chapter One (section I), there is a paucity of Biblical citations in Paul's ethics as compared to Paul's doctrine, the numerous occasions where Paul does quote Scripture to express or support a moral admonition ought to be recognised, as by Koch, Ellis and Verhey, as a sizeable element in his use of Scripture.[22]

*Scriptural Citations in Pauline Ethics*

| | |
|---|---|
| Proverbs 25:21-22 | Romans 12:20 |
| Leviticus 19:18 | Rom 13:9 & Gal 5:14 |
| Exodus 20:13-15, 17; | } Rom 13:9 |
| Deut 5:17-19, 21 | } Rom 13:9 |
| Isaiah 49:13; 45:23 | Romans 14:11 |
| Jeremiah 9:23-24 | 1 Cor 1:31 & 2 Cor 10:17 |
| Deuteronomy 17:7, etc | 1 Corinthians 5:13 |
| Genesis 2:24 | 1 Corinthians 6:16 |
| Deuteronomy 25:4 | 1 Cor 9:9 and 1 Tim 5:18 |

---

[20] Schreiner, 'Abolition and Fulfillment of the Law', 54. Cf. T.J. Deidun, *New Covenant Morality*, 175-83.
[21] See Westerholm, *Israel's Law and the Church's Faith*, for a full and informed defence.
[22] Koch, *Die Schrift*, 296-98; Ellis, *Paul's Use*, 125; Verhey, *The Great Reversal* (cf. 110: "Paul frequently cites the Jewish Scriptures in contexts of moral admonition").

| | |
|---|---|
| Psalm 24:1 | 1 Corinthians 10:26 |
| Isaiah 52:11-12 | 2 Corinthians 6:17 |
| Exodus 16:18 | 2 Corinthians 8:15 |
| Psalm 112:9 | 2 Corinthians 9:9 |
| Exod 20:12 & Deut 5:16 | Ephesians 6:2-3 |

The topics covered by these citations touch upon the main themes of Paul's paraenesis, including personal vengeance, boasting, giving, financial support, sexual immorality, obedience to parents, eating food sacrificed to idols, and sanctification in general. It is data of this kind that forces C.K. Barrett to arrive at the opposite conclusion to Hanson (see quotation, Chapter One, I):

> There is in the New Testament far more halakic development, far more moral and disciplinary regulation, than is sometimes recognised, and much (though not all) of this is explicitly founded on Old Testament passages.[23]

However, quotations are only a reliable measure of the most explicit level of usage. To accurately diagnose the extent to which Paul's ethics is 'infected' with Scripture, it is not enough just to note the most obvious symptom (explicit citation). Four observations arising out of our research warn against assuming that counting quotes is a reliable method for assessing Paul's dependence upon the Scriptures and concluding that Scripture is not a crucial and formative source for Paul's ethics.

First, there are examples in Paul's ethics in which he has been profoundly influenced by the Scriptures, but has not quoted them at all. There are no quotations in 1 Corinthians 6:1-11 or 7:1-40, yet in both cases Scripture is nevertheless an elemental source.

Secondly, when Scripture is quoted in Paul's ethics, it is often at the heart, rather than being on the fringes, of his argument. For example, the Deuteronomic expulsion formula in 1 Corinthians 5:13b is the veritable 'tip of an iceberg' of Scriptural usage, pointing to Paul's use of the laws of Deuteronomy concerning covenant exclusion in 1 Corinthians 5. And in 1 Corinthians 6:12-20, Paul's exhortation concerning harlotry is in part a creative teasing out of the implications of Genesis 2:24 which he quotes in 6:16.

Thirdly, there is a precedent in Paul's day for texts of an ethical

---

[23] Barrett, 'The Interpretation of the Old Testament in the New', 399.

character to use Scripture broadly without quoting it often. A parcel
of texts which could be described as Jewish moral teaching of the
first century and earlier, which form some kind of background for
Paul's ethics (see Chapter Two), evidence an intricate and unmistaka-
ble relation to the Scriptures without many direct citations of Scripture.
This material expresses the moral demands of Torah, yet Karl-Wilhelm
Niebuhr found only one exact LXX citation in his survey of over
forty texts (Exod 20:17 in 4 Macc. 2:5).[24] In Paul's case the genre
of his ethical instruction means that he had no need to appeal to
Scriptural authority. His authority "to build up and tear down" rested
in his Christ-given apostolic office (2 Cor 13:10; cf. 10:8; 1 Cor 9:1).
The Corinthians were wont to obey Paul's instructions not because
they were explicitly tied to Scripture, but because he had "the Spirit
of God" (1 Cor 7:40). Paul told the Corinthians that what matters
most is "keeping the commandments of God," which is how he
described his own instruction in 1 Corinthians 14:37 ("what I am
writing to you is a command of the Lord").[25]

Fourthly, since Paul's use of Scripture may in part have been
mediated to him by early Jewish parænesis, this indirect dependence
upon Scripture cannot be recognized in his ethics simply by noting
quotations of Scripture, since its influence is more subtle and diffuse
(see Chapter Two).

We are contending that there is a better explanation for the dispro-
portionate number of quotations of Scripture in the doctrinal as opposed
to the ethical sections of Paul's epistles than supposing it betrays Paul's
independence from Scripture. It is suggested simply by observing the
topics in which Paul does include Scriptural quotations. Most quotations
of Scripture in Paul's letters, the 80% plus, as D.-A. Koch argues,
accumulate around precisely the issues where Paul's theology departs
most dramatically from previous exegetical traditions within Judaism,
such as christology, the Law, the election of Israel and the inclusion
of the Gentiles.[26] Romans 9-11, for example, which deals with these
very subjects, contains almost a third (29% by Moody Smith's count)

---

    [24] Niebuhr, *Gesetz und Paränese*, 234.
    [25] In 2 Thessalonians 3:14ff., Paul regards obedience to his instructions as prerequi-
site to continued church fellowship. See Longenecker, *Paul: Apostle of Liberty*, 196-
20; Westerholm, *Law*, 214-15; B. Holmberg, *Paul and Power: The Structure of Authority
in the Pauline Epistles*.
    [26] Koch, *Die Schrift*, 257ff.

of Paul's citations of Scripture![27] Paul cites Scripture most commonly when in the throes of controversy.[28] It was when Paul was pressed to defend the new community's legitimacy and continuity with Scripture that we find him quoting Scripture most often. Since this apologetic purpose is absent when Paul is attempting to regulate conduct in his churches, it is to be expected that Scripture is cited less often and less explicitly.

## IV. WRITTEN FOR OUR INSTRUCTION

There is one last possible objection to our thesis which, if correct, would seriously undermine it. Perhaps Paul's dependence upon the Scriptures for ethics was unwitting or even reluctant? Maybe Paul did not regard the Jewish Scriptures highly as a source for his ethics, but 'like an alcoholic trying to kick the habit, found himself unable to resist a drink'. We should probably let Paul answer for himself. The bulk of this study has been concerned with Paul's practice with respect to ethics and Scripture. What of Paul's precept on the same subject? In 1 Corinthians 4:6; 9:10; 10:6,11; 14:34 and Romans 7:12; 15:4 Paul confesses his profound dependence upon the Scriptures as a Christian ethical teacher.[29]

In 1 Corinthians 4:6 Paul urges the Corinthians to learn from the example of Apollos and his own example "not [to go] beyond the things which are written," μὴ ὑπὲρ ἃ γέγραπται. The most natural interpretation of this rather difficult phrase is to take it, along with

---

[27] Koch lists 66 instances of Paul's use of citations introduced by explicit introductory formulae; 22 occur in Romans 9-11.

[28] This point has been recognised by several scholars. Eg. D. Moody Smith, 'The Pauline Literature', 274: "The reason for Paul's heavy use of the Old Testament in Romans and Galatians are obvious enough. Paul must counter arguments advanced by Judaisers directly"; Barrett, *Essays on Paul*, 154-70 argues that most of the Old Testament texts in Galatians 3 and 4 are cited by Paul because they were being used by his opponents. Cf. Barnabas Lindars, 'The Old Testament and Universalism in Paul', 513: "Paul makes frequent appeal to the Old Testament [in Romans 9-11] of necessity, for he could not hope to gain a hearing for his revolutionary ideas otherwise"; cf. the title of C.F.D. Moule's chapter four in *The Birth of the New Testament*: "The Church explains itself: the use of the Jewish Scriptures."

[29] It is remarkable that this impressive little collection of texts has received so little attention in studies which doubt the importance of the Law or the Scriptures for Paul's ethics. Every one of them is conspicuous by their absence, for instance, from Westerholm, *Israel's Law*, and Hamerton-Kelly, 'Sacred Violence'. Even Tomson, *Paul*, ignores these texts, preferring instead to highlight 7:17-24 and 9:19-23.

Morna D. Hooker, to refer to Scripture, in particular the quotations found in the previous context, namely Isaiah 29:14 in 1:19, Jeremiah 9:23f in 1.30f. and Job 5:13/Psalm 94:11 in 3:19-20.[30] Understood in this way, 4:6 instructs the Corinthians not to go beyond the exhortations found in and constructed from the Scriptures to boast exclusively in the Lord (not in human leaders) and to recognise the unity of the people of God. Thus, if our interpretation is deemed correct, we have in 4:6 a remarkable statement about the sufficiency of the Scriptures for Christian conduct. To avoid the party spirit and the sin of pride (the subject of 1:10-4:21), Paul says what one must do is "live according to Scripture" (4:6; RSV).

A kindred thought is found in 1 Corinthians 9:10 where Paul, having quoted Deuteronomy 25:4 in 9:9 to strengthen his case for financial support, states that this Scripture "speaks by all means [πάντως; cf. Romans 3:9; Luke 4:23] for us . . . it was written for us." Paul affirms that an obscure Torah text about fair treatment to oxen is applicable to the regulation of Christian behaviour. When Paul says Deuteronomy speaks δι ἡμᾶς, he does not mean simply for Christian labourers (contra Findlay, Ellicott), but for all Christians, since the following application of the law is made to the Corinthians (Conzelmann). Leaving aside Paul's controversial exegesis and application of the Deuteronomy text,[31] it is worth noting the high status he accords the witness of the Law of Moses on the practical matter of support. Though his claim to support is undergirded at various levels (common experience, 9:7; justice, 9:11-12; temple practice, 9:13; the Lord's command, 9:14), the use of ἢ καὶ in 9:8 to introduce the argument from the Law stresses its superiority (at least over the first argument). Paul does not simply speak on human authority (κατὰ ἄνθρωπον), but can appeal to "that which stands written." Rather than being revoked, Paul views Deuteronomy 25:4, a text which most Christians would regard as obsolete civil law, as instructing Christians. This sentiment is congruent with Romans 7:12 which states that "the Law is holy, and the commandment is holy and just and good," and with 1 Corinthians 14:34 where Paul claims that the Law (either Genesis 3:16; chs. 1

---

[30] Hooker, 'Beyond the Things which are Written: An Examination of 1 Cor. iv. 6'. Perhaps the Scriptural allusions in 2:9 and 3:9 should also be included.

[31] See D. Instone Brewer, '1 Cor 9.9-11: A Literal Interpretation of Do Not Muzzle the Ox', for the view that Paul's use of Deuteronomy 25:4 has rabbinic parallels and should not, in fact, be labelled allegory.

and 2 or the thrust of the whole Law) supports the practice of all the churches regarding the subordination of women.[32]

In 1 Corinthians 10:11 (cf. 10:6) Paul claims that the Exodus events (cf. Exodus and Numbers) which Paul recites in 10:1-10 (in a manner reminiscent of Ps 78, Deut 32, Neh 9 and Acts 7[33]) were written down with a goal in mind, namely, the ethical instruction and correction of Christians.[34]

Thus in these six texts (1 Cor 4:6; 9:10; 10:6,11; 14:34; Rom 7:12; 15:4) Paul underscores *the relevance of the Scriptures for ethics* with reference to passages found in Genesis, Exodus, Numbers, Deuteronomy, Job, Psalms, Isaiah, and Jeremiah, material encompassing Biblical narrative, poetry, prophecy, wisdom and law. This is why Paul can say in Romans 15:4 (with immediate reference to Ps 69:9 [10] quoted in 15:3) that "*whatever* (ὅσα) was written in former days was written for our instruction",[35] διδασκαλία.[36] There is ample and good evidence in the accepted Pauline corpus of a positive orientation to the Scriptures on matters of conduct.

The immense theological contribution of 1 Corinthians to a number of areas is widely recognised. Three recent studies of the theology of the epistle by Ralph P. Martin, Gordon E. Fee and Victor Paul Furnish underscore the doctrines of God, Christ, salvation, eschatology,

---

[32] The view that 14:34-35 are a non-Pauline interpolation (see Fee for a full defence) is based mainly on the supposed contradiction with 1 Corinthians 11. But since this is susceptible to a variety of explanations, the interpolation view is at best very difficult to prove. Furthermore, no manuscript lacks the verses, and Metzger, *A Textual Commentary on the Greek New Testament*, 565 has offered a reasonable explanation for the Western tradition's placement of verses 34-35 after verse 40.

[33] Cf. Fee, 442.

[34] νουθεσία/νουθετέω are favourite Pauline words to denote moral appeal that leads to amendment; 1 Corinthians 4:14; Romans 15:14; Ephesians 6:4; Col 1:28; 3:16; 1 Thessalonians 5:12,14; 2 Thessalonians 3:15; Titus 3:10; Acts 20:31.

[35] In Romans 15:4 Paul indicates that the Scriptures inculcate endurance and faithfulness and provide a strong incentive to continue in Christian hope. Also present, as seen within the immediate context, is the notion that Paul uses Scripture for moral exhortation, to foster brotherly unity and oneness of mind. Thus, although the Greek of Romans 15:4 and 1 Corinthians 10:11 is different, the RSV is not amiss to translate them both as indicating that Scripture was "written for our instruction."

[36] BAGD, 191 make the plausible suggestion that b. Sanhedrin 73a underlies the usage of διδασκαλία with a preposition in Romans 15:4 and 2 Timothy 3:16. It seems that Paul's presupposition was that not only has God spoken through the Scriptures (cf. the common perfect tense introductory formula, γέγραπται, "it stands written"), but that He still speaks through them (cf. the introductory formulae present tense λέγει with various subjects, "the Scriptures/God/He says").

the church, and ethics in this regard.[37] However, if we combine the considerable collection of biblical quotations and allusions in 1 Corinthians, not to mention biblical motifs, ideas and vocabulary, which represent Paul's practice, with the statements in 1 Corinthians 4:6; 9:10; 10:6,11; 14:34 which disclose Paul's precept, we ought to add the doctrine of Scripture to this list. 1 Corinthians has much to teach concerning Paul's positive orientation towards the Scriptures, especially in matters of Christian conduct.

The Scriptures, Paul says, were written "for us" and "for our instruction." It is true that Scripture is, for Paul, witness to the gospel, *Zeuge des Evangeliums* (the title of D.-A. Koch's book on Paul's use of Scripture and the emphasis of almost every book and article on the subject). However, if the evidence of this study is valid, and if 1 Corinthians 5-7 is a representative sample, then the Scriptures are for Paul not only witness to the gospel (Rom 3:21), but also guide for ethical conduct, written for our instruction (1 Cor 10:11).[38]

---

[37] Martin, *Word Biblical Themes: 1,2 Corinthians*; Fee, 'Toward a Theology of 1 Corinthians'; Furnish, 'Theology in 1 Corinthians: Initial Soundings'. 1 Corinthians 4:6; 9:10; 10:6,11; 14:34 are not discussed in these treatments.

[38] 2 Timothy 3:15-17 states this double purpose of the Scriptures (cf. C.J.H. Wright, *Living as the People of God*, 16): the Scriptures 1. "make you wise for salvation" (3:15) and 2. are "profitable for teaching, for reproof, for correction, for training in righteousness, that the man of God may be complete, equipped for every good work."

APPENDIX

# THE ORIGIN AND MEANING OF
# 1 CORINTHIANS 10:22B

## I. Introduction

The concluding words of Paul's warning concerning the perils of idolatry in 1 Corinthians 10:1-22 form a rhetorical question which expects an emphatically negative response (note μὴ): μὴ ἰσχυρότεροι αὐτοῦ ἐσμεν; 'are we stronger than he?' Gordon Fee is not alone among commentators when he admits that 'the precise intent' of this question is 'puzzling.'[1] What has a comparison of the strength of believers with the strength of God to do with idolatry? Is there some connection between God's power and his jealousy? Whereas a good case has been made for the indebtedness of Paul's teaching in 10:1-13 and 14-22a to certain Old Testament traditions, verse 22b remains somewhat inexplicable.

A number of commentators take the question as an ironic, if not sarcastic, reference to 'the strong' in the Corinthian church, who possessed the 'knowledge' (cf. 8:1) that 'an idol is nothing in the world' (8:4), were convinced that 'food will not commend us to God' (8:8) and thus felt free to attend idolatrous temple meals. For example, in 1937 R. St. John Parry found in 10:22b 'a clear reference to οἱ ἰσχυροι, with tremendous irony.'[2] J. Héring, Gaston Deluz and C.K. Barrett make the same identification.[3] This interpretation is, however, unlikely since Paul does not use the term 'strong' in 1 Corinthians to refer to a group (as he does in Romans 14)[4] but as characteristic of the Corinthian attitude in general (cf. 4:10).[5] If Paul gives a label to the group more likely to eat idol food in 1 Corinthians 8-10 it is to do with γνῶσις, 'knowledge.'[6] In 1 Corinthians 8-10 the two

---

[1] Fee, 474.
[2] Parry, 153.
[3] Héring, 97; Deluz, *A Companion to 1 Corinthians*, 131; Barrett, 238.
[4] *Contra* W.M. Meeks, '"And Rose Up to Play"; Midrash and paraenesis in 1 Corinthians 10:1-22', 73: 'Paul labels the two sides of the controversy "the strong" and the "weak".'
[5] Cf. Hans Conzelmann, 174.
[6] Peter J. Tomson, 193.

groups are 'the weak' (in conscience) and 'the knowing.' Thus, an ironic rebuke of the adherents to the latter position would not allude to their strength but to their knowledge. To rebuke them Paul could have said: Are we more knowledgeable than he? Paul's warning in 10:22b in fact takes in more than one group in Corinth; he asks, 'are we, ἐσμεν (not 'are you,' ἐστε) stronger than he?' 10:22b is addressed to all the Corinthians.

A. Robertson and A. Plummer list several Old Testament parallels to 10:22b which they consider to have influenced Paul: 'Job ix. 32, xxxvii. 23; Eccles. vi.10; Isa. xiv.9; Exek. xxii.14; some of which passages may have been in the Apostle's mind.'[7] It is true that some of these passages contain comparable sentiments to 10:22b: 'The Almighty— we cannot find Him: He is exalted in power' (Job 37:23); 'He cannot dispute with him who is stronger than he is' (Eccl. 6:10); 'Woe to the one who quarrels with his Maker' (Isa. 45:9); 'Can your heart endure, or can your hands be strong, in the days that I shall deal with you? I, the LORD, have spoken and shall act' (Ezek. 22:14).

However, the fact that none of them concerns idolatry and/or the jealousy of God makes them less relevant to 1 Corinthians 10. Nonetheless, it is clear from verses 1-21 that Paul's mind was moving along Old Testament lines. It is the contention of this short study that an investigation of the Scriptural background to these verses (10:1-21) suggests a likely origin for 10:22b, and also clarifies its precise intent, significance and force.

## II. The Origin of 1 Corinthians 10:22B

In 10:1-22 Paul delivers an urgent warning: Christians who participate in meals alongside pagans engaged in idolatrous activity share in the worship of demons and run the risk of provoking the Lord to jealousy.[8] Verses 1-13 make the point that even the most ideal environment does not supply certain protection from the temptations and perils of idolatry with reference to a number of Exodus events (recorded

---

[7] Robertson/Plummer, 218. We could add Isaiah 10:15 to this list.

[8] Whether 8:1-13 also concerns pagan temple worship (Fee's view) or, along with 10:23-11:1, addresses the broader issue of marketplace idol meat (the majority of commentators) should not detain us here. For a full discussion see Bruce N. Fisk, 'Eating Meat Offered to Idols: Corinthian Behavior and Pauline Response in 1 Corinthians 8-10 (A Response to Gordon Fee)'.

in Exodus and Numbers).[9] Verses 14-22 expressly forbid attendance at pagan temple feasts by insisting that in such a sacred meal, as in the Lord's Supper, the participants share in the worship of the deity, and by declaring that such worship is offered to demons. Paul's words in verses 20 and 22a recall Deuteronomy 32:17 and 32:21 respectively. These points of contact have led A.T. Hanson to conclude that '1 Cor. 10.14-21 is a Christian midrash on Deut. 32.17-21,' by which he means that when Paul wrote 10:14-21 he was reflecting upon the contemporary relevance of the Deuteronomy passage.[10] The Old Testament passages which inform both 10:1-13 and 10:14-21 contain elements which could have given rise to Paul's question in 10:22b.

Numbers 14 is a passage that forms part of the background to 10:1-13 (with 14:22-23, 28-30 cf. 1 Cor 10:5, 9-10) which refers to the strength of God. In chapter 14 the people of Israel accept the majority report of the spies who had investigated the Promised Land and rebel against the Lord by grumbling and refusing to take possession of the land (14:1-10). The Lord proposes to destroy the nation and start afresh with Moses and his descendants (14:11-12). In 14:13-19 Moses successfully persuades God to relent, refering to his power in the exodus and in forgiveness and judgement:

> Then the Egyptians will hear of it, for by your strength (LXX: τῇ ἰσχύι σου) you brought up this people from their midst; But now, I pray, may your power (ἡ ἰσχύς σου) O Lord, be great, just as you have declared: the Lord is slow to anger and abounding in lovingkindness, forgiving

---

[9] The section, as Fee, 442 observes, is very similar to Psalm 78, Nehemiah 9:5-37 and Deuteronomy 32:1-43, which also employ God's rejected mercies in Israel's early history to warn a present generation. The pervasive presence of Old Testament traditions in verses 1-11 has led some to argue that they had prior existence as a Christian or Jewish midrash (or homily) -see e.g., W.A. Meeks, '1 Corinthians 10:1-22'; cf. E.E. Ellis, *Prophecy and Hermeneutic in Early Christianity: New Testament Essays*, 156, n.36. However, the section's perfect fit in the present context and the lack of an extant piece that parallels 10:1-11 in more than a few respects indicates that Paul composed it himself.

[10] Hanson, *Studies in Paul's Technique and Theology*, 115, 167. Hanson, 115 also believes that Deut. 32:14 ('with the finest of the wheat and of the blood of the grape you drank wine') would have pointed Paul to the Christian sacred meal mentioned in 1 Corinthians 10:16-17,21. Cf. Meeks, '1 Corinthians 10:1-22', 72: Paul 'did find in Deuteronomy 32 phrases that were suggestive for his admonition to the Corinthian Christians.' P.D. Gardner, 'The Gifts of God and the Authentication of a Christian: An Exegetical Study of 1 Corinthians 8:1-11:1', 186, points out that when Paul uses παραζηλόω in 1 Cor. 10:22 and Rom. 10:19 'Deuteronomy 32:21 was his source.'

iniquity and transgression, but he will by no means clear the guilty (cf. Ex. 34:6-9).

According to these verses the Lord's power is shown in forgiveness (Israel escapes total annihilation) and also in judgement (14:21ff; the generation of rebels die in the desert). Thus Numbers 14 establishes a connection between God's strength (ἰσχύς) and his destruction of the rebellious among his people, a link which is implicit in 1 Corinthians 10:22b.

When we turn to Deuteronomy 32, that 'rich and vigorous poem'[11] to which Paul alludes in 1 Corinthians 10:14-21,[12] we find not only the strength of God, but also the strength of foreign gods and of God's people implicated in the question of divine discipline. The Song depicts Israel's future in gloomy terms: newly acquired wealth would lead the people into apostasy, illiciting severe judgement from the Lord.[13] In verses 15-18 it is Israel's prosperity which leads her to abandon God, the source of her benefits. She 'kicks against' her master in rebellion, like a stubborn donkey. God's determination to judge his wayward people appears in verses 21ff.

A purpose of God's judgement will be to impress upon the nation their lack of strength and the Lord's great power. Verse 30 depicts Israel's impotence without the Lord's help: one man will chase a thousand Israelites; two will put ten thousand to flight.[14] Verses 36-38 indicate that judgement will bring an end to Israel's strength, including any they may have derived from 'the gods': The Lord will

---

[11] P.W. Skehan, 'The Structure of the Song of Moses in Deuteronomy', 163. In this article Skehan defends the unity and integrity of Deuteronomy 32:1-43. This defence is supported by Peter C. Craigie, *The Book of Deuteronomy* (Grand Rapids, Eerdmans 1976).

[12] Paul's complete familiarity and high regard for the chapter is seen further in his quotation of verse 21 in Rom. 10:19 and verse 35 in Rom. 12:19. Hanson, *Paul's Technique*, 115, is right to conclude that Deut 32 is 'a passage which we know that Paul studied carefully.' The last words of Moses found in the closing chapters of Deuteronomy exercised a wide influence in early Judaism. For example, Meeks, '1 Corinthians 10:1-22', 66, notes that the fourth-century Samaritan midrash on sections of the Pentateuch, the *Memar Marqah*, devotes an entire book to the exposition of the song, cross-referencing verses from Exodus and Numbers (see esp. 4:4,8). Deut 30-33 are also prominent in the biblical exposition of Philo and Josephus and in the Dead Sea Scrolls.

[13] The brighter note that ultimately the Lord would deliver his people and take vengeance on their enemies concludes the song, but it is not relevant for our purposes here.

[14] For similar imagery, though with God's people and her enemies in reverse positions see 1 Sam. 18:7; Isa. 30:17.

desist from punishment 'when he sees their strength is gone' (NIV 32:36).[15] Peter C. Craigie explains:

> Since Israel's defection was largely a result of the arrogance of believing in their own *strength*, that arrogance and belief in *human strength* had to be totally demolished before the people were in a position to realize their need of *God's strength*. The rhetorical question posed in vv. 37-38 is designed to create awareness that other possible sources of *strength* were also useless" (italics added).[16]

These notions tally well with other verses in Deuteronomy. The description of God in 10:17, which serves as the basis for a proper attitude towards God (cf. 10:16) and a warning not to 'turn aside and serve other gods . . . [lest] the Lord's anger be kindled against you' (11:16-17), is noteworthy: 'the Lord your God is God of God's and Lord of Lords, the great, mighty (ἰσχυρὸς) and fearful God.' Deuteronomy 8:17-20 strikes a similar note. In a warning against idolatry the nation is alerted to the sin of presumption, of thinking that her accomplishments were achieved by her own power: 'But you shall remember the Lord your God, for it is he who is giving you power (ἰσχὺν) to make wealth' (8:18a).

The theme of God's strength and the strength of his people is reinforced in the Targumim of Deuteronomy 32. That Paul knew targumic traditions of interpretation of this chapter is suggested by the use he makes of the chapter in Romans 11.[17] Whereas in the MT the dominant name for God in the chapter is "the Rock" (cf. 32:4,13,15,18,30,31,37), a unique appellation in the Pentateuch, the Targumim employ several titles which interpret 'rock' as a figure for God's strength (The LXX translates צור by θέος):[18]

---

[15] Paul could well have asked in 10:22b 'are they, εἰσιν (i.e., foreign gods) stronger than he?'
[16] Craigie, *Deuteronomy*, 387.
[17] See Hanson, *Paul's Technique*, ch. 6.
[18] Cf. Andrew Chester, *Divine Revelation and Divine Titles in the Pentateuchal Targumim*, esp. the full list of titles 352ff.
  Abbreviations for the Targumim:
L = MS B.H., fol. 1, of the Universitätsbibliothek, Leipzig
N = Codex Neofiti (Vatican Library)
Nur = Codex I of the Stadtbibliothek, Nuremberg
O = Targum Onqelos
P = MS 110 of the Bibliotheque nationale, Paris
PJ = Targum Pseudo-Jonathan
V = MS Ebr. 440 of the Vatican Library.

(1) 'The Strong One' -         Deut. 32:30  (N,VNur,L,O,PJ)
                               Deut. 32:37  (N,O,PJ)
                               Deut. 32:31  (O)
(2) 'The Strong One whose deeds are perfect' -
                               Deut. 32:4  (O,PJ,PVNurL)
(3) 'The Strong One who redeemed them' -
                               Deut. 32:15  (O,PJ)
(4) '(The Fear of) the Strong One who created you' -
                               Deut. 32:18  (O,PJ,N,VNurL)
(5) 'The Strong One of Israel' -
                               Deut. 32:31,31(PJ)
(6) 'The Strong God of Israel in whom they put their trust' -
                               Deut. 32:37  (N,VNurL)
(7) 'The Strong One in whom they put their trust' -
                               Deut. 32:37  (PJ)

Of the approximately 109 divine titles and epithets in the Pentateuchal targumim (see Chester's list) the above six are virtually unique to Deuteronomy 32.[19] 'Strength' as a divine title and attribute would certainly have been well known to Paul, maintaining some currency in Jewish circles up to his day. In Greek literature examples include ἰσχυρός, Wis. 6:8; ἰσχύς, Arist. 192; Wis. 12:16-18; 16:16; ἰσχύω, Wis. 11:21.[20] Among synonyms for God in Rabbinic literature we may note אדיר ('Mighty'); נבורה ('Might'); and תוקפיהון דישׂראל ('The Strength of Israel').[21] The New Testament uses ἰσχύω to depict Christ's superior power over various others (John the Baptist: Mark 1:7; par.; demons: Mark 3:27; par.).

The notion of strength is also inserted in other places in the Targumim of Deuteronomy 32. The Fragment Targumim (ed., M.L. Klein) explain the discipline of verse 30 in terms of Israel losing her strength:

> When Israel toiled in the (study of the) Torah and fulfilled the commandments, then one of them would rout a thousand, and two of them would chase away ten thousand; but because they sinned and brought about wrath before Him, the Strong One has forsaken them.

---

[19] The only exceptions are as follows: (1) Gen. 49:24 (N,PVNur); and 'The Strong One of Isaac/Jacob'—Gen. 31:42,53; 49:24 (N); Gen 49:24 (O).

[20] Cf. Ralph Marcus, 'Divine Names and Attributes in Hellenistic Jewish Literature, *American Academy for Jewish Research: Proceedings 1931-32*, Philadelphia, 43-120, esp 80.

[21] See A. Marmorstein, *The Old Rabbinic Doctrine of God: I. The Names & Attributes of God* (London, Oxford University Press 1927) 64, 82 and 107 for references.

In verse 11 O, PJ and N add 'strength' to the description of God's pinions. In the explanation of Israel's rebellion in verse 11, O notes that Israel 'grew strong' and in verse 13 it describes the land of Israel as containing 'strong places' and boasting 'strong defences.' PJ and O depict God when provoked to jealousy in verse 22 as sending a 'wind as strong as fire' (MT has simply 'a fire').

In Deuteronomy 32, especially in the Targumim, the question of Israel's participation in idolatry and the Lord's jealousy and discipline is set in terms of strength and power. Israel follows other gods when they feel strong (cf. 1 Cor. 10:11, 'Let him who thinks he stands') and in response, the Lord purposes to show himself strong by punishing the Israelites. It is this material which represents a likely origin for Paul's question in 1 Corinthians 10:22b. Paul warns the Corinthians that it is not possible to provoke the Lord to jealousy with impunity: surely we are not stronger than the Strong One! Paul's question is designed not only to underscore the impotence of believers (the view of most commentators), but also to stress the omnipotence of God. Paul sees the provocation of God's jealousy as arousing his power, a discernible theme of Deuteronomy 32. Thus we may extend Hanson's observation of the indebtedness of 1 Corinthians 10:14-21 to Deuteronomy 32 to include verse 22.[22]

### III. THE MEANING OF 1 CORINTHIANS 10:22B

Having established that Paul's words in 10:22b arise out of a biblical milieu, a look at a couple of related biblical themes may assist in the attempt to locate their precise meaning. The belief of Paul and Deuteronomy 32 that idolatry arouses God's jealousy is, of course, a sturdy Old Testament theme with a long history. It is introduced in the second commandment (Ex 20:5; Deut. 5:9) and in Exodus 34:14 ('Do not worship any other god, for the Lord whose name is Jealous, is a jealous God') it is the explanation of the divine name, 'Jealous.' In fact, all the Pentateuchal references to God's jealousy have to do with idol-worship (cf. also 1 Kings 14:22 and the references below). An idol worshipped in Jerusalem in Ezekiel 8:3 is called 'the image of jealousy, which provokes to jealousy' (cf. Ezek. 16:38,42; 23:25).

---

[22] 1 Corinthians 10:1-22 is thus a choice example from start to finish of the dependence of Paul's parænesis upon the Scriptures, which is precisely what he states in 10:6,11 (Scripture was 'written for our instruction').

Furthermore, the conviction that God's jealousy inevitably leads him to stern action is also deeply rooted in the Old Testament.[23] God's jealousy, based upon his love for those he has redeemed at great cost, motivates him to judge his people; Nahum 1:2, 'The Lord is a jealous God and avenges.' The Old Testament is replete with texts in which God's jealousy leads him to destroy the faithless among his people:

Deut. 6:14-15   'Do not follow other gods . . . for the Lord your God, who is among you, is a jealous God and his anger will burn against you and he will destroy you from the face of the land.'

Josh. 24:19-20  'He is a jealous God. . . . If you forsake the Lord and serve foreign gods, he will turn and bring disaster on you and make an end of you.'

Ps. 78:58-64    'They aroused his jealousy with their idols. When God heard them he was very angry; he rejected Israel completely. . . .'

Zeph. 1:18      'In the fire of his jealousy the whole world will be consumed.'

Read in this light 1 Corinthians 10:22b turns out to be a frightening threat of judgement upon those Corinthian Christians who provoke God to jealousy, if not upon the church in Corinth as a group on account of the behaviour of some of its members (hence Paul's 'are *we* stronger than he?').[24] Paul states, not just, do not defy God (for he is supreme), but do not tempt God, he is ready to judge powerfully. Paul is convinced that the God of the Jewish Scriptures is unchanged in his attitude to idolatry.

In the context of the religious pluralism of Paul's day 1 Corinthians 10:22b sounds a solemn note and brings the discussion in 10:1-22 to a climax.[25] Amidst the pressures to be open, tolerant and accommodate other faiths of the early Empire some Corinthian Christians were quite unaware of the real danger of becoming guilty of idolatry by association. Before Paul turns to the relation of the Corinthians

---

[23] In Proverbs 27:4 ('Wrath is cruel, anger is overwhelming, but who can stand before jealousy') the power of jealousy is almost 'proverbial.'

[24] On corporate responsibility and judgement in the Old Testament and in 1 Corinthians 5 see the author's 'Corporate Responsibility in 1 Corinthians 5'.

[25] Uncompromising and forthright comments also close the sections on unity (1:18-4:21; see 4:21) and incest (5:1-13; see 5:13b).

to their neighbours (10:23ff.), he culminates his argument of their relationship with God himself with the warning that to provoke God to jealousy is to risk his punitive intervention. Thus in the teaching of 1 Corinthians, verse 22b of chapter 10 should be placed alongside 5:13b and 11:29-32, and recognised as a text which deals with the discipline of the church in the 'strongest' terms.[26]

---

[26] Recent accounts of the theology of 1 Corinthians by Gordon E. Fee, 'Towards a Theology of 1 Corinthians'; Ralph P. Martin, *Word Biblical Themes: 1, 2 Corinthians*; and Victor Paul Furnish, 'Theology in 1 Corinthians: Initial Soundings', neglect this point.

# BIBLIOGRAPHY

1. *Primary Sources*

*Aboth de Rabbi Nathan.* Edited by S. Schechter. Vienna: Lippe; London: Nutt; Frankfurt: Kauffmann. 1887.
*Ante-Nicene Christian Library: Translations of the Writings of the Fathers down to A.D. 325.* Edited by A. Roberts and J. Donaldson. 24 Vols. Edinburgh: T. & T. Clark, 1867-72.
*The Apocrypha of the Old Testament: Revised Standard Version.* The Oxford Annotated Apocrypha. Edited by B. M. Metzger. New York: Oxford University Press, 1977.
*The Apocryphal Old Testament.* Edited by H.F.D. Sparks. Oxford: Clarendon, 1984.
*The Apostolic Fathers. Text and Translation.* Translated by K. Lake. LCL. 2 Vols. Cambridge, MA: Harvard University Press; London: Heinemann, 1912-1913.
Baillet, M.; Milik, J.T. et al. *Discoveries in the Judaean Desert.* Vols. 1-7. Oxford: Clarendon, 1955-1982.
*The Bible in Aramaic: Based on Old Manuscripts and Printed Texts.* Edited by A. Sperber. 4 Vols. Leiden: Brill, 1959-68.
*Biblia Hebraica Stuttgartensia.* Edited by K. Elliger and W. Rudolph. New edn. Stuttgart: Deutsche Bibelgesellschaft, 1977.
*Biblia Patristica. Index des citations et allusions bibliques dans lat littérature patristique.* 3 Vols. Paris: Centre d'analyse et de documentation patristiques, 1975-81.
*The Dead Sea Scrolls in English.* Edited and Translated by G. Vermes. 3rd edn. Harmondsworth: Penguin, 1987.
*The Fathers According to Rabbi Nathan.* Translated by Judah Goldin. New Haven: Yale University Press, 1955.
*Gregori Nysseni opera.* Edited by E. Gebhardt. Leiden, 1967.
*Die griechischen christlichen Schriftsteller.* Edited by K. Holl. Leipzig, 1922.
*The Hebrew Text of the Book of Ecclesiasticus.* Edited by I. Lévi. Semitic Study Series 3. 3rd edn. Leiden: Brill, 1969.
*Hebrew-English Edition of the Babylonian Talmud.* Edited by I. Epstein. 20 vols. London: Soncino, 1972-1984.
Hennecke, E. *New Testament Apocrypha.* 2 vols. Edited by W. Schneemelcher. Translation edited by R. McL. Wilson. London: Lutter worth, 1963-1965.
Herford, R. Travers. *Pirke Aboth: The Tractate 'Fathers', from the Mishnah, Commonly Called 'Sayings of the Fathers'.* 2nd edn. New York: Jewish Institute of Religion/Bloch. 1930.
Jenkins, C. 'Documents: Origen on 1 Corinthians', *JTS* 9 (1908): 353-72.
*Josephus.* Text and Translation. Translated by H. St. J. Thackeray (vols. 1-5), Ralph Marcus (Vols. 5-8) with Allen Wikgren (Vol. 8), and Louis H. Feldman (Vols. 9-10). LCL. London: Heinemann; Cambridge, MA: Harvard University Press, 1926-1965.
Knibb, Michael A. *The Book of Enoch: A New Edition in the Light of the Aramaic Dead Sea Fragments.* 2 Vols. Oxford: Clarendon, 1978.
*Mekilta de-Rabbi Ishmael.* Edited by J. Z. Lauterbach. 3 Vols. Philadelphia: Jewish Publication Society of America, 1933-1935.
*Midrash Rabbah.* Edited by H. Freedman and M. Simon. 10 Vols. London: Soncino, 1939.
*The Mishnah.* Translated by H. Danby. Oxford: OUP, 1933.
*Mishnayoth.* Edited by P. Blackman. 7 Vols. New York: Judaica Press, 1964.
Montefiore, C.G. and Loewe, H. *A Rabbinic Anthology.* London: Macmillan, 1938. [Repr. New York: Schocken, 1974]

*Novum Testamentum Graece*. Edited by E. Nestle et al. 26th edn. (revised). Stuttgart: Deutsche Bibelstiftung, 1981.

*The Old Testament Pseudepigrapha*. Edited by J. H. Charlesworth. 2 Vols. Garden City: Doubleday, 1983-1985.

*Patrologiae cursus completus—series Graeca*. Edited by J.P. Migne. Paris, 1857-66.

*Philo*. Text and Trnslation. Translated by F.H. Colson (Vols. 2, 6-10) with G. H. Whitaker (Vols. 1, 3-5); and by Ralph Marcus (Supplements 1-2). LCL. London: Heinemann; Cambridge, MA: Harvard University Press, 1929-1953.

*Septuaginta: Id est Vetus Testamentum graece iuxta LXX interpretes*. Edited by A. Rahlfs. 2 vols. in 1. Stuttgart: Deutsche Bibelgesellschaft, 1935.

*Septuaginta: Vetus Testamentum Graecum Auctoritate Academiae Scientiarum Gottingensis editum*. 16 Vols. Göttingen: Vandenhoeck & Ruprecht, 1931-

*Sifre on Deuteronomy*. Edited by L. Finkelstein. New York: Jewish Theological Seminary of America, 1969 [=1939].

*Sifre: A Tannaitic Commentary on the Book of Deuteronomy*. Translated by R. Hammer. New Haven/London: Yale Univeristy Press, 1986.

*Talmud Yerushalmi*. Krotoshin: 1866. [Reprinted Jerusalem: Shiloh, 1967.]

*The Targums of Onkelos and Jonathan ben Uzziel on the Pentateuch with the Fragments of the Jerusalem Targum; From the Chaldee*. Translated by J. W. Etheridge. New York: Ktav, 1968.

*The Testaments of the Twelve Patriarchs: A Critical Edition of the Greek Text*. Edited by M. de Jonge. PVTG 1:2. Leiden: Brill, 1978.

*Tosephta: Based on the Erfurt and Vienna Codices*. Edited by M. S. Zuckermandel. 2nd edn. Jerusalem: Bamberger & Wahrmann, 1937.

*The Tosefta*. Translated by J. Neusner. 6 Vols. New York: Ktav, 1977-83.

Yadin, Yigael. *The Temple Scroll*. 3 vols. and supplementary plates. Jerusalem: Israel Exploration Society, 1983.


2. *Secondary Sources* (Works Cited)

Aageson, J. W. 'Paul's Use of Scripture: A Comparative Study of Biblical Interpretation in Early Palestinian Judaism and the New Testament with Special Reference to Romans 9-11'. D.Phil Thesis, Oxford University, 1983.

Alexander, Philip S. 'Jewish Law in the Time of Jesus: Towards a Clarification of the Problem'. In *Law and Religion: Essays on the Place of the Law in Israel and Early Christianity by members of the Ehrhardt Seminar of Manchester University*. Edited by Barnabas Lindars. Cambridge: James Clark and Co., 1988. pp. 44-58.

Alford, Henry. *The Greek Testament: with a critically revised text: a digest of various readings: marginal references to verbal and idiomatic usage: prolegomena: and a critical and exegetical commentary*. Volume II. Cambridge: Rivingtons, 1881.

Allison, D.C. 'The Pauline Epistles and the Synoptic Gospels', *NTS* 28 (1982): 1-32.

Alter, R. 'A Literary Approach to the Bible', *Commentary* 60 (1975): 70-77.

Amir, Yehoshua. 'Authority and Interpretation of Scripture in the Writings of Philo'. In *Mikra: Text, Translation, Reading and Interpretation of the Hebrew Bible in Ancient Judaism and Early Christianity*. CRIadNT II,i. Assen: Van Gorcum, 1988. pp. 421-53.

Anderson, A.A. 'Psalms'. In *It is Written: Scripture Citing Scripture. Essays in Honour of Barnabas Lindars*, ed. D.A. Carson and H.G.M. Williamson. Cambridge: CUP, 1988. pp. 56-66.

Anderson, Arnold A. 'Law in Old Israel: laws concerning adultery'. In *Law and Religion: Essays on the place of the Law in Israel and Early Christianity*. Edited by Barnabas Lindars. Cambridge: James Clarke & Co., 1988. pp. 13-19.

Argyle, A.W. 'The Influence of the Testament of the Twelve Patriarchs Upon the New Testament', *ExpTim* LXIII (1951/52): 256-58.

Aschermann, H. 'Die paränetischen Formen der "Testamente der zwölf Patriarchen" und ihr Nachwirken in der frühchristlichen Mahnung'. Diss. Theol. Berlin, 1955.

Aune, D.E. 'Bride of Christ', *ISBE* II: 546-47.

Badenas, Robert. *Christ the End of the Law: Romans 10.4 in Pauline Perspective.* JSNTSS 10. Sheffield: JSOT Press, 1985.

Baeck, L. 'The faith of Paul', *JJS* 3 (1952): 93-110.

Bailey, D.S. *The Man-Woman Relation in Christian Thought.* London. 1959.

Bailey, K.E. 'The Structure of 1 Corinthians and Paul's Theological Method with a Special Reference to 4:17', *NovT* 25 (1983): 152-81.

Bailey, K.E. 'Paul's Theological Foundation for Human Sexuality: 1 Cor. 6:9-20 in the Light of Rhetorical Criticism;', *NESTThRev* 3 (1980): 27-41.

Balch, David L. '1 Cor 7:32-35 and Stoic debates about marriage, anxiety and distraction', *JBL* 102 (1983): 429-39.

—— 'Household Codes'. Chapter 2 in *Greco-Roman Literature and the New Testament: Selected Forms and Genres.* SBL Sources for Biblical Study 21. Edited by David E. Aune. Atlanta, Georgia: Scholars Press, 1988. Pp. 25-50.

Bammel, Ernest. 'Ein Beitrag zur paulinischen Staatsanschauung', *TLZ* 85/11 (1960): 837-40.

—— 'Paulus, der Mose des Neuen Bundes', *Theologia* 54 (1983): 399-408.

Barclay, John M. G. 'Mirror-Reading a Polemical Letter: Galatians as a Test Case', *JSNT* 31 (1987): 73-93.

—— *Obeying the Truth: A Study of Paul's Ethics in Galatians.* SNTW. Edinburgh: T. & T. Clark, 1988.

Barnett, Paul. *Bethlehem to Patmos: The New Testament Story.* London: Hodder and Stoughton, 1989.

Barnikol, E. 'Römer 13: Der nichtpaulinische Ursprung der absoluten Obrigkeitsbejahung von Römer 13:1-7', *Texte und Untersuchungen* (Berlin) 77 (1961): 65-133.

Barr, James. *Old and New in Interpretation: A Study of the Two Testaments.* London: SCM, 1966.

Barrett, C.K. *Essays on Paul.* London: SPCK, 1982.

—— *The First Epistle to the Corinthians.* 2nd Edn. Black's NT Comm. London: A. & C. Black, 1971.

—— 'The Interpretation of the Old Testament in the New'. In *The Cambridge History of the Bible.* Edited by R.R. Ackroyd and C.F. Evans. Cambridge: CUP, 1970. I: 377-411.

Bartchy, S. Scott. *First-Century Slavery and 1 Corinthians 7:21.* SBL DS 11. Missoula, Montana: University of Montana, 1973.

Barton, George Aaron. *A Critical and Exegetical Commentary on the Book of Ecclesiastes.* ICC. Edinburgh, 1908.

Barton, John. *Oracles of God: Perceptions of Ancient Prophecy in Israel after the Exile.* London: Darton, Longman and Todd, 1986.

—— *People of the Book: The Authority of the Bible in Christianity.* The Bampton Lectures for 1988. London: SPCK, 1988.

—— 'Review of R.T. Beckwith's, *The Old Testament Canon of the New Testament Church and its Background in Early Judaism,*' *Theology* 90 (1987): 63-65.

Batey, Richard A. *New Testament Nuptial Imagery.* Leiden: E.J. Brill, 1971.

—— 'Paul's Bride Image: A Symbol of Realistic Eschatology', *Int* 17 (1963): 176-82.

Baumgarten, J. *Paulus und die Apokalyptik: Die Auslegung apokalyptischer Überlieferungen in den echten Paulusbriefen.* WMANT 44. Neukirchen: Neukirchener Verlag, 1975.

Bazak, Jacob. 'Judicial Ethics in Jewish Law'. In *Jewish Law Association Studies III: The Oxford Conference Volume.* Edited by A.M. Fuss. Atlanta, Georgia: Scholars Press, 1987. pp. 27-40.

Beale, G. 'Revelation'. In *It is Written: Scripture Citing Scripture: Essays in Honour of Barnabas Lindars.* Edited by D.A. Carson and H.G.M. Williamson. Cambridge: CUP, 1988. pp. 318-36.

Becker, J. *Untersuchungen zur Entstehungsgeschichte der Testamente der Zwölf Patriarchen.* AGJU 8. Leiden: E.J. Brill, 1970.

Beckwith, R.T. *The Old Testament Canon of the New Testament Church and its Background in Early Judaism.* Reading: SPCK, 1985.

—— Review of John Barton's *Oracles of God: Perceptions of Ancient Prophecy in Israel after the Exile'*, *VT* 41/4 (1991): 385-95.

Berg, Sandra Beth. *The Book of Esther: Motifs, Themes and Structure.* SBLDS 44. Missoula: Scholars Press, 1979.

Berger, Klaus. *Die Gesetzauslegung Jesu: Ihr historischer Hintergrund im Judentum und im Alten Testament. Teil I: Markus und Parallelen.* WMANT 40. Assen: Neukirchener Verlag, 1972.

Bergren, Richard Victor. *The Prophets and the Law.* Cincinnati: Hebrew Union College/ Jewish Institute of Religion, 1974.

Bertowitz, Luci and Squitier, Karl A. (eds). *Thesaurus Linguae Graecae: Canon of Greek Authors and Works.* Oxford, 1986.

Best, Ernest. '1 Cor 7:14 and Children in the Church', *Irish Biblical Studies* 12 (1990): 158-66.

—— *One Body in Christ: A Study in the Relationship of the Church to Christ in the Epistles of the Apostle Paul.* London: SPCK, 1955.

Beyer, Klaus. *Semitische Syntax im Neuen Testament.* Band I. Satzlehre Teil 1. Göttingen: Vandenhoeck & Ruprecht, 1968.

Bicknell, E.J. *A Theological Introduction to the Thirty-nine Articles of the Church of England.* London: Longmans, 1955.

Bilde, Per. *Flavius Josephus between Jerusalem and Rome: His Life, His Works and their Importance.* JSPSS 2. Sheffield: JSOT Press, 1988.

Black, M. 'The Tradition of Hasidaean-Essene Asceticism: Its Origins and Influence'. In *Aspects du Judéo-Christianisme: Calloque de Strasbourg 1964.* Paris: Presses Universitaires de France, 1965.

Blass, F., Debrunner, A. and Funk, Robert W. (translation). *A Greek Grammar of the New Testament.* London 1961.

Blidstein, Gerald J. ''Atimia: A Greek Parallel to Ezra X.8 and to Post-Biblical Exclusion from the Community', *VT* 24 (1985): 357-60.

Boecker, H.J. *Redeformen des Rechtsleben im Alten Testament.* WMANT 14. Neukirchen: Neukirchener, 1970.

Bömer, Franz. *Untersuchungen über die Religion der Sklaven in Griechenland und Rom.* 4 Bde. Mainz: 1957-63.

Borgen, P. 'Catalogues of Vices, The Apostolic Decree and the Jerusalem Meeting'. In *Essays in Tribute to Howard Clark Kee: The Social World of Formative Christianity and Judaism.* Edited by J. Neusner, P. Borgen, E.S. Frerichs and R. Horsley, 1988.

Boswell, John. *Christianity, Social Tolerance, and Homosexuality.* Chicago and London, 1980.

Bowersock, G.W. *Roman Arabia.* London: Harvard University Press, 1983.

Brewer, D. Instone. *Techniques and Assumptions in Jewish Exegesis before 70 CE.* TSAJ 30. Tübingen: J.C.B. Mohr (Paul Siebeck), 1992.

—— '1 Cor 9.9-11: A Literal Interpretation of *Do Not Muzzle the Ox.*' *NTS* 38/ 4 (1992): 554-65.

Bring, Ragnar. *Christus und das Gesetz: Die Bedeutung des Gesetzes des Alten Testaments nach Paulus und sein Glauben an Christus.* Leiden: E.J. Brill, 1969.

Brock, Sebastian. 'The Two Ways and the Palentinian Targum'. In *A Tribute to Geza Vermes: Essays on Jewish and Christian Literary History.* Edited by Philip R. Davies and Richard T. White. *JSOTSS* 100. Sheffield: Sheffield Academic Press, 1990. pp.139-52.

Brooke, George J. *Exegesis at Qumran: 4QFlorilegium in its Jewish context.* JSOT Supp. Ser. 29. Sheffield: JSOT Press, 1985.

Brooten, Bernadette J. 'Paul and the Law: How complete was the Departure?', *Princeton Seminary Bulletin Supplement* 1 (1990): 71-89.

Bruce, F.F. 'Paul and the law in recent research.' In *Law and Religion: Essays on the Place of the Law in Israel and Early Christianity*. Edited by Barnabas Lindars. Cambridge: James Clark & Co., 1988. pp. 115-25.

—— 'Review of *Die Tugend- und Lasterkataloge im Neuen Testament* by Siegfried Wibbing', *JTS* 11 (1960): 389-91.

—— *1 and 2 Corinthians*. NCB. London: Oliphants, 1971.

—— *Paul: Apostle of the Free Spirit*. Grand Rapids: Eerdmans, 1977.

—— *Romans*. Tyndale NT commentaries. Revised Edition. Leicester: IVP, 1985.

—— *This is That: The New Testament Development of Some Old Testament Themes*. Exeter: The Paternoster Press, 1968.

Brueggemann, Walter. *Genesis: A Bible Commentary for Teaching and Preaching*. Atlanta, Georgia: John Knox Press, 1982.

Buber, M. *Zwei Glaubensweisen*. Munich, 1950.

Büchler, Adolph. *Types of Jewish-Palestinian Piety from 70 B.C.E.to 70 C.E.—The Ancient Pious Men*. New York: KTAV, 1968.

Bultmann, Rudolph. *Theologische des Neuen Testaments*. Tübingen: J.C.B. Mohr (Paul Siebeck), 1954.

—— *Theology of the New Testament*. 2 vols. Trans. Kendrick Grobel. New York: Charles Scribner's Sons, vol. 1, 1951; vol. 2, 1955.

—— 'Significance of the Old Testament for the Christian Faith'. Trans. Bernhard W. Anderson. In *The Old Testament and the Christian Faith*. Edited by Bernhard W. Anderson. New York: Harper & Row, 1963. pp. 8-35 (orig. in *Glauben und Verstehen*, 1933).

Burkill, T.A. 'Two into One: The Notion of Carnal Union in Mark 10:8; 1 Cor 6:16; Eph 5:31', *ZNW* 62 (1971): 115-20.

Burkitt, F.C. *Early Christianity Outside the Roman Empire*. Cambridge, 1899.

Buss, Martin J. 'The Distinction Between Civil and Criminal Law in Ancient Israel. In *Proceedings of the Sixth World Congress of Jewish Studies*. Jerusalem: World Union of Jewish Studies, 1977. 1:51-62.

Byrne, B. 'Sinning Against One's Own Body: Paul's Understanding of the Sexual Relationship in 1 Corinthians 6:18', *CBQ* 45 (1983): 608-16.

Cambier, J. 'La Chair et l'Esprit en 1 Cor 5:5', *NTS* 15 (1968-69): 221-32.

Campbell, Jonathan. 'The Use of Scripture in CD 1-8,19,20'. Oxford D.Phil Thesis, 1991.

Carmichael, C. *The Laws of Deuteronomy*. London: Cornell University Press, 1974.

Carpenter, H.J. 'Popular Christianity and the Theologians in the Early Centuries', *JTS* 14/2 (1963): 294-310.

Carrington, Philip. *The Primitive Christian Catechism: A Study in the Epistles*. Cambridge: CUP, 1940.

Catchpole, David R. 'Paul, James and the Apostolic Decree', *NTS* 23 (1977): 428-44.

Chadwick, Henry. *The Early Church*. London: Penguin Books, 1967.

Charlesworth, James H. 'The Pseudepigrapha as Biblical Exegesis'. In *Early Jewish and Christian Exegesis: Studies in Memory of William Hugh Brownlee*. Edited by Craig A. Evans and William F. Stinespring. Atlanta, Georgia: Scholars Press, 1987. pp. 139-52.

—— *The Old Testament Pseudepigrapha and the New Testament: Prolegomena for the Study of Christian Origins*. SNTSMS 54. Cambridge: CUP, 1985.

Chartles, R.H. *The Testaments of the Twelve Patriarchs*. London, 1908.

Chavasse, Claude. *The Bride of Christ: An Enquiry into the Nuptial Element in Early Christianity*. London: Faber and Faber, 1939.

Chester, Andrew. 'Citing the Old Testament'. In *It is Written: Scripture Citing Scripture: Essays in Honour of barnabas Lindars*. Edited by D.A. Carson and H.G.M. Williamson. Cambridge: CUP, 1988. pp. 141-69.

—— *Divine Revelation and Divine Titles in the Pentateuchal Targumim.* Tubingen: J.C.B. Mohr (Paul Siebeck), 1986.

Childs, Brevard S. *Exodus.* London: SCM, 1974.

—— *The New Testament as Canon: An Introduction.* London: SCM, 1984.

Coats, G.W. 'The Joseph Story and Ancient Wisdom: a Reappraisal', *CBQ* 35 (1973): 285-97.

Collins, A.Y. 'The Function of "Excommunication" in Paul', *HTR* 73 (1980): 251-63.

Collins, John J. 'Chiasmus, the "ABA" Pattern and the Texts of Paul'. In *Studia Paulinorum Congressus Internationalis Catholicus.* Rome, 1963.

Collins, John J. 'Review of Karl Wilhelm Niebuhr's *Gesetz und Paränese*', *CBQ* 51/4 (1989): 752-53.

Collins, John J. *Between Athens and Jerusalem: Jewish Identity in the Hellenistic Diaspora.* New York: Crossroad, 1983.

Collins, Raymond F. 'The Unity of Paul's paraenesis in 1 Thess 4.3-8 and 1 Cor 7.1-7 , a significant parallel', *NTS* 29 (1983): 420-29.

Conzelmann, Hans. *1 Corinthians.* Trans. James W. Leitch. Philadelphia: Fortress, 1975.

—— *An Outline of the Theology of the New Testament.* Transl. John Bowden. London: SCM, 1969.

Corriveau, Raymand. *The Liturgy of Life.* Paris: Brouwer, 1970.

Countryman, L.W. *Dirt, Greed and Sex: Sexual Ethics in the New Testament and their Implications for Today.* London: SCM, 1989.

Craigie, Peter C. *The Book of Deuteronomy.* Grand Rapids: Eerdmans, 1976.

Cranfield, C.E.B. *A Critical and Exegetical Commentary on the Epistle to the Romans.* 2 vols. ICC. Edinburgh: T. & T. Clark, vol. 1, 1975, reprinted with corrections, 1980; vol. 2, 1979.

Crouch, James E. *The Origin and Intention of the Colossian Haustafel.* Göttingen: Vandenhoeck & Ruprecht, 1972.

Cummins, Tony. 'Paul, Salvation and the Temple of Jerusalem: A Study of the Socio-Political Dimension of Pauline Soteriology'. Forthcoming Oxford D.Phil Thesis.

Daube, David. 'Alexandrian Methods of Interpretation and the Rabbis.' In *Festschrift for H. Lewald.* Basel: Helbing and Lichteholm, 1953. pp. 27-44.

—— 'Pauline Contributions to a Pluralistic Culture: Re-Creation and Beyond?' In *Jesus and Man's Hope.* vol. II. Edited by D.G. Miller and D.K. Hadidian. Pittsburgh: Pittsburgh Theological Seminary, 1971.

—— 'Rabbinic Methods of Interpretation and Hellenistic Rhetoric', *HUCA* 22 (1949): 239-65.

—— 'A Reform in Acts and its Models'. In *Jews, Greeks and Christians: Religious Cultures in Late Antiquity—Essays in Honor of William David Davies.* Edited by Robert Hamerton-Kelly and Robin Scroggs. Leiden: E.J. Brill, 1976. pp. 151-63.

—— 'Concessions to Human Sinfulness in Jewish Law', *JJS* 10 (1959): 1-13.

—— 'Participle and Imperative in 1 Peter'. An Appended Note in *The First Epistle of St. Peter*, by Edward Gordon Selwyn. London: MacMillan & Co. 1946. pp. 467-88.

—— *The Exodus Pattern in the Bible.* London: Faber and Faber, 1963.

—— *The New Testament and Rabbinic Judaism.* London: Athlone Press, 1956.

Davies, Philip R. 'Halakhah at Qumran'. In *A Tribute to Geza Vermes: Essays on Jewish and Christian Literature and History.* Edited by Philip R. Davies and Richard T. White. Sheffield: JSOT Press, 1990. pp. 37-50.

Davies, W. D. *Torah in the Messianic Age and/or the Age to Come.* JBL Monograph Series 7. Philadelphia: Society of Biblical Literature, 1952.

—— *Paul and Rabbinic Judaism: Some Rabbinic Elements in Pauline Theology.* Philadelphia: Fortress Press, 1980 (orig. 1948).

De Jonge. H.J. 'The Testaments of the Twelve Patriarchs and the New Testament.' In *Studia Evangelica.* Edited by K. Aland, 1959. pp. 546-56.

de Lacey, D.R. 'οἵτινές ἐστε ὑμεῖς: The Function of a Metaphor in St Paul'. In *Templum Amicitiae: Essays on the Second Temple presented to Ernst Bammel*. Edited by William Horbury. JSOTSS 48. Sheffield: Sheffield Academic Press, 1991. pp. 391-409.
de Vaux, Roland. *Ancient Israel*. 2 Volumes. New York: McGraw-Hill, 1965.
de Young, James B. 'A Critique of Prohomosexual Interpretations of the Old Testament Apocrypha and Pseudepigrapha', *Bib Sac* 147/588 (1990): 437-54.
Deidun, T.J. *New covenant Morality in Paul*. Analecta Biblica 89. Rome: Biblical Institute Press, 1981.
Deissmann, Adolf. *Light from the Ancient East*. Trans. L. R. M. Strachan from the 4th (1923) German edn., 1927; reprint edn. Grand Rapids: Baker, 1978.
Delcor, Mathias. 'The Courts of the Church of Corinth and the Courts of Qumran'. In *Paul and Qumran: Studies in New Testament Exegesis*. Edited by Jerome Murphy-O'Connor. London, 1968. pp. 69-84.
Deluz, Gaston. *A Companion to 1 Corinthians*. London: Darton, Longman and Todd, 1963.
Derrett, J. Duncan M. '"Handing over to Satan": An Explanation of 1 Cor 5:1-7'. In *Studies in the New Testament*. vol. 4. Leiden: E.J. Brill, 1986. pp. 167-86.
——— 'Judgement and 1 Corinthians 6', *NTS* 37/1 (1991): 22-36.
Dexinger, F. 'Der Dekalog im Judentum', *Bibel und Liturgie* 59 (1986): 86-95.
Dibelius, M. *An die Kolosser, Epheser an Philemon*. HNT 12. 3rd ed. rev. by H. Greeven. Tübingen: J.C.B. Mohr (Paul Siebeck), 1953.
Dillard, Raymond B. *2 Chronicles*. WBC 15. Waco, Texas: Word Books, 1987.
Dimant, Devorah. '4QFlorilegium and the idea of the Community as Temple'. In *Hellenica et Judaica: Hommage A Vantin Nikiprowetzky*. Edited by A. Caquot, M. Hadas-Lebel and J. Riaud. Leuven-Paris: Editions Peeters, 1986. pp. 165-89.
——— 'Use and Interpretation of Mikra in the Apocrypha and Pseudepigrapha'. In *Mikra: Text, Translation, Reading and Interpretation of the Hebrew Bible in Ancient Judaism and Early Christianity*. CRIadNT II,i. Assen: Van Gorcum, 1988. pp. 379-419.
Dodd, C.H. *According to the Scriptures: The Sub-structure of New Testament Theology*. London: Nisbet, 1952.
Dodd, C.H. *Gospel and Law*. Cambridge, 1963.
Dumbrell, William J. *The Faith of Israel: Its expression in the books of the Old Testament*. Apollos. Leicester: IVP, 1988.
Dungan, D.L. *The Sayings of Jesus in the Churches of Paul*. Fortress, 1971.
Dunn, J.D.G. 'Works of the Law and the Curse of the Law (Galatians 3:10-14)', *NTS* 31 (1985): 523-42.
Dunn, James D. G. *Romans*. 2 vols. WBC 38A, 38B. Dallas: Word Books, 1988.
——— *The Living Word*. London: SCM, 1987.
Dunstan, G.R. 'Hard Sayings—V. 1 Corinthians 6:16, *Theology* 66/522 (1963): 491-93.
Easton, Burton Scott. *The Pastoral Epistles: Introduction, Translation, Commentary and Word Studies*. London: SCM, 1948.
Eaton, Michael A. *Ecclesiastes: An Introduction*. Tyndale Comm. Downers Grove: IVP, 1983.
Elert, W. 'Redemptio ab hostibus', *TLZ* 72 (1947): 265-70.
Ellicott, C. *St. Paul's First Epistle to the Corinthians with a Critical and Grammatical Commentary*. London, 1887.
Ellingworth, Paul and Hatton, Howard. *A Translators Guide on Paul's First Letter to the Corinthians*. London: United Bible Societies, 1985.
Ellis, E. Earle. 'The Old Testament Canon in the Early Church'. In *Mikra: Text, Translation, Reading and Interpretation of the Hebrew Bible in Ancient Judaism and Early Christianity*. CRIadNT II,i. Assen: Van Gorcum, 1988. pp.653-90 (= Chapter One of *The Old Testament in Early Christianity: Canon and Interpretation in the Light of Modern Research*. WUNT 54. Tübingen: J.C.B. Mohr [Paul Siebeck], 1991).
——— 'Paul', *New Bible Dictionary Revised*. Edited by J.D. Douglas. London: IVP, 1962. pp. 943-55.

—— *Paul's Use of The Old Testament.* Grand Rapids, Michigan: Eerdmans, 1957.
—— *Prophecy and Hermeneutic in Early Christianity: New Testament Essays.* Tübingen, J.C.B. Mohr (Paul Siebeck), 1978.
Endres, John C. *Biblical Interpretation in the Book of Jubilees.* CBQMS 18. Washington: The Catholic Biblical Association of America, 1987.
Epstein, L.M. *Sex Laws and Customs in Judaism.* 1949; reprint New York, 1967.
Eron, Lewis John. 'Ancient Jewish Attitudes Towards Sexuality: A Study of Ancient Jewish Attiutdes Towards Sexuality as Expressed in the Testaments of the Twelve Patriarchs'. PhD Thesis, Temple University, 1987.
Evans, Craig A. and Sanders, James A. (eds.) *Paul and the Scriptures of Israel.* JSNTSS 83. SSEJC 1. Sheffield: JSOT Press, 1993.
Fee, Gordon E. *The First Epistle to the Corinthians.* NICNT. Grand Rapids, Michigan: Eerdmans, 1987.
—— '1 Corinthians 7:1 in the NIV', *JETS* 23 (1980): 307-14.
—— 'Toward a Theology of 1 Corinthians.' In *SBL Seminar Papers: Annual Meeting 1989.* Edited by David J. Lull. Atlanta, Georgia: Scholars Press, 1989. pp. 265-81.
Feldman, Lous H. 'Use, Authority and Exegesis of Mikra in the Writings of Josephus.' In *Mikra: Text, Translation, Reading and Interpretation of the Hebrew Bible in Ancient Judaism and Early Christianity.* CRIadNT II,i. Assen: Van Gorcum, 1988. pp. 455-518.
Ferguson, Everett. *Backgrounds of Early Christianity.* Grand Rapids: Eerdmans, 1987.
Findlay, G.G. 'St. Paul's First Epistle to the Corinthians'. In *The Expositior's Greek Testament.* London: Hodder and Stoughton, 1900.
Fishbane, Michael. 'Use, Authority and Interpretation of Mikra at Qumran'. In *Mikra: Text, Translation, Reading and Interpretation of the Hebrew Bible in Ancient Judaism and Early Christianity.* CRIadNT II,i. Assen: Van Gorcum, 1988. pp. 339-77.
—— *Biblical Interpretation in Ancient Israel.* Oxford: Clarendon Press, 1985.
Fishburne, C.W. '1 Corinthians III. 10-15 and the Testament of Abraham', *NTS* 17 (1970): 109-15.
Fisk, Bruce N. 'Eating Meat Offered to Idols: Corinthian Behavior and Pauline Response in 1 Corinthians 8-10 (A Response to Gordon Fee)', *TrinJ* 10 (1989): 49-70.
Fitzmeyer, J.A. 'Paul and the Law'. In *To Advance the Gospel.* New York, 1981. pp. 185-201.
Forkman, Göran. *The Limits of the Religious Community.* Lund: CWP Gleerup, 1972.
Fraade, Steven D. 'Ascetical Aspects of Ancient Judaism'. In *Jewish Spirituality: From the Bible Through the Middle Ages.* Edited by Arthur Green. New York: Crossroads, 1985. pp. 253-88.
Freedman, David Noel 'The Nine Commandments: The Secret Progress of Israel's Sins', *Bible Review* V/6 (1989): 28-42.
Fuller, Reginald H. '1 Cor. 6:1-11. An Exegetical Paper', *Ex Auditu* 2 (1986): 96-104.
Fung, Ronald Y.K. 'Some Pauline Pictures of the Church', *EvQ* 53 (1981): 89-107.
Furnish, Victor Paul. *II Corinthians.* Anchor Bible 32A. Garden City, New York: Doubleday, 1984.
—— *The Love Command in the New Testament.* London. SCM, 1973.
—— *Theology and Ethics in Paul.* Nashville: Abingdon, 1968.
—— 'Theology in 1 Corinthians: Initial Soundings.' In *SBL Seminar Papers: Annual Meeting 1989.* Edited by David J. Lull. Atlanta, Georgia: Scholars Press, 1989. pp. 246-64.
—— *The Moral Teaching of Paul.* Nashville, 1979.
Gadamer, Hans-Georg. *Truth and Method.* New York: The Seabury Press, 1975.
Gager, John G. *Moses in Greco-Roman Paganism.* SBLMS 16. New York: Abingdon Press, 1972.
Gardner, P.D. 'The Gifts of God and the Authentication of a Christian: An Exegetical Study of 1 Corinthians 8:1-11:1', Unpublished PhD Thesis, Cambridge University 1989.

Garnsey, P. *Famine and Food Supply in the Graeco-Roman World: Responses to Risk and Crisis*. Cambridge: CUP, 1988.

Gaston, Lloyd. *No Stone on Another: Studies in the Significance of the Fall of Jerusalem in the Synoptic Gospels*. NovTSup 23. Leiden: E.J. Brill, 1970.

Gereboff, J. *Rabbi Tarfon: the Tradition, the Man and early Rabbinic Judaism*. Brown Judaic Studies 7. Missoula: Scholars Press, 1979.

Gerleman, Gillis. 'Studies in the Septuagint, III. Proverbs', *Lunds Universitets Arsskrift*. N.F. Avd. 1. Bd. 52. Nr. 3, Lund. C.W.K.. Gleerup, 1956. pp.1-63.

Ginzberg, Louis.*The Legends of the Jews: Volume 2*. Philadelphia, 1948.

Gloch, J.Ph. *Die Gesetzesfrage im Leben Jesu und in der Lehre des Paulus*. Karlsruhe & Leipzig, 1885.

Godet, F. *St Paul's First Epistle to the Corinthians*. Edinburgh, 1886.

Goodenough, E.R.*The Jurisprudence of the Jewish Courts in Egypt: Legal Administration by the Jews under the Early Roman Empire as Described by Philo Judaeus*. New Haven, 1929.

Gräbe, P.J. 'Die verhouding tussen indikatief en imperatief in die pauliniese etiek: enkele aksente uit diskussie sedert 1924', *Scriptura* 32 (1990): 54-66.

Grafe, E. *Die paulinische Lehre vom Gesetz nach den vier Hauptbriefen*. Leipzig, 1893.

Grant, Robert M. 'Holy Law in Paul and Ignatius.' In *The Living Text: Essays in Honour of Ernest W. Saunders*. Edited by Dennis E. Groh and Robert Jewett. London: University Press of America, 1985. pp. 65-71.

Gräßer, E. *Der Alte Bund im Neuen: Exegetische Studien zur Israelfrage im Neuen Testament*. Tübingen, 1985.

Grotius, Hugo. *Annotationes in Novum Testamentum*. Edited by E. von Windheim. Erlangen, 1756 (orig. 1646).

Hamerton-Kelly, R.G. 'Sacred Violence and "Works of Law": Is Christ then an Agent of Sin? (Galatians 2:17)', *CBQ* 52/1 (1990): 55-75.

Hanson, Anthony Tyrrell. *Studies in the Pastoral Epistles*. London: SPCK, 1968.

—— *Studies in Paul's Technique and Theology*. London: SPCK, 1974.

—— *The Living Utterances of God: The New Testament Exegesis of the Old*. London: Darton, Longman and Todd, 1983.

Harnack, Adolph (von). 'Das Alte Testament in den paulinischen Briefen und in den paulinischen Gemeinden', *Sitzungsberichte der Preußischen Akademie der Wissenschaften*, Berlin (1928): 124-41 (= *Kleine Schriften zur alten Kirche*, Vol. 2, Leipzig 1980, 823-41).

—— *Marcion*. Leipzig: J.C. Hinrichs, 1921.

Harris, G. 'The Beginnings of Church Discipline: 1 Corinthians 5', *NTS* 37/1 (1991): 1-21.

Harris, R. *Testimonies: Part I* (Cambridge, 1916), *Part II* (Cambridge, 1920).

Hart, J.H.A. *Ecclesiasticus: The Greek Text of Codex 248*. Cambridge: CUP, 1909.

Hartman, Lars. 'Code and Context: A Few Reflections on the Parenesis of Colossians 3:6-4:1'. In *Tradition and Interpretation in the New Testament: Essays in Honor of E. Earle Ellis for His 60th Birthday*. Edited by Gerald F. Hawthorne with Otto Betz. Grand Rapids, Michigan: Eerdmans and Tübingen: J.C.B. Mohr (Paul Siebeck), 1987. pp. 236-47.

Harvey, A.E. 'Review of *The Sentences of Pseudo-Phocylides* edited by P.W. van der Horst', *JTS* 30 (1979): 543-46.

—— *Strenuous Commands: The Ethic of Jesus*. London: SCM Press, 1990.

—— 'The Testament of Simeon Peter'. In *A Tribute to Geza Vermes: Essays on Jewish and Christian Literary History*. Edited by Philip R. Davies and Richard T. White. *JSOTSS* 100. Sheffield: Sheffield Academic Press, 1990. pp. 339-54.

Hay, David M. 'Moses Through New Testament Spectacles', *Int* 44/3 (1990): 240-52.

Hays, Richard B. *Echoes of Scripture in the Letters of Paul*. New Haven/London: Yale University Press, 1989.

Hengel, Martin. *Judaism and Hellenism: Studies in their Encounter in Palestine during the Early Hellenistic Period.* 2 vols. Trans. John Bowden. Philadelphia: Fortress, 1974.
—— *The Pre-Christian Paul.* Tran. John Bowden. London: SCM Press, 1991.
—— 'Zwischen Jesus und Paulus. Die 'Hellenisten', die 'Sieben' und Stephanus (Apg 6,1-15; 7,54-8,3)', *ZTK* 72 (1975): 151-206.
Herbert, A.S. 'Marriage in the Bible and the Early Christian Church: I. The OT Foundations', *ExpTim* LIX (1947): 12-13.
Herford, R Travers. *Talmud and Apocrypha: A Comparative Study of the Jewish Ethical Teaching in the Rabbinical and Non-Rabbinical sources in the Early Centuries.* London: The Soncino Press, 1933.
Héring, Jean. *The First Epistle of Saint Paul to the Corinthians.* Transl. A.W. Heathcote and P.J. Allcock. London: Epworth, 1962.
Herz, N. 'A Hebrew Word in Greek Disguise: 1 Cor vii.3', *ExpTim* 7 (1895/96): 48.
Heth, William Alexander. 'Matthew's "Eunuch Saying"' (19:12) and its Relationship to Paul's Teaching on Singleness in 1 Corinthians 7'. ThD Thesis, Dallas Theological Seminary, 1986.
Hillyer, Norman. '1 Corinthians'. In *The New Bible Commentary Revised.* Edited by D. Guthrie and J.A. Motyer. London: IVP, 1970. pp. 1049-74.
Holladay, William L. *Jeremiah 1: A Commentary on the Book of the Prophet Jeremiah Chapter 1-25.* Philadelphia: Fotress Press, 1986.
Hollander, H.W. and de Jonge, M. *The Testaments of the Twelve Patriarchs: A Commentary.* Leiden: Brill, 1985.
Hollander, H.W. *Joseph as an Ethical Model in the Testaments of the Twelve Patriarchs.* Leiden: Brill, 1981.
Holmberg. B. *Paul and Power: The Structure of Authority in the Pauline Epistles.* CBNT 11. Lund, 1978.
Holtz, Traugott. 'Zur Frage der inhaltlichen Weisungen bei Paulus', *TLZ* 106 (1981): 385-400.
—— 'Die Bedeutung des Apostelkonzils für Paulus. *NovT* 16(1974): 110-48.
—— 'Zum Selbstverständnis des Apostels Paulus', *TLZ* 91 (1966): 321-30
—— 'Zur Interpretation des Alten Testaments im Neuen Testament', *TLZ* 99 (1974): 19-32.
—— *Geschichte und Theologie des Urchristentums: Gesammelte Aufsätze.* Edited by Eckart Reinmuth and Christian Wolff. Tübingen: J.C.B. Mohr (Paul Siebeck), 1991.
Hooker, Morna D. *From Adam to Christ: Essays on Paul.* Cambridge: CUP, 1990.
—— '"Beyond the Things which are Written": An Examination of 1 Cor iv. 6', *NTS* 10 (1963/64):127-32.
Horbury, William. '1 Thessalonians ii.3 as Rebutting the Charge of False Prophecy', *JTS* 33 (1982): 492-508.
—— 'Herod's Temple and "Herod's Days"'. In *Templum Amicitiae: Essays on the Second Temple presented to Ernst Bammel.* Edited by William Horbury. Sheffield: JSOT Press, 1991. pp. 103-49.
—— 'The Twelve and the Phylarchs', *NTS* 32 (1986): 503-27.
—— 'Extirpation and Excommunication', *VT* 35 (1985): 13-38.
—— 'New Wine in Old Wine Skins: IX. The Temple', *ExpTim* 86 (1974/75): 36-42.
—— 'Old Testament Interpretation in the Writings of the Church Fathers'. In *Mikra: Text, Translation, Reading and Interpretation of the Hebrew Bible in Ancient Judaism and Early Christianity.* CRIadNT II,i. Assen: Van Gorcum, 1988. pp. 727-87.
—— 'Paul and Judaism' [Review of *Paul and Palestinian Judaism*, by E. P. Sanders]. *ExpTim* 89 (1977-78): 116-118.
—— 'The Benediction of the *Minim* and Early Jewish-Christian Controversy', *JTS* 33/1 (1982): 19-61.
Horsley, G.H.R. *New Documents Illustrating Early Christianity: A Review of Greek Inscriptions and Papyri published in 1978.* Vol. 3. Sydney: Macquarie University, 1983.

Houlden, J.L *Ethics and the New Testament.* London: Penguin, 1973.
Howard, George E. 'Christ the End of the Law. The Meaning of Romans 10:4ff',
       *JBL* 88 (1969): 331-37.
—— *Paul: Crisis in Galatia: A Study in Early Christian Theology. SNTSMS* 35. Cambridge:
       CUP, 1979.
Howard, J.K. 'Christ Our Passover: A Study of the Passover-Exodus Theme in 1
       Corinthians', *The EvQ* 41 (1969): 97-108.
Hubbard, D.A. 'Ethics: OT Ethics', *ISBE* 2:165-69.
Hübner, H. 'Anthropologischer Dualismus in den Hodayoth?', *NTS* 18 (1972): 268-84.
—— 'Paulusforschung seit 1945. Ein kritischer Literaturbericht'. In *Aufstieg und
       Niedergang der Römischen Welt.* Teil II Principat. Band 25.4 Religion. Edited by
       Wolfgang Haase. Berlin: Walter de Gruyter, 1987. pp. 2649-2840.
—— *Das Gesetz bei Paulus: Ein Beitrag zum Werden der paulinischen Theologie.* FRLANT
       119. Göttingen: Vandenhoeck & Ruprecht, 1978. (ET: *Law in Paul's Thought.* Trans.
       James C.G. Greig; ed. John Riches. SNTW. Edinburgh: T. & T. Clark, 1984.)
Hugghins, Kenneth, W. 'An Investigation of the Jewish Theology of Sexuality
       influencing the references to homosexuality in Romans 1:18-32'. PhD Thesis,
       Southwestern Baptist Theological Seminary, Texas, 1986.
Hughes, H. Maldwyn. *The Ethics of Jewish Apocryphal Literature.* London: Robert Culley,
       1909.
Hughes, Robert Bruce. 'Textual and Hermeneutical Aspects of Paul's Use of the
       Old Testament in 1 and 2 Corinthians'. PhD Thesis, University of Edinburgh, 1978.
Hurd, J.C. *The Origin of 1 Corinthians.* London: SPCK, 1965.
Hurley. J.B. 'Man and Woman in 1 Corinthians'. Cambridge University PhD Thesis,
       1973.
Jones, Peter R. 'The Apostle Paul: Second Moses to the New Covenant Community'.
       In *God's Inerrant Word: An International Symposium On the Trustworthiness of Scripture.*
       Edited by John Warwick Monthomery. Minneapolis: Bethany Fellowship, Inc.,
       1974, pp. 219-41.
Junod, E. 'La formation et la composition de l'Ancien Testament dans l'Église grecque
       des quatres premiers siecles'. In *Le Canon de l'Ancien Testament: sa formation et son
       historie.* Ed. by S. Amsler, *et al.* Geneva: 1984. pp. 105-51.
Kallas, J. 'Romans xiii 1-7; An Interpolation', *NTS* 11 (1965): 365-74.
Kamlah, E. 'Frömmigkeit und Tugend: Die Gesetzetypologie des Josephus in C.Ap,
       145-295'. In *Josephus-Studien.* Edited by O. Betz, K. Haacker and M. Hengel.
       Göttingen, 1974. pp. 220-32.
Kamlah, Ehrhard. *Die Form der Katalogischen Paränese im Neuen Testament.* WUNT 7.
       Tübingen: J.C.B. Mohr (Paul Siebeck), 1964.
Käsemann, Ernst. *Paulinische Perspectiven.* Tübingen, 1973.
—— *Commentary on Romans.* Trans. and edited by Geoffrey W. Bromiley from the
       fourth (1980) German edn. Grand Rapids: Eerdmans, 1980.
Kaufmann, Stephen. 'The Structure of Deuteronomic Law', *Maarav* 1/2 (1978): 105-58.
Kee, H.C. 'The Ethical Dimensions of the Testaments of the Twelve Partriarchs
       as a Clue to their Provenance', *NTS* 24 (1978): 259-70.
Kellermann, D. 'חמס', *TDOT* 4:487-93.
Klein, G. *Der älteste Christliche Katechismus und die Jüdische Propaganda-Literatur.* Berlin, 1909.
Klein, George L. 'Hos 3:1-3 - Background to 1 Cor 6:19b-20?', *Criswell Theological
       Review* 3/2 (1989): 373-75.
Kleinknecht, Karl Theodor. *Der leidende Gerechtfertigte: Die alttestamentlich-jüdische Tradition
       vom 'leidenden Gerechten' ind ihre Rezeption bei Paulus.* WUNT 2.13. Tübingen: J.C.B.
       Mohr (Paul Siebeck), 1984.
Klinzing, G. *Die Umdeutung des Kultus in der Qumrangemeinde und im Neuen Testament.*
       Göttingen, 1971.
Knierim, Rolf P. 'Customs, Judges and Legislators in Ancient israel'. In *Early Jewish
       and Christian Exegesis: Studies in Memory of William Hugh Brownlee.* Edited by Craig

A. Evans and William F. Stinespring. Atlanta, Georgia: Scholars Press, 1987. pp. 3-15.

Knox, J. *The Ethic of Jesus in the Teaching of the Church: Its Authority and Relevance*. London, 1961.

Koch, Dietrich-Alex. *Die Schrift als Zeuge des Evangeliums: Untersuchungen zur Verwendung und zum Verständnis der Schrift bei Paulus*. BHT 69. Tübingen: J.C.B. Mohr (Paul Siebeck), 1986.

Kohler, Kaufmann. 'Didache or the Teaching of the Twelve Apostles', *The Jewish Encyclopedia* 4 (1903): 585-88.

—— 'Essenes', *The Jewish Encyclopedia* 5 (1903): 224-32.

Krupp, K. 'Das Verhältnis Jahwe-Israel im Sinne eines Ehebundes'. Unpublished PhD thesis, Freiburg, 1972.

Kruse, Colin G. 'The Offender and the Offence in 2 Corinthians 2:5 and 7:12', *EvQ* 88/2 (1988): 129-39.

Küchler, Max. *Frühjüdische Weisheitstraditionen*. Orbis Biblicus Et Orientalis 26. Göttingen: Vandenhoeck & Ruprecht, 1979.

Kugel, James L, and Greer, Rowan A. *Early Biblical Interpretation*. Philadelphia: Westminster Press, 1986.

Kühl, E. 'Stellung und Bedeutung des alttestamentlichen Gesetzes im Zusammenhang der paulinischen Lehre', *ThStKr* 67 (1894): 120-46.

Kümmel, Werner Georg. *Das Neue Testament: Geschichte der Erforschung seiner Probleme*. Freiburg/München: Karl Alber, 1958.

Ladd, George Eldon. 'Paul and the Law'. In *Soli Deo Gloria: Festschrift for William Childs Robinson*. Edited by J. McDowell Richards. Richmond: John Knox, 1968. pp. 50-67.

Lampe, G.W.H. 'Church Discipline and the Interpretation of the Epistles to the Corinthians'. In *Christian History and Interpretation: Studies Presented to John Knox*. Edited by W.R. Farmer, C.F.D. Moule and R.R. Niebuhr. Cambridge: CUP, 1967. pp. 337-61.

Laney, J. Carl. 'The Biblical Practice of Church Discipline', *Bib Sac* 143 (1986): 353-64.

Lang, Friedrich. *Die Briefe an die Korinther*. NTD. Göttingen: Vandenhoeck & Ruprecht, 1986.

Lauterbach, J. 'Midrash and Mishnah'. In *Rabbinic Essays*. New York: Ktav reprint, 1973. pp. 163-256.

Legrand, Lucien. *The Biblical Doctrine of Virginity*. London: Geoffrey Chapman, 1963.

Leiman, S.Z. *The Canonization of Hebrew Scripture: The Talmudic and Midrashic Evidence*. Hamden, CT, 1976.

Lenski, R.C.H. *The Interpretation of St. Paul's First and Second Epistles to the Corinthians*. Minneapolis: Augsburg, 1963 (orig. 1937).

Levine, Etan. *The Aramaic Version of the Bible: Contents and Context*. Berlin/New York: Walter de Gruyter, 1988.

Liddell, Henry George and Scott, Robert A. *Greek-English Lexicon*. 9th Edn. Oxford: Clarendon Press, 1940.

Lieberman, Saul. *Greek in Jewish Palestine: Studies in the Life and Manners of Jewish Palestine in the II-IV Centuries C.E.* New York: Philipp Feldheim, 1965.

Lightfoot, J.B. *Notes on Epistles of St. Paul*. London: Macmillan and Co., 1895.

Lillie, W. 'The Pauline House-Tables', *Exp Tim* 86 (1974/75): 179-83.

Lindars, Barnabas (ed). *Law and Religion: Essays on the Place of the Law in Israel and Early Christianity*. Cambridge: James Clark Co., 1988.

—— 'The Old Testament and Universalism in Paul', *BJRL* 69/2 (1987): 511-27.

Lindars, Barnabas. *New Testament Apologetic: The Doctrinal Significance of the Old Testament Quotations*. London: SCM, 1961.

Lindemann, Andreas. 'Die biblischen Toragebote und die paulinische Ethik'. In *Studien zum Text und zur Ethik des Neuen Testaments: Festschrift zum 80. Geburtstag von Hein-*

*rich Greeven.* Edited by Wolfgang Schrage. Berlin: Walter de Gruyter, 1986. pp. 242-65.

Lohse, Eduard.*The Formation of the New Testament.* Transl. by Eugene Boring. Nashville: Abingdon, 1981.

—— *Theoligische Ethik des Neuen Testaments.* Stuttgart: W. Kohlhammer, 1988.

Longenecker Richard. *Biblical Exegesis in the Apostolic Period.* USA: Eerdmans, 1975.

—— *Paul, Apostle of Liberty: The Origin and Nature of Paul's Christianity.* New York: Harper & Row, 1964; reprint edn. Grand Rapids: Baker, 1976.

—— *Galatians.* WBC 41. Dallas: Word Books, 1990.

Lowenthal, E.I. *The Joseph Narrative in Genesis.* New York: KTAV, 1973.

Löwy, M. 'Die paulinische Lehre vom Gesetz', *MGWJ* 47 (1903): 322-39; 417-33, 534-44; 48 (1904): 268-76, 321-27, 400-16.

Luhrmann, Dieter. 'Paul and the Pharisaic Tradition', *JSNT* 36 (1988): 75-94.

Lyonnet, Stanislas, and Sabourin, Leopold. *Sin, Redemption and Sacrifice: A Biblical and Patristic Study.* Rome: Biblical Institute Press, 1970.

Lyons, George. *Pauline Autobiography: Towards a New Understanding.* SBLDS 73. Atlanta: Scholars Press, 1985.

Maccoby, H. 'Neusner and the Red Cow', *JSJ* 21/1 (1990): 60-75.

Malan, F.S. 'The Use of the Old Testament in 1 Corinthians', *Neo* 14 (1981): 134-70.

Malherbe, Abraham J. 'Paul: Hellenistic Philosopher or Christian Pastor?', *ATR* 68 (1986): 3-13.

Malina, Bruce J. *The New Testament World: Insights from Cultural Anthropology.* London: SCM Press, 1983.

Marcus, Ralph 'Divine Names and Attributes in Hellenistic Jewish Literature', *American Academy for Jewish Research: Proceedings 1931-32*, Philadelphia, 43-120.

Mare, W.H.*1 Corinthians.* EBC. Grand Rapids: Eerdmans, 1976.

Marmorstein, A.*The Old Rabbinic Doctrine of God: I. The Names & Attributes of God.* London: Oxford University Press, 1927.

Marshall, I. Howard. 'Church and Temple in the New Testament', *TynBull* 40.2 (1989): 203-22.

—— *1 and 2 Thessalonians*, NCBC. London: Marshall, Morgan and Scott, 1983.

Marshall, L.H. *The Challenge of New Testament Ethics.* London, 1946.

Martin, Brice L. *Christ and the Law in Paul.* NovTSup 62. Leiden: Brill, 1989.

Martin, R.P. 'ἀρετή', *NIDNTT* 3:925-32.

Martin, R.P. *Word Biblical Themes: 1,2 Corinthians.* London: Word Publishing, 1988.

McArthur, H. 'Celibacy in Judaism at the Time of Christian Beginnings', *Andover Univ Sem Stud* 25/2 (1987): 163-81.

McBride, S. Dean. 'Transcendent Authority: The Role of Moses in Old Testament Traditions', *Int* 44/3 (1990): 229-39.

McComiskey, T. 'πενθέω', *NIDNTT* 2:421-23.

McDonald, James I.H. *Kerygma and Didache: The Articulation and Structure of the Earliest Christian Message.* Cambridge: CUP, 1980.

McKane, William. *Proverbs: A New Approach.* London. 1970.

McKeating, H. 'Sanctions against Adultery in Ancient Israelite Society with some Reflections on Methodology in the Study of Old Testament Ethics', *JSOT* 11 (1979): 57-72.

McNamara, Martin.*Targum and Testament—Aramaic Paraphrases of the Hebrew Bible: A Light on the New Testament.* Shannon, Ireland: Irish University Press,1968.

Meeks, Wayne A.*The First Urban Christians: The Social World of the Apostle Paul.* New Haven/London: Yale University Press, 1983.

—— *The Moral World of the First Christians.* Philadephia: Westminster, 1986.

—— '"And Rose Up to Play"; Midrash and paraenesis in 1 Corinthians 10:1-22', *JSNT* 16 (1982): 64-78.

Merk, O. *Handeln aus Glauben: Die Motivierungen der paulinischen Ethik*. Marburg: N.G. Elwert, 1968.

Metzger, Bruce M. *A Textual Commentary on the Greek New Testament*. London: United Bible Societies, 1971.

Meyer, H.A.W. *Critical and Exegetical Handbook to the Epistles to the Corinthians*. Vol. I. 1 Corinthians 1-8. Transl. D. Douglas Bannerman. Edinburgh: T. & T. Clark, 1884.

Michel, Otto. *Paulus und seine Bibel*. Darmstadt, 1972 (Orig. 1929).

Miguens, Manuel. 'Christ's 'Members' and Sex', *Thomist* 39 (1975): 24-48.

Milgrom, J. 'Two Kinds of Hatta't Sacrifice', *VT* 26 (1976): 333-37.

Miller, J.I. 'A Fresh Look at 1 Corinthians 6.16f. ' *NTS* 27 (1980): 125-27.

Minear, Paul. 'Christ and the Congregation: 1 Corinthians 5-6', *RevExp* 80/3 (1983): 341-50.

Mitten, Leslie C. 'New Wine in Old Wine Skins: IV. Leaven', *ExpTim* 84/11 (1973): 339-43.

Moiser, J. 'A Reassessment of Paul's view of marriage with reference to 1 Cor. 7', *JSNT* 18 (1983): 103-22.

Moo, D.J. 'Paul and the Law in the Last Ten Years', *SJT* 40 (1987): 287-307.

Moore, A.L. *The Parousia in the New Testament*. Supp to NT 13. Leiden: E.J. Brill, 1966.

Moore, George Foot. *Judaism in the First Centuries of the Christian Era: The Age of the Tannaim*. 3 Volumes. Cambridge: Harvard University Press, 1927-30.

Morris, Leon. *1 Corinthians*. Revised Edn. Tyndale NT comm. Leicester: Eerdmans, 1985.

—— *The Epistle to the Romans*. Grand Rapids: Eerdmans, 1988.

Moule, C. F. D. 'Obligation in the Ethic of Paul'. In *Christian History and Interpretation: Presented to John Knox*, ed. W.R. Farmer, C.F.D. Moule, and R. R. Niebuhr. Cambridge: CUP, 1967. pp. 389-406.

—— *An Idiom Book of New Testament Greek*. Cambridge: CUP, 1959.

—— *The Birth of the New Testament*. Third Edition. San Francisco: Harper and Row, 1982.

Moule, H.C.G. *The Epistle of Paul the Apostle to the Romans with Introduction and Notes*. The Cambridge Bible for Schools and Colleges. London: CUP, 1884.

Moulton, James Hope. *Grammar of New Testament Greek: Prolegomena*. Volume 1. 3rd Edn. Edinburgh: T. & T. Clark, 1908.

Münchow, Christoph. *Ethik und Eschatologie: Ein Beitrag Zum Verständnis der frühjüdischen Apokalyptik mit einem Ausblick auf das Neue Testament*. Göttingen: Vandenhoeck & Ruprecht, 1981.

Murphy O'Connor, J. 'Freedom or the Ghetto (1 Cor. viii, 1-13; x, 23-xi,1)', *RB* 85 (1978): 543-74.

—— 'Corinthian Slogans in 1 Corinthians 6:12-20', *CBQ* 40 (1978): 391-96.

—— The divorced woman in 1 Cor 7:10,11", *JBL* 100 (1981): 601-6.

—— *St. Paul's Corinth: Texts and Archaeology*. Wilmington: Michael Glazier, 1983.

Neill, Stephen, and Tom Wright. *The Interpretation of the New Testament 1861-1986*. 2nd edn. Oxford: University Press, 1988.

Neusner, Jacob *A Religion of Pots and Pans: Modes of Philosophical and Theological Discourse in Ancient Judaism: Essays and a Program*. BJS 156. Atlanta, Georgia: Scholars Press, 1988.

Newsom, Carol A. '4Q370: An Admonition Based on the Flood', *RevQ* 13/49 (1988): 23-43.

Newton, Michael. *The Concept of Purity at Qumran in the Letters of Paul*. Cambridge: CUP, 1985.

Nickelsburg, G.W.E. 'The Bible Rewritten and Expanded'. In *Jewish Writings of the Second Temple Period: Apocrypha, Pseudepigrapha, Qumran Sectarian Writings, Philo, Josephus*. Edited by M.E. Stone. CRINT 2/2. Assen: van Gorcum and Philadelphia: Fortress, 1984. pp. 89-156.

Niebuhr, Karl-Wilhelm. *Gesetz und Paränese: Katechismusartige Weisungsreihen in der frühjüdischen*

*Literatur*. WUNT 28. Tübingen: J.C.B. Mohr (Paul Siebeck), 1987.
—— *Heidenapostel aus Israel: Die jüdische Identität des Paulus nach ihrer Darstellung in seinen Briefen*. WUNT 62. Tübingen: J.C.B. Mohr (Paul Siebeck), 1992.
Nieder, L. *Die Motive der Religiös-sittlichen Paränese in den paulinischen Gemeindebriefen: Ein Beitrag zur Paulinischen Ethik*. MTSHA 12. München: Karl Zink Verlag, 1956.
Nikiprowetzky, V. 'Le Nouveau Temple', *REJ* 130 (1971): 5-30.
—— 'Temple et Communeauté', *REJ* 126 (1967): 7-25.
Nissen, Andreas. *Gott und der Nächste im Antiken Judentum*. Tübingen: J.C.B. Mohr, 1974.
O'Brien, Peter T. *Colossians, Philemon*. WBC 44. Waco, Texas: Word Books, 1982.
—— *Introductory Thanksgiving in the Letters of Paul*. NovTSup 49. Leiden: Brill, 1977.
O'Neill, J.C. *Paul's Letter to the Romans*. Middlesex: Penguin Books, 1975.
Oepke, Albrecht. 'κρύπτω', *TDNT* 3 (1965): 957-1000.
Olshausen, Hermann. *Biblical Commentary on St. Paul's First and Second Epistles to the Corinthians*. Trans. John Edmund Cox. Edinburgh: T. & T. Clark, 1850.
Osten-Sacken, Peter von der. *Evangelium und Tora: Aufsätze zu Paulus*. München: Chr. Kaiserverlag, 1987.
Parry, R. St. John. *The First Epistle to Paul the Apostle to the Corinthians*. Cambridge: 1937.
Parsons, Michael. 'Being Precedes Act: Indicative and Imperative in Paul's Writing', *EvQ* 88.2 (1988): 99-127.
Perk, J. *Handbuch zum Neuen Testament: Alttestamentliche Parallelen*. Düsseldorf: Verlag "der Pflug", Julius Nüttgens, 1947.
Petersen, William L. 'Can ἀρσενοκοῖται be Translated by "Homosexuals"? (1 Cor. 6.9; 1 Tim. 1:10)', *VC* 40 (1986): 187-91.
Pfitzner, Victor C. 'Purified Community-Purified Sinner: Expulsion from the Community according to Matthew 18:15-18 and 1 Corinthians 5:1-5', *AusBR* 30 (1982): 34-55.
Phillips, A. 'Another Look at Adultery', *JSOT* 20 (1981): 3-25.
Phillips, Anthony. *Ancient Israel's Criminal Law: A New Approach to the Decalogue*. Oxford: Basil Blackwell, 1970.
Philonenko, M. *Les interpolations chrétiennes des Testaments des Douze Patriarches et les manuscrits de Qoumran*. Paris, 1960.
Phipps, W.E. '1 Cor 7:1', *NTS* 28 (1982): 125-31.
Piper, John. *'Love Your Enemies': Jesus' love command in the synoptic gospels and in the early Christian paraenesis. A history of the tradition and an interpretation of its uses*. SNTSMS 38. Cambridge: CUP, 1979.
Plumptre, E.H. *Ecclesiastes*. The Cambridge Bible for Schools and Colleges. Edited by J.J.S. Perowne. Cambridge: CUP, 1898.
Prat, F. *The Theology of Saint Paul. I.* Transl. J.L. Stoddard. London/Dublin, 1945.
Prior, David. *The Message of 1 Corinthians: Life in the Local Church*. Leicester: IVP, 1985.
Procksch, D. 'ἅγιος', *TDNT* 1 (1964): 88-97.
Rabinowitz, Abraham Hirsch. 'Commandments, the 613', *Encyclopaedia Judaica* 5 (1972): 759-83.
Räisänen, H. *Paul and the Law*. Philadelphia: Fortress Press, 1983.
Ramsey, P. *Basic Christian Ethics*. London, 1950.
Reinmuth, Eckart. *Geist und Gesetz: Studien zu Voraussetzungen und Inhalt der paulinischen Paränese*. TA XLIV. Berlin: Evangelische Verlagsanstalt, 1985.
Rendall, R. 'Quotation in Scripture as an index of Wider Reference', *EvQ* 36 (1964): 214-21.
Rengstorf, K.H. 'Die neutestamentlichen Mahnungen an die Frau, sich dem Manne unterzuordnen'. In *Verbum Dei manet in Aeternum: Festschrift für O. Schmitz*. Edited by W. Foerster. Witten: Luther, 1953. pp. 131-45.
Rhyne, C. Thomas. *Faith Establishes the Law*. SBLDS 55. Chicago: SBL, 1981.
Richardson, P. '"I say, not the Lord": Personal Opinion, Apostolic Authority, and the development of Early Christian halakah', *TynBull* 31 (1980): 65-86.

Ricoeur, Paul. 'Narrative Identity', *Philosophy Today* 35.1 (1991): 73-81.
—— *Hermeneutics and the Human Sciences.* Edited and Transl. by John B. Thompson. Cambridge: CUP, 1981.
Robertson, A.T. *A Grammar of the Greek New Testament in the Light of Historical Research.* 3rd Edn. New York: Hodder and Stoughton, 1919.
Robertson, Archibald and Plummer, Alfred. *A Critical and Exegetical Commentary on the First Epistle of St. Paul to the Corinthians.* ICC. Edinburgh: T. & T. Clark, 1914.
Roetzel, Calvin J. *Judgement in the Community: A Study of the Relationship Between Eschatology and Ecclesiology in Paul.* Leiden: E.J. Brill, 1972.
Rogerson, J.W. 'The Hebrew Conception of Corporate Personality: A Re-examination', *JTS* 21 (1970): 1-16.
—— 'The Interpretation of the Old Testament in the New'. In *The Study and Use of the Bible.* Edited by Paul Avis. Basingstoke: Marshall Pickering, 1988. pp. 3-13.
Rosner, Brian S. '"οὐχὶ μᾶλλον ἐπενθήσατε"—Corporate Responsibility in 1 Corinthians 5', *NTS* 38/3 (1992): 470-73.
—— 'A Possible Quotation of Test. Reuben 5:5 in 1 Corinthians 6:18a', *JTS* 43/1 (1992): 123-27.
—— 'Moses Appointing Judges: An Antecedent to 1 Cor 6.1-6?', *ZNW* 82.3/4 (1991): 275-78.
—— 'Temple and Holiness in 1 Corinthians 5', *TynBull* 42.1 (1991): 137-45.
Safrai, Shumel. 'Halakha'. In *The literature of the Sages.* Edited by Shmuel Safrai. Assen/Maastricht: Van Gorcum, 1987. pp. 121-209.
Saito, Tadashi. *Die Mosevorstellungen im Neuen Testament.* Bern: Verlag Peter Lang, 1977.
Sampley. J. *And the Two Shall Become One Flesh: A Study of Traditions in Ephesians 5:21-33.* SNTSMS 16. Cambridge: CUP, 1971.
Sanday, W. and Headlam, A.C. *The Epistle to the Romans.* ICC. 5th edn. Edinburgh, 1920.
Sanders, E. P. *Paul and Palestinian Judaism: A Comparison of Patterns of Religion.* Philadelphia: Fortress, 1977.
—— *Paul, the Law, and the Jewish People.* Philadelphia: Fortress, 1983.
—— *Paul.* Oxford: OUP, 1991.
Sandmel, Samuel. 'Parallelomania', *JBL* 81 (1962) 1-13.
—— *The Genius of Paul: A Study in History.* 3rd Edn. Philadelphia: Fortress, 1979 (orig. 1958).
Sandnes, Karl Olav. *Paul—One of the Prophets?—A Contribution to the Apostle's Self Understanding.* WUNT 2.43. Tübingen: J.C.B. Mohr (Paul Siebeck), 1990.
Schechter, S. and Taylor, C. (eds.) *The Wisdom of Ben Sira: Portions of the Book of Ecclesiasticus.* Cambridge: CUP, 1899.
Schnabel, Eckhard J. 'Law and Wisdom: in the Mishnaic System', *BTB* 17/3 (1987): 104-11.
—— *Law and Wisdom from Ben Sira to Paul: A Tradition Historical Enquiry into the Relation of Law, Wisdom and Ethics.* WUNT 16. Tübingen: J.C.B. Mohr (Paul Siebeck), 1985.
—— 'Wie hat Paulus seine Ethik entwickelt? Motivationen, Normen und Kriterien paulinischer Ethik', *The European Journal of Theology* 1:1 (1992): 63-81.
Schnelle, Udo. '1 Kor 6:14—eine nachpaulinische Glosse', *NT* 25 (1983): 217-19.
Schoeps, Hans Joachim. *Aus Frühchristlicher Zeit: Religionsgeschichtliche Untersuchungen.* Tübingen: JCB Mohr (Paul Siebeck), 1950.
Schoeps, Hans Joachim. *Paulus: Die Theologie des Apostels im Lichte der jüdischen Religionsgeschichte.* Tübingen: J.C.B. Mohr (Paul Siebeck), 1959.'
Schrage, Wolfgang. 'Die Stellung zur Welt bei Paulus, Epiktet und in der Apokalyptik: 1 Kor 7:29-31', *ZTK* 61 (1964): 125-54.
—— 'Zur Ethik der neutestamentlichen Haustafeln', *NTS* 21 (1975): 1-22.
—— 'Zur Frontstellung der paulinischen Ehebewertung in 1 Kor 7,1-7', *ZNW* 67 (1976): 214-34.

—— 'Ethische Tendenzen in der Textüberlieferung des Neuen Testaments'. In *Studien zum Text und zur Ethik des Neuen Testaments: Festschrift zum 80. Geburtstag von Heinrich Greeven*. Edited by Wolfgang Schrage. Berlin/New York: Walter de Gruyter, 1986. pp. 374-96.

—— *The Ethics of the New Testament*. Transl. David E. Green (German, 1982). Edinburgh: T & T Clark, 1988.

Schreiner, Thomas R. 'The Abolition and Fulfillment of the Law in Paul', *JSNT* 35 (1989): 47-74.

Schroeder, D. 'Die Haustafeln des NT: Ihre Herkunft und ihr theologischer Sinn'. PhD Thesis, Hamburg, 1959.

—— 'Lists, Ethical', *IDB Sup*, 546-47.

Schubert, K. 'Die jüdisch-christliche Oekumene: Reflexionen zu Grundfragen des christlich-jüdischen Dialogs', *Kairos* 22 (1980): 1-33.

Schulz, Siegried.*Neutestamentliche Ethik*. Zürich: Theologischer Verlag, 1987.

Schürer, Emil. *Geschichte des jüdischen Volkes im Zeitalter Jesu Christi. III* (4th edn). Leipzig, 1909.

—— *The History of the Jewish People in the Age of Jesus Christ 175 B.C.-A.D. 135*. 3 vols. Revised and edited by G. Vermes, F. Millar, M. Black, and M. Goodman. Edinburgh: T. & T. Clark, 1973-1987.

Schutter, William L. *Hermeneutic and Composition in 1 Peter*. WUNT 2/30. Tübingen: J.C.B.Mohr (Paul Siebeck), 1989.

Schweitzer, Albert. *The Mysticism of Paul the Apostle*. Transl. W. Montgomery. New York: Seabury Press, 1968.

Schweizer, E. 'Die Weltlichkeit des Neuen Testaments: die Haustafeln'. In *Beiträge zur alttestamentlichen Theologie, Festschrift für Walther Zimmerli zum 70. Geburtstag*. Edited by H. Donner, R. Hanhart and R. Smend. Göttingen: Vandenhoeck & Ruprecht, 1977. pp. 397-413.

—— 'Traditional ethical patterns in the Pauline and post-Pauline letters and their development (lists of vices and house tables)'. In *Text and Interpretation: Studies in the New Testament presented to Matthew Black*. Edited by E. Best and R. McL.Wilson. Cambridge: CUP, 1979. pp. 195-209.

—— *Church Order in the New Testament*. London: SCM, 1961.

Schweizer, E. *The Good News According to Matthew*. Transl. David E. Green. London: SPCK, 1975.

Scroggs, Robin. 'Paul: Σοφός and Πνευματικός', *NTS* 14 (1967): 33-55.

—— *The New Testament and Homosexuality: Contextual Background for Contemporary Debate*. Philadelphia: Fortress Press, 1983.

Seebass, H. 'ἅγιος', *NIDNTT* I (1976): 223-29.

Seeberg, Alfred. *Der Katechismus der Urchristenheit mit einer Einführung von Ferdinard Hahn*. Theologische Bücherei 26. München: Chr. Kaiser Verlag, 1966 (originally 1903).

Sellin, Gerhard. 'Hauptprobleme des Ersten Korintherbriefes'. In *Aufstieg und Niedergang der Römischen Welt*. Teil II Principat. Band 25.4 Religion. Edited by Wolfgang Haase. Berlin: Walter de Gruyter, 1987. pp. 2940-3044.

Selwyn, Edward Gordon. *The First Epistle of St. Peter*. London: MacMillan & Co., 1946.

Shaver, Judson R. *Torah and the Chronicler's History Work: An Inquiry into the Chronicler's References to Laws, Festivals, and Cultic Institutions in Relationship to Pentateuchal Legislation*. Brown Judaic Studies 196. Atlanta, Georgia: Scholars Press, 1989.

Skehan, P.W. 'The Structure of the Song of Moses in Deuteronomy', *CBQ* 13 (1951): 159-170.

Smith, D. Moody. 'The Pauline Literature'. In *It is Written: Scripture Citing Scripture. Essays in Honour of Barnabas Lindars,* ed. D.A. Carson and H.G.M. Williamson. Cambridge: CUP, 1988. pp. 265-291.

—— 'The Use of the Old Testament in the New'. In *The Use of the Old Testament in the New and Other Essays: Studies in Honor of William Franklin Stinespring*. Edited by James M. Efird. Durham, N. C.: Duke University Press, 1972. pp. 3-65.

Snodgrass, Klyne. 'Spheres of Influence: A Possible Solution to the Problem of Paul and the Law', *JSNT* 32 (1988): 93-113.

Spicq, Ceslaus. *Théologie morale du NT.* 4th ed. EtB. Paris: Lecoffre, 1965.

Stachowiak, L,R. 'Paraenesis Paulina et Instructio de duobus spiritibus in 'Regula' Qumranensi', *Verbum Domini* 51 (1963): 245-50.

Stamm, J.J. and Andrew M.E. *The Ten Commandments in Recent Research.* SBTSS 2. London: SCM, 1967.

Stauffer, Ethelbert. 'γαμέω, γάμος,', *TDNT* 1:648-57.

Stein, A. 'Wo trugen die korinthischen Christen ihre Rechtshändel aus?', *ZNW* 59 (1968): 86-90.

Steiner, A. "Warum lebten die Essener asketisch?', *BZ* 15(1971): 1-28.

Stockhausen, Carol K. *Moses'Veil and the Glory of the New Covenant: The Exegetical Substructure of 1 Cor. 3,1-4,6.* Analecta Biblica 116. Rome: Pontifical Institute, 1989.

Stone, M.E. 'Apocalyptic Literature'. In *Jewish Writings of the Second Temple Period: Apocrypha, Pseudepigrapha, Qumran Sectarian Writings, Philo, Josephus.* Edited by M.E. Stone. CRINT 2/2. Assen: van Gorcum and Philadelphia: Fortress, 1984. pp. 383-441.

Strack, H.L. and Stemberger, G. *Introduction to the Talmud and Midrash.* Transl. Markus Bockmuehl. Worcester: T & T Clark, 1991.

Strack, H.L. and Billerbeck, Paul. *Kommentar zum Neuen Testament aus Talmud und Midrasch.* 7 vols. Munich: Beck, 1922-1961.

Strobel, A. 'Das Aposteldekret in Galatien: zur Situation von Gal. 1 und 2', *NTS* 20 (1974): 177-90.

Strugnell, J. 'Notes En Marge Du Volume V des "Discoveries in the Judaean Desert of Jordan"', *RevQ* 7(1970): 163-276.

Stuhlmacher, P. 'Christliche Verantwertung bie Paulus aund seinen Schülern', *EvT* 28 (1968): 165-86.

Stuhlmueller, C. *Creative Redemption in Deutero-Isaiah.* AnBib 43. Rome: Pontifical Biblical Institute, 1970.

Suffrin, A.E. 'Asceticism, Jewish', *ERE* 2 (1909): 97-99.

Sundberg, A.C. *The Old Testament of the Early Church.* Cambridge, MA, 1964.

Sweet, J.P.M. *Revelation.* Pelican commentaries. London: SCM, 1979.

Talbert, C.H. 'Paul on the Covenant', *RevExp* 84 (1987): 299-313.

—— *Reading Corinthians: A New Commentary for Preachers.* London: SPCK, 1987.

Thackeray, Henry St. John. *The Relation of St. Paul to Contemporary Jewish Thought.* London: Macmillan and Co. 1900.

Theissen, Gerd. *The Social Setting of Pauline Christianity: Essays on Corinth.* Edited and Translated by John H. Schütz. Philadelphia: Fortress Press, 1982.

Thielicke, Helmut. *Theological Ethics: Foundations.* Volume 1. Philadelphia: Fortress Press, 1966.

Thielman, Frank. *From Plight to Solution: A Jewish Framework for Understanding Paul's View of the Law in Galatians and Romans.* NovTSup 61. Leiden: Brill, 1989.

Thiselton, A.C. 'The meaning of σάρξ in 1 Corinthians 5:5: A Fresh Approach in the Light of Logical and Semantic Factors', *SJT* 26(1973): 204-28.

Thompson, Michael. *Clothed with Christ: The Example and Teaching of Jesus in Romans 12.1-15.13.* JSNTSS 59. Sheffield: JSOT Press, 1991.

Thornton, T.C.G. 'Jewish Bachelors in New Testament Times', *JTS* 23 (1972): 444-45. 'Satan—God's agent for punishing', *ExpTim* 83:5 (1972): 151-2.

Tomson, Peter J. *Paul and the Jewish Law: Halakha in the Letters of the Apostle to the Gentiles.* Assen/Maastricht: Van Gorcum, 1990.

—— 'The names Israel and Jew in Ancient Judaism and in the New Testament', *Bijdragen* 47 (1986): 120-40, 266-89.

Tripp, David Mark. 'An interpretation of Romans 13:1-7 in light of sapiential and apocalyptic traditions'. PhD Thesis, Southwestern Baptist Theological Seminary, 1987.

Turner, Nigel. *A Grammar of New Testament Greek. Volume 4: Style.* Edinburgh: T. & T. Clark, 1976.
—— *Grammatical Insights into the New Testament.* Edinburgh: T. & T. Clark, 1965.
Ulonska, H. 'Die Funktion der alttestamentlichen Zitate und Anspielungen in den paulinischen Briefen'. Ph.D dissertation, Münster, 1964.
Urbach. Ephraim E. *The Sages: Their Concepts and Beliefs.* 2 vols. Transl. by Israel Abrahams. Jerusalem: Magnes Press, The Hebrew University, 1979.
van der Woude, A.S. 'Review of Karl Wilhelm Niebuhr's *Gesetz und Paränese*', *JSJ* 20 (1989): 100-4.
van der Horst, P.W. 'Pseudo-Phocylides and the New Testament', *ZNW* 69 (1978): 187-202.
van Unnik, W.C. 'Die Rücksicht auf die Reaktion der Nicht-Christen als Motiv in der altchristlichen Paränese'. In *Judentum, Urchristentum, Kirche: Festschrift für Joachim Jeremias.* Edited by W. Eltester BZNW 26. Berlin: Töpelmann, 1964. pp. 221-34.
Vanderkam, James C. 'Review of Karl Wilhelm Niebuhr's *Gesetz und Paränese*', JBL 108/3 (1989): 514-16.
Verhey, Allen. 'Ethics: NT Ethics'. *ISBE* 2: 173-83.
—— *The Great Reversal: Ethics and the New Testament.* Grand Rapids, Michigan: Eerdmans, 1984.
Vermes, Geza. 'A Summary of the Law by Flavius Josephus', *NovT* 24 (1982): 289-303.
—— *Jesus the Jew: A Historian's Reading of the Gospels.* London: Collins, 1973.
Vielhauer, P. 'Paulus und das Alte Testament'. In *Studien zur Geschichte und Theologie der Reformation: Festschrift für Ernst Bizer.* Neukirchen, 1969. pp. 33-62.
Vischer, Lukas. *Die Auslegungsgeschichte von 1 Kor 6,1-11.* Tübingen: J.C.B. Mohr, 1955.
Viviano, B. *Study and Worship: Aboth and the New Testament.* Leiden: E.J. Brill, 1978.
Vögtle, A. *Die Tugend- und Lasterkataloge im Neuen Testament: exegetisch, religions- und formgeschichtlich untersucht.* NTAbh 16. Münster: Aschendorff, 1936.
von Campenhausen, Hans. *The Formation of the Christian Bible.* Transl. John Austin Baker. London: Black, 1972.
von Dehson, Christian D. 'Sexual relationships and the church: An exegetical study of 1 Corinthians 5-7'. PhD Thesis, Union Theological Seminary, 1987.
von Rad, Gerhard. *Genesis, a Commentary.* Philadelphia, 1961.
—— 'The Joseph Narrative and Ancient Wisdom'. In *The Problem of the Hexateuch and Other Essays.* Edinburgh, 1965. pp. 292-300.
Walton, John H. 'Deuteronomy: An Exposition of the Spirit of the Law', *Grace Theological Journal* 8/2 (1987): 213-25.
Ward, R.B. 'Musonius and Paul on Marriage', *NTS* 36/2 (1990): 281-89.
Watson, F. *Paul, Judaism and the Gentiles: A Sociological Approach.* SNTSMS 56. Cambridge: CUP, 1986.
Watts, Rikki E. 'The Influence of the Isaianic New Exodus on the Gospel of Mark.' PhD Thesis, Cambridge University, 1990.
Weidinger, K. *Die Haustafeln: Ein Stück urchristlicher Paränese.* UNT. Leipzig: J.C. Hinrichs, 1928.
Weinfeld, Moshe. 'Judge and Officer in Ancient Israel and the Ancient Near East', *Israel Oriental Studies* 7 (1977): 65-88.
—— 'The Decalogue: Its Significance, Uniqueness, and Place in Israel's Tradition'. In *Religion and Law: Biblical-Judaic and Islamic Perspectives.* Edited by Edwin B. Firmage, Bernard G. Weiss and John W. Welch. Winona Lake: Eisenbrauns, 1990. pp. 3-47.
—— 'What makes the Ten Commandments Different?', *Bible Review* April (1991): 35-41.
Weingreen, J. 'Rabbinic Type Commentary in the LXX Version of Proverbs'. In

*Proceedings of the Sixth World Congress of Jewish Studies. 1973*, Volume 1. Edited by Avigdor Shinan. Jerusalem: Jerusalem Academic Press, 1977. pp. 407-15.

Wendland, Heinz-Dieter. *Ethik des NT.* GNT 4. Göttingen: Vandenhoeck & Ruprecht, 1978.

Wenham, Gordon. *The Book of Leviticus.* NICOT. Grand Rapids: Eerdmans, 1976.

—— 'The Old Testament Attitude to Homosexuality', *ExpTim* 102/12 (1991): 359-63.

Wenschkewitz, H. 'Die Spiritualisierung der Kultusbegriffe Tempel, Priester und Opfer im Neuen Testament', *Angelos* IV (1932): 70-230.

Wernle, P. *Die Anfänge unserer Religion.* Tübingen/Leipzig, 1904.

Westerholm, Stephen. 'The Law and the "Just Man" (1 Tim. 1:3-11)', *StTh* 36 (1982): 79-95.

Westerholm, Stephen. 'Letter and Spirit: The Foundation of Paul's Ethics', *NTS* 30 (1984): 229-248.

—— *Israel's Law and the Church's Faith: Paul and His Recent Interpreters.* Grand Rapids: Eerdmans, 1988.

Wibbing, S. *Die Tugend- und Lasterkatologe im Neuen Testament und ihre Traditionsgeschichte unter besonderer Berücksichtigung der Qumran Texte.* BZNW 25. Berlin: Töpelmann, 1959.

Wickert, Ulrich. 'Einheit und Eintracht der Kirche im Präskript des ersten Korintherbriefes', *ZNW* 50 (1959): 73-82.

Wild, Robert A. 'Review of *Geist und Gesetz* by Eckart Reinmuth', *CBQ* 49 (1987): 678-79.

Williamson, H.G.M. *1 and 2 Chronicles.* NCBC. London: Marshall, Morgan & Scott, 1982.

Wills, Lawrence M. *The Jew in the Court of the Foreign King: Ancient Jewish Court Legends.* Harvard Dissertations in Religion 26. Minneapolis: Fortress Press, 1990.

Wimbush, V.L. *Paul the Worldly Ascetic: Response to the World and Self-Understanding according to 1 Corinthians 7.* Mercer University Press, 1987.

Winter, Bruce W. 'Secular and Christian Responses to Corinthian Famines', *TynBull* 40 (1989): 86-106.

—— 'Civil Litigation in Secular Corinth and the Church: the Forensic Background to 1 Corinthians 6.1-8', *NTS* 37/4 (1991): 559-72.

Wiseman, D.J. 'Law and Order in Old Testament Times', *Vox Evangelica* 8 (1973): 5-21.

Wright, C.J.H. *God's People in God's Land: Family, Land, and Property in the Old Testament.* Exeter: Paternoster, 1990.

—— *Living as the People of God: The Relevance of Old Testament Ethics.* Leicester: IVP, 1983.

—— 'The People of God and the State in the Old Testament', *Themelios* 16/1 (1990): 4-10.

Wright, David F. 'Homosexuality: The Relevance of the Bible', *EvQ* 61/4 (1989): 291-300.

—— 'Homosexuals or Prostitutes? The Meaning of ἀρσενοκοῖται (1 Cor .6:9, 1 Tim. 1:10)', *VC* 38 (1984): 125-53.

—— 'Translating ἀρσενοκοῖται (1 Cor. 6:9; 1 Tim. 1:10)', *VC* 41 (1987): 396-98.

Wright, N.T. 'The New Testament and the "state"', *Themelios* 16/1 (1990): 11-17.

Wright, N.T. *Colossians and Philemon.* Tyndale NT Comm. Leicester: IVP, 1986.

Wright, Robert J. 'Boswell on Homosexualty: A Case Undemonstrated', *ATR* 66 (1984): 79-94.

Yarbrough, O.L. *Not Like the Gentiles: Marriage Rules in the Letters of Paul.* SBLDS 80. Atlanta, 1985.

Yaron, R. *Introduction to the Law of the Aramaic Papyri.* Oxford, 1961.

Yohannan, J.D. *Joseph and Potiphar's Wife in World Literature: An Anthology of the Story of the Chaste Youth and Lustful stepmother.* Norfolk, Conn., 1968.

Zaas, Peter S. 'Catalogues and Context: 1 Corinthians 5 and 6', *NTS* 34 (1988): 622-29.

—— '"Cast Out the Evil Man from Your Midst"', *JBL* 103/2 (1984): 259-61.

Zerbe, Gordon. *Non-Retaliation in Early Jewish and New Testament Texts.* JSPSS 13. Sheffield: JSOT Press, 1993.

Zeiner, Georg. 'Die Verwendung der Schrift im Buch der Weisheit', *TTZ* 66 (1957): 138-52.

Zerwick, M. and Grosvenor, M. *A Grammatical Analysis of the Greek New Testament.* Rome: Biblical Institute Press, 1979.

Zerwick, M. *Biblical Greek.* SPIB 114. Rome: Biblical Institute Press, 1963.

Ziesler, J. A. *Pauline Christianity.* Oxford: OUP, 1983. Σῶμα in the Septuagint', *NovT* 25 (1983): 133-45.

Zöckler, O. 'Asceticism, Christian', *ERE* 2 (1909): 73-80.

Zuntz, G. 'The Critic Correcting the Author', *Philologus* 99 (1955): 295-303.

—— *The Text of the Epistles: A Disquisition upon the Corpus Paulinum.* The Schweich Lectures, 1946. London: OUP, 1953.

# INDEX OF AUTHORS

# INDEX OF REFERENCES

## I. Old Testament

| | | | |
|---|---|---|---|
| 17:8-13 | 97 | 26:10 | 184 |
| 17:12 | 65 | 26:13 | 88 |
| 18:8-13 | 184 | 26:18 | 135 |
| 18:15 | 103 | 27-28 | 64, 66 |
| 18:19 | 113 | 27 | 32, 46, 53 |
| 19:11-13 | 48 | 27:9-10 | 87 |
| 19:13 | 65, 66 | 27:14 | 70 |
| 19:16-20 | 84 | 27:15-26 | 47 |
| 19:15-19 | 89 | 27:16 | 48 |
| 19:16-20 | 92 | 27:20 | 72, 82, 92, 160, 178 |
| 19:16-19 | 48 | | |
| 19:17 | 84 | 28 | 84 |
| 19:18-19 | 69 | 28:30 | 158, 159 |
| 19:19 | 63, 65, 93 | 29:19-21 | 67, 68 |
| 19:20a | 84 | 30 | 53 |
| 20:5-7 | 159, 175 | 30:12-13 | 165 |
| 21:8 | 65 | 30:19 | 170 |
| 21:9 | 65, 66 | 31:9-10 | 159 |
| 21:18-21 | 48 | 31:16 | 128 |
| 21:20-21 | 69 | 32 | 193, 197-201 |
| 21:21 | 23, 63, 65, 93 | 32:16ff | 119 |
| 22:13-29 | 124 | 32:17-19 | 197 |
| 22:13-21 | 160 | 32:17-21 | 197 |
| 22:14 | 144 | 32:21 | 197 |
| 22:19 | 168 | 34:9 | 102 |
| 22:21 | 93, 124 | | |
| 22:21b | 80, 143 | *Joshua* | |
| 22:22 | 48, 65, 83, 124 | 1:16-20 | 102 |
| 22:24 | 23, 65, 83 | 3:7 | 102 |
| 22:28-29 | 168 | 4:14 | 102 |
| 22:30 | 72, 133, 178 | 6:18 | 64 |
| 23 | 13, 74, 80 | 7 | 72, 90 |
| 23:1 | 74, 82, 83, 92, 160 | 7:1 | 67 |
| 23:1-8 | 92, 178 | 7:12 | 64, 76 |
| 23:2-9 | 54, 73, 74, 75, 81, 83 | 7:15 | 65, 76 |
| | | 7:20 | 90 |
| 23:2 | 74 | 7:25 | 64, 76 |
| 23:3 | 74 | 7:26 | 67 |
| 23:4-6 | 74 | 17:15 | 88 |
| 23:9-14 | 158 | 22:16-18 | 67 |
| 23:14b | 66 | 22:20 | 67 |
| 23:17-18 | 178 | 23:1-24:28 | 53 |
| 23:17 | 127, 128 | 23:12-13 | 72 |
| 23:17 | 124 | 23:12 | 173 |
| 24 | 174, 175 | 23:16 | 65 |
| 24:1-4 | 166, 171, 172, 175, 178 | 24:19-20 | 202 |
| 24:1 | 167 | *Judges* | |
| 24:3 | 171, 172 | 2:17 | 127, 128 |
| 24:5 | 175 | 6:25 | 64 |
| 24:7 | 63, 65, 93 | 6:28 | 64 |
| 24:14 | 100 | 6:30 | 64 |
| 25:1 | 100, 104 | 7:4 | 88 |
| 25:4 | 6, 178, 188, 192 | 8:27 | 128 |
| 26:2 | 184 | 8:33 | 128 |

## II. New Testament

## III. Apocrypha and Pseudepigrapha

## IV. QUMRAN LITERATURE

## V. RABBINIC LITERATURE

## VI. OTHER JEWISH LITERATURE

## VII. GREEK AND ROMAN LITERATURE

## VIII. EARLY CHRISTIAN WRITINGS

**Brian S. Rosner** (Ph.D., University of Cambridge) is lecturer in New Testament at the University of Aberdeen.